Letters from Sardis

Letters from Sardis

by George M. A. Hanfmann

Harvard University Press   Cambridge, Massachusetts   1972

To
Ilse
Henry and Catharine
All Sardians
and
Supporters of Sardis

Preface

The book really owes its origin to Ilse; for she had collected all the letters with some illustrations and gave them to me for a birthday present. I showed the collection to Maud Wilcox, humanities editor at Harvard University Press, and this led eventually to its publication. Ruth Stanford Thomas did much fundamental work on text, captions, and illustrations and looked after the progress of the manuscript to its final stage. Jane A. Scott helped out at crucial junctures. Fikret K. Yeğül kindly drew the maps. And Ilse stepped in whenever help was needed.

Ilse, as the reader has guessed, is Mrs. Hanfmann. A husband cannot very well write extensively about his wife's attainments in such letters as these but both as official recorder and unofficial counselor for human relations she was very much part of it all. *Meter Kastron,* "Mother of the Camp," seems a good description of her functions over fourteen years (the title appears in the dedicatory inscription of the Roman Gymnasium we found—applied to empress Julia Domma).

A. Henry Detweiler and Catharine S. Detweiler shared with us the joys and worries of the Sardis project from its inception. Henry came into the picture one hot August evening in 1955 via a long distance call by which he as President of the American Schools of Oriental Research approved our request for sponsorship by the Schools. His last letter to me, written on December 16, 1969, approved on behalf of Cornell the publication of these *Letters.* He died on January 30, 1970. Gallant, optimistic, and of whirlwind efficiency Henry as Associate Director worked unceasingly for Sardis with

vii

Catharine backstopping him in this as in so many other of his diversified activities.

This is the place to thank our friends at Cornell who have maintained successfully a partnership of such long duration: Thomas Canfield, James W. Yarnell, Robert and Marcia Ascher, and especially Stephen W. Jacobs, who succeeded Detweiler as Associate Director. We think gratefully of the collaboration with the Corning Museum, with Paul Perrot as curator, then as director, and with Axel von Saldern and Robert H. Brill as researchers. At Harvard, John Coolidge really set the Sardis project in motion by asking me incautiously after he became Director of the Fogg Museum whether I should not have an excavation sometime. His successors, Agnes Mongan and Daniel Robbins have always shown sympathy and understanding. The list of those to whom we are indebted is long and will be recited elsewhere, but by the third line of my dedication, I want to convey my thanks to all who worked at Sardis—Americans and Turks, scholars, students, and workmen.

It will be perhaps more obvious from the reading of these *Letters* than from official reports how much we owe to the help and hospitality of Turkey and the Turkish people. To the Ministries of Education and Culture and to the Department of Antiquities we express our gratitude for the privilege of working at Sardis and for much assistance over the years. We hope that the results of our work will add worthily to the historic patrimony of Turkey's unsurpassed "Loom of History."

I say something in the Introduction about the financial support given to us by many people and institutions; to all of them go our thanks. The last line of the dedication is meant to suggest that the *Letters from Sardis* is really their book.

The *Letters* constitute a running account of the development of our excavations at Sardis. The final publication has begun to appear but it will be a long time before all evidence becomes completely available, and even longer before a definitive summation can be attempted. We hope that with their many illustrations and explanatory captions the *Letters* may in the meantime serve as an introduction and informal survey of what has been done at Sardis from 1958 through 1971.

December 1971   George M. A. Hanfmann

Contents

Letters from Sardis

Introduction

In Classical antiquity "Golden Sardis" was a name to conjure with. "I do not care for the gold of king Gyges," cried the Greek adventurer and poet Archilochus defiantly; but the rest of the ancient world did. The kings of Lydia of the Mermnad Dynasty from Gyges to fabulous Croesus (ca. 680–547 B.C.) made Sardis the Paris of the ancient world. The Greek poetess Sappho of Lesbos laments that she cannot get the colorful Lydian hat from Sardis for her daughter Cleis; Xenophanes warns the citizens of Colophon against the useless luxuries of soft living they have learned from the Lydians; and Alcman, writer of choral songs for Sparta, proudly proclaims someone's metropolitan sophistication: "You are not a country hick . . . but a man from the heights of Sardis."*

Herodotus, who knew Lydia well, made the Lydian kingdom the subject of his most fascinating stories, and the collision of Lydia and Persia an example of the first encounter of East and West. He draws unforgettable pictures of Sardis and its court: how the wife of Candaules was seen in the nude by Gyges and gave him the choice "kill and be king—or be killed"; how Alcmaeon of Athens, friend of Croesus, was given permission to take as much gold out of Croesus' treasury as he could carry, and how he staggered out, his mouth full of gold dust, his clothes and boots spilling over with gold (VI. 125); how the Athenian sage Solon refused to call Croesus the happiest of all men and was proved right in the end; and how Croesus was about to be burned on a pyre but was saved by the magnanimity of his conqueror, the Persian king Cyrus (I.86–88). These stories have become

*All major literary sources for Sardis and the Lydians have been collected by John G. Pedley in *Ancient Literary Sources on Sardis*, Sardis Monograph 2 (Cambridge, Harvard University Press, 1972).

1

common property of the European and the Islamic worlds.

For a century and a half, the kings of Lydia ruled a kingdom extending from the Aegean to Iran. They sent messengers to Assyria, they allied themselves with Babylon and Egypt. By skillful combination of religious and financial propaganda, they enlarged their influence in the Greek world. They ruled this empire from their well-nigh impregnable citadel at Sardis, some 65 miles inland from the coast of Turkey, in the rich Hermus plain (Gediz Çay), under the foot of the towering Tmolus mountain.

"The land Lud I took, their king I killed"—such was the terse account given by Cyrus, the conquering king of Persia, after he overthrew Croesus and captured the citadel in 547 B.C. As *Sfarda*, Sardis became the seat of the most important Western satrapy, the western terminal of the famous Royal Road along which mail couriers sped from the distant capitals of Susa and Persepolis toward the Mediterranean. The King of Kings trod on purple rugs woven at Sardis, and piled up gold from Sardis in his treasury.

In 499 B.C. the Ionians marched across the Tmolus and burned Sardis, starting the great wars between Persia and the Greeks. "Though they took the city, they did not succeed in plundering it; for, as the houses in Sardis were most of them built of reeds, and even the few which were of brick had a reed thatching for their roof, one of them was no sooner fired by a soldier than the flames ran speedily from house to house . . . The Lydians, and such Persians as were in the city, enclosed on every side by the flames . . . came in crowds into the market-place, and gathered themselves upon the banks of the Pactolus. This stream, which comes down from Mount Tmolus, and brings the Sardians a quantity of gold-dust, runs directly through the market-place [*agora*] of Sardis, and joins the Hermus. So the Lydians and Persians, brought together in this way . . . were forced to stand on their defence; and the Ionians, when they saw the enemy in part resisting, in part pouring towards them in dense crowds, took fright, and . . .

Plate I The Acropolis of Sard

went back to their ships" (V.101). In revenge, the Persians mustered their huge armies against Greece in the Sardian plain, and Aeschylus writes of Lydian charioteers from golden Sardis as Persian allies (*Persae* 40–48).

Themistocles and Alcibiades and many other famous Greeks passed through Sardis on their way to the Persian court. When the tide of power reversed and began to flow from west to east, the efficient general and historian Xenophon went to Sardis on his famous march with the Ten Thousand (401 B.C.) (*Anabasis* III. i.8). In 334 came Alexander the Great who captured the great citadel without a fight (Arrian *Anabasis* I. 17.3f.).

As key fortress and capital, Sardis became a bone of contention among the Successors of Alexander; kings from Macedon, Syria, and Pergamon contended for the city. The Seleucid dynasty of Syria transformed the Lydian capital into a typical Greek city (c. 270–190 B.C.), and it is they who built the huge Temple of Artemis (*Figure 1*). Later in this period came another dramatic change in the history of Sardis. Prince Achaeus, discovered to be conspiring against Antiochus III, was besieged for two years (215–213 B.C.) on the citadel, and was finally captured and killed (Polybius *Historiae* VII. 15–17). Antiochus first severely punished the city and then refounded it on a Hellenistic urban plan. Under the kings of Pergamon (180–133 B.C.), then under the Romans (beginning 133 B.C.), Sardis was still a major government and industrial center, famous for gold-woven textiles.

A fierce earthquake struck the region in A.D. 17 (Tacitus *Annales* II. 47) but the city came back with the help of the emperors Tiberius and Claudius, who gave liberally to restore it. As metropolis of Asia, seat of many wealthy and influential families, it led a peaceful and prosperous existence under the emperors Trajan and Hadrian, and the Antonines and Severans.

Meantime another kind of fame was to attach itself to Sardis. In Obadaiah (20) mention is made of exiles from Jerusalem "in Sepharad"; most scholars now believe that Sepharad is Sardis (*Sfard* in Lydian and Persian). Thus there were perhaps Hebrews in Sardis under the Persian rule in the fifth century B.C. After the uprising of the Lydians who sided with Achaeus in 215–213 B.C., Antiochus III brought 2000 Jewish veterans with their families from Mesopotamia to Lydia, "to guard the most important fortresses," of which Sardis surely was the chief. A sizable Jewish community must have formed at Sardis. The Jewish historian Josephus writes that they had a place of worship and sent much temple tax to Jerusalem (*Antiquitates Judaicae* XIV. 235, 260; XVI. 171). It is in the ambient of such Jewish congregations that Christian groups began to organize. By the time of Nero, St. John of the Revelation addressed the church of Sardis as one of the seven earliest Christian communities of Asia Minor (*Revelation* 3.1). By mid-second century, one of the important early church fathers, Melito (ca. A.D. 140–190), whose eloquent treatise "On the Lord's Passion" has survived, was bishop of Sardis, and presented an apology for Christianity to the emperor Marcus.

The dangerous decline of the Roman Empire, and especially an attack by the Goths in 253, shook Asia Minor, and we hear of bad conditions in the Lydian countryside. Under Constantine (306–337) security was restored and there was considerable building activity in the fourth century. A great scare for Sardis came when another attack of the Goths threatened in 399 but the flooding of the Hermus river stopped the attackers. From inscriptions it seems that Sardis, a metropolitan see, was still flourishing in the sixth century.

The Arab invasion in the early eighth century reached Sardis; and later historians made brief mention of battles between Byzantines near the city; then the Turks appear. A very curious episode is related, in which the Turks and the Byzantines for a while divided the citadel on the Acropolis (1304). But the city declined rapidly. In 1369, the Patriarch of Constantinople wrote that Sardis "formerly reckoned among the greatest and first . . . now does not even preserve the appearance of a city . . . but has become a field of obliteration and destruction instead of a paradise of luxury"; and he transferred the metropolitan see to Philadelphia (Alaşehir).*

Thereafter only small Turkish villages remained around Sart, as the place was now called.

This much was known from written history, and like twin magnets, the fame of the kingdom of Croesus and his treasure, and the reputation of Sardis as one of the "Seven Churches of Asia" drew the attention of the Western world. The learned Renaissance traveler and humanist Cyriacus of Ancona correctly identified the ruins of "the regal city of Croesus," which he visited in 1446. He measured the "immense columns" of the Temple of Artemis (he thought it was the temple of Sardian Zeus). Remembering Herodotus, he tried to pan gold in the Pactolus. The general location of Sardis was also known to fifteenth century cartographers.

The Reverend Thomas Smith, who thought that "antiquity threw the purest light on Christianity," went to Sardis in 1671 and published "A Survey of the Seven Churches of Asia." Like the patriarch in 1369, he laments the impoverished state of Sardis and its few Christians who have no church nor priest, whose houses are "few and mean." He thought he recognized "a great church" east of the castle (Acropolis), and another church converted into a mosque.

Accounts more scientific in nature, sometimes accompanied by drawings made on the spot, were published by several travelers in the eighteenth and early nineteenth centuries. The first excavations of significance were carried out in 1853 by German consul H. Spiegelthal, who successfully tunneled the huge mound of Croesus' father Alyattes, and by the famous British archaeologist George Dennis, who between 1868 and 1882 dug up many chamber-

*Fr. Miklosich and Io. Müller, *Acta et Diplomata Graeca Medii Aevi* (Vienna, 1860), I, no. cclv, pp. 509–510.

tombs in the Royal cemetery of Bin Tepe (Thousand Mounds). Dennis also ran a big trench through the Artemis Temple, discovering an overlifesize head of the Roman empress Faustina, now in the British Museum.

Then came the remarkable effort of the First Sardis Expedition, led by Howard Crosby Butler (1872–1922). Professor of Art and Archaeology at Princeton, Butler had done distinguished work in the study of architecture of Christian churches in Syria (1901, 1904, 1912); upon invitation of the Turkish government he turned his attention to Lydia and Sardis. "Archaeologists the world over had long wished that excavations should be undertaken at Sardis, the chief city of ancient Lydia . . . The antiquity of the site, its importance in history, and its geographical position made it appear almost certain that Sardis held the keys to many difficult historical and archaeological problems." So wrote Butler in justifying "The Need of Excavations at Sardis."

As backers of his enterprise Butler enlisted in his American Society for the Excavation of Sardis some of the financial giants of the age: J. Pierpont Morgan, Allison V. Armour, R. Garrett, Edward S. Harkness, Archer M. Huntington—some forty founders, fellows, and members. He showed remarkable technical ingenuity in bringing a complete small-gage railroad with locomotive and crane out to Sardis—part of the crane is still sitting as melancholy memento at the Temple of Artemis. The staff of Butler's first season (1910) consisted of two engineers, two inscription specialists, himself as director, and some three hundred workmen. The sweep and style of the First Sardis Expedition have become legendary among colleagues and natives. We still hear tales of how expedition members always dressed in formal clothes for dinner, how Butler galloped around on a black stallion, how he sat above the temple excavation and blew a whistle to stop or start work, and how he introduced field telephones to communicate with diggers in the remote cemetery hills across the Pactolus. I should add that in fifteen years of our experience with Sardis we have gained profound respect for the capabilities and the powers of observation of this extraordinary archaeologist. One has really to be on the spot to appreciate fully many of his remarks and observations which do not seem very striking when one just reads them over in his reports or in the two volumes of final publication which he lived to complete.

Quite naturally, Butler tackled first the Temple of Artemis of which two columns were still rising over a desolate field. In the relatively short span of five campaigns from 1910 through 1914, he and his small staff freed the wonderful structure, fourth largest Ionic temple known, which had been nearly completely buried under landslides. Butler assigned it to the Late Classical age of Greek architecture.

His second major effort was devoted to the hundreds of rock-cut tombs in the cliffs of the western hills (Necropolis Hill) of the Pactolus. This enterprise was less closely supervised, and never mapped—which though most regrettable, is not surprising, for these are precipitous cliffs. His foremen opened 1107 graves; only about 70 had any objects. Ancient grave robbers had visited almost all; but at least two were intact and one yielded a glorious array of gold plaques stitched to a garment, gold plaques which we today know to be Lydo-Persian in style, made by jewelers of the satrapal court of Sardis. Being relatively well preserved, Butler's grave assemblages provided the first glimpse of the material culture of the Lydians.

Butler's extensive long-range plans were suddenly upset by the outbreak of the First World War. After the war, conditions in western Turkey were very unsettled. By spring of 1921, the excavation house had been damaged and many finds destroyed. Butler died on his way back from Sardis where he had been planning the campaign for 1922. His junior colleague Theodore Leslie Shear, later to achieve even greater renown as director of the Agora excavation at Athens, had a remarkably promising campaign in 1922 but was abruptly stopped by the Turkish-Greek war. With this, field activities at Sardis came to a halt, although publication proceeded for some years thereafter. The Society for the Excavation of Sardis appears to have dissolved in the 1930's.

George Henry Chase (1875–1952), John E. Hudson Professor of Archaeology at Harvard, had gone to Sardis in 1914 to study the pottery found during the five seasons. He, like Butler had counted on going back after the war. A very competent student of Greek pottery, Chase published two fine articles on vases from Sardis; then, as "Chippy" Chase himself related with a twinkle in his merry brown eyes, he "went down the gutters of administration," winding up as Dean of the Graduate School of Arts and Sciences. The occasion of this pronouncement was in 1938, when he asked me, then a Junior Fellow at Harvard, to share with him the publication of the vases found at Sardis. I had studied at Johns Hopkins with another staff member of the Sardis Expedition, David M. Robinson, who together with William H. Buckler had published a thorough volume on the Greek and Latin inscriptions of Sardis. I also met Buckler, a Baltimorean who lived mostly in Oxford, a precise and meticulous scholar whose volume on Lydian inscriptions (1925) was a milestone in the study of that newly emerging tongue. In Princeton, T. L. Shear (who died in 1945) was most generous in making available his records of 1922 and his collection of literary sources on Sardis, and the colleagues in charge of the official Sardis archive at the university were most helpful.

My own interest in Sardis had been kindled long before by an occurrence in the history of Lydia as famous as Croesus or St. John but much more obscure. In one of the most violently disputed chapters of his history (I.94), Herodotus tells how the Lydians in times of a legendary king Atys, son of Manes, had a dreadful famine; how to forget hunger they invented dice and all sorts of games; and how finally one half of them took to ships, sailed to Italy, and became the mysterious Tyrrhenoi or Etruscans. I had started my archaeological career as an Etruscologist and like so many others I had the optimistic hope that Lydia might yet yield the key to the mystery of the Etruscan language and the origins of the people. Might not the huge necropolis of Bin Tepe several miles north of Sardis, where the Lydian kings were buried, yield some clue to link Lydians and Etruscans, especially since its mounds seemed (at least in illustrations) so similar to the mounds of ancient Etruscan cemeteries north of Rome?

Together with Chase I studied the material brought from the Sardis Excavations to the Metropolitan Museum of New York in 1916. Then on a journey to the excavations at Tarsus for Hetty Goldman and the Institute for Advanced Study, Princeton, in 1947–48, Mrs. Hanfmann and I did some detective work at Istanbul and Izmir museums. It became clear that while jewelry, coins, and some of the pottery were saved, much other material had perished when the Princeton excavation house was destroyed and its wooden parts and contents carried away.* Clearly the "collection of bronze mirrors, ivory and bone," much pottery, and all lamps and glass were lost —apparently just smashed into the ground. Some sculptures and other objects were also missing.

The Princeton House long stood as a picturesque ruin. We had hoped to preserve part of it, but it was demolished, allegedly after further damages by earthquake, in April 1969.

It was May 1948 when we went out to Sardis, in spring rain. The cobbled medieval east-west highway wound across the Pactolus on a wooden bridge. There were but a few houses along the southward path up to the Artemis Temple. We sat high up above the ruins with the village blacksmith who was our guide. "Americans are rich," said he, programmatically. "No, they are not." "But you are here" (meaning, "you are rich enough to travel"). We

*Shortly before his death, H. C. Butler gave a brief account of losses which seems to have been borne out since. *Sardis I*, preface dated August 1921.

tried to explain about grants and fellowships. He sighed, too courteous to contradict; then his eyes lit up as he looked upon the mighty temple and the red cliffs honeycombed with chambertombs. "But Croesus was a very rich man," said he triumphantly.

I was now determined that a new excavation of Sardis was needed. Butler had proclaimed as his major aim the study of Lydian culture. He saw in Sardis "an important pool in the stream of influence which flowed from Mesopotamia to Greece" and "a clearing house between the Orient and Greece on a route as old as ancient civilization" (*Sardis I*, p.2). By finding a number of inscriptions in the Lydian tongue at the Temple of Artemis and the cemetery he had proved that the Lydian capital was in the same general area as the big later Hellenistic, Roman, and Byzantine ruins. He had hoped to find at the temple what the British had found at the Artemis Temple at Ephesus (1901–02), an archaic level with rich finds. Yet this archaic level never became clearly defined in the temple area. The new knowledge of Lydian culture came almost entirely from objects found in the few dozen tombs, most of them previously disturbed and plundered. In fact, Butler had not been able to determine the exact location of the Lydian city of Sardis itself; only once, just before the outbreak of the war, did he come upon what he thought were Lydian buildings in a dry brook northeast of the temple (Northeast Wadi; see Map 3, no. 16). In 1922 T. L. Shear started testing there and on the Acropolis, but had to leave. He did have, however, one of the most extraordinary strokes of luck in the annals of archaeology. He found literally "a pot of gold," a little Lydian pot, so-called "lydion," with 36 gold pieces of Croesus, in the crack of a Roman tomb which was apparently built right into an earlier Lydian grave—and which the Romans had missed!

We were certainly not going to object to treasures but treasures were not our aim when we began the Harvard–Cornell–American Schools of Oriental

Research expedition to Sardis. "The prime objective of any research at Sardis is the Lydian city of Croesus and his predecessors . . . which remains completely unknown." This was the statement we made in our proposal of 1958. Beyond that we envisaged the study of the development of all human settlements in the Sardis area, from Stone Age through the earlier Islamic phases. "Here astride the major road into Asia, Mediterranean and Eastern peoples, cultures, and religions met and interacted . . . Thus Sardis is uniquely suited to demonstrate the modern multi-disciplinary approach in which humanists and scientists open new vistas upon the history of humanity." We hoped to reconstitute here a case history of urbanism in a vital region between East and West.

According to literary sources, the city of Croesus held such major targets as the temples, the agora described by Herodotus, the mint, where the earliest coins in the world were made, and, above all, the palace of Croesus whose archives must have contained correspondence with Assyria, Egypt, Babylon, Media, and most of the Greek states and sanctuaries.

After I revisited Sardis in 1953 and 1957, the second time with Dean A. H. Detweiler of Cornell, it became clear that the city of the Persian satraps (547–334 B.C.), and the Hellenistic and Roman cities also had remained virtually unknown. Even the few considerable ruins visible above ground had not been scientifically described or surveyed (theater, stadium, Early Christian and Byzantine churches and public buildings, Byzantine city wall). The towering, picturesque Acropolis of Sardis, presumably harboring the earliest settlement, was said by Shear to contain Greek and Lydian strata but nothing had been recorded. Indeed, nothing was known about even the bold Byzantine or Late Roman fortress crowning the Acropolis, although it had been searched for inscriptions.

The situation was even more tantalizing at the gigantic cemetery at Bin Tepe and the Gygean Lake behind it, the latter mentioned earlier than Sardis, by Homer in the *Iliad*. Spiegelthal had made an assault on the Alyattes mound, and Dennis had opened but did not publish various chamber graves. (Some were drawn and published by the distinguished French architectural historian A. Choisy, but their location was not indicated.) Meantime, modern irrigation was rapidly changing the appearance of the entire Hermus plain and of the cemetery. A canal into the lake had raised the level of the water. Prehistoric pile dwellings allegedly seen in the lake and collections of Prehistoric stone implements gave hints that here, perhaps, were to be found the earliest settlements of the Sardian Plain. Ancient writers wrote about a famous sanctuary of Artemis Koloe which was somewhere near the lake.

We could hope, too, to find either in the city or out at Bin Tepe the evidence to resolve some major controversies which had resulted from the decipherment of the Royal archives of the Hittite kings at Hattusa (Boğazköy). Some scholars thought that Hittites had penetrated Lydia. Others saw in it the kingdom of Assuwa which, in turn, gave the name of Asia to the entire continent. Others thought that the region might have belonged to another Indo-European group, the Luvian. Others pointed to Herodotus' statement that the dynasty of the sons of Herakles had assumed rule over Lydia and Sardis 505 years before the accession of the Mermnad Dynasty and king Gyges (680 plus 505 would make it 1185 B.C.), and suggested that Mycenaean Greek heroes wandering about after the fall of Troy might have seized the region; and others yet thought the forerunners of the Etruscans might have lived at Sardis when it was still called Hyde (Strabo says that Sardis and its citadel was originally called Hyde; *hut* being "four" in Etruscan the name was thought to mean "Tetrapolis").

Such were some of the problems and prizes we had considered. On behalf of the Fogg Museum of Art at Harvard I had made a proposal to the Bollingen Foundation. Its President, J. D. Barrett, suggested that we should try to secure the sponsorship of the American Schools of Oriental Research. Albert Henry Detweiler of Cornell was then President of the Schools. A veteran of many Near Eastern digs, including Tepe Gawra, Seleucia on the Tigris, Gerasa, and Doura, he embraced the proposal with enthusiasm and subsequently Cornell University, especially the College of Architecture, of which Detweiler was Associate Dean, joined the project. He became its field adviser and later associate director.

The Bollingen Foundation had stipulated that its grant should be matched by Harvard and Cornell jointly. Under the Harvardian system of ETOB ("each tub on its own bottom"), I had to find the means; and thus came into being the Supporters of Sardis, an informal group, whose contributions came to carry the show through its ups and downs. Future sociologists may find it of interest that starting from 47 the first year, the Supporters came to include over four hundred people by 1970, compared to Butler's thirty-nine helpers. To communicate with these friends, I started writing letters from the field, usually three each season; and another letter went to the members of the American Schools of Oriental Research. It is these letters, pared down, that constitute the book which follows. They encompass the immediate preparations and the campaigns from 1958 to 1971. For the period described the project was financed initially by the Bollingen Foundation (1957–1965), then by the Old Dominion Foundation (1966–1968); by university grants from Cornell University (1958–1967); by grants from Corning Museum of Glass (1960–1971); the Loeb Classical Library Foundation (1965–1970); the Ford Foundation by training grant to Cornell University (1968–1972); the Department of State under Public Law 480 (1962–1965); the National Endowment for the Humanities (1967–1971); and several Fogg Museum Funds, primarily the Sardis Expedition Fund and the Sardis Synagogue Fund to which some 400 friends have contributed. From the beginning Turkish colleagues and students took part. Altogether, 197 staff members from 42 institutions worked at Sardis during this period.*

*See the Staff List, pp. 331–343.

Our initial plan was to have two phases: Phase A, 1958–1960, in which we would test various promising areas and lay the groundwork for extensive operations; and a Phase B, at that time estimated to last three more seasons, which would include large-scale excavation of big urban areas and "a cooperative study of Sardis and the Sardian region in collaboration with institutions concerned with ecological research and economic and religious history."

This is where our story begins. I should like to warn the reader that it was not possible to keep our illustrations completely in chronological sequence. This would have meant much repetition, as each major sector advanced a little more each season. We have tried to meet the needs of scholars and students for systematic knowledge in our preliminary reports in the *Bulletin of the American Schools of Oriental Research (BASOR)*. The letters were meant to give the highlights of our dig and our finds; they were also meant to let our friends take part in our work and our life.

Chronology

5000?–2000 B.C.	Early farmers settle in the Hermus valley. Early Bronze Age burials (2500—2000 B.C.) found in 1967 on south shore of Gygean Lake by Sardis expedition.	Prehistoric Period
1500–1300 B.C.	Large urn with cremation burial and a circular hut prove that people lived or traded in the city area.	Late Bronze Age (Hittite and Mycenaean)
1400–1200 B.C.	Royal archives of Hittites at Boğazköy mention kingdoms of Assuva and Masa, possibly in the region of Sardis.	
1185 B.C.	According to Herodotus, a new dynasty established at Sardis by the "Sons of Herakles."	
1200–900 B.C.	So-called "Mycenaean," "Sub-Mycenaean," and "Protogeometric" pottery, partly imported from Greece, partly imitated locally, found ca. 10 m. below present surface in "Lydian Trench" (Map 3) in 1966. Warrior bands from Greece roaming on Aegean coast after the fall of Troy may have seized the rule in Sardis.	
ca. 1000 B.C.	Emergence of painted pottery, recognizable as Lydian.	Lydian "Iron Age"
ca. 680 B.C.	Gyges founds the dynasty of Mermnads; sends embassies to Assyria; fights invading nomad tribes (Cimmerians) 660–645 B.C.; dies in battle at Sardis, 645 B.C.	Lydian Kingdom

15

ca. 670 B.C.	"Gold strike":—Gyges and Sardis become famous for gold. Sardis a world capital.	
645–561 B.C.	Kings Ardys, Alyattes. Invention of first coins.	
561–547 B.C.	Rule of Croesus. Lydian Kingdom from Dardanelles to Sangarios to south coast. Defeated by King Cyrus of Persia, besieged and killed October—November 547 B.C. Treasure of Croesus allegedly taken to Gazaca in eastern Iran.	
547–334 B.C.	Sardis as capital of the satrapy of Sfarda (Biblical Sepharad) and western Persian empire.	Persian Period
499 B.C.	Ionian Greeks attack and burn Sardis.	
401 B.C.	Xenophon and the Ten Thousand at Sardis. Altar of Artemis mentioned.	
334 B.C.	Alexander the Great captures Sardis without a fight, admires the triple defenses of the citadel, builds temple to Zeus Olympios.	Hellenistic
ca. 300 B.C.	Sardians attack Sacred Embassy from Artemis of Ephesus.	
ca. 300 B.C.–A.D. 17	Sardis as Hellenistic Greek city. Lydian language abandoned; Greek city constitution. Theater, stadium, gymnasia built.	
282 B.C.	Battle of Cyroupedion—Seleucus defeats Lysimachus of Macedon.	
270–ca. 190 B.C.	Sardis as a capital of Seleucid kingdom.	
215–213 B.C.	King Antiochus III besieges his uncle Achaeus in the citadel, murders	

	Achaeus, destroys city; then permits new "foundation" (*synoikismos*) under his viceroy Zeuxis. Settles Jewish families from Mesopotamia and Babylon. Defeated by Romans in 188 B.C.	
188–133 B.C.	Sardis under kings of Pergamon.	
46–28 B.C.	Roman decrees concerning Jewish community at Sardis.	Roman
A.D. 17	Sardis leveled by earthquake. Helped by Emperors Tiberius and Claudius (who gave aqueduct, ca. A.D. 50)	
A.D. 20–200	Replanning and urban renewal by Romans. Greatest area, largest population (possibly over 100,000).	
ca. 50–60	Church of Sardis addressed in the *Revelation*.	
166	Visit of Emperor Lucius Verus.	
ca. 400–616	Early Byzantine Sardis. Urban renewal, repairs; churches at Artemis Temple and at east edge of city ("D").	Early Byzantine
ca. 616	Persian king Chosroes II destroys lower city of Sardis.	
ca. 650–700	Severe earthquakes bring down Sardis buildings; landslides from citadel.	Middle Byzantine (A.D. 616–1072)
seventh century	Acropolis citadel built of remains of ancient buildings.	
718	Arab attack.	
ca. 1200	Byzantine church ("E") built at **Pactolus North**.	
ca. 1300	Turks occupy Sardis. Turk-Byzantine joint occupation of citadel.	Islamic

1368	Metropolis transferred to Philadelphia.	
1405	Conquest of Tamerlane.	
ca. 1420	Last traces of continuous occupation of Acropolis.	
1446	Italian traveler, Cyriacus of Ancona, reports on "temple of Zeus" and inscriptions.	Era of study and excavation
ca. 1680	Turkish traveler Evliya Çelebi, mentions Sart as a *kaza* (county seat).	
1910–1914, 1922	American excavations under Howard Crosby Butler, Princeton University. Excavates Artemis Temple, 1100 graves.	
1958–	Excavations of Fogg Museum of Harvard University and Cornell University sponsored by American Schools of Oriental Research.	
1964–	Restoration work in collaboration with Department of Antiquities, Ministry of National Education, Republic of Turkey.	

Map 1

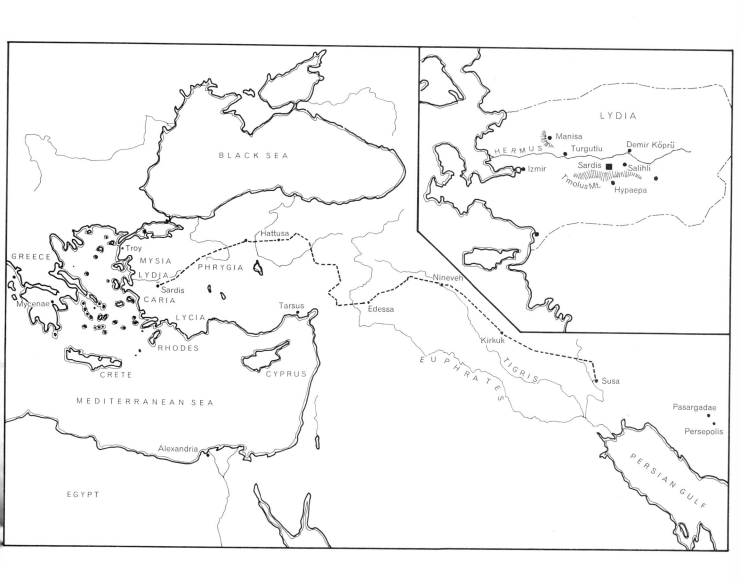

GREECE

BLACK SEA

Troy

MYSIA

PHRYGIA

Hattusa

LYDIA

Sardis

CARIA

Mycenae

LYCIA

Tarsus

Nineveh

Edessa

RHODES

CYPRUS

Kirkuk

CRETE

MEDITERRANEAN SEA

EUPHRATES

TIGRIS

Susa

Pasargadae

Persepolis

Alexandria

PERSIAN GULF

EGYPT

LYDIA

HERMUS

Manisa

Turgutlu

Demir Köprü

Izmir

Sardis

Salihli

Tmolus Mt.

Hypaepa

Map 2

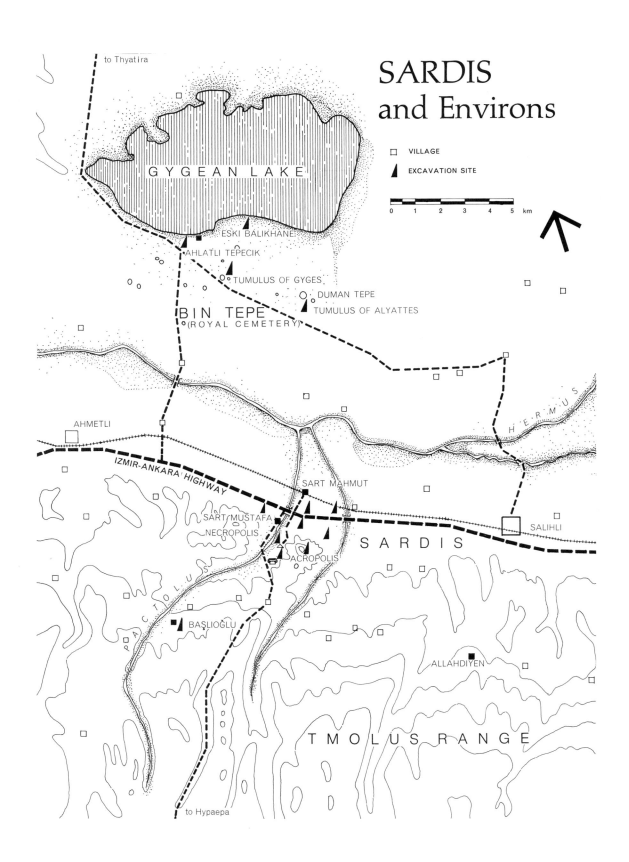

to Thyatira

SARDIS
and Environs

□ VILLAGE

◤ EXCAVATION SITE

0 1 2 3 4 5 km

GYGEAN LAKE

ESKI BALIKHANE

AHLATLI TEPECIK

TUMULUS OF GYGES

DUMAN TEPE

TUMULUS OF ALYATTES

BIN TEPE
(ROYAL CEMETERY)

HERMUS

AHMETLI

IZMIR-ANKARA HIGHWAY

SART MAHMUT

SART MUSTAFA

NECROPOLIS

SARDIS

SALIHLI

ACROPOLIS

PACTOLUS

BAŞLIOGLU

ALLAHDIYEN

TMOLUS RANGE

to Hypaepa

Map 3

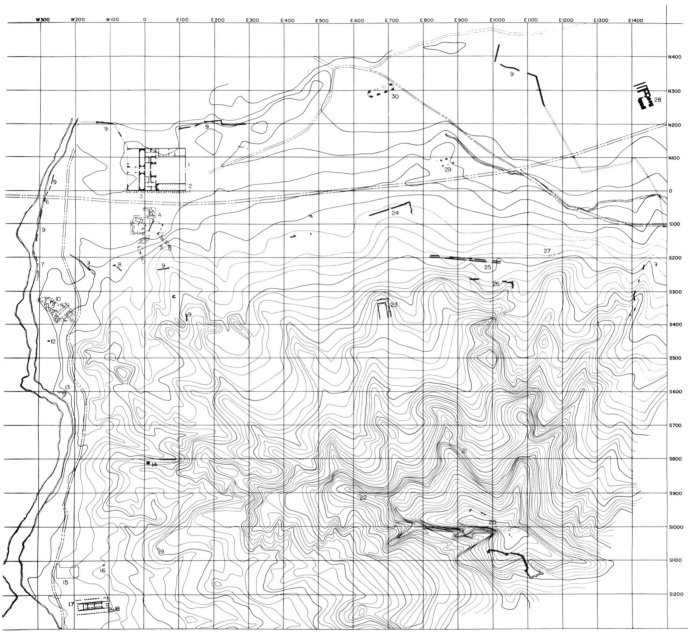

mag. N

0 50 100 150
meters

1	Gymnasium	11	Church 'E'
2	Synagogue	12	Peacock Tomb
3	Byzantine Shops	13	Pactolus Cliff
4	House of Bronzes	14	Pyramid Tomb
5	Upper Terrace	15	Expedition Headquarters
6	Roman Bridge	16	Northeast Wadi
7	Pactolus Industrial Area	17	Temple of Artemis
8	Southwest Gate	18	Church 'M'
9	Byzantine City Wall	19	Kagirlik Tepe
10	Pactolus North	20	Acropolis

21	Tunnels
22	'Flying Towers'
23	Byzantine Fortress
24	Roman Civic Center 'A'
25	Roman Stadium
26	Theater
27	'Odeion'
28	Complex 'CG'
29	Building 'D' (Church)
30	Roman Building 'C'

MASTER

URBAN PLAN

JANUARY 1970

1958

Istanbul   April 12, 1958

I am writing this report the night before my return to America while things are fresh in my mind. The thousand lights of Istanbul are spread amphitheatrically through the night as I look down on the hills of the two banks of the Golden Horn from the heights of Tepebashi.

You may want to hear about Sardis first. I found it as impressive as ever in scenery (*Figures 1–5*) and antiquity. I had never seen it this early in the year, and in some ways it looks grander, more awe-inspiring, at this time when spring contends with winter. Snow still lay on the highest tops of the Tmolus range and vaporous, torn clouds floated along its wooded flanks. Wetness—and wet it was two out of three days—brings out different aspects of the ruins, in fact even different and new ruins. On the last of my visits I conceived the injudicious—in light of the weather—idea of cutting across the high green field to follow the ancient city wall, which is preserved to considerable height and forms a clearly defined support of the great scarp that limited the ancient city in Byzantine and Roman times. A brook flows along the foot of this mighty wall which together with the supporting part reaches heights of thirty feet. From this vantage point I saw three new ruins —new to me, that is, though they are certainly too big to be easily overlooked.

I was frequently drenched to the bones. Drying out at the stove of the *kahvehane* ("coffee house" and social center) of the lower village of Sart Mahmut gave an occasion to talk to the villagers. I found the people of that village keenly interested in the possibility of excavation work. Labor is one aspect which looks encouraging. In addition to the lower village of Sart Mahmut, said to have about a thousand inhabitants, there is the upper village

Figure 1 (left)—Looking west from the Acropolis over the Pactolus valley before the Harvard-Cornell excavations. In center, Artemis Temple and precinct. Above, the Pactolus River bed lined with trees, and beyond, Necropolis Hill with hundreds of rock-cut Lydian graves, which Artemis was supposed to protect. Left center, ruins of the Princeton Expedition House; empty space right of the Temple became the site of our camp.

Figure 2 (right)—Looking east from west bank of the Pactolus toward the eroded pinnacles of the Acropolis. The last units of the camp, a work room and storage shed for objects, are being built.

of Sart Mustafa, of about half the size (see Map 2). There seems to be no question but that we can get the fifty or so workmen which is all I think we can schedule for this campaign.

To revert to archaeology of Sardis, its soil keeps bringing up an ever new harvest of sculptural and architectural fragments. The peasants, too, are building their new houses with ancient fragments, giving natural preference to well-cut pieces of masonry; but I have seen occasional decorated fragments and one of our incidental pastimes may well be a little checking to see if any important pieces or inscriptions are among these "spoils."

In the Museum of Manisa (Figure 7) I was shown a half-dozen new pieces of sculpture from Sardis, and the District Commissioner of Salihli led us to the men's room at City Hall to point out a handsome marble leg with a lion's head, also from Sardis. The most fascinating find was made four years ago by peasants quarrying stones on the steep bank of the "gold-bearing Pactolus" torrent (see Map 2). This was a beautiful archaic torso (Figure 8), now in Manisa, the first statue of a human figure from the time of Croesus. I thought we ought to see the exact findspot—visions of an archaic temple precinct replete with archaic statuary rising before my covetous eye. Regrettably, the archaic piece was found in the wall of what seems to be either a Roman house or a Roman tomb—and thus it was not in its original location. However, the walls and floors—"the Room of the Archaic Statue" had a black and white mosaic floor—are very clearly exposed in the cut made by the Pactolus and would make a worthwhile and not too difficult sector, these structures being only one to ten feet below modern surface. Our future excavation commissioner, Kemal Ziya Polatkan, who is director of the Manisa Museum, and I will publish the piece shortly.*

Archaeology, on this trip, had to take a back seat to the preparations for archaeology. I had flown off on March 20 at the height of a snowstorm at Idlewild. Upon arrival in Istanbul, I arranged for the opening of an account

*G. M. A. Hanfmann and K. Z. Polatkan, "Three Sculptures from Sardis in the Manisa Museum," Anatolia 4 (1959): 55–60, pls. 9–10.

Figure 3—Acropolis of Sardis seen against the Tmolus range. Izmir to Ankara State Highway is the modern successor to the Persian Royal Road which began in Susa near the Indian Ocean and terminated in Sardis near the Mediterranean, a distance of 1800 miles.

in Manisa, the ancient Magnesia ad Sipylum and now the seat of the governor (*vali*) and administration of the province in which Sardis is located. I then went to Ankara to discuss such matters as appointment of commissioner, construction of an expedition house, arrival and customs clearance of our supplies, and applications for educational permits for import of vehicles. I finally reached Ankara but only after: the plane flight was canceled because of snowstorm; the Ankara express train which I had then made in hot haste was wrecked spectacularly on the shores of an angry lake; the first taxi we took to escape from the immobilized train toward the Ankara highway collapsed with a flat tire; a bus got us to Adapazari in pouring rain at 3 A.M. —when everything was shut down tight; a taxi, finally found to go the 330 kilometers to Ankara, had to give up halfway because passes over Bolu Dağ were snowbound; another bus finally made it from Düzce—arriving at Ankara 4:15 P.M., still twelve hours ahead of the first train to come through after the wreck.

The warm hospitality and kindness of various friends and acquaintances made the stay in Ankara very pleasant. Negotiations with Kâmil Su, Director General of Antiquities and Museums, were most cordial. Unfortunately, rising costs forced revision of plans for the excavation house and museum. The architect of the department, Avni Kirkağaçioğlu, and his staff made a revised plan and drawings within three days.

I then commuted for several days between Manisa, Salihli, and Sardis, mostly accompanied by our commissioner, Kemal Ziya Polatkan. Kemal Bey is a genial person, and very ambitious for the Sardis excavation. Last summer he was commissioner for the Austrian excavation at Ephesus which is run with a tremendous amount of machinery such as tractors, conveyor belts, and trucks, and before his optimistic vision the excavation at Sardis is assuming a like stature.

The trip was undertaken to set things in motion and this has been done. It would be unwise, however, to assume that the unexpected will not happen or that everything will happen as expected.

Figure 4—In 1960, almost nothing was visible of the Marble Court and Synagogue, which after excavation became outstanding features of the Roman gymnasium area (above the modern highway; compare Figure 226). The central building and later the whole area were called "B" following the designation set by the Princeton Expedition in 1910. In foreground across the highway, the first trenches are being cut in the Lydian Market area (left). On the right is the Early Byzantine "House of Bronzes" after which the sector was named "HoB." In the background is the rich plain of the Hermus River (Gediz Cay).

The house-building project undertaken jointly by the Ministry of Education (Department of Antiquities) and the Sardis Expedition is in principle agreed upon. Plans are drawn, and the competent *tekniker* of the Department of Education in Manisa, Ismail Kuralay, has agreed to supervise and has made a detailed estimate. The Governor of Manisa, the Lieutenant Governor, and the Director of Education have appointed a building committee of three. For a while it looked as if construction would start around April 15, but the cost to be shared approximately 50–50 was shown by the detailed estimate to exceed the funds available this year, because the share of the Ministry of Education is available only in two budgetary years.

Through the efficient cooperation of my friend of last year's trip to Bin Tepe, the *Kaymakam* (District Commissioner of Salihli), the school building at Sardis has been placed at our disposal. In the village we are renting the house of a school teacher and her mother, whom we are evicting for the summer.

Preparations have been made for the arrival of supplies, and Mehmed Ali Yeğenoğlu, an Izmir merchant, formerly a teacher, recommended by Everett Blake of the American Girls' College, has agreed to purchase and store (at a fee) equipment that we have planned to secure in Turkey.

Kemal Bey and I ascertained the facts about ownership of fields on or adjacent to ruins we may plan to excavate this or next year. I think we more or less bought the "City Gate"; at any rate, money has been left for this purpose with our commissioner.

A sobering fact and one that makes emphatic the need for more supporters and more support has emerged during this trip. Prices in Turkey have gone up 10 to 15 percent, thus putting pressure on what seemed a liberal budget when it was drawn up last year. This will hit us where it hurts an excavator most—in the size of the working force, and to some degree, in the extent of equipment that we can use (for example, rent of trucks or other earth-moving equipment). Again and again I am impressed by the great promise

but also the great size of Sardis. Whatever we do this year, we are certain to need more, I should say many more, workmen next year.

Sardis   Summer 1958

The Archaeological Exploration of Sardis, sponsored by the American Schools of Oriental Research in partnership with Cornell University and the Fogg Art Museum of Harvard University, is now well along in its first campaign. Early in June Mrs. Ilse Hanfmann, recorder, John Washeba, conservator, Donald P. Hansen, archaeologist, and I as field director, all of Harvard, arrived in Izmir. With the vigorous help of our Turkish commissioner, Kemal Ziya Polatkan, we set up camp in the village school at Sart Mustafa (*Figure 6*). The location of our headquarters amidst the green trees and under the shadow of a slender minaret is indeed picturesque, offering beautiful views of the bold crags of the Sardis Acropolis (*Figure 2*), of the nearly sheer red wall of Necropolis Hill (*Figure 1*, so named after the many Lydian tombs found at its foot), and finally across to the gigantic mound of king Alyattes visible beyond the wide Hermus plain.

To secure additional living quarters for the staff and sufficient working and storage space, we annexed and refurbished the "official room" (*köy odasi*) of the village and a sizable village house. Our renovation of the "official room" created such enthusiasm among the villagers that they contributed additional materials for the embellishment of the building, which henceforth received the nickname of "Kresus Palas."

During late June and early July frequent arrivals completed the roster of the staff. We were happy to welcome to our ranks our field adviser, the President of the American Schools of Oriental Research, A. Henry Detweiler. Other members of the staff during the current campaign are Thomas H. Canfield, Cornell University, architect; Marion Dean Ross, University of Oregon, architect; Sherman E. Johnson, Church Divinity School of the

Figure 5 (left)—Clouds over the Royal Cemetery of Bin Tepe. In the center of the photograph is the mound (BT 63.1) of king Gyges (died 645 B.C.); it was dug by the expedition from 1963 to 1966. This picture was taken from the top of the mound of king Alyattes, father of Croesus.

Figure 6 (right)—The Acropolis of Sardis and the village of Sart Mustafa, where we set up camp in the village school until our house was built.

Pacific, archaeologist and epigrapher; Mrs. Catharine S. Detweiler, numismatist; and Baki Öğün, archaeologist of the University of Ankara, who was also assigned by the Department of Antiquities the function of assistant commissioner. Mrs. Jean Johnson has been doing invaluable work, especially in the cataloging and recording of glass and lamps. Finally, we have added to our staff as draftsman and general helper Güven Bakir of the Manisa Museum.

Don Hansen came to us straight from the Oriental Institute excavations at Nippur; Sherman and Jean Johnson are veterans of El Jib; Dean Ross has done architectural field work for the National Park Service; Baki Öğün has participated in the excavations of many Turkish sites.

Sardis   June 1958

The summer heat is upon us and the humidity is not so little. We have been leading a somewhat strange life alternating between spells of hectic activity and unavoidable periods of sitting and waiting. Still, despite the fact that we had to start from scratch without the American equipment, we have managed to get ourselves established at Sart Mustafa. More important is the accomplishment of getting the excavation started on schedule. On June 20 we began to dig alongside the Temple of Artemis (*Figures 9–10*; Map 3, no. 17). On June 25, we had our first thrilling find—a Lydian inscription (*Figure 11*). It was on a black-glazed sherd, deeply incised. Only four letters preserved (not a four-letter word, I hope).* It was very encouraging that one of our as yet little trained pickmen not only spotted the piece but recognized its importance.

We are finding sizable numbers of Lydian sherds, more perhaps already

*RLAM is the reading accepted by R. Gusmani, *Lydisches Worterbuch* (1964), no. 57. The meaning is unknown.

Figure 7 (left)—Muradiye Mosque in Manisa, sixteenth century, built by the famous Turkish architect Sinan. In the building next to it, the former religious school (Medresse) is the Manisa Museum, where many of the Sardis finds may be seen.

Figure 8 (right)—A beautiful archaic torso of the Croesan era (ca. 550 B.C.) was found by chance on the bank of the Pactolus in 1954. Hoping to find more archaic sculptures and perhaps an archaic sanctuary, we started digging in this spot in 1960. Torso is now in the Manisa Museum.

than were recorded by the First Sardis Expedition. Our trench *(Figure 10)* is laid parallel and some 10 meters distant from the south side of the great Artemis Temple, and is about 9 by 15 meters. When our digging was stopped temporarily by the great Bayram (holiday) on Friday, we had gone down about 1.20 meters below the so-called "Lydian level" which H. C. Butler, the leader of the First Sardis Expedition, had exposed along this side of the Temple. Among the vase fragments are some that may be as early as the eighth century B.C., but the bulk of Lydian and a few Greek (or Greek type) fragments would do for anything between the late seventh and the fifth centuries B.C. A Lydian bronze earring has also turned up.

This sector is quite a sight *(Figure 9)* with workmen shoveling, sifting the earth into sieves, and wheelbarrows going in procession to and from the Pactolus bank—all raising clouds of dust. The workmen have a little shelter with a huge earthen jar (pithos) set into the ground in the shadow while we have what is known here as a *çardak*, a sort of arbor thrown together out of tree branches which are taken with leaves and so form a fairly solid shadowing roof. We have a little water jar, the same shape as the old amphorae; we have all been most impressed with the way in which these porous jars keep the water cool by evaporation.

Don Hansen has been carrying the major burden of the supervision of the field work and is doing a wonderful job—not only in the actual direction of the digging but also in showing our workmen how to dig. Jack Washeba has been alternating between carpentry and archaeology. He was in charge of a very necessary and, as it turned out, very hot assignment—to clear the brush and wildlife out of the "City Gate" area *(Figure 22* and Map 3, no. 28). Inasmuch as the locals firmly believe that this place is infested with all species of scorpions and serpents, the final solution was to dig a fire ditch around the area and then burn down the vegetation. I was not there, but Jack says the workmen looked like something out of Hades—small wonder if you add the

Figure 9—Beginning excavations at the Artemis Temple, June 20, 1958. At this stage wooden wheelbarrows were used to dump excavated earth on the edge of the Pactolus. Setting levels for the trench is architect D. Ross (in tropical helmet), followed by chief foreman Hasan Koramaz (in cap) and rod boy; archaeologist D. Hansen (in cap) peers out of the trench. In the background, Byzantine waterpipe leading to reservoir and Temple.

heat of the brush to the summer midday blaze. Operations at the "City Gate" will now begin in earnest. (We had deferred that sector because we waited for more workmen and because there was an additional negotiation to be completed concerning our right of way from the highway through a cotton field—we are renting the strip and paying for the equivalent of the harvest.)

Ilse Hanfmann has set up the records, largely with substitute materials. The flood of objects begins to rise and we shall be glad to see some additional members arriving on the scene. Our Turkish "trainee," actually a colleague with a number of years of digging experience, Baki Öğün, of the Department of Antiquities, should be arriving tomorrow; of the architects, Dean Ross has already gone into action. We have managed to borrow a level from the Surveyors' Office in Manisa, and the architect who is building the excavation house, Ismail Kuralay, very kindly brought it to Sardis and took points and levels for our trench; Dean was in on this operation (*Figure 9*). The long-awaited "Expeditor" with our equipment finally made port in Izmir on June 28 so we now can look forward to an eventual reunion with our equipment.

In addition to recording things archaeological, Ilse also has the task of making life possible for archaeologists. It turned out to be something of a job to convert into livable units the various village rooms that we have either annexed or rented, particularly as practically any kind of item needed involves a trip to either Salihli or Izmir—a bit of a problem for the presently carless expedition. We have been bumming rides into Salihli and renting a truck for return with the loot. The jeep (if and when released by customs) will make a big difference.

We have taken on the usual, unavoidable retinue—cook and helper, man to go into Salihli, several guards to guard the equipment at the sectors, a boy to assist Jack in his carpentry and laboratory. The most interesting character

Figure 10 (left)—Trench south of Artemis Temple, seen from the west. On the right is the Byzantine drain, and Levels II, III, and IV. The Artemis Temple and the Acropolis are in the background.

Figure 11 (middle)—Potsherd with Lydian graffito, our first Lydian inscription, was found in Level II, trench south of Artemis Temple.

Figure 12 (right)—Lydian terracotta die from Level III, trench south of Artemis Temple. The cube measures one inch. Herodotus reported that the Lydians invented many games to forget their hunger during a famine.

is a venerable patriarch who guards the supplies in the tent*—his name is Yakup Çauş ("Sergeant"-foreman) and he was with the First Sardis Expedition from 1912 on.

Sardis   August 1, 1958

At the beginning of July we had to pause briefly to celebrate the Kurban Bayrami commemorating the sacrifice of Isaac. All through the moonlit night the drums were beating at the upper and lower village, and some of our younger members were induced by their local friends to join in the men's dancing at the small kahvehane.

We have begun to develop our program of combining investigation of large buildings visible above ground with soundings designed to test promising areas. The large structure known as Building B *(Figures 15, 16;* Map 3, no. 1) was briefly alluded to by Butler. It had been much admired by early travelers, who saw in it the palace of Croesus, but it has never been excavated or recorded. With its two long apsidal halls, its intricate system of pillars, niches, and arches, and its central unit which may have had a dome, this complex presents a great challenge to the student of architectural history. Standing firm amidst clouds of dust which violent winds blow across this knoll, Tom Canfield has been conducting both a precise architectural survey and the digging, assisted by various members of the staff. With huge amounts of debris to be moved, we are hard at the work of clearing part of the southern facade and the long eastern flank. Already fruitful developments have occurred. A most remarkable yet puzzling find was made in the dead center of the southern apse. On a shelf or podium which goes round

---

*"The tent" is a circus tent which we borrowed from the American Girls' College in Izmir. Its erection by the joint forces of everybody from the District Comissioners down was a great event in the life of the village of Sart Mustafa.

the apse, there was found a large curving marble base *(Figures 17, 18)*, which, as its monumental inscription informs us, originally carried a statue of the emperor Lucius Verus (A.D. 161–169). The dedicant, Claudius Antonius Lepidus, known from another Sardian inscription, held the high office of Chief Priest of Asia.

As far as objects are concerned, our most productive area developed when a row of rooms came to light directly south of the facade of the big building *(Figure 19)*. Pottery, glass, nails, iron implements, and, above all, great numbers of coins, chiefly Byzantine, have come from all three levels that we have been able to distinguish so far. From the lowest, perhaps Early Byzantine (fifth to sixth century) level, we retrieved the fragments of a small Roman statue of Attis, which had been broken up and used as bedding for a floor.

A mile to the east two walls of mighty limestone masonry, three to four courses high, formed an intriguing ruin. Noting briefly its existence, Butler had speculated that this might be the eastern city gate of Sardis, where the famous Royal Road of the Persians entered the city *(Figure 22)*. Optimistically, we thought of it as a "limited objective" that might well be attained within the scope of one campaign. Now, a month later, and some six meters down into the ground, we know better. The grandiose structure was found to have a large arched main gate. Devoting himself single-mindedly to this task, Dean Ross has been freeing the eastern part of the building to which there is a western counterpart. Cascades of blocks weighing some two to three tons had fallen from the building at various times, and lacking appropriate machinery our workmen have been performing Herculean deeds with crowbars and levers to move these obstacles out of the excavation. That the big gate was flanked by several smaller arches was clear. Recently it became apparent that one extended into a half-dome. The latest surprise came yesterday when another mighty arch began to emerge *under* the great

arched gateway. We can trace the later history of the building through squatter's ash floors and a brick structure built into the gate after the passage had been blocked up, but we have yet a long way to go before we can appraise with certainty the original date and design. Certain it is that its austere grandeur evokes visions which rival Piranesi's fancies in his famous Carceri.

While a few fragments of sculpture and a half-dozen inscriptions have come to light in the excavations proper, our coming to Sart has focused the flow of accidental finds. Sherman Johnson has combined with greatest efficiency the duties of excavator, photographer, and epigrapher. His careful examination of the inscriptions now at Sardis lists a total of some sixty believed to be new, all but two in Greek. He has also ascertained that some fifty inscriptions published in *Sardis VII, Part I*, are still at Sart.

A stepped trench dug by Don Hansen on Kagirlik Tepe (see Map 3, no. 19), northeast of and above the Artemis Temple, revealed a cemetery of Roman and probably Early Christian times. Another sounding was started today in an area across the highway from Building B, where according to our calculations an important part of the ancient city was located.

What I can hardly convey in this letter is the tremendous number and variety of the ruins of ancient Sardis. A full circuit from our headquarters in Sart Mustafa to the Artemis precinct, to Kagirlik, to Building B, to the "City Gate" (CG) is a matter of at least three miles (see Maps 2 and 3). In the early "heroic" days of the excavation this circuit was walked by the staff two, three, or even four times—no joke in the glaring heat of noon.

Our relations with the local authorities, the District Commissioner and other officials at Salihli and the many officers of the Province of Manisa, have been most cordial. Indeed, His Excellency, the Governor (Vali) of Manisa visited the excavation on the second day and several times since. The Commissioner of Education has let us use his office as headquarters during visits

Figure 14—A Turkish brickmaker and his product. The mudbricks, cut and dried in the back yard, went into the construction of the showers.

to Manisa. Acting on behalf of the Ministry of Education, his department has joined forces with the expedition in the construction of the permanent excavation house and compound, which is now going up (*Figures 2, 13*). Unfortunately we shall not be able to enjoy the new quarters this year, since the excavation house will be completed after our departure. We hope, however, to be able to store some of our equipment in the basement, which should be completed in September.

The Americans at Izmir and also at the great dam project of Demir Köprü have been much interested in our work, as have the Turkish magazines and newspapers. (We may appear in the Turkish "Life"—no relation to the American.) Donald B. Eddy, the American consul, has shown the utmost kindness as well as exemplary efficiency in dealing with the various problems we have brought before him, and American officers of the NATO command have been most helpful to the expedition. It may be fairly said that the importance of our undertaking for cultural relations between Turkey and the United States is appreciated in many circles.

As we were readying our camp we were skillfully piloted through the proper channels of Turkish economic life by our commissioner. Glass, sugar, tea, concrete, and at times gasoline are subject to special allocation permits. By careful combing of the teeming, still rather Oriental market of Izmir and of the prosperous, cotton-growing center of Salihli we found suitable substitutes for many American products and also learned a good deal about local tools and products. We have now a much clearer picture of the possibilities of supplying the expedition, and the operation is running smoothly. Scholarly and diplomatic visitors begin to arrive in increasing number.

The season at Sardis will continue until September, but even now we feel certain that the results of the first, partly exploratory campaign justify the plan of a long-term, large-scale excavation of this magnificent site.

Sardis   August 1958

The last four weeks our excavation has been running on all cylinders. What a pleasure it is to see every section of the staff now busy at full capacity and getting first-rate results. The liberation of our nonconsumable supplies from customs set off the march, sending our three architects on their great rounds of surveying and mapping, according to the Detweiler Surveying system.*

Both our big buildings are good examples of architectural design, yet totally different—the massive "City Gate" with its series of huge arches and stupendous masonry; and Building B excelling in intricacies of apses, pillars, brick arches, and goodness knows what yet. Growing apace out of the ground in the Artemis precinct is Butler's so-called Lydian Building. That too is proving to be a much deeper and larger affair than it looked at first sight—not merely a row of shops or a store.

Jack Washeba, who had been working with stopgap materials, has swung into action. He is cramped for space in his laboratory (formerly a stable) by the boxes we have to store there, but it does look and work like a laboratory. With the aid of two young Turkish boys (both now make a point of wearing aprons) he has been getting excellent results with coins and metal objects. Catharine Detweiler, as our numismatist, has been able to identify many of them now that I borrowed Wroth's *Byzantine Coins* from Paul Underwood† on a flying trip to Istanbul. We just had our first important result—a sealed

---

*Henry Detweiler wrote a handy and popular *Manual of Archaeological Surveying* (1948) which was required reading for Sardis architects.

†Paul Underwood, professor of Byzantine archaeology at Dumbarton Oaks, was Director of the Byzantine Institute at Istanbul.

Figure 15 (left)—Workmen with horsecart begin excavation of Building B, the Roman gymnasium complex north of highway in Hermus Plain. An unequal struggle—wooden wheelbarrows and one-horse carts trying to remove tons of debris.

Figure 16 (right)—Commissioner Kemal Ziya Polatkan (in tropical helmet), his assistant Muharrem Taǧtekin, and a workman examine ruins of Building B before excavations.

hoard of coins of Heraclius—which dates the second level of a row of Byzantine Shops (*Figure 19*). Ray Winfield Smith,* who came here on a one day visit, tells me that this is the first time that Byzantine glass (of which we have been finding not only fine vessels but also window panes) will be so accurately dated by coins and periods.

Sherman Johnson has gone after the local epigraphic material—sixty new inscriptions, so far. With the arrival of the supplies, he has started making both paper and pliotex squeezes—in fact the big Verus inscription (*Figure 18*) is just being "squeezed."

Finally, the expedition house is growing and we have proceeded to plan a compound for next year. It is clear that the staff is going to increase (we shall have had fifteen members instead of the planned ten by the end of this season) and there is talk in various circles of making this a center for Turkish-American student study in archaeology. Henry Detweiler thinks that this is what the American Schools of Oriental Research should aim at.

It is tremendously hot but dry here—and nearly cold at night. There is a great fruit season on: delicious honeydews and peaches as well as fine seedless grapes. We are given quite a lot of them regularly by the village well-wishers. Automobiles having become a regular sight here, the village kids have acquired the civilized disease of riding on the bumpers—together with chickens that run back and forth in front of the cars, herds of sheep, and donkeys that will not get up from the middle of the road, they create considerable traffic hazards.

We shall probably work on the "City Gate" until August 15, then shift the workmen from there to the construction of the compound wall around the new house—the "City Gate" (which is currently producing evidence that it served as a glass factory in Byzantine times) will take a lot of recording. On the other sectors, work will go on until September 1.

*Eminent expert and collector of glass. See the catalog *Glass from the Ancient World: The Ray Winfield Smith Collection* (Corning, New York, 1957).

Sardis   August 12, 1958

In order to explore some areas of ancient Sardis, we decided to let Don Hansen, who is our soundings specialist, have a fling at a new spot. Originally we had in mind a field on a slope where the ancient city wall begins to climb upward to the Acropolis. Ancient Lydian sherds found on the surface promise a rich harvest, and we hope to dig that area next year if we can get the land. But for now we decided on a trial trench right by the highway, across from Building B and the Byzantine Shops (Map 3, no. 3) which we have been excavating for the past few weeks. We thought we might find in the new sounding the main street of Sardis, which must have come through the hollow. Also, our architects pointed out that it would be very much easier to plot the new excavation if it could be tied to the grid designed for Building B.

Hardly had Don's crew set to work—he has trained the best pickmen we have—than ancient walls began to appear practically under the melons (*Figure 4*). It was really amazing that anything could grow five to ten inches over an ancient structure. Interesting finds were made from the start, but the walls looked like a labyrinth. And then, as Don patiently cleaned and cleared this welter, there appeared lying in the earth the wholly visible shape of an ancient bronze vase. This happened during the last hour of work, too late for the delicate operation of extraction. We appointed a laborer to guard the treasure during the night. Actually nearly all of Don's workmen spent part of the night on the site—such was their enthusiasm. The next morning found all of us hopping up and down, for not one but three bronze vessels were coming out, one of them a large bronze basin, or brazier. This was found in a basement room, while the findspot of the other bronzes was

shown by a huge jar in its corner to be a storage room (*Figures 24 and 25*). Since then in the same small space of a few square feet there have appeared two curious bronze vessels provided with chains for suspension, one hexagonal, the other round, apparently lamps, though we cannot discount the possibility that they were incense burners (censers) such as are still being used in the ritual of the Eastern Greek church. Lying on the floor next to them was a most remarkable bronze object shaped somewhat like a shovel with hollow handles but decorated with a cross on top and two dolphins on its sides (*Figure 23*). These three objects are solid cast; but a bronze flagon, which came to light the same day, and two bronze vases found the day before are all of hammered bronze.

One room in the first story of this "House of Bronzes" (Map 3, no. 4) had a floor paved with the biggest tiles we have seen; traces of painted walls—unfortunately only in small shattered fragments—are visible. An elaborately patterned marble floor has been revealed in another room at the basement level.

We have freed only one corner of this palatial dwelling. As the digging progresses, anything I write today may be superseded tomorrow. The size of the basements and the richness of their contents suggest the residence of an important personage. The Early Christian objects—and to many of our visitors Sardis is first and foremost one of the "Seven Churches that are in Asia" (*Revelation* 1.4)—induce us to speculate that this may have been the bishop's palace, since beginning in the second century important bishops are known at Sardis. The coins found so far are of the age of Constantine and his sons. In the two remaining weeks of digging we propose to follow the basement which has yielded the spectacular collection of bronze vases.

The find establishes with certainty the location of a great urban area with important dwellings just east of the modern and ancient bridges over the Pactolus torrent.

The House of Bronzes seems to have been built in the late Hellenistic or Early Roman times—both on account of structural technique and of the Hellenistic or Roman objects which we have found. It was later remodeled, and the spectacular collection of bronzes belongs to this later phase in the life of the dwelling. That such valuable objects were abandoned and never recovered bespeaks a violent catastrophe. Indeed traces of a fierce conflagration are evident throughout the house.

Something much earlier than any of the objects from the House of Bronzes turned up a few days ago in the big Building B some forty yards to the south. It is a gaily painted archaic architectural terracotta, quite possibly of the time of Croesus. It cannot have come from very far away. We have not tried this season to reach the bottom of the walls of B, much less to go deep down below this huge structure; for we do not want to destroy important monuments illuminating an intriguing phase in the life of ancient Sardis —even if they are "late" monuments. We feel that we have located the center of the city, and with patience we shall be able to unfold the entire panorama of its history.

Fresh breezes have begun to blow down the Hermus plain, and we have been treated to the unwonted sight of the Tmolus range hidden under thunderous clouds. It is the time of most delicious honeydew melons. Grapes, too, are spread out in bright green rugs over the edges of the fields, where they are left drying to become raisins. Mrs. Hanfmann took an hour off recently to work in the neighbor's vineyard as a vintager and earned our dessert.

As the season advances, objects keep pouring in at a great rate. We shall stop digging gradually between August 20 and September 1, to allow time for recording and preparation of excavated monuments for the winter season. The "City Gate," where we have gone down deep and steeply (*Figure 22*), will need to have an irrigation ditch diverted from its eastern face, or

Figure 20 (left)—Terracotta head of a blond barbarian with a "Phrygian" cap, belongs to the class of sculpture known as Hellenistic grotesques. Height 0.05 m. Found in the Byzantine Shops area, it indicated that earlier strata lay underneath.

Figure 21 (right)—In the seventh century the Sassanian Persians were overrunning Asia Minor until emperor Heraclius (A.D. 610–641) counterattacked. Dozens of big bronze coins of Heraclius were found at Sardis, especially in the Byzantine Shops. None is later than A.D. 616, the year Persians may have taken Sardis and destroyed the lower city. This was the end of Classical Sardis. This coin is a bronze half follis of Heraclius, struck at Cyzicus in A.D. 612–613. Inscribed DN (*Dominus Noster*, Our Lord) HeRaCLIus PERPetuus AUGustus; shows a cuirassed bust of the emperor holding a cross.

else the winter torrents will pour into it, as they have done more than once before in its long history. Building B will need to have its excavation slopes banked so that the water will run off easily and not bring down the rubble. Our deepest pits in the Artemis precinct will have to be filled in, and something must be done to protect the sector with the House of Bronzes against clandestine digging, now that the melon field is known to contain "treasures."

All this involves much negotiation about land rights and purchases, and probably payment for an additional guard—unromantic but essential aspects of archaeology.

We are also facing the task of folding up all of our equipment and putting it into temporary storage in the basement of the new excavation house and in the village or in Manisa. The walls of the new excavation house are nearly finished (*Figure 13*). Its sight gives us a feeling of permanence; we shall really be "at home" next year. Our architects, Henry Detweiler and Tom Canfield, are starting to lay out a compound (Map 3, no. 15) around the house and plan the necessary service structures as well as additional living space for next year. The compound will go up the slope in several terraces. The size of the excavation house was determined by what we could afford last year. The compound is planned to meet additional urgent needs, which we can now state with considerable precision. Some of the structures are absolute musts for the next campaign—a house for the guard, toilets, showers, several rooms to house staff members, and at least one sizable storage and work room. The overall plan calls for a laboratory, a pottery and storage room, and a structure to house the sculptures and inscriptions now scattered all over the vast area of Sardis. Should we not be able to find the means for all the structures, we plan to make use of native temporary shelters known as *çardaks*. They are airy and ideal for summer use. We cannot, of course, leave either our materials or the objects out in the open during the

Figure 22—Originally thought to be a City Gate (hence labeled "CG"), this building turned out to be a bath complex, deeply buried by flood deposits. The "Main Arch" of the west facade is seen here.

cold and the rains of winter, and we are under an obligation to provide the facilities which would eventually make possible a Sardis Museum. Other concrete needs have emerged out of the experience of this campaign. Machinery for the moving of heavy stones is vital. We have been able to transport fairly large amounts of rubble, smaller stones, and earth with horse-drawn carts, but we must have the proper equipment for lifting and dragging the blocks of two and three tons in the "City Gate" and in the area on both sides of Building B.

P.S. The day after these lines were written we found in the basement of the House of Bronzes the marble statue of a pagan god, perhaps Bacchus, and a number of imposing stone bowls. A marble basin was filled with a substance which—according to our conservator, Jack Washeba—seems to be sulphur. Suggestions as to what it might have been used for will be welcomed.

Cable to John Coolidge, Director, Fogg Museum

Transmit following Pinkerton Cornell supporters of Sardis. Climaxing a two months search American archaeologists claimed today to have located the Lydian city of Sardis, the capital of Croesus. Large gaily painted jars (*Figure 26*) and some house walls were the tip that the great city of golden Lydia had been found. The discovery was made within a few yards of the Izmir-Salihli highway near the wealthy Early Christian residence discovered last week (*Figure 4;* Map 3, no. 4). Commenting on the find Professor Detweiler of Cornell, field adviser of the expedition, said "this is what we have been looking for. The concentration of large heavy vases proves conclusively that we are within the inhabited area of the city." Professor Hanfmann of Harvard, field director, added that the discovery demonstrates that the an-

cient city of Croesus lies under the ruins of the Roman city and disposes of the old theory that it was located in the side valley of the Pactolus.

Cambridge   September 17, 1958

I had meant to write this letter at Sardis, but our last days "on location" proved to be extremely hectic. The big schoolroom and the schoolyard were a chaos of boxes, wheelbarrows, pickaxes, and more boxes. We were working feverishly to pack part of our finds for shipment to the museum at Manisa (*Figure 7*), another lot was to be stored in the village, and all of the excavation equipment was to be "winterized" and stowed away. The weather, which had treated us to temperatures of 110–115° during the last two weeks of the campaign, made an aboutface. Rain began to pour steadily and cold winds blew from the heights of Tmolus, disrupting our plans for out-of-doors packing. Nor was this the only disruption. Every couple of hours or so, a taxi with journalists would drive up and we would be cajoled into posing with our trophies—such as were not yet packed up. Our first move was always to explain that we had *not* found the treasure of Croesus, and, indeed, believed that Cyrus had taken it long ago.* Now the belief that the treasure of Croesus still lies hidden at Sardis is almost an article of faith with many people in Turkey; and when the Associated Press carried a dispatch that we had found the site of the city of Croesus, there was a rush to see what we had done with the treasure. Indeed, the first intimation we had was the appearance at midnight of two armed state troopers, who stated that they had been dispatched by higher authorities to guard the treasure,

*Herodotus, who lived a hundred years after Croesus, implies that Cyrus took Croesus' treasure. The Byzantine historian Theophanes says that it was kept near Gazaca in Iran.

Figure 24—A view of the House of Bronzes at the end of the 1958 campaign. In right foreground is a Lydian potter's shop and kiln, seventh century B.C. Receding on left, the Early Byzantine basement Room 1 (with big jar), Rooms 2 and 5, and staircase 3—all built a thousand years later than the Lydian shop.

and asked why our commissioner had not reported the find and its contents. Our genial Kemal Bey replied with greatest good humor that if the gentlemen would show him the treasure, he would be the first to report its contents in detail.

Those of you who have seen my cable will want to know what the jubilation was all about. Now here is what happened. All through the campaign we had striven to find the Lydians but they kept eluding us. Our trench south of the Artemis Temple (*Figure 10*) showed that quite early Lydian remains must have existed higher up on the Acropolis slope, but what we found were only sherds that had been carried down by a torrent. When we excavated a building in the southern part of the Artemis precinct, we found what one might call a Late Lydian level of ashes and sherds, because the pottery continued the traditions of the Lydian age; but historically these finds belong to the time of the Persian domination, to the fifth and fourth century B.C. Underneath was the same riverbed that we had encountered in our first trench, and the evidence seems conclusive that the sacred precinct of Artemis with its great temple was first established in its present location during the Persian era.

Our predecessor, Howard Crosby Butler, had looked in vain for the Lydian city. The only place where he had encountered early Lydian remains was on a terrace northeast of the Artemis Temple. This led him to advance the theory that the archaic Sardis, of which Herodotus writes with such liveliness, was located up the Pactolus valley, near the Temple. We had checked on the place where he found early Lydian sherds and may yet do something about it. But it did not look too promising, and Butler never claimed to have found very consistent or extensive Lydian material.

We had tried a sounding above the Artemis Temple, at Kagirlik Tepe (see Map 3, no. 19), and found nothing but Roman and Early Christian graves.

It had been my view right along that the Lydian city was somewhere

44

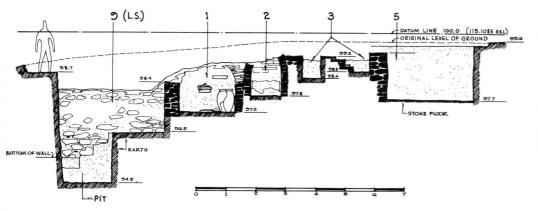

Figure 25—Section of the House of Bronzes. "L.S." designates the Lydian potter's shop. A great array of bronzes was found in the vaulted basement of Room 1. Another vault, Room 2, served as a grave where many human bones were found. Room 5 has a beautiful marble-paved floor and contained a marble table (see Figure 34).

within the general area later occupied by the Hellenistic, Roman, and Byzantine Sardis. This is a mile away from the Artemis Temple, at the northern foot of the Acropolis, on a platform dominating the broad Hermus plain. The modern highway from Izmir-Turgutlu to Salihli runs through this area in east-west direction, and its medieval predecessor followed a similar course (Map 2).

When we started on the colossal Building B, which lies just south of the highway, and some 300 yards west of the Pactolus torrent, we had intended to go several meters down from the modern surface to test this hypothesis. But as we came instantly upon the Byzantine Shops *(Figure 19)* with their rich, varied contents, we had to give up the idea.

After some prospecting late in July and early in August just across the highway from Building B, where the fields rise in three platforms toward the Byzantine city wall, we found evidence of Lydian presence in the shape of sherds scattered over the surface. The most abundant crop appeared on the highest platform, right below the city wall; but time was getting short, negotiations about land rent or purchase would be time-consuming, and Henry Detweiler and Tom Canfield pointed out that it would be much easier to plot and record a trench if it were right across the highway from Building B. So on August 2 Don Hansen started and, as you know by now, almost immediately hit upon the Roman and Early Christian House of Bronzes *(Figures 23–25)*. We reaped rich rewards but the Lydians had once more eluded us.

Under the agreement with the owner of the field, we were free to make a trial dig, without charge, within an area of 15 by 25 meters. By August 18 Don had excavated all of the House of Bronzes that could be legitimately, or even liberally, viewed as fitting into such an area; and yet the house spread into all directions. The sector was scheduled to close on August 24. Don would have liked to pursue further some of the rooms of the house which

were yielding such remarkable treasures, but I thought that unless and until we had bought the field, we could not expand any further. There were a few yards left between the excavated part of the House of Bronzes and the highway. We decided to "go down."

Next day, shortly before work was to stop, I was passing by. Beaming, our commissioner shouted, "Mr. Professor, une belle surprise!" and ran off toward the solitary tree which served to provide shade for drinking water and pot washing. Out of the earth of the small trench peered several majestic necks of vases, still upright *(Figure 26)*; and Don came back with unmistakably early Lydian sherds that had just been washed. Here were the Lydians.

We were still cautious and batted the facts back and forth. "Looks good, but could they have been thrown in with the fill?" "I think we are coming on a floor"—and so we were. Although my instinct was to jump up and down for joy, we held back. But two days later there could be no doubt. In the small space of not more than 15 by 9 feet were a dozen large vase necks and upper bodies, pot stands, the characteristic "lydia." So tightly packed an array of pottery could not have been placed by chance, and our workmen had the same idea as ourselves—a pottery shop. The owner must have been a pot mender as well as vendor; for several of the vases had been carefully repaired *(Figure 27)*—or were in process of being repaired. The stone foundations of two walls could be traced, and eventually there emerged, in the corner, a canal of stones *(Figure 25)* leading to a circular construction of which the upper part seemed to curve as if to make a dome. This reminded me irresistibly of the Iron Age pottery kilns which I had seen at Tarsus. Large and imposing as the Lydian pots were, the most helpful find was a fine Greek sherd decorated with a frieze of wild goats *(Figure 28)*. This kind of pottery is well-known and studied, so that I had no hesitation in determining its date as the last quarter of the seventh century B.C. The workshop, then, seems to have flourished around 600 B.C., at the time of Croesus'

Figure 27—This Lydian "waveline hydria" (water jar) from the Lydian pot shop was broken in antiquity and repaired by inserting lead clamps into holes drilled on both sides of the breaks. The extensive mending suggests the jar was of considerable value to the Lydian potter.

father, king Alyattes. For reasons which we do not know, it was suddenly abandoned.

We had been incredibly lucky in finding this shop with its contents, if not intact, at least not much damaged or disturbed. For the Roman builders of the House of Bronzes had sunk one of their walls clear down through the Lydian floor, and another wall, while it ended high up above the Lydian room (*Figure 25*), yet impeded any thought of sideways expansion of our dig, since we would have had to bring down this sizable block of concrete.

I had granted a two-day extension to this our final enterprise. It gave us an opportunity to dig a small pit (*Figure 25*) to see what might be lurking under the Lydian shop. We found no other building underneath but only a slope of earth. There, however, and in the corner under the presumed kiln, the earliest stage of Lydian pottery appeared in a number of sherds, largely black and grey monochrome ware, but also some painted sherds, black on red and black on buff. Under this was river sand. Potters need water, and so presumably there was water nearby—it is not impossible that the Pactolus, in those early days, ran east of its present course and thus through the area which we are investigating.

This is the first time that a considerable amount of Lydian material has been found in association with definite architectural remains. Our assumption is now that this region was part of the Lydian city, and from surface finds and stray finds around Building B we believe that the city will be found to extend on both sides of the present highway. We have taken steps to secure the land, and we are particularly eager to excavate the platform near the Byzantine city wall, uphill from our Lydian shop. While nobody can predict how well the Lydian remains have survived under the later buildings, it is encouraging to note that they are not, at least, as deeply buried as seemed from other chance finds. For the floor of the Lydian shop was only 7–8 feet below the modern surface.

The search for the site of the Lydian city, then, seems to have ended; but

Figure 28—This fragment of a jug decorated with grazing (left) and striding wild goats, was made on the Greek island of Rhodes, ca. 625–600 B.C., and exported to Sardis. Its discovery in the Lydian shop indicates that the potter was in business in the late seventh century B.C.

the *excavation* of the Lydian city is only about to begin. This will be a long and important task for our future campaign, and we shall need all the help that our supporters can give us, to do justice to this great challenge.

Some other interesting developments made the last days of digging exciting. Our excavation of Building B had at long last proceeded to a point where we were able to probe for the floor of this building, and to try to solve the mystery of the placing of the Lucius Verus inscription. Here the acute, architecturally trained eye of our field adviser, Henry Detweiler, was able to discern new facts which led us to revise radically our earlier opinions. As Henry himself is as yet suspending judgment, I shall not divulge his conclusions except to say that the building was seen to have had a beautifully made floor with marble pavement, and that the walls, too, appear to have been revetted with marbles of various colors. The base with the Verus inscription was built especially for the purpose of placing the inscription in its center, and this platform, too, appears to have been revetted with marble (*Figures 17–18*).

Finally, I must mention an important piece, although it was not found in our excavation. Following a report from the farmers, our commissioner brought in a beautiful funerary stele (*Figure 29*). It shows the deceased woman named Matis together with a little girl; the woman takes an ornament from the jewelry box, in a scene made familiar by Attic funerary reliefs. An epitaph of four lines in verse appears above the relief. The piece was found one kilometer west of the modern bridge over the Pactolus (Map 3, no. 6—Roman bridge near the modern one), in a location which suggests that the sepulcher was alongside the ancient road which led westward out of Sardis. This fine piece of sculpture, which I believe to be Early Hellenistic, gives a very promising notion of the kind of finds that a systematic exploration of Sardis may produce.

48

Figure 29—Grave stele, found in vineyards less than one mile west of Sardis, shows a woman named Matis and her little girl or servant bringing a box of jewels. A Greek poem is carved above. Greek speech and art were replacing Lydian in the third century B.C. Height 1.56 m. Photographed in the school yard at Sardis; now in Manisa Museum.

Figure 30—The idyllic Pactolus brook where Lydians once panned gold; now the village women of Sart Mustafa wash expedition laundry. In winter the brook turns into a raging, flooding torrent.

1959

Ankara   July 1–2, 1959

I am writing this from the hospitable office of the United States Information Service in Ankara, having flown up for some official business. This is the story of our arrival and the first week of digging.

"Look at this!"—Ilse, Don Hansen, and I cried out in unison; but we did not mean the same thing. I was amused by two storks solemnly approaching us in the manner of a reception committee looking for all the world as if they were dressed in coat-and-tails. Don and Ilse had been looking ahead to the house gleaming white on the brow of the hill, rising over the Pactolus gorge in the clear June sky. "Our" house, finished at last *(Figure 46)*.

The green mountainsides of the wooded Tmolus Mountain stood forth in romantic grandeur in the glory of the evening sun. Rhododendron bushes were violent blotches of red against the tan and beige of the Pactolus bed. Soft white clouds lay against the twin peaks where Dionysus was born in the golden age of gods.

Don's star pickman, Ahmet Avcikaya, came running down the road. He had been serving as a guard of the house in our absence. It was not long before the servants assembled, broad grins on their usually stolid faces. They had installed kitchen and crockery and there were beds and chairs in the rooms; there were, to be sure, also mounds of unopened crates and boxes. Our commissioner, Kemal Bey, together with Arthur Steinberg had managed to transport from various chickenyards, stables, and village rooms the belongings of the expedition which we had stored in the village over the winter.

Arthur had managed an even greater feat in piloting the expedition supplies through customs prior to our arrival. Things would not have been true to form though, if everything had gone without hitches; I am told that for a while a vital permit was lost by the appropriate ministry. Still and all, it was a blessing not to have to worry about the next day's or the next week's battle with customs. On the other hand, we have at the time of writing a generator strike-bound in Naples, a truck presumably in transit from Courbevoie to Marseilles, and a Landrover of uncertain status in Pakistan, surely a kind of record of international dispersal for an expedition working in Turkey.

We miss the truck and its crane most—for good reasons. As we went out to look at last year's digs and came to the "City Gate" (CG), my heart fell. I had not quite remembered how big those fallen stones were and how many. Here, too, Arthur has galvanized things into action, putting into practice a suggestion of our foreman. We have bought some wooden rails, really just trees, and some rollers. Now the workmen heave the stones onto the rollers which run (more or less) on the wooden rails. This primitive "Steinberg Railway" has been accomplishing great things, and the workmen seem to get a kick out of its operation. Incidentally, this device is what many scholars believe was used by the Egyptians to build pyramids.

We began our second campaign officially on June 26; actually, we had started cleaning the excavation two days before. On the whole, the various sectors have come through the winter pretty well. Somebody threw a stone at the Verus inscription causing minor damage; somebody else busted one of the marble containers with sulphur found in the House of Bronzes; and a lot of somebody elses must have gone after the terracotta drain pipes; but there has been no serious damage to the buildings.

Currently, Don Hansen is continuing on the House of Bronzes, which he has so spruced up and cleaned that it outshines our new excavation house. Already some remarkable objects have come to light, for instance, a bronze

Figure 31—Terraced digging at "Pactolus Cliff," on the east bank of the river, where a winter landslide brought to light fragments of marble sculpture (taken August 1960). The walls at the bottom are Lydian. The workmen are digging at the level of the Roman cemetery, second to third century, our era.

brooch with glass inlay. Dave Mitten first tackled the east and west sides of Building B and is now starting into the new Byzantine Shops at the south side of the building. Arthur Steinberg was in charge of CG, where Mario Del Chiaro, newly arrived from Rome, will be taking over. The plan is for Don to keep at the House of Bronzes, exploring both its Roman-Early Christian and its Lydian levels; then he will go uphill to open a new trench in an area which we hope will be important.

New eyes can sometimes see things which escape those familiar with a dig. Al Shapiro, student of architecture from Cornell, has noticed something in the House of Bronzes that we failed to see last year. On the wall of the vaulted room 2 *(Figure 25)* next to the one where we found the Early Christian bronzes last year (room 1), he believes he can discern an incised medallion with what may be the beginning of a cross. Such a monumental Christian symbol, perhaps preliminary incision for a painting, would greatly bolster our belief that an important Christian personage dwelled in this residence.

Al has taken on Henry Detweiler's assistant of last year and another Turkish boy and has been hard at work on a grid and levels. Sporting a sun helmet and a tentative blond beard he is heard yelling with gusto, "Sol, sağ" (left, right), and other Turkish terms needed for surveying in fine Cincinnati Turkish. He and his Turkish rodmen seem to understand each other perfectly.

Dave Mitten is the enthusiast of the expedition; while others relax after the hot day in the trenches, he is ranging uphill and down, loading himself with sherds until he comes back panting under his archaeological load.

We found here welcome new additions to our unexcavated antiques—described as No Ex ("not excavated")—especially a lovely female head *(Figure 32)* and some sarcophagus fragments from a cave-in of the Pactolus bank *(Figure 31)* during the winter.

Figure 32 (left)—This head of a Roman girl from a sarcophagus of the second century was one of the pieces which prompted the beginning of excavations at Pactolus Cliff.

Figure 33 (right)—Marble basin, originally a cooling tank, was later decorated with Christian crosses. The crosses allude to the salutary power of water of life in baptism. The date of the crosses is fifth or sixth century, four hundred years after the Church of Sardis is mentioned by St. John.

Our associate director, Henry Detweiler, arrived at Izmir June 29. Good friend that he is, he came to meet me at the railroad station, where our famous "oto-ray" (diesel train) gets in at night (our usual way into town on free days). We had come to Izmir for a party which American Consul and Mrs. Eddy gave for us. The Governor of Izmir was there and a Turkish air force General as well as a notable Turkish literary figure known as "The Fisherman of Halicarnassus." We were warmly received at this party, as we are now at Ankara. Last year we were a novelty and one-day wonder; this year, we are old friends. If I may hazard a guess, people have confidence that we are an established and going concern. Indeed, at the Department of Antiquities, which I visited yesterday (July 1), there was evident satisfaction about the very close collaboration in such matters as the building of the excavation house and compound and about the fact that in staff size and in some other ways we seem to have blossomed into the largest foreign excavation in Turkey.

The new house has much to do with this feeling of permanence. It is very nicely finished, and the rooms are larger than they looked to us last year during construction. Immediately upon arrival, we launched a campaign of furniture building, mostly shelving for supplies and objects. We have started the contractor on the building of a laboratory and four rooms on the upper terrace of the compound. Mounds of bricks are lying behind the house and cement is being mixed everywhere. There is hope that these indispensable additions may be finished in time for use during the latter part of the season. We are hanging on, however, to the "Croesus Palace," the village "guest house" near the village school, to take care of the overflow of staff. Much remains to be done; only half of the compound wall has been built and we can hardly get around putting up some sort of storage for the larger excavation equipment and objects.

I wish I could detail some of our adventures and strange happenings—the bulldozer that kept us awake all night; the flooding of a house that has no

water; the shenanigans of our ailing jeep and the remarkable makeshift abilities of the Turkish mechanics; but this would be too unarchaeological. I will only record that we had the sudden if somewhat disruptive honor of entertaining at an hour's notice a delegation of some twenty French *sousprefets* who were touring Turkey.

And I promise a shorter and more excavatorial letter next time.

Sardis   July 15, 1959

Just before we left Sardis last year, we outlined the long line of Byzantine Shops *(Figure 19)*, without actually excavating them. I may have mentioned at the time that a very fine rectangular marble basin or tank was found; but we covered it up again. It was as well we did, for the surprises hidden around it would have been too much in the hectic final week of last summer's dig. This summer, when Dave Mitten began to uncover the new shops, he found on the outside of this basin a most exciting thing *(Figure 33)*. Two large crosses had been carved on the two front slabs and another large marble lying just outside had very much the same shape as later baptismal (or holy water) fonts. The crosses are carved on reused slabs—one of them had a checkered history, for the wreath of a pagan honorary inscription is on top, a funerary pagan inscription was carved over that original one, and the second inscription is bisected by the huge Christian cross. The other slab has caused us literally to stand on our heads, particularly Arthur Steinberg, who was determined to read the original pagan inscription, and the Christians had put it upside down. Standing on your head in temperature well over 90 degrees is quite a feat, even though Arthur is using a beach umbrella to give him protection. Anyway, the pagan inscription is in verse and all we can make out is that it is a votive dedication to (probably) "gods of our fathers."

The baptistry had been a shop and quite possibly the marble tank was there before it became a baptistry. For a while it was fed in very progressive manner by water pipes of the Late Roman water system. The "font" may have come into use after the pipes were stuffed up.

The shop has at least in part a marble floor. Two more brick floors are known to lurk beneath but we shall take good care to record first this remarkable adaptation of a commercial establishment to religious uses.

The long line of shops (Figure 96) begins to look impressive and there is not doubt that we have here a real shopping center. The main avenue, to be sure, is covered partly by modern highway, partly by unexcavated ground between the Byzantine shops and the House of Bronzes, just the other (south) side of the modern highway.

Dave Mitten, who found the "baptistry," also had the thrill of finding a small but neat torso of Athena in another shop.

In the meantime, Don Hansen has been patiently and delicately uncovering the fascinating but difficult House of Bronzes. The most interesting room at the moment is a large hall (Figure 34) with a patterned floor of cut marble, its central design circular. Don has just cleaned its marble doorway and found the iron door sockets in place and a surprisingly elaborate lock. Yesterday, too, there came to light a sumptuous marble table, or at least parts thereof—a leg shaped like a lion leg plus a lion head growing out of floral chalice on top, the top a marble slab with a peg fitting into a hole on top of the leg. The other "leg" seems to be an Ionic column. An inscription inscribed on the base seems to speak of a "sumptuous house," perhaps a reference to the House of Bronzes. There is an inscription set into the floor, too, but that is quite certainly re-used and not completely excavated yet.

So far, the House of Bronzes has produced only smaller bronzes; one is a lamp or vessel, and another, a brooch with glass inlay, is of artistic import.

Because of the many later walls above and around, Don has been able to extend only a little the area of the Lydian shop which created such a stir last

year (*Figures 24, 26*). There is no doubt however that the Lydian walls and Lydian levels of the seventh and sixth centuries B.C. continue below the later structures.

Mario Del Chiaro has sailed with great efficiency into the task of excavating CG, formerly known as "City Gate." What looked like unshapely hillocks of rubble is emerging as a sequence of high walls to the north of the great masonry oblong we dug last year. They were covered by tremendous floods and we cannot as yet guess how high those walls stand. I thought we had one of our problems licked when we got permission from everybody to use a bulldozer that belongs to the state government in order to run a long ramp from the highway to the dig. But the very night before the operation was scheduled the bulldozer broke down, and it is now sitting ignominiously in front of our house, some essential parts of it having been taken away for repair. Two days ago Henry and I visited the huge dam construction at Demir Köprü; subsequently we got permission from Süleyman Demirel, then Director General of Public Waterworks, Ankara, to borrow from them a five-ton crane to move those huge stones at CG. This morning three men appeared to negotiate the preliminaries. Mindful of the bulldozer's fate I am keeping my fingers crossed.

The Demir Köprü project inspires us with both awe and envy. Where last year there was only a little trickle of a river, there is now a majestic lake some ten miles long. We went on the day the dam proper was declared officially complete (though work will continue on the power station), and so had a great guided tour, through the courtesy of Mehmet Yavaş, Director of Waterworks of our region. The envy, needless to say, refers to the great organization and equipment that has literally moved mountains.

The truck generously ordered for us by a benefactor has been held up in France and its current whereabouts are as of today unknown.

After some hectic work by Ilse, our commissioner, Don Hansen, and my-

Figure 35—An inscription, reused as base in the marble-paved hall (Figure 34), was a dedication to the native moon god Mên Axioteinos.

self, we have succeeded in making the new house livable—and believe me, it certainly is a difference from last year. Henry Detweiler supervised with ingenuity the installation of window and door screens, thereby reducing our fly population from legions to individuals.

On the upper terrace, the same contractor's crew that built the house is putting up four additional rooms and the laboratory. They are no speed-demons and take some pushing but we hope for the best. As the wall round our quarters is less than half complete, we are rather exposed to invasions of all comers to the Artemis Temple. Among our adventures have been the rescue of one taxi and one private car from the Pactolus and transporting a sick woman to the station.

This year we have for the first time taken on students from Harvard and Cornell. There is a good deal of zip and zest, and our Turkish commissioner, who likes jokes and kidding, gets along famously with the boys and is learning English a lot faster than before. Conversely, it is a pleasure to report that Arthur Steinberg, Dave Mitten, and Alan Shapiro are all making remarkable progress in "Basic Turkish." We have also taken on as drafts-man a young Turkish student, Hamdi Baysoy, son of the local district attorney.

We have had strange weather with two large thunderstorms. The last one was terrific. Instead of a little trickle in a wide dry bed (*Figures 30, 31*), the Pactolus became a roaring red-brown flood, stones pelting down its tributaries from the mountains. Henry, Arthur, Kemal Bey, and I were coming back from the Demir Köprü Dam at the time and somehow escaped, but poor Mario was caught excavating some Lydian graves high on the west bank of the Pactolus, and had to make a detour of nearly two miles to get back to the house.

In a few days we shall open the sector uphill, in an area for which we had high expectations last year.

Figure 36—Early Byzantine beaker of bluish glass found in a niche in the north wall of the marble-paved hall in the House of Bronzes (Figure 34).

Sardis   August 1, 1959

We are just past the midway point of this, our second campaign of digging at the ancient capital of Lydia, and work is going forward on five sectors of the far flung site. As the tempo rises, discoveries crowd each other. Yesterday and today brought us the first life-size, indeed larger than life-size, marble statues. A Roman official and his wife *(Figure 38)* were lying foot to foot right under the entrance to the shelter used as sector headquarters by Don Hansen and Arthur Steinberg—and only a foot or so underground, at that.

With a staff of seventeen, and half a dozen household personnel, there was plenty to do to set up our headquarters and its various adjuncts, such as *çardaks*. Vigorous steps were taken to produce the needed permanent establishment for the laboratory and additional housing; I am happy to say that as I look out of the window I see before me a red brick building on the upper terrace of our compound which should be ready and occupied within a week *(Figure 46,* background).

The new compound, which enjoys a beautiful view of the great Temple of Artemis, is a beehive of activity with masons starting the urgently needed working and storage building and carpenters preparing shelves for the never ending flood of new objects.

Now to the excavations. In the House of Bronzes, which yielded such spectacular finds last year, we have nearly quadrupled the excavated area. We can now more clearly discern an important unit which includes a paved street or entrance way, the working area dug last year, a tiled room, and then an imposing hall with a marble floor and various marble furnishings

Figure 37—Early Byzantine poly-candelon, a bronze chandelier, from a room in the House of Bronzes.

(Figure 34). Among them is a dedication to the moon god Mên, probably re-used *(Figure 35).* A Christian hexagonal censer and a bronze chandelier of "Coptic" type *(Figure 37)* as well as various utensils of iron, glass *(Figure 36),* and bronze also have come to light in this hall. Beyond it is a room, again marble-paved, which seems to have been rebuilt to accommodate an apse to the east. Henry Detweiler surmises that a raised platform may have been part of a bishop's throne and the whole room a house chapel. It is difficult to enumerate either the rooms or the finds of this area. I will note only that the funerary inscription of a centurion Theodorus came to light in one room, and a Christian cross of the same kind that one finds in the Temple of Artemis (to exorcise pagan demons) in another.

The Lydian shop, which adjoins the House of Bronzes and, indeed, may lie amidst its walls *(Figures 24–26),* was taken by us last year as proof that the Lydian city was located along the modern highway (a successor to the Royal Road). As it turns out, we were fantastically lucky in lighting upon the one spot where the Lydian level could be readily reached and freed. The yield of Lydian pottery continues, but the walls are much disrupted. Yet there is no doubt that the level continues under the later buildings.

To the northwest of the House of Bronzes, Don Hansen and Arthur Steinberg have come upon a cemetery of Roman brick graves and some very neat Hellenistic chamber tombs with stucco walls that imitate masonry and couches provided with head and shoulder rests. They are interesting as an indication that the Hellenistic city did not extend as far to the west as the Lydian and the Roman.

Under the direction of Tom Canfield we are now seeking to determine the history of the large complex of which both the great apsidal Building B and the shops were but one part *(Figures 4, 15–19).* By the end of the campaign I hope to be able to report on its complicated history. The building itself was most luxurious in its decoration of marbles and mosaics. Its huge spaces and

60

Figure 38—Headless statues of a Roman official and his wife lying foot to foot were found near our House of Bronzes shelter. Such honorary statues were reused by inserting new heads.

its intricate water system will contribute much to the now hotly debated question of the forerunners of Byzantine architecture.

Last summer we had tackled a mysterious building of large, not to say colossal stone masonry, which we dubbed CG *(Figure 22)*, on the theory that it was a city gate. Under the energetic direction of Mario Del Chiaro we now have cleared what looked like rubble heaps to the north. These have revealed themselves as well built rubble walls of a circular room, and several other large units—all buried under flood deposits of deluge proportions. Our progress had long been barred by the problem of the huge fallen stones. As forecast in my previous letter, we were able to borrow on its "day off" the 25-ton Bucyrus crane and its crew from the great Demir Köprü Dam project. It was a great day for us to see this giant swing through the air the blocks estimated to weigh from one to two and a half tons *(Figure 39)*. In one day it cleared out virtually all of the major obstacles.

We are now tackling CG on a broad front and building ramps to avoid the ever present danger of cave-ins which we would run if we continued our steep descent—so far we had only excavated the upper story of this complex!

An unscheduled but effective excavation known as "Pactolus Cliff" *(Figure 31,* Map 3, no. 13) has developed out of a landslide into the torrent bed of the Pactolus which occurred last February. Our guards and peasants have picked up a number of fragments of a columnar Roman sarcophagus of the so-called Lydian* type *(Figure 32)*. Initial examination of the surface yielded little. But when a peasant brought a beautiful horse head, which seems Hellenistic in style, we started a dig. We were rewarded by the dis-

*A great medievalist, C. R. Morey, called a group of finely worked Roman sarcophagi made between A.D. 160 and 220 "Lydian" because the sarcophagus of Claudia Antonia Sabina and several other marble caskets of this kind were found in Sardis and other cities of the Roman province of Lydia; they are not the work of early Lydians. *The Sarcophagus of Claudia Antonia Sabina, Sardis V, Part I* (1924), p. 2.

Figure 39 (left)—Crane aids excavation along the east face of bath complex CG by removing tons of heavy fallen masonry.

Figure 40 (right)—East facade of CG with Main Arch in foreground as it appeared one month after beginning operations shown in Figure 39. The newly arrived Citroën truck could remove twenty times as much earth as the horse carts it replaced.

covery of parts of a monumental structure, some of them decorated with lion legs and two inscribed "MA." After the landslide was explored, Mario Del Chiaro excavated the top of the cliff, where remains of a Roman building, a Hellenistic chamber tomb, and Lydian sherds are currently vying for our attention.

Both Anthony Casendino and Al Shapiro are hard at work on the architectural recording of these varied ruins. Al and Mario Del Chiaro also took part in some tomb-digging in Butler's so-called Great Necropolis of Lydian rock-cut graves (*Figure 1*) on the west bank of the Pactolus (Map 2). Last summer, Ilse Hanfmann and Lenore Keene saw evidence of recent grave digging. More was evident this summer. Our follow-up on three graves yielded Lydian terracotta sarcophagi *in situ* and a few vases. Evidently either Butler or some earlier grave digger had anticipated both ourselves and our illicit competitors. However, as very few Lydian tombs have ever been satisfactorily published, our four-day dig was not in vain.

P.S. Great rejoicing. Our long awaited truck and crane has arrived in Izmir.

Sardis   August 20–21, 1959

I had set today as the deadline for something special to happen—and within 20 minutes we found a golden earring in a Roman grave and an intact vase on a Lydian floor. Then Dave Mitten found a statue of Bacchus.

No "treasures" in the accepted sense have appeared. But I must tell you how we almost found one. In the interior of the huge Building B, there appeared, quite deep under the fallen debris, an earthen jar tightly closed with a leaden lid. It was so heavy that two people could hardly lift it. With his usual optimism our commissioner proclaimed that this must be at the

Figure 41—Entrance to Hellenistic chamber tomb in Pactolus Cliff sector featured a large stone lintel found in situ.

very least a hoard of coins. To be quite official, we let him open the jar on the terrace of the excavation house in the presence of a crowd of witnesses. Kemal Bey pried open the lid and there appeared some fragments of bronze with gold-like dust thinly sprinkled upon them. Underneath was earth. How did it get in under the tight lid? Indefatigably did Kemal Bey dig into the jar. More and more earth came out and finally stones, one bigger than another. Some just barely fit through the neck of the jar. Looking at our own disappointed faces we all started roaring with laughter. The only explanation of our strange find we can offer is that in antiquity someone substituted earth and stone for what must have been both heavy and valuable contents.

However, we have had a fine harvest of non-treasures. The small excavation on the Pactolus Cliff proved rewarding in immediate returns and long-range prospects. After we had sifted the debris fallen into the riverbed and extracted the enigmatic monument inscribed MA, Mario Del Chiaro noticed another block of the monument on top of the cliff. Threading his way skillfully through a maze of walls, Mario uncovered and clearly outlined a Byzantine structure, Roman burial vaults, and a beautifully preserved Hellenistic tomb (which we now call the "Tomb of the Lintel"; *(Figure 41)*. Underneath it all he came upon not less than three phases of Lydian structures *(Figure 31)*. One of them is a tantalizing corner of monumental construction. The highest (and latest) of the Lydian walls is overlaid by ashes, indicating a violent conflagration—one thinks of that fateful year of 499 B.C. when the Ionians set all of Sardis aflame and thus started the war between Greece and Persia.

Last year and again this year—in very delicate probing operations—Don Hansen found Lydian dwellings along the Izmir-Salihli highway. Mario's dwellings are in the side valley of the Pactolus. The Lydian city, then, did extend for perhaps as much as a mile up the torrent bed (see Map 3, *Figure 134*).

Figure 42—Hellenistic amphora with lid from "Tomb of the Lintel" (Figure 41). Height 0.40 m. Typical of mold-made relief pottery, the vase imitates silver ware and is decorated in registers with amorini and wreaths. Head of Lydian queen Omphale (?) on shoulder. Perhaps locally made.

Among the memorable finds at the Pactolus are wall paintings (flowers) in the Roman burial vaults. Again from the vaults came an expressive marble head of a man wearing a crown with twelve small heads (*Figure 43*). I was reminded of the portraits of the Emperor Diocletian, famous as a restorer of the Empire and persecutor of Christians. However, Louis Robert, our epigrapher consultant, remarked on his visit that crowns of this kind were worn by priests of the Roman imperial cult. The Hellenistic tomb yielded a masterpiece of painted relief pottery (*Figure 42*), recomposed with great skill by our conservationist John Washeba and his assistants. The large vase, clearly imitating silver work, is adorned with a dynamic head of Omphale with the lionskin of Herakles as well as many small figures and ornaments.

An important sector has been developing within the last few days in the rectangular area east of Building B. Initiated upon the request of our senior architect, Tom Canfield, as part of the architectural study of B and its surroundings, this large trench has already revealed the traces (tons of them) of a mighty and richly decorated colonnade. The most striking fragments are those of two large Corinthian capitals, each adorned with a spirited head—one with a laughing faun (*Figure 44*), the other with an Athena. I have just brought the latter to the excavation house on our new truck.

Here a word about the Citroën truck. After various delays and adventures, it arrived at Izmir and partly through the good services of Chaplain J. McLeroy finally reached Sardis on August 6. Henry Detweiler showed his usual technological acumen in fathoming the functions of all the buttons and levers. He was, to be sure, stimulated by the desire to get at the generator which after its long odyssey had arrived at the same time and was reposing in one of the truck's dumping caissons. Anyway, Henry pushed the right buttons, the caisson plus generator rose majestically through the air and came gently down to earth. Henry also saw to it that the generator (a small one) was properly installed and the house and laboratory wired. The truck

Figure 43—From a Roman mausoleum found in Pactolus Cliff, head of bearded man with crown of twelve small diademed heads or busts, variously interpreted as emperors or the twelve Great Gods. Height 0.17 m. Manisa Museum.

has been busy, both at earth removal (*Figure 40*) and at lifting stones—it has brought in safely the monument to "MA," the two big Roman statues, and the two Corinthian capitals.

To complete our technological survey: The day before the truck arrived the decrepit bulldozer from the Highway Department was revived and worked one day at CG, long enough to make a fine ramp. Then it went off to another job and promptly died again.

West of the Building B, we have in the last few days begun to trace what seems to be an important system of piers, perhaps of Hellenistic date. In the interior of B, we have dug through one of the most massive floors and underpinnings known to man and are going down in a pit to see if we can find earlier structures underneath. Bits of seventh century pottery keep the dream of Lydian buildings alive here. Other pits, nearly thirty feet deep, have been dug in the corner of the Byzantine Shops and in the House of Bronzes. Two of them have produced evidence of what may be Bronze Age cultures.

Don Hansen is particularly addicted to these pits which we finally had to let go—we would have had to shore them if we went any deeper. Don had had quite a time disentangling Early Christian marble halls; Roman tile graves; Hellenistic chamber graves with very appealing little bedrooms, one couch always with head and shoulder rest, the other without (one must be for husband, the other for wife; but we cannot figure out which is which); and corners of Lydian rooms.

Don was also in charge of the three digs on the flat-topped "Upper Terrace" south of the House of Bronzes (see Map 3, no. 5). This terrace by the city wall, with its magnificent views, has failed to come up with the hoped-for palaces. We are exploring the footing of the towering city wall and going down hill in a series of steps which have led so far to a Roman villa. From the huge layers of debris which constitute the top of this hillock there have come multitudes of interesting objects—feminine toilet articles, fragments of wall paintings, and a charming ivory figurine of a sleeping amorino.

66

Figure 44—Corinthian column capital with laughing faun, late second century, our era, found in an area east of central complex Building B. Height of head 0.23 m. Manisa Museum.

After elaborate preparations designed to permit safe digging, we have launched a final (or semi-final?) assault on the mysterious building CG. It now also rejoices in the nickname of "arch factory" for not a day goes by but a new arch comes to light. At something like 35 feet below the highest preserved point, we have hit the water table. It is clear by now that the original structure of powerful masonry was only the first phase. Under the Roman Empire it became the center of a vast complex, perhaps a great bathing establishment, of which we find the walls going off in all directions (*Figure 54*). The terrible floods that submerged these structures so deeply have also preserved them. We have excavated, for example, a very fine staircase resting on brick arches—but I should hesitate to say what floor we happen to be on.

Our home ground brigade has been strengthened by the arrival of Jim McCredie, experienced as archaeologist and photographer. He and "Greenie," Crawford Greenewalt, Jr., are working as a team to photograph the highly diversified offerings that our sector men bring home. The recording section has been increased in a welcome way by the freely volunteered services of Mrs. J. D. Hancock, wife of the resident engineer of the Demir Köprü Dam project. She is helping Mrs. Hanfmann in the last hectic rush to keep the recording abreast of the excavation.

We had a staff picture taken just before our associate director, Henry Detweiler and our numismatist, Catharine Detweiler, departed on August 19 (*Figure 46*). The truck, the jeep, Arthur Steinberg and his Landrover, and the two Mercedes cars belonging to Jim McCredie and Mrs. Hancock, the eighteen staff members, half a dozen household members, and the workmen who are building our storage and workroom structure, who quickly got into the act, were quite a sight when all lined up. We were sorry to see the Detweilers go. Henry has been a mainstay of this expedition from the beginning and a source of both administrative wisdom and practical resourcefulness. Catharine devoted herself wholeheartedly to her coins throughout her stay and is probably the only member of the expedition who managed to get everything done that had to be done—and did the job clearly, efficiently, and well. The general exodus will begin September 1 and last until September 12.

To sum it up, this second campaign has brought considerable enlightenment on long-range prospects and problems as well as the definite establishment of a real base for our expedition which will be adequate to the tasks posed by the vast and as yet barely touched site of Sardis.

Sardis   September 26, 1959

It never fails. We were on our last day of large-scale digging when Dave Mitten brought the news that a great Imperial inscription was beginning to show up in fragments in the area east of Building B. I chased out and had a hasty look. Sure enough, there were letters of majestic size on fragments of a marble entablature. "You cannot go home today," said I jokingly to Arthur Steinberg, who had taken an enlightened and keen interest in our inscriptions and had cataloged them for later publication by Louis Robert. Arthur was scheduled to depart that afternoon. It was his turn now to dash out to the dig, and upon return he said to me with greatest seriousness: "You are right, I have to stay." And stay he did, getting both a reasonable reading and a squeeze of the major fragments. SEBASTOI KAI IOULIAI SEBASTE (I), "Augustus and Ioulia Augusta," are the key words, meaning "To the Emperor and the Empress Ioulia." Judging by the character of the letters, the inscription cannot be earlier than the second century; and empresses named Julia are known around that time only in the dynasty of the Severans. Of these Julia Domna (died A.D. 217), the beautiful, intelligent, and ambitious wife of the Emperor Septimius Severus is the most likely candidate.

The inscription, recording the dedication of a building to an emperor and an empress, was placed above a mighty triple gate located to the east of the central part of Building B and composed of great piers with rich architectural

Figure 45—Marble-paved public latrine with supports for seats projecting from west wall, in the area west of Building B. Some seats were found and a lot of small change and glassware. Early Byzantine period.

ornaments, imposing in size and splendid in execution—torded columns, entablatures with fine floral ornament, and the like. We found these architectural parts, as well as the fragments of the inscription, as they had fallen during the building's final destruction, whether by human or natural agency *(Figure 53)*. This sector, comprising the rectangular area to the east of B, had been going like wildfire in the last days of the dig. It was Tom Canfield's architectural eye that had divined under the unshapely hillocks of earth a large structure leading to the center of B. As supervisor of the area he laid out the plan of attack, and the actual excavation carried out by Dave Mitten vindicated Tom's surmise. I reported in my previous letter that we had found a colonnade which must have formed the eastern boundary of this complex, with double half-columns, probably in two stories, and an incredible number of architectural ornaments of remarkable quality. Tom conjectures that a court area lies between this colonnade and the newly discovered gate. Next summer we shall certainly want to put much of our effort into this exciting sector.

Surprise of a very different kind awaited us in the area west of Building B. Here we took up an alignment formed by large marble blocks, expecting to find the western boundary of what is obviously another large building complex. We found the alignment all right, but in front of it there appeared before our astonished eyes a magnificently constructed public latrine *(Figure 45)*—with most elaborate provisions for water and drainage, and a few marble seats still near their original position. Our workmen greatly admired this display of advanced standards of sanitation. We have been a bit puzzled why there should be so many coins (did they charge admission?) and fine glass vases. Coming in the last moment, these finds added to Dave's heavy burdens—and those of the recording department—but we still had time to ascertain from the coins that this establishment, like the Byzantine Shops, continued to function through the sixth century.

On August 21, a whirlwind and dust storm within a matter of minutes made night of day. It must have been in a storm like this that Apollo miraculously concealed and carried away Croesus from the fire death. The storm was followed by a downpour of several hours which flooded most of our excavations and nearly wiped out our deep pits. Fortunately, work on these had already stopped, but some of the Lydian areas near the House of Bronzes remained lakes that slowly turned to mud. We were considering where we might borrow pumps, but eventually things dried out, and we were able to finish the planned digging and clean up most of the mud from this deluge.

The official large-scale digging stopped on August 30, but we went slightly overtime until September 5 with a couple of small crews to clear up some special points. Thus we dug up the north apse of Building B, again upon Tom's suggestion. It turned out to have the same platform as the south apse, but—alas—no Imperial statue base preserved upon it.

In order to make maximum use of the truck and of Nuri, its trusty operator, we kept some workmen going at CG, the truck hauling large amounts of earth off the south end and also managing occasional big stones. The dramatic assault of men and machines upon the building came to a spectacular end when water began to gush out wherever we reached a level some thirty feet below the surface of the plain. We purchased a pair of huge boots and tried underwater exploration by touch—Mario Del Chiaro, who directed the last couple of weeks, Greenie, and myself. During the 1959 campaign we descended one story down from last year's excavation. Under the east side of the "Main Arch" and north of it we have found what seems to be a furnace for heating a bathing establishment. The only indication as to when this huge extension was made is given by a Roman lamp of a type current from the third to the fifth century, our era.

In the meantime, Don Hansen was adding some intricate and important bits of evidence to our knowledge of the Lydian levels near the House of

Bronzes—the most important discovery was a nearly complete Lydian room which yielded some fine Greek vases, notably part of a Rhodian jug with a dashing dog.

As usual, the last week was a hectic one, with our recorders, Ilse Hanfmann and Evelyn Hancock, our draftsman Güven, and our two photographers, Greenie and Jim McCredie, doing work at top speed. It was also a time of major effort for our architectural team, which under Tom Canfield's guidance did some highly productive work. Their work was not only arduous but at times perilous, as when Al Shapiro and Tony Casendino suspended themselves as well as their plumbbobs and tapes from the precipitous projections of CG some forty feet above the excavations.

After working hours we took time off to look at various areas with a view to the 1960 campaign. We shall certainly want to explore further the steep east bank of the Pactolus, now that our Pactolus Cliff test has taught us that Lydian strata are only masked by Roman buildings along its cliffs. Twice we went up to the breathtakingly beautiful Acropolis. We shall probably tackle this great citadel of Sardis next season. It may well be that we shall find ourselves wishing, if not for wings, at least for light metal scaffolding there. You feel that if you take another step you might be walking on air, and you would be, too, with those precipices all around you.

The new storage and work building (which is also to house the jeep) is nearly finished and a garage for the truck and another vehicle (someday that Landrover from Pakistan may yet come) is going up. A little house for the generator is also being built. The building program has been completed; our commissioner Kemal Bey has promised to take care of the completion of the walls of the compound. We shall have to lick the problem of unruly plumbing. Yes, we have plumbing—pipes leading from a large tank under the roof of the showers into the house, the laboratory, and the toilets. The process of installation was often dramatic; its results sometimes traumatic, especially to the users of showers and toilets. In some rosy future, it would be worthwhile to find water and bring it into our compound; at present, we pay several dollars a day for the "water wagon." Yet to be done is the landscaping and planting of trees.

During the last phase of the dig we had an increased number of visitors. Several groups touring early Christian sites of Asia Minor called at the camp. It was a pleasure to welcome the first of the Supporters of Sardis to make the pilgrimage to our site—Professor and Mrs. George Bates of the Harvard Business School and University of Istanbul, and Mr. William R. Engstrom of the First Boston Corporation. But another of our most valued friends, Dr. Lillian Malcove, had the misfortune to arrive unannounced on our "free" day when all the staff members were away, and was barred from seeing the house and finds by our zealous if misguided houseboy. This leads me to remark that we do have a "free" day, which happens to be Wednesday because that is the day when our workmen want to go to the market in Salihli. Most members of our staff—sometimes all of them—then go on trips to other sites. So if you plan to visit Sardis write or telegraph beforehand to Sart Amerikan Hafriyat Heyeti, P.K. 7, Salihli. There is a better than 50 percent chance that the communication will reach us.

On September 1, the Director General of Antiquities, Kâmil Su, and the Assistant Director, Ahmet Dönmez, came to inspect the site and the camp. They were visibly impressed by the magnitude of the results already attained, and made it clear that they will be very much interested in an early start on a program of consolidation and restoration of the buildings and monuments which we uncover, a program which should also include certain minimum measures for cleaning, conservation, and beautification of the area of the Artemis Temple.

1960

Sardis   July 1, 1960

We started on schedule June 26. By now all four vehicles are working, some 120 workmen are digging, and "the gang's all here." Four weeks ago things did not look nearly so hopeful. Although a cable exchange with the new consul at Izmir, Kenneth Byrnes, was reassuring, members of our staff made their departures in the face of considerable uncertainty.* But we have met no impediments, and even such delays as might be expected from changes of top government personnel did not affect any matters vital to the expedition.

Mrs. Hanfmann and I flew to Istanbul on June 11 and then to Izmir. Gus Swift, who had come ahead to fight the Battle of the Customs, had performed most efficiently; the first shipment was already cleared and in the garage at Sardis. Even the nearly mythological Landrover had safely arrived and was being repaired after its journey from Karachi. Nuri, our driver and mechanic, was still getting the jeep and Citroën truck in readiness, so we made our entry by taxi. At Sart we found an unshaven but joyous Kemal Bey on hand to greet us, as well as the house staff. Kemal Bey, our commissioner, had labored several days to clean up after an unusually stormy winter. He had stayed after the last campaign until November to see through the construction of several buildings. Now we were overcome by the sight of gleaming white doors and windows; the huge dimensions of the garage, which on the inside looks like a double-pedimented temple; the attractive new work-and-storage unit, which with its nice light would do credit to a

---

*On May 27, 1960, the Turkish Armed Forces took over the government. Tanks were still stationed at various points in Istanbul when we arrived there in June.

museum; and the new kitchen, which Kemal managed to maneuver in between the garage and the generator house. It was much needed, for the small one in the house was crowded beyond capacity by the cook, cook's helper, foreman, and houseboys. The camp looks impressive, and we hope for many years' good use of it. Even though major facilities were in order, the first ten days had to be spent unpacking furniture and utensils for eighteen people, putting up screens, going to Izmir to release the Landrover and to Manisa to register it, to Izmir to clear the second shipment, to Manisa to greet the new Governor, and to Salihli to greet the District Commissioner.

Meantime our staff members were coming in like homing pigeons—Don Hansen lugging his luggage half a mile from the coffee house in hottest sun, Dave Mitten and Greenie from Athens, Bob Whallon and Mehmet Bolgil from Istanbul, then Tony Casendino and a few days later Charlie Rogers and Bob Mayers from Athens. Almost everybody arrived at a time and in a way different from that foreseen. Claire Albright missed me in Izmir, took the bus past the dig to Salihli and returned by taxi.

Before the campaign got under way, there were short but intensive wage negotiations. Last year we had kept the wage rates of the first campaign though prices had gone up because of the devaluation of the lira. This year a wage increase was unavoidable and thoroughly justified. We had to raise wages about 12 percent, plus tax resulting from the increase. The first day only 65 workmen appeared but we now have the labor force we expect to maintain. We started on three "old" sectors, the large gymnasium complex B, the House of Bronzes area, and CG (alias City Gate). With the arrival of a 1956 Ford truck generously donated by the patron saint of our motor fleet, it has become possible to use one truck in the B area and another at CG.

Mario Del Chiaro is beginning to dig down in the Pactolus Cliff where he found three Lydian strata last year deep between Hellenistic and Roman tombs *(Figure 31)*. Unfortunately, the raging Pactolus has brought down

74

Figure 47—An imposing structure of yellow limestone and green sandstone thought in 1960 to be a Hellenistic fortress tower. It has since been identified as a remnant of Lydian terracing for a palace on the Acropolis. A staircase rose along wall at left. A second wall was discovered in 1971 directly above the first. See Figure 229.

the Tomb of the Lintel *(Figure 41)* in part, and we are now bringing down the rest of it to get at the Lydian levels.

Some discoveries were made prior to the beginning of the digging. Greenie succeeded where we had failed for two seasons: he rediscovered the tomb described by Butler as the Persian Tomb (now known as the Pyramid Tomb; *Figure 62,* Map 3, no. 14). This is so far the only major monument of Persian rule at Sardis, and Greenie plans to dig for objective evidence of its date, for Butler gave it to the Persians only on architectural comparisons with the tomb of King Cyrus at Pasargadae.

Tony Casendino, Mehmet Bolgil, Don Hansen, and Greenie came panting down the slopes of the Acropolis one evening with shouts of joy. They had found a beautifully built wall quite unknown before *(Figure 47,* Map 3, no. 20). The betting is that it may be part of the Hellenistic fortress on the citadel. We are making plans to excavate there as well as on the central platform of the Acropolis. We find again that car-driving and smoking (as in Cambridge) does not put one in good shape for Acropolis ascent. It will be a reducing regimen for the diggers and architects who have to operate up there.

Among the "presents" collected by our guard during our absence is a nice torso, already carefully cleaned by Burriss Young in his laboratory, which he has set up in a very orderly fashion. A long inscription recording various honors for some deserving citizen has turned up, and finally, a crude but quite astonishing frieze that shows people riding on bulls. The frieze does not look like ordinary representations of Roman circus games; more likely this ancient "rodeo" illustrates some local religious rite. Kemal Bey has taken the relief to the Manisa Museum.

Things are going smoothly in all departments. The architects under Tony Casendino have been putting down grids and have started on sections of CG. Tony and Charlie Rogers have set up the Rotolite copying device, which will be a great help to the architectural work. Bob Whallon has

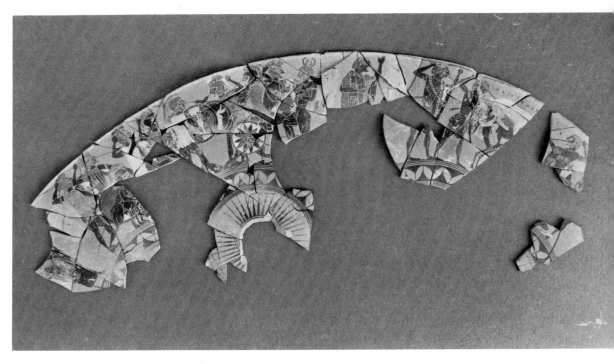

shown considerable technological talent—he is keeping alive our temperamental refrigerator and has put into effective operation the camera generously lent us by H. Dunscombe Colt. Bob is helping Greenie with photography. Claire Albright is firmly installed in the recording section. Gus Swift will be administrative officer of the expedition and has been digging at CG.

We had the pleasure of welcoming here the Turkish-American Association of Izmir, to whom Gus gave a conducted tour. We have had visits from several members of the NATO forces, and two French colleagues, architects of the Mari Expedition. Two extracurricular events gave us pleasure of a very different kind. We went to Salihli to view the best belly dancer of Turkey (an attraction discovered by the enterprising Mehmet Bolgil) and were rewarded by an evening of Turkish music in which audience and performers were of equal interest—the affair taking place in an outdoor cinema, with spectators on balconies and walls of the houses around. The other venture was a climb and scramble up the slopes of the Tmolus into a most romantic gorge, from which marble was supposedly quarried for the Artemis Temple. This breathtaking place would be a major tourist attraction in many a country. A picturesque touch was added to our return when our equestrian guide triumphantly carried off Claire Albright behind him on his horse. We hoped she would ride into camp in this manner so we could see the expression on Kemal Bey's face, but she elected to dismount before.

I want to say something about the activities of the Sardis project during the nine months between the 1959 and 1960 campaigns. At Cornell, Tony Casendino under Tom Canfield's supervision prepared the plans and drawings for the preliminary reports, while at the Fogg, Miss Frederica Appfel of France and Tangiers, Mrs. Sükran Umur of Istanbul, and Mrs. Claire Albright did a great job on the records under Mrs. Hanfmann's guidance. We had also a student assistant, Dennis Egnatz, under the Faculty Aid

Program, and some photographic work was done by Miss Bonnie Solomon, who is working for the Fine Arts Department. For two years, Miss Margaret Golding had devoted herself wholeheartedly to the important task of collecting ancient sources and descriptions of travelers concerning Sardis. A protracted illness during the last year exhausted her powers, and she passed away on May 31. On behalf of the Sardis Expedition I want to record our great indebtedness for her work and our sorrow at losing a gentle and good friend.

Cambridge   September 1960

Perhaps it was not purloined, but it certainly disappeared—the newsletter I wrote at Sardis late in August. So here I am now, writing with less immediate impression, but, to compensate for it, with knowledge of the entire 1960 campaign.

When last I wrote, we were just hitting our stride. The work gained speed and momentum all through July. Don Hansen, architects Tony Casendino and Bob Mayers, visitors, and donkeys were streaming up and down the steep path to the Acropolis. Just before I left for my flying trip to Germany late in July, I was presented at tea with a box mysteriously wrapped and tied with the cord of Tom Canfield's bathrobe. The contents made me whoop with joy, for here were fragments of a most exquisite Attic black-figure drinking cup, with inscriptions (*Figures 48, 49*). Don had found it on the Acropolis in a "pocket" of early material just above native rock. When put together the fragments yielded a drinking cup made in Athens at the time when Croesus ruled over Lydia (561–547 B.C.). One side depicts a battle scene, the other the legend of the Calydonian boar hunt in which the heroine Atalante took part. On the interior is part of the signature of the artist who painted this elegant jewel of archaic draftsmanship. It was

probably broken at the time the Persians stormed the citadel and captured King Croesus. All through August Don trenched and pitted on the central and southern platforms of the citadel. He discovered, among other things, a remarkable archaic relief of a lion, part of a marble throne—whether of the goddess Cybele or of a king is not known. This, however, was found in a Byzantine cistern. Apparently the Byzantines leveled and filled over the entire central platform. The loose fill and rock became at times dangerous and the depth of the accumulations quite unpredictable. One cave-in nearly led to tragedy; and few would care to duplicate the feat of Tony Casendino squinting through the theodolite while standing on a razor ridge of the northwest slope (Plate I). The way it looks now, we shall have to dig our Acropolis as the Acropolis at Athens was dug—square meter by square meter. Enough fine objects and early pieces have come up to make it worthwhile, even though hope for coherent early buildings is much diminished.

On the Pactolus, meanwhile, Mario Del Chiaro was commuting with giant strides from the ever more precipitous Pactolus Cliff to the rapidly developing new sector "Pactolus North" (Map 3, no. 10). His efficiency never faltered—nor did his luck. Even when he had to remove a broken wall he would find a Roman tomb with the prettiest terracottas, such as an elegant Venus and a goddess on horseback. The final aspect of the Pactolus Cliff (Figure 31) was quite something—part of a colorful Late Roman or Early Byzantine mosaic floor at the very top, and twenty feet below at the base an early wall of river stones from somewhere around 1000 B.C. You may recall that what set us off on this sector were three short stretches of Lydian walls found last year. Now Mario had at least three distinct Lydian levels, one probably a street with parts of two large buildings and walls nearly 30 feet long. The only trouble is that the walls run off into steep unexcavated banks of the trench—and the village houses all around make immediate expansion difficult.

Figure 50—Mosaic with ornamental design in five colors decorates floor of a Late Roman (ca. A.D. 400) bath in Pactolus North, a sector opened in 1960 on the east bank of the Pactolus.

Things went even better in the short three weeks of digging at Pactolus North (see Map 3, no. 10)—a spot upstream from the modern highway bridge and downstream from Pactolus Cliff, which we picked because an archaic statue *(Figure 8)* was found there in 1954. First we had quite a research in land deeds on our hands until it was ascertained that the land "upstairs," currently serving as threshing floors of the village, was Treasury land and that the land in the riverbed below, on which we had to dump, had been only temporarily used by the villagers as a vegetable garden for the school teacher. Right off the bat, virtually on the surface, Mario uncovered rooms of a Roman villa with mosaic floors *(Figure 50)*—pretty ones, with ornamental designs in five colors. These we had to let be—we have covered them up for the winter in hopes of securing expert workmen to lift them next year. Going down through the less ornamental parts of the late structures, we discovered that the Roman walls *(Figure 75)* sat right on Hellenistic walls and these in turn on earlier walls still. Two of the most auspicious discoveries were made here. First, a beautiful terracotta relief which we call "Portrait of a Lydian as a Young Man" (Plate II)—white-skinned like a woman and with earrings, but unmistakably bearded, and wearing a gorgeous purple cloak. The second, and to me the sensational find, was the appearance of a curious structure, preserved to over six feet: two curving walls with a passage between—either two apsidal walls or two parallel towers. The sherds found at its base make it certain that it was built in the Persian era after the Ionians had burned Sardis in 499 B.C., for the burned layer runs off its base. This is the first monumental urban building of the Persian era we have found; we are inclined to think of it as part of defenses to secure the crossing of the Pactolus, but it is too early to be sure. What is exciting is the knowledge that we are in the monumental zone of the city. My own surmise is that the archaic agora of Sardis, the one Herodotus describes as being astride the Pactolus, lies between this sector and the

Figure 51 (left)—Ten unsold Lydian lamps lying on a small part of a shop floor preserved in the Lydian Market, House of Bronzes area.

Figure 52 (right)—Architect Robert Mayers using plane table (right) and level (left) in the Lydian Market, House of Bronzes area. "Plane tabling" is a rapid method for getting measured sketch plans in the field; they are later redrawn to scale in the drafting room. The plane table is standing on wall which enclosed the Market on the east. The big wall in background is Roman.

expanding excavation in the area of the House of Bronzes (see Map 3, *Figure 134*).

The House of Bronzes area *(Figure 4)* kept us on tenterhooks to the very end of the campaign. Proceeding with tenacity and determination, Gus Swift first uncovered a sizable stretch of Lydian levels, and then descended into the bowels of the earth to pursue the quest of pre-Lydian Sardis. The Lydian structures, small and partly disrupted, produced heaps of pottery comparable to the "Potter's Workshop" of 1958, and in another place a pile of Lydian lamps *(Figure 51)*. We interpret these as part of a shopping area comparable to the open air markets of modern Turkish towns; and the teasing thought is that these may be the shops at the eastern fringe of the agora. Our first archaic Greek silver coin and bits of imported Near Eastern glazed wares appeared here. However, the pit was the thing. Digging through a deep flood deposit, Gus came upon one earth floor after another. Archaeologists will have plenty to discuss and debate, but we believe we have a continuous sequence of settlements spanning the darkest period in the history of Asia Minor, from the Late Bronze Age of the thirteenth century B.C. to about 700 B.C., the beginning of the historical dynasty of the Mermnads. This, to my knowledge, is unique for Western Asia Minor. A great burned level occurs in the early twelfth century B.C., the time when, according to Herodotus, "the sons of Herakles" established their rule over Lydia—the time, too, when the Hittite kingdom perished in the violent migrations that threw all the Aegean and much of the Near East into turmoil. By the time the dig ended, Gus was down to thirty-five feet below surface, and it took two ladders and some acrobatics to reach the bottom of the pit, which narrowed from about fifty to about three square meters. At this point another riverine deposit was coming up. Whether the earlier Bronze Age settlements lie underneath we shall not know without greatly enlarging the trench.

Charlie Rogers, sporting an elegant straw hat with a feather, and Bob

Mayers had a busy time measuring and drawing ever new walls and ever deeper stratigraphic mysteries in the House of Bronzes and Pactolus areas *(Figure 52)*, but they kept right up with the pace of excavation.

The "big stuff" was of course in the area of Building B *(Figure 4)*. Our plan here was dictated to some degree by exigencies of traffic and land ownership. To get the two trucks near the actual digging, we ran a kind of circular highway through the ruins, over the tops of the walls *(Figure 116)*. As long as we did not own the field to the east, we could not tackle the important entrance court (now known as Marble Court) whose existence we had surmised from last year's trenches which ran right upon the land boundary. The field had to be secured from eleven heirs! After two weeks of preliminary conversation, an agreement was reached, but to round up the eleven heirs was something else again. Kemal Bey and I managed to capture and load into the jeep nine men, women, and children; when we had secured the tenth heir we found that the eleventh heiress had gone to a nearby village. The jeep was sent in pursuit and the heiress picked up en route—but by the time we returned to the Land Deed office, several other heirs had wandered off. In the end, the purchase was duly signed, and we tackled what turned out to be one of the most impressive examples of Roman Imperial architecture in Asia Minor. The great marble facades of this court were, however, toppled and twisted in wild mountains of marble *(Figure 53)*—and some of the pieces weighed several tons. At this point our associate director, Henry Detweiler, who arrived in August for a two weeks' stay, appeared most opportunely on the scene. With Dave Mitten, Henry quickly worked out an efficient system for moving and sorting the masses of marbles. About two thirds of the court are now cleared. We also established crucial points in the plan of the two large arcaded halls flanking the marble court and in the vast colonnaded court which extends for some hundred yards to the east. This marble court, rivaling Baalbek, will necessitate close study and reconstruction first in drawing and eventually *in natura*. We shall need increased

Figure 53 (left)—Ruins of Marble Court emerging in the Gymnasium area. Jumble of huge marble pieces overthrown by earthquake foreshadows the mammoth task ahead.

Figure 54 (right)—Extending northward from a hall of massive limestone masonry the Roman-Byzantine bath complex CG had a circular towerlike unit and large rooms built of rubble. The walls were covered with frescoes imitating multicolored marble paneling, later removed to the Manisa Museum. Superimposed arches (as in the corner) gave rise to the nickname "arch factory."

facilities for earth removal and equipment with greater lifting reach and capacity to undertake this task.

Our first essays in restoration have taken place in the Temple of Artemis and at the structure CG. Our operations in the temple, conducted by Mehmet Bolgil and Burriss Young, were on a small scale: a clean-up of the eastern cult cella and reconstruction of the image base. Yet they have already improved the appearance of this noble structure. We plan to proceed westward to the other units of the shrine. Here, too, ways and means for lifting and resetting of very heavy blocks will have to be found.

The local master mason and his crew, who had the task of repairing the rubble walls and brick arches of the bathing establishment CG, seemed to know exactly how it was done. We have taken the precaution of adopting a distinctive style of raised joins and are inscribing the date of restoration, to prevent posterity from confusing our handicraft with that of the Romans. The mysteries of CG became ever more complicated; it lived up to its nickname of "arch factory" in a manner surprising even to most hardened admirers of arches and vaults. At the very end it produced a surprise: fragments of wall paintings (*Figure 54*). These gave an opportunity for field work both to conservator Burriss Young and his laboratory assistants and to our admirable draftsman Güven Bakir.

This brings me back to the compound. Here the recording department was organized in the new workroom building with Mrs. Hanfmann and Mrs. Claire Albright laboring indefatigably against the ever new waves of objects arriving from the seven sectors. Claire left late in July and Mrs. Christina Del Chiaro took over with equal efficiency. The "depot" also became a sort of exhibition room: we put out a selection of finds to gratify the curiosity and interest of numerous visitors. Another part of the establishment was preempted by Bob Whallon's collection of human and animal bones. After his arrival on August 9, Axel von Saldern found space here to work on glass

wares from our three seasons. Cheerful and obliging, Axel became a good friend to all of us, setting an example of scholarly cooperation and giving freely of his expert knowledge of ancient glass. Another branch of scientific cooperation was represented by Ken Frazer, who for several days collected archaeomagnetic samples for a group of scientists in Cambridge, England.

On August 6 we had the pleasure of greeting John D. Barrett of the Bollingen Foundation and Ernest Brooks of the Old Dominion Foundation. Despite some misadventures en route and the hottest spell at Sardis, the visitors went gamely through the arduous ascent to the Acropolis and a concentrated guided tour of the premises and sectors. As the grant from the Bollingen Foundation has been the cornerstone of the whole Sardis project, we were happy indeed to be able to show what had been accomplished in the relatively brief span of three summers. Several of the Supporters found their way to Sardis, almost invariably followed rather than preceded by telegrams announcing their arrival. (Note: there are two kinds of telegrams in Turkey: *Acele*, "Urgent," and the other kind which gets sent as circumstances permit.)

Life in camp was not all archaeology. Following the terms of the Milton grant, Bob Whallon carried on a sociological study of Turkish village life, making phenomenal advances in Turkish and learning to play the native guitar-like *saz* to the admiration of native and foreigner alike. He and Dave Mitten even managed to enlighten the villagers about the satellite Echo, whose nightly jerkings across the starry Lydian sky were watched from our terrace by most of the staff, while Bob Mayers and Charlie Rogers contributed astronomical lore. Burriss undertook the collection of bugs for an American doctor in Izmir, a pursuit which led to nightly alarums and excursions as spiders and scorpions were discovered about the premises. The highlight of night life was reached when Bob and Dave let loose a hedgehog in the excavation house; it went on a rampage among the *gazos* (soft drink) and aspirin bottles, and they decided it was better off elsewhere.

Bob's, Dave's, and Don's friendliness with the villagers paid off in archaeological dividends—they received numerous tips about antiquities kept here and there in the village. Some of the workmen proceeded to make sketches and even to copy inscriptions. Our "No Ex" (not excavated) holdings were thus increased by some really important items: an archaic Lydian relief apparently from a small sanctuary of which we were later shown the findspot, a colossal head of a Roman emperor, a handsome relief of a flying Eros, to mention but a few. We have not yet started on a systematic survey of the vicinity, or even systematic follow-up of the leads of these chance finds. That there is much to be done in this line is shown by the discovery by Bob Whallon of a rock-cut (apparently Classical) relief in a marble gorge of the Tmolus, and the spotting of an ancient site in the plain near the village of Mersindere by Greenie and Güven. It was Greenie too who in addition to his duties as photographer and his dig of the Persian tomb found time to verify some village tales about subterranean passages in the north slope of the Acropolis.

This, the third season, has brought much new knowledge and a clearer definition of the great potential and great challenges of Sardis. The deep sounding in the House of Bronzes area has opened exciting possibilities for early periods. We seem to have "boxed in" an extremely promising area of the Lydian city in the western part of the site. We have proved that important Lydian and Persian finds may be expected all along the Pactolus. We have tested the Acropolis and know now both the possibilities and the difficulties. And we have made progress on the excavation of two large Roman complexes in the plain. With the fourth season we shall enter upon the phase of continued systematic excavation of larger areas, though we shall continue testing in order to discover whether the archaic city extended into the central and eastern part of the site.

1961

Sardis   July 4, 1961

Today is the Fourth of July, but since yesterday was the first payday we did not have time to make this a holiday. The only constructive contribution to celebration was by Charlie Rogers who had secretly made a colorful poster of fireworks and newspaper clippings, and thus kept alive the spirit of the occasion. Most of our crowd will be taking off for Izmir today—the first "free" day.

The season has started with a bang: on the very first morning of digging (June 26) Greenie, just arrived from Gordion, found our first Lydian gold. A lovely granulated gold bead, a tiny silver hawk (rather like the Egyptian Horus hawks), and an agate with a gold wire attachment were the treasures he produced at lunchtime before our astonished eyes (*Figure 57*). We have been blowing no horns about this because we do not want another "gold rush" on the part of the populace who are already too willing to credit us with the discovery of gold treasures. Even so, a delegation from the Turkish press soon appeared. They were very reasonable, however, and did not overdo the treasure hunt inquiries. Then too, what we got are "graverobbers' leavings." Unfortunately for us, it is during the winter rains that washouts are apt to reveal the location of graves. Our unlicensed colleagues had somehow spotted two Lydian graves (*Figure 56*), and one of them must have been that one-in-five-hundred rarity, an unplundered or at least incompletely plundered grave. The new expedition guard, Ahmet Avcikaya, and the government excavation guard, Ali Riza (our former cook), heard about it, and then our commissioner pointed the graves out to us on a pre-

excavation tour. The decision to complete the graverobbers' work paid off: in addition to the jewels some very nice painted pottery came to light, notably two drinking cups decorated with birds and fish *(Figure 58)*. Fish must have been a subject of some interest to the Sardian vase painters of the seventh century B.C., for last year we found some nice ones on sherds from the Acropolis.

At a place called Haci Oğlan Mevki (Map 2) we dug out two monumental bathtub-shaped sarcophagi with roof-like lids *(Figure 60)*. These, too, had been spotted by Ali Riza while he was working in the field of our former water-wagon man. Lying at the foot of a flat-topped hill, the spot commands a beautiful view northward, over the modern highway and across the Hermus plain to the Royal Cemetery of Bin Tepe. As usual, our cheerful commissioner, Kemal Bey, was full of the most optimistic auguries; almost as usual, the reality failed to live up to them. The heavy lids of the caskets were still on, but somebody had broken in through holes in the sides and had left us several vases plus three considerably pushed around skeletons. One of our two pairs of newlyweds, Willy and Elaine Kohler, did a most meticulous job of sifting and cleaning the contents. Elaine, our anthropologist, did a study of the skeletal remains in situ. Bonnie Solomon took complete photographic coverage of the opening and then devoted an hour to collecting the skeletal remains of a mouse which had strayed into one sarcophagus. The sarcophagi did however contribute something: the coin finds seem to prove that this hitherto poorly known type does belong to the Early Hellenistic period.

Twofold activity has developed in the House of Bronzes area: Gus Swift is currently descending on a broad front to the Lydian levels; and the Early Byzantine House of Bronzes is being repaired, since winter damage made the need for consolidation only too obvious. When the workmen turned

over a slab which lay in a basin of Unit 7—the working basement area excavated by Don Hansen during our first season—they found a marble relief of a river god, certainly from a fountain (*Figure 63*).

After his grave-digging success Greenie has ascended the Acropolis and is making a new trench there. So far he has uncovered some late walls and several graves (the latter are to be connected perhaps with a crusader coin).

Don Hansen is now widening the Pactolus North sector which gave us our first Persian building last year. Dave Mitten, fresh from digging at Isthmia (Corinth), has already freed much of the remaining part of the great Marble Court at gymnasium B, ably assisted by Chris Reagan who is also keeping an eye on inscriptions. Already two large and several small fragments of the Byzantine poem(s?) have appeared. We have also tried to oblige a wandering crew of Yale men who are trying to follow the Royal Road and are looking for it in front of B. So far the most we have is the medieval road, if that.

Burriss Young has made his laboratory a place not only for work but also for the orderly dispensing of various supplies. He lost one valuable assistant when two soldiers with bayonets appeared and presented the Turkish equivalent of Selective Service greetings to Arif Akyel who had been a great help in the laboratory for three years. However, with his pedagogical acumen, Burriss detected a possible (in fact two possible) replacements, and they are now being trained. One of them knows English and is doing double duty teaching Turkish and getting into the routine.

The letter would not be complete without its vignette on wildlife. Citations went to Burriss and Tony Casendino for evicting a centipede from Elaine Kohler's violin case; and to Bonnie Solomon and Burriss for successfully raising a family of swallows whose nest was destroyed by the violent rain and thunderstorms which prevailed during our first days here. A truck

Figure 57—"Graverobbers' leavings." Lydian jewelry sieved out of the Indere graves: small silver pendant in shape of Egyptian hawk, Height 1.75 cm.; oblong agate bead with gold wire loop, Length of wire 2.7 cm., Diameter of bead 1.05 cm.; melon-shaped granulated gold bead, Weight 2.35 grams.

stopped by the House of Bronzes to offer me a wild boar which they had tied to their spare tire—apparently the truck had run over it. And the dwellers on the upper terrace maintain that a coyote or wild dog serenades them nightly.

Sardis   July 25, 1961

I was waiting for something special to happen—and it did.

I had come across the sun-parched foothills of the citadel from the Pactolus Cliff, where we are uncovering a beautiful colored mosaic with the assistance of Reha Arican, a specialist who came from Istanbul to supervise the lifting; and on to Pactolus North, where Don Hansen has found an elegant Roman bath flanked by much earlier Lydian houses; and so past Gus Swift's huge trench, which is producing great quantities of Lydian pottery; and finally arrived at the House of Bronzes where our young architects, Charlie Rogers and Stu Carter, were crouched over our pottery dump studying vases. I picked them up and we went to get some levels for our spectacular "Road Trench" (*Figure 64*). Here Dave Mitten has uncovered, in rapid succession, the late medieval, the Middle (?) Byzantine, and finally the imposing Roman road, which is paved with huge stones and flanked by a majestic colonnade with mosaics. This was the "Fifth Avenue" of Sardis, and the successor to the famed Royal Road of the Persian kings.

Charlie and Stu went to work, and just as they were painting the fourth level mark a shout went up from the workmen—and there was my something special. A beautiful marble head, lying face down in the debris over the Roman road. The head of a bearded man with wavy locks, breathing an almost fanatic, expressive spirit—which has led some scholars to describe

88

Figure 58—Lydian skyphos with fish motif from Indere grave. Style and shape imitate Greek pottery from Corinth.

this kind of "Proto-Byzantine" sculpture as "soul portraits"—and yet retaining in the modeling something of the refined vitality of Hellenistic sculpture *(Figure 65)*.

Bonnie Solomon was summoned and immortalized the scene from all sides and angles. Even the workmen were excited about the finely preserved "heykel" (image).

Next to the Lydian gold jewels of our first day *(Figure 57)*, this is certainly our most distinguished artistic find this season—but we have had others: the fragments of a grandiose Hellenistic relief which unfortunately the Byzantines chiseled down to use in a pavement at Pactolus North; and the head fragments of the colossal statue of Antoninus Pius, which Burriss Young found in the little church behind the Artemis Temple (Map 3, no. 18). For strangeness, Gus Swift's find takes the prize—a gaily painted phallus of respectable Lydian antiquity. Just today there is news that a gold earring has been found in the Early Christian or Early Byzantine "Peacock Tomb" (Map 3, no. 12), along with the one well-preserved wall painting. At this very moment Don Hansen is opening the sarcophagus found in the bottom of the tomb.

This Peacock Tomb has been quite an enterprise. First Burriss Young and his assistants nearly fainted from the fumes of the cleaning medium; then Marga Rogers was almost incarcerated there while making exact drawings (and now water colors) of the lovely Early Christian or Early Byzantine wall paintings *(Figure 61)*.

All our mosaics are being cleaned. Reha Bey uses a very effective technique to lift them and has already raised two *(Figure 66)*. It is a majestic sight to see a parade of workmen carrying the mosaic on a stretcher, led by Reha Bey wearing a Napoleonic hat made of newspaper.

Our geophysicist, David Greenewalt, has just left. We had a bit of trouble

Figure 59 (left)—This bronze plaque was found in the Lydian Market (House of Bronzes) area. It seems to be a mold over which thin foil might be beaten. The edges are unfinished, arguing for local bronze casting at Sardis (see the unfinished ibex plaque, Figure 77). Width ca. 2 inches. Lydian or Lydo-Persian.

Figure 60 (right)—Sifting earth in one of the big sarcophagi found at Haci Oglan Mevki ("place of the youth who made a pilgrimage to Mecca"), about one-half mile west of Pactolus North. Their bathtub shape is a Lydian survival in the Hellenistic Age. The lid (left) resembles a house roof.

getting him and his equipment in, but with the help of the American Consulate General it was managed. Dr. Greenewalt went around sticking electrodes into sundry locations assisted by a monkey-faced boy, one of our workmen, who is also known as the "Court Musician" because of his prowess with the *saz*, a native stringed instrument. The results of the geophysical venture have been sufficiently encouraging to make a continuation for two seasons desirable.

Professor Stephen Jacobs of Cornell arrived and strengthened the architectural, and particularly the architectural-historical, aspect of our enterprise. Steve has already acquired the native yellow headgear. He has been turning over the huge marble blocks in the Marble Court, classifying them in preparation for the reconstruction. He has also gotten into the problems of the Artemis Temple and the little church behind it *(Figure 67)*. His genial interest in all things Turkish has made him many friends.

The social highlight of the season was a great wedding feast in Salihli. It was preceded by an almost catastrophic event: the sudden resignation of the cook just before we were to entertain the District Commissioner for dinner and the Governor for lunch. Kemal Bey, however, rushed to town and returned with a cook, and the two notables were entertained in style. As return engagement the District Commissioner invited the whole expedition staff to attend a wedding, *the* wedding at the nearby town of Salihli. As our cavalcade of four cars lined up in front of the Army Officers' Garden, we saw that we would not be lonely. From the flood-lit and streamered concrete dancing floor in the center hundreds of faces seemed to blend into the outer darkness. And in fact, more than a thousand people witnessed the marriage of the daughter of the director of the Agricultural Bank. A loud-speaker periodically announced that the official who was to perform the ceremony would be late, but that did not seem to bother anyone. When dancing began the expedition members took the opportunity to participate—though it must

Figure 61—Gaily painted peacocks, flowers, birds, and garlands adorn the walls of a well-preserved barrel-vaulted mausoleum, the "Peacock Tomb," of the Early Christian era, built on the east bank of the Pactolus, south of Pactolus North.

be said that none of them lasted through the dance in which two partners press an apple between their foreheads while dancing.

The ceremony was a civil one performed by the Mayor, and the District Commissioner, our host, was a witness. Afterwards there was the presentation of gifts and other traditional Turkish features. We presented our flowers and compliments to the bride and her family. Another friend of ours treated us to a dance performed with bayonets—that's when we left.

Work has been stepping up in all departments. The recorders now sally forth to help empty the many boxes collected in the field. Elaine Kohler has virtually an anatomical museum; some of it of "human interest," such as the nineteen-year-old young man who was thrown violently into a hole in Don Hansen's Roman bath—and stayed there until studied by Elaine. Coins pour in for classification by Dave Mitten; the prize among them is a gold solidus which Greenie found on the Acropolis. He also found there quite a large building, probably part of the Early Byzantine fortress. Conservation work has been finished on the House of Bronzes and Byzantine Shops, and is currently going forward in the church behind the Temple of Artemis (*Figure 67*; see also *Figures 197, 198*). In the temple itself Willy Kohler is supervising a skilled crew who are operating a hoist and winch to re-set the image base of the east cult room. Charlie Rogers and Stu Carter are roaming over hill and dale putting down a grid over the entire area. Chris Reagan is finishing the excavation of the Pyramid Tomb (*Figure 62*) which we found last year and which may have an interesting background—if the tomb is really that of the romantic couple Abradatas and Pantheia, eulogized by Xenophon.*

*In his romantic "Education of Cyrus," Xenophon, who marched with the Ten Thousand from Sardis in 401 B.C., tells of faithful and beautiful Pantheia, who killed herself over her husband's body. He was a Persian nobleman who fell battling the Lydians when Cyrus defeated Croesus. Cyrus built for him a tomb "high above the Pactolus" (*Cyropaedia* VII. iii. 3–16).

92

Figure 62—"Pyramid Tomb," found by the Princeton Expedition in 1914 and rediscovered by the Harvard-Cornell group in 1960, was further excavated in 1961 and 1969. The stepped monument, built in a recess carved in the hard red clay of a hillside east of Pactolus Cliff, may have served as model for Persian architecture such as the tomb of king Cyrus at Pasargadae, where Lydian captives were taken after the fall of Croesus.

Cambridge   September 1961

"Footage excellent" ran a telegram we received shortly before our departure from Sardis. Thus culminated a hectic episode that proved once more that Sardis is a place where the unexpected always happens. The proposal to film the expedition had come from David G. Briggs, USIS officer in Ankara, and after a week of messages to and from Sardis, Izmir, Ankara, and Istanbul, a film crew from the Turkish company A.D.S. showed up a day early—an event unheard of in the annals of arrivals at our camp.

It was the last day of Greenie's dig on the Acropolis, so we made the cameramen climb the citadel immediately. Henry Detweiler and I kept them company. Their spirits, flagging from the fierce heat, were revived by the magnificent sweep of perilous precipices unfolding before their camera—though they were eternally grateful that we had commandeered a donkey to carry the equipment they had at first boldly volunteered to lug up.

Next day, the film crew and C. K. Waters from USIS Istanbul, who had come with them, got a real workout. From dawn to dusk they went indefatigably from one sector to another, recording all the varied activities. The "film festival" ended at the camp with the camera men shooting Bonnie Solomon's photography, Burriss Young's Turkish laboratory assistants, and Ilse Hanfmann's recording crew (Elaine Kohler and Alice Swift), while they in turn were being shot with still cameras by nearly every member of the expedition. Details of the use of this (black and white, no sound track) material are under discussion. On our way back, Ilse and I did see in Istanbul the preliminary versions for a three-minute news spot and an eleven-minute documentary. We are hopeful that eventually Harvard and Cornell will get prints of the latter.

Figure 63 (left)—Probably from a fountain, this Roman relief of a river god was reused in a dyeing (?) basin in the Early Byzantine House of Bronzes. Sculptor's tools, mallet and chisel, are incised in upper left corner.

Figure 64 (right)—Marble-paved Main Avenue of Sardis south of the Byzantine Shops, 50 feet wide and flanked by colonnade lies partly under the modern highway. The avenue was meagerly restored by the Byzantines after A.D. 616; its Ottoman replacement was in use until 1952. (The contemplative archaeologist is C. H. Greenewalt, Jr.)

Just a couple of days before, we had the great pleasure of welcoming to our camp the American Consul General at Izmir, Kenneth A. Byrns, and Mrs. Byrns. Mr. Byrns had been most helpful on a number of occasions and we were happy to be able to show him what our project is accomplishing both scientifically and by way of Turkish-American cultural cooperation.

Around August 20 the heat wave began finally to break, and the last-minute outpouring of finds set in. No less than four capitals strikingly adorned with heads of satyrs, gorgons, and other divinities were found in the Marble Court of the gymnasium complex, where Steve Jacobs with his little helper Hüseyin (the son of the District Commissioner of Salihli) were laboring valiantly to record the hundreds of richly ornamented architectural pieces. Meantime, the wonderful marble-paved "Fifth Avenue" of Sardis uncovered by Dave Mitten became the scene of both excavation and construction. Our construction crew was building a retaining wall for the modern highway to permit us to leave exposed the step of the colonnade flanking the Roman road to the south. At the same time Greenie was digging a deep pit through a disrupted part of the avenue to see if any earlier roads might be found underneath *(Figure 64)*. No Hellenistic or Persian Royal Road came to light during his descent of some 20 feet; but there were lots of Lydian sherds in the earth layers interspersed with water-laid deposits—much the same kind as Gus Swift had encountered last year in his deep pit in the House of Bronzes area some two hundred feet to the south. Next year we intend to free another section of the great avenue to find out if a major street branched off from it. At that time we shall look again for earlier roads—this year's probe was not really wide enough to be conclusive.

Meantime, the Lydian commercial and industrial area in the House of Bronzes region (it will be officially known as "Lydian Trench" henceforth) kept pouring out intact Lydian vases, charming parts of terracotta reliefs, bronze plaques *(Figure 59)*, and molds for bronze casting. Gus Swift, his

daughter Noye, and indeed a good part of his family labored here with Willy Kohler amidst the dust storms to cope with the intake of material and bring some order into the chaotic tangle of rubble walls. The lineaments of two shops are clear; they in turn seem to align with a large building in the northwest corner *(Figure 76)* as yet only partially known. Dating problems get more and more complicated. Did the Persians build the big structure? Did Hellenistic coppersmiths have a huge burned circular area aglow with their furnaces?

Neither could Don Hansen complain of lack of complexities. As we left it, his Pactolus North sector *(Figure 75)* has rooms with mosaics at the south end, a contemporary Late Roman bath in the middle, and in between and to the north first the richest collection of water pipes going, presumably from a Roman reservoir that distributed water into the city; then Persian apsidal structures, one with a wonderful circular well nearly thirty feet deep which began to function again the minute it was excavated; finally, Lydian rooms, again with a well. The Late Roman or Early Byzantine bath is a most elegant affair and eloquent testimony for the prosperity of Sardis at a time when the Western Roman Empire was disintegrating. Again and again, Sardis shows how continuous was the development from the Roman to the Byzantine era in Asia Minor, and our excavation may well become one of the most important sites for this transition. Here we must mention the delightful visit of A. H. S. Megaw, field director of the Byzantine Institute. His enthusiasm for the Byzantine buildings of Sardis, both excavated and unexcavated, was contagious, and his acumen in architectural observation invaluable. Inter alia, he suggested that the southern bastion of the Acropolis is a highly interesting example of Early Byzantine military architecture, and that the unexcavated building "D," whose four piers stick up south of the modern highway (Map 3, no. 29), may be a great church from Justinian's time.

The last two weeks we had a galaxy of scholarly visitors. Professor and

Figure 65 (left)—The "soul portrait": a magnificent Late Roman marble portrait head was found face down where it had been tamped into the roadbed during Byzantine construction of Sardis' major east-west street (Figure 64). It probably belonged originally to a statue honoring an important official, orator, or philosopher; ca. A.D. 260–280.

Figure 66 (right)—Cleaned mosaics with intricate patterns were lifted from Pactolus North structure (see Figure 50) and stacked against the camp wall.

Mrs. Laroche, famed in Hittite studies, arrived just in time to inspect three inscriptions incised on potsherds of the sixth century B.C. found by Gus and Willy in the Lydian Trench, and to pronounce them not Lydian but Carian. As king Gyges employed Carian mercenaries (who went all the way to Abu Simbel), the matter is most intriguing. Our epigraphists, Professor and Mrs. Louis Robert, gave their usual masterly, not to say magicianly, demonstration. The most striking coup was the decipherment of a much effaced and poorly written Byzantine inscription—it turned out to invoke the curses of the 318 Fathers of the Nicene Council on anyone who violates the burial. Another remarkable item recorded the story of a man who had failed to give to a god the present he had promised if he succeeded in marrying "the woman I love" (the god punished him). Robert was enthusiastic about the new part of the great Byzantine inscription which has appeared on the north side of the Marble Court of the Gymnasium. He pointed out that it gives, in prose, facts about the Byzantine reconstruction of the Marble Court —facts the Byzantine poems we found on the south and west sides fail to provide. Thus there is a date (unfortunately not identifiable, as it is an *indictio* date) and important architectural terms. I may add here that Dave Mitten and Chris Reagan have in cooperation with Henry Detweiler and Steve Jacobs freed some more parts of the original Roman dedicatory inscription of the Marble Court *(Figure 117)*—it keeps adding important historical information: a proconsul of Hellas, a consular woman, and another lady, one Flavia Politte, being mentioned among the benefactors who contributed to the construction.

Virtually every visitor has hailed this Gymnasium complex as one of the greatest monuments of Roman Imperial architectural design. It will be a goal of future campaigns to complete excavation of its major features. Then for the reconstruction—for which Steve Jacobs is now laying research foundations.

Figure 67—Beginning restoration of the small Early Christian church (ca. A.D. 400) known as Church M, adjoining the southeast corner of the Artemis Temple. Darkened rings around columns in center of photograph reveal how deeply the church and temple were buried by landslides.

We are looking forward to a big season in 1962: the investigation of the main artery of the city, a large-scale effort at the Gymnasium complex, enlargement of the sectors where we got Lydians (House of Bronzes and Pactolus North), a probe in depth at least in the House of Bronzes, a detailed study of the Late Roman bath, and, we hope, the opening of at least one, if possible two, new sectors to find out what was going on in the central and eastern parts of the city, so far left untouched. Then there is also the Acropolis and especially the amazing and hazardous tunnel on its northern side, which we inspected this year. Its exploration will require considerable effort and skill—at present only two out of maybe ten of its serpentine passages are accessible. We hope to continue our geophysics project, and have applied for a permit to start on the Royal Cemetery of Bin Tepe.

Plate II Painted portrait of a Lydian, part of a terracotta frieze possibly from a Lydian shrine or building. It was a stray find in debris of a Pactolus North structure leveled by Persians for one of their buildings. Height, a little over three inches.

1962

Sardis   July 8, 1962

"Jacob, son of . . ." We cannot agree whose son, since the slightly incised writing is damaged. Anyway, we seem to have found "Jacob's Bargain Basement." This is what the Byzantine shop excavated by David Mitten and John Pedley turns out to be. The inscription on a water jar was spotted early this morning by Ilse Hanfmann. Now photographer Vincent Wickwar is immortalizing the shop, which is all cleaned up and nearly ready for business *(Figure 68)*.

The interest of the inscription is in the Hebrew name. It may, of course, be the name of a Christian, but Sardis is known to have had a considerable Jewish community; Josephus quotes decrees of Julius Caesar and Augustus commanding officials not to forbid the Jews of Sardis "to assemble together according to the custom of their forefathers" (*Antiq. Jud.* xiv.235, 260, xvi.171).

The shop was excavated in order to test how far along the main marble avenue the shopping center might extend. We now know that the colonnaded street *(Figure 64)*, mosaics, and the shops behind extended for at least 500 feet and there is as yet no end in sight.

Across the road, Gus Swift has been going down since June 13 and has now reached the Lydian levels. A welcome "first" in the Roman-Hellenistic fill above was our first Hellenistic silver coin, either of Alexander the Great or one of his immediate successors. Here in the House of Bronzes area we have put into operation our first stretch of the railroad. As usual, the problem of finding skilled operators seemed baffling, and as usual the required

Figure 68—The first sign of a Jewish community at Sardis: "Property of Jacob the Elder" (of the Synagogue) was incised on the shoulder of a storage jar found in this shop. The jar's lit-up lower part is seen lying between the left wall and a bronze wine jug standing on a big tray. Fragments of two bronze balance scales were found in the store, but it is not known what Jacob was selling.

experts were found within our labor force. The venerable "Black Mehmet," who had worked on the small-gage railroad of the Princeton Expedition before the First World War, became our principal railroader. A second stretch is now being put into operation in Mario Del Chiaro's Pactolus North sector.

It was Mario Del Chiaro who found our nicest Lydian piece so far. Maintaining a tradition established in 1960, when on his first step into this sector he kicked up a Lydian painted terracotta frieze, Mario on his second day there this year found another attractive example of this archaic Lydian sculpture—two lions walking away from each other. He has been going like a whirlwind in an area of nearly 1000 square meters between last year's trench on the Pactolus edge and a small building of which the interesting domes are lying on the ground. This was called "E" by the First Sardis Expedition (*Figure 75*). There was a brief flurry of excitement when an alignment of marble blocks appeared at the edge of the building, but Henry Detweiler rightly saw that they were re-used as a leveling course for what looks to be a small Byzantine church. Henry is studying the structure and finds it intriguing—it is of course yet to be fully excavated.

Greenie, and later Güven Bakir, tackled our most dramatic objective, the tunnels Greenie discovered two years ago in the cliffs on the north side of the Acropolis (*Figures 69–70*). In length these Sardis tunnels already have the famous one at Mycenae beat, but we do not as yet know who made them or why, nor how far they may still go on.

Between June 17 and 30 arrivals followed each other thick and fast until the staff shot up to over twenty and the labor force to about two hundred. These two weeks culminated a year of suspense, alarums, and excursions, in preparation for the 1962 campaign. The principal cause of this stir was the agreement finally signed in April by the United States government

Figure 70—Plan and section of the Acropolis Tunnels. Elevation (right) shows shearing of the cliffside in a landslide (earthquake?).

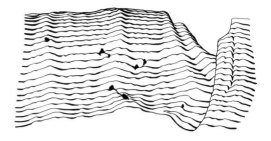

PARTIAL EAST ELEVATION OF ACROPOLIS
TUNNEL OPENINGS IN BLACK — NO SCALE

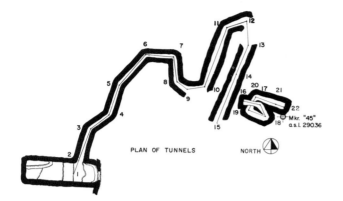

PLAN OF TUNNELS   NORTH

with Harvard College; its essence is that under Public Law 480,* to promote intercultural cooperation, the State Department, through the American Embassy in Ankara, will make available each year to the joint Harvard–Cornell–American Schools of Oriental Research Expedition at Sardis a grant in Turkish currency. Out of this grant most of the requirements of the Turkish budget may be met (not included, for instance, are land purchase and heavy equipment); in addition, several special projects are to be undertaken, notably the appointment of three Turkish student trainees and collaboration with a Turkish specialist in anthropology, zoology, or geology. Dollar expenses, well over half the budget, continue to be met from private funds. The award of this grant is a gratifying sign of recognition of the contribution made by the Sardis Expedition to American-Turkish relations; it imposes even greater responsibility upon our staff to represent the United States in a manner worthy of this confidence.

Right after the conclusion of the agreement there was a rush to secure all sorts of documents and to start negotiations with the appropriate Turkish authorities. Gus Swift, of the Oriental Institute, Chicago, administrative officer of the expedition, who was appointed the second representative of Harvard College for the grant, traveled to Cambridge to be briefed and then departed straightway, reaching Istanbul on June 1 and Izmir on June 4. Proceeding with his usual great good sense and aided effectively by our ever active commissioner Kemal Ziya Polatkan, Gus opened the camp and had most problems well in hand by the time I arrived.

In the meantime, correspondence by letter and cable with Earle H. Balch, cultural attaché in Ankara, bore fruit. A meeting to appoint Turkish trainees took place in Istanbul on June 14, attended by two representatives of the

*P.L. 480, Agricultural Surplus Act, provided that payments by foreign countries in their own currencies owed to the United States for agricultural products could be used for grants to American cultural enterprises.

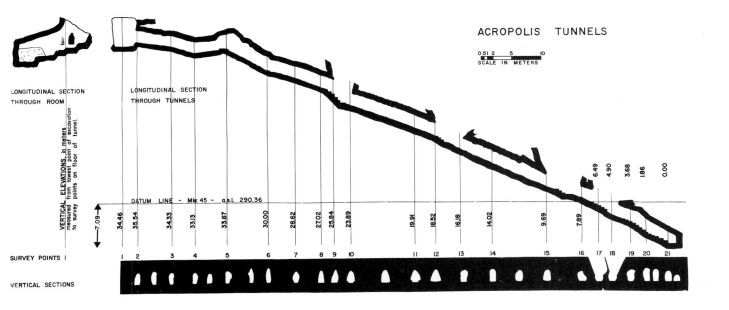

ACROPOLIS TUNNELS

Department of Antiquities, Necati Dolunay and Professor Afif Erzen, Ralph C. Talcott, cultural affairs officer and American Consul in Istanbul, and myself. The office of the cultural attaché had sent out an announcement about traineeships, and despite the shortness of time, nine applications were received. Güven Bakir, University of Ankara, Mehmet Ergene, Robert College, and Asim Erdilek, Izmir College, were chosen and are now at Sardis working very happily with us.

It was harder to capture the actual grant. For procedural reasons, the check had to wander back and forth between Ankara and Salihli, and as luck would have it, the banks added Manisa and Izmir to the stops in this odyssey. We heaved a sigh of relief when a telegram came June 21 announcing that the money was available; it was the very day on which, according to Turkish law, the check was to lapse.

Another bit of the confusion which periodically punctuates, not to say punctures, the life of our enterprise occurred the day the current Director General of Antiquities came to visit. It all began when a driver with jeep appeared and told our commissioner that the Governor wanted him to go immediately to Alaşehir and Kula, places some distance away. Hardly had Kemal Bey left than two tired strangers appeared and revealed themselves as the Director General and a lawyer friend—for whom the jeep had been intended. Burriss Young, who had just arrived from America, was dispatched in our jeep to recapture our commissioner. Finally it was all straightened out and the Director General inspected the camp and gave oral permission for construction of the rooms for Turkish trainees. Written permission came yesterday and we are now trying to catch up with this enterprise. For the time being two of the trainees are housed in an improvised partitioned room in the pottery and recording shed.

Having had more than our usual share of visa and related difficulties, we were awaiting with bated breath the arrival of Stuart Carter and David

Figure 71—Archaic Lydian painted terracotta relief tile of winged Pegasus found in gravel fill under Byzantine floor on top of the Acropolis. Hundreds of such tiles must have adorned the buildings of the Croesan citadel.

Stieglitz from Cornell, for they were bearing a torpedo-sized tube with all our architectural drawings. They made it safely and after a rigorous refresher course by Henry in the Detweiler method of archaeological surveying they have gone about triangulating and leveling. At the moment they are up at Willy Kohler's bailiwick, the Acropolis. Mehmet Ergene, who studies civil engineering, is working out with the architectural team.

In my letters to the Sardis secretary, Miss Loomis, I have been running a regular paragraph entitled "Current Crisis." Lest it should be missed I shall tell you that the generator went on the blink, so Henry Detweiler and Mehmet Ergene, the two electrical experts, have just made a trip to Izmir and returned carrying with them in triumph a new generator. We hope to recondition the old one sufficiently to run up lamps in the tunnels.

P.S. Of course, right after I sent off the newsletter things began to show. Yesterday Gus found our first silver siglos (early Persian coin), and I found a small hoard of Islamic silver coins on the Acropolis. Today, John Pedley found more Byzantine bronzes (a very pretty scale with weight), Mario found some others around his church, and Willy Kohler came triumphantly from the Acropolis with a beautiful Lydian terracotta tile of a Pegasus (*Figure 71*), doubly encouraging as a fine piece in itself and a sign that something Lydian may yet turn up on the citadel.

Sardis   July 1962

There were seven hundred of them, Turkish cadets from Ankara War College. Seventeen buses were lined up in front of the excavation house, and military formations marched along the Pactolus. Despite the glaring sun four "companies" made the rounds of all major excavation sectors, led by two of our Turkish trainees, Güven Bakir and Mehmet Ergene, by Dean

Figure 72—Our largest guided tour. Seven hundred Turkish cadets of the War College in Ankara arrive at Sardis from summer camp near Izmir on a cultural tour. Dean Burriss Young of Harvard (in Roman imperatorial posture) explains the Acropolis above.

W. C. Burriss Young of Harvard *(Figure 72),* and by me. The cadets had come from their summer camp near Izmir from which they make weekly trips to places of cultural interest. We were happy to have been included and had very enjoyable conversations with Colonel Paksoy and other officers. This was the most numerous of the many visitations that Sardis has seen this season.

Karl F. Brauckmann, director of USIS in Izmir, took a very helpful interest in our work and sent an interviewer and photographer to interview our three Turkish trainees. Subsequently, on my visit to Ankara, Voice of America interviewed Asim Erdilek, one of the trainees, and so if you are in the Mediterranean you may hear about Sardis in either Turkish or English.

We were able to start digging somewhat earlier than usual, since Gus Swift, Mario Del Chiaro, and Crawford Greenewalt, Jr.—Greenie—arrived early and immediately went to work on their sectors. Despite various obstacles, Henry and Catharine Detweiler appeared on the scene exactly as scheduled, on June 30. Henry reorganized architectural recording, studied a remarkable Byzantine church now being excavated at the Pactolus North sector, and found time to install a new generator. His vigor is unbeatable. One of the unforgettable sights of this campaign was that of Henry pivoting on tiptoe on a ledge over a precipice in order to get the best "shot" of the tunnels.

Such acrobatic feats were part of excavation of the tunnels, a dramatic enterprise supervised by Greenie and Güven Bakir. A bastion-like projection from the north side of the Acropolis harbors a spiraling tunnel, of which we have so far explored and freed about 100 meters. The turns have fallen away from the upper three windings (see 1–15 on the plan, *Figure 70)* of which the topmost ends next to a large chamber cut into the rock *(Figure 70,* number 1)*.* Downward, the tunnel proceeds so steeply that because of difficulties of bringing the earth upward and poor air circulation we had to

105

defer its exploration. This leaves the purpose of the tunnels a mystery, although the most likely guess is that they went to some hidden source of water. Since the roof of the tunnel had collapsed and waters of many centuries had rushed through, no definite conclusions can yet be drawn from the objects found which range from Lydian to Byzantine and which have revealed no stratification. There is hope, however, that if the bottom and the final goal of the tunnel are reached next season its date, too, may become more definite.

Developments have been rapid in other major sectors. As we reach the half-season mark, Gus Swift is about to start his descent from the Lydian levels into deeper strata at the House of Bronzes (Figure 81). His clearing of the overburden and of the very interesting building C (Figure 76) has brought noteworthy results for the refinement of the history of the area and had given us our first silver coin of Alexander, our first siglos, and, just now, a charming bronze ibex with folded-under feet, much like the type known from ivories in Ephesus (Figure 77). Although unfinished, it is even nicer in style than the bronze boar found on the Acropolis in 1960; both have identical round loops attached at the back and must have been used for the same purpose.

In the Pactolus North sector Mario Del Chiaro is clearing an area of nearly 1000 square meters (see plan, Figure 75). It is bounded on the east by a very interesting Byzantine church (E). What appears to be a street is flanked by a long building on the south and an array of units with mosaic floors on the north. The mosaics are the most ambitious we have yet found. One has a circular motif in the center encircled in turn by four blue dolphins (Figure 74) and features, in other panels, dogs hunting a stag and a hare. Another room has an eagle and various animals, all in five colors (Figure 73). In this sector, too, the descent—to the Persian and Lydian levels—is beginning.

In the excavations of the Gymnasium (Building B) and the adjacent

Figure 73 (left)—Two great eras of Sardis emerge at Pactolus North: digging the Persian and Lydian houses 10–15 feet under Roman "Street of Pipes" (compare Figures 75 and 66). Roman and Byzantine bath with eagle mosaic is at the right and remains of early Christian buildings are at top left.

Figure 74 (right)—Mosaic with rotating dolphins separated by Neptune's tridents was distinguished by remarkable variations of blue. It belongs to the farthest room in Pactolus North bath seen in Figure 73.

marble-paved avenue, we have now proved that the shops flanking the avenue on the north extend for at least 130 meters. David Mitten has made a test in depth and just now, several meters below the Early Byzantine shops (ca. A.D. 400–615), there has appeared a fine marble stair of three steps, probably Hellenistic or very Early Roman in date.

To the north of the shops, somewhat to our surprise, instead of the expected colonnade around the palaestra, lies a building with mosaic floors which extends about 20 meters north-south. It was all revetted with reused marbles and its south wall featured a dedicatory inscription *(Figure 84)* mentioning *skoutlosis* (marble revetment) and *zographia* (painting).

Stephen Jacobs of Cornell has resumed the work at the great Severan Marble Court of the Gymnasium. Here as well as at Pactolus North our work is greatly benefiting by the purchase of second-hand Decauville lorries and track. Our architectural team this year, with Steve Jacobs as senior architect, includes Stuart L. Carter and David Stieglitz of Cornell and a Turkish trainee, Mehmet Ergene, who by virtue of his thorough training in surveying and his ever ready helpfulness is a welcome addition.

We are looking forward to cooperation with Docent Dr. Enver Bostanci, successor to the late Professor M. Şenyürek as head of Institute of Palaeo-anthropology, Ankara, and with Professor Sabri Doğuer, Professor of Veterinarian Faculty, University of Ankara.

David Greenewalt has arrived and is proceeding with his geophysical exploration. We hope to extend it shortly to the Royal Cemetery of Bin Tepe, where the location of the corridors leading to burial chambers presents both a particular challenge and a very important prize, should the technique for detection of underground structures prove successful.

In order to fulfill more effectively our obligations toward the trainees and to profit ourselves, we have begun a seminar after working hours. In a "double-header" Henry Detweiler spoke on archaeological surveying, and

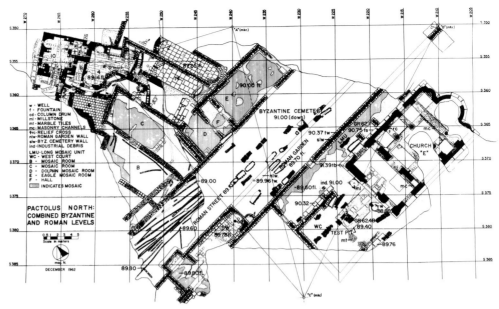

Figure 75—Plan of Pactolus North showing partly the same remains as Figure 73. Rooms E (with Eagle Mosaic), F, and D (with dolphins) are seen on the right in Figure 73. Not shown in this plan are the Lydian and Persian levels (seen in Figure 73 on the left).

Mrs. C. S. Detweiler on numismatics. Greenie, who has participated in the work at Gordion as well as at Sardis, spoke on Phrygian-Lydian relations, and a field trip was made to study the theater, stadium, and nearby monuments. One of our trainees, Asim Erdilek, is offering Turkish lessons to expedition members.

It remains to express our thanks to Mrs. Detweiler for her valiant numismatic work; this year the finds have been very numerous and many of the issues may eventually prove of interest for history of local coinage in the Hellenistic, Roman, and Byzantine eras.

Sardis   August 9, 1962

We have started at Bin Tepe (*Figure 5*, Map 2). Perhaps it is better to say: we have started nibbling at Bin Tepe. The Lydian kings well knew how to guard the stark, solitary grandeur of their resting places. During the past ten years the Hermus trough has been transformed from swampy marshes into a network of well-irrigated cotton fields, and wheat fields have now advanced to the foot of many of the burial mounds. Still, the trip to Bin Tepe is guaranteed to shake the stuffing out of any vehicle. And the sun beats down mercilessly on the towering mounds and the sloping sweeps of land between them. In return, the views of the citadel of Sardis to the south and the Lake of Gyges to the north are breathtaking (*Figures 5, 106*).

On July 26, David Greenewalt, our commissioner Kemal Bey, David's temporary geophysical amanuensis Mustafa Sezgin, and I went out to Bin Tepe in our *dolmuş*, a hired Volkswagen microbus. We first went to the villages to collect three mayors and several landowners, a process which took some time and several rounds of tea. We then held, very literally, a "summit conference"; it took place on the summit of one of the mounds. There is,

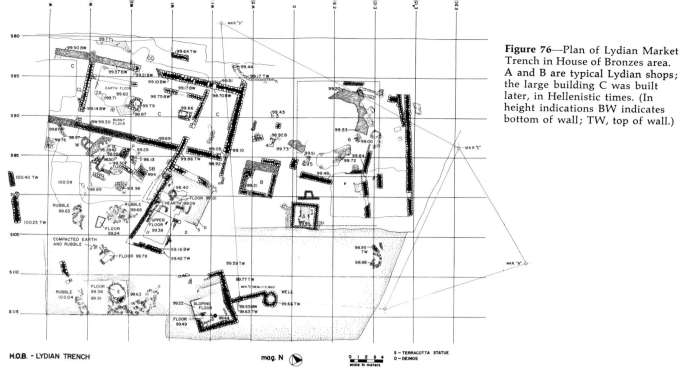

Figure 76—Plan of Lydian Market Trench in House of Bronzes area. A and B are typical Lydian shops; the large building C was built later, in Hellenistic times. (In height indications BW indicates bottom of wall; TW, top of wall.)

unfortunately, some question whether the Treasury owns the mounds and if so, which. We have gone ahead under interim permission of the landowners.

The major purpose of the current work is to help the testing of electrical resistivity measurements which Dr. Greenewalt is carrying on. However, one of the landowners, modern enough to have a jeep, has pointed out to us two open mounds. One of them had the first stone chamber I have ever seen intact, and the stone work is just beautiful. This we plan to excavate and record. John Pedley is just launched on this project, together with Muharrem Tağtekin, our second commissioner, who was appointed by the Department of Antiquities for the Bin Tepe project. Turan Alper, a trainee who is studying physics, has also come out occasionally to assist Dr. Greenewalt.

There are only a few workmen out there, "The Tunnelers," so known from their previous underground activity. They are a gay, young bunch and after their really risky underground ventures they do not seem to be fazed by the hazards of Bin Tepe (the first thing to come out of the grave were two poisonous snakes!). The logistics are formidable. We have built one of the usual mat-and-pole shelters and have got hold of one old medieval conical type tent for the workmen. Yet the mound which we are excavating is too far away to commute and we must have portable "shadow casters" to survive. Bringing water in sufficient quantity will be a problem. So far, we are commuting in the hired *dolmuş* (the trip takes over one hour each way). The present accommodations will have to do for the small force of this season. Next year we shall have to plan a camp by the spring in the middle of this six-mile-long cemetery and send out from there "task forces" with shadow shelters, water, and so forth.

"Professor Bikini wants you." This was the report of our young gate guard (he was hired on the suspicion that he might be able to speak French). The gentleman, who wore shorts (though not *that* short), turned out to be Elias Bickerman, the eminent historian from Columbia University. We had

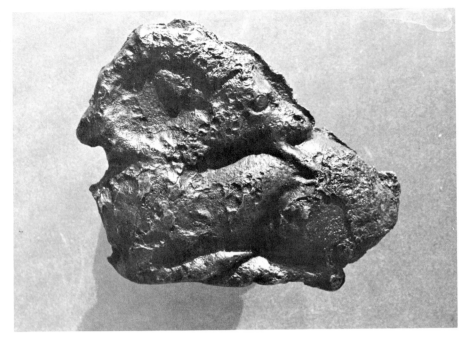

Figure 77—Legs folded under, head turned back, this lively ibex is a bronze plaque with two loops attached to back, perhaps for reins. Similar "folded legs" animals are known in Iran and Scythia but there was a workshop in Asia Minor making these little animal plaques in Perso-Lydian style, perhaps even at the market in Sardis, since the piece is unfinished. Width a little over two inches, sixth–fourth century B.C.

a most stimulating discussion about the many sets of Lydian pots *(Figure 78)* which continue to come out of the Lydian Trench in the House of Bronzes area. Professor Bickerman rightly suggested that it would be a rare coincidence for as many as thirty people to sit down and eat exactly the same meal—namely a small animal—and drink the same drink (probably wine). His idea is that we are dealing with a sacral or ritual communal meal. There are fascinating vistas of Lydian religion opening here, particularly if the poor animals turn out to be puppies—for the one peculiar god we know about was "Hermes the Dog Throttler," "Cynanches" in Greek, "Candaules" in Lydian.

There are many fascinating developments in Gus Swift's trench. The large Building C yields ever new evidence for its complicated history *(Figure 76)*; the deep digging is going down well beyond the level of the Cimmerian invasion. The most recent discoveries were peculiar round pits with channels, probably of the seventh century B.C. Even more surprising was the result of removing a Roman lime-kiln patch—underneath was a real "nest" of beautifully wrought small Doric column capitals *(Figure 79)*, seven of them, enough for three sides of a small peristyle court. Gus surmises that they were being worked on by a master mason, but why they were piously preserved rather than burned to lime remains an enigma.

We believe we have found the Synagogue of Sardis. Dave Mitten had started a trench northward from Jacob's Shop, mentioned in the last letter. We had fully expected to find a colonnade which should go around all four sides of the gymnasium court. Instead of it there appeared a wall luxuriously revetted with marble and fragments of a long inscription *(Figure 84)*. The inscription records that somebody whose name has been lost, his wife Regina, and his children gave from the bounties of Almighty God *(Pantokratoros tou Theou)* the complete marble decoration and painting (of the building?). A large mosaic floor spreads northward for many meters—much

110

Figure 78—One of thirty sets of pots used in a ritual meal (similar to American Thanksgiving turkey dinner?), perhaps for Lydian (war?) god Candaules ("Dog Throttler"). The set always had a jug for pouring, a cup, a plate, and a jar, often with newborn puppies' bones. Iron knives were for carving. The pots are typical examples of Lydian black-red painted and gold (mica)-dusted pottery (jar). Most sets came from House of Bronzes (Lydian Market) area. 600–550 B.C.

too wide for a colonnade. So far had the efforts of Dave as archaeologist and J. Pedley as epigraphist carried us, when suddenly a most carefully wrought marble platform with steps began to appear *(Figure 83, right)*. I happened to be on duty when the evidence was found—a relief with a seven-branched candle-stick and tree *(Figure 85)*, and an inscription in Hebrew letters *(Figure 86)*. The discoveries have continued thick and fast but at the moment we have so much to uncover that we have as yet no clear idea of the overall plan or of the exact date of the structure.

"The fountain of the synagogue" is mentioned in an inscription of Sardis. Personally, I think the probability is very strong that we have found the synagogue (or a synagogue), but there is yet too much to be learned. For this reason we want no premature publicity.

Mario Del Chiaro's grand sweep in the Pactolus North sector *(Figure 75)* has given us, in rapid succession, a Middle Byzantine church, a Byzantine cemetery, a court or precinct paved with mosaics (Late Roman or Early Byzantine?), a street (with all the waterpipes of a Roman system underneath), and several rooms of the house which adjoins the small bath excavated in 1961. The mosaic floors of the house are spectacular—four dolphins in a circle, animals chasing each other in one room; an eagle, sea-dog monsters, animals and birds in another. A fine Hellenistic altar has been found built into the street wall. Now Mario has dug himself into the Persian level *(Figure 73)*, and has already come forth with a Lydian inscription (on a pot) which features twice the famous Lydian "8" sign which has been used often to link the Lydians with the Etruscans.

The two or even four pronged attack on the Gymnasium (Building B) area continues. Prior to his exploit detailed above, Dave Mitten had descended through the Byzantine shops to find, some ten feet below, a tantalizing marble bench—which shows that structures with different orientation lie below the marble-paved Roman avenue. Steve Jacobs is pushing on with

the gigantic task of studying the Severan Marble Court. The stone and railroad crews have been proving their mettle in evacuating the giant blocks while Steve in a yellow *küfiyah* (headgear) and his new assistant, Necati, in a baseball cap go around studying and numbering every block.

Stuart Carter, David Stieglitz, and Mehmet Ergene are clambering in and around the eagle aeyrie known as the "Tunnel Shelter." A team of Turkish surveyors had done the ground work and now the boys are finishing up. The setting is as inspiring as the heat is sweltering. We always have a heat wave in August but this one is as torrid as the record one in 1958.

This makes martyrs out of those unsung heroes, the photographers, who have to stand for hours in the sun squinting at the never-ending parade of objects needing photography. Vincent Wickwar reports that yesterday the cameras were too hot to handle. He and Mike have been carrying on in the face of all obstacles. Mike has also revealed most desirable talents as diagnostician of the never-ending ailments of our cars and generators.

Vehicles have been breaking down with monotonous regularity—they are not getting any younger. A pall of gloom settled over the entire labor force when the Citroën truck broke its half axle. The workmen have come to regard the green giant towering against the purple hills of Sardis as the special hallmark of the expedition. Our driver-mechanic Nuri swore fiercely that he will not have this *araba* (literally "cart") laid up. He dashed off and borrowed the axle from the only other Citroën to be found within a radius of 100 miles, and subsequently had another axle machined at Izmir.

Sardis   September 6, 1962

We had found no gold all season, but we found gold two days after we stopped digging. Workmen straightening out an earth embankment to build

a protective wall came upon a stone weight, and under it a stunningly beautiful gold coin of the emperor Theodosius II (A.D. 408–450).

This postscript in gold to the 1962 campaign came after what seemed like an exciting enough finale. On the very last morning a Prehistoric burial of the fourteenth century B.C. appeared in Gus Swift's deep trench (*Figure 82*). Gus and Elaine Kohler spent nearly the whole day excavating the burial jar (*Figure 81*), precious to us as confirmation that people lived at Sardis in the time of the Hittites.*

Three mosaic inscriptions showed up at the same time in Dave Mitten's Synagogue. The mosaics contributed to the display of amazing historical knowledge and epigraphic fireworks put on for our benefit and that of the Sardis Synagogue on August 31 and September 1 by Louis and Jeanne Robert, ably assisted by John Pedley, who had managed to keep track of the niagara of inscription fragments the Synagogue kept pouring out. As yet we have been able to clear only half of the Synagogue, and will have to wait for next year to determine the exact position of some crucial features. In the meantime we take pride in Professor Robert's enthusiasm over the prospect of the first large synagogue scientifically excavated in Asia Minor, and in his pronouncement that its inscriptions shed a flood of light on the religious, social, and economic milieus of synagogues in this part of the world.

Some results of the Roberts' detective work:† the Synagogue was built

*Coming so late in the season, Gus Swift's great discovery did not quite receive its due in the Letters. Of the three great descents undertaken by Gus in 1960, 1962, and 1966, this was the only one to reach a Prehistoric settlement earlier than the Mycenaeans (thirteenth century B.C.). (*Figures 76, 81–82.*) The wattle and daub huts and cremation burials he found in 1962 cannot be very closely dated but cremation burials are known both from the Hittite area in the fifteenth-fourteenth century and from Troy VI. That these were small primitive huts built right over the burials of the ancestors may indicate that Sardis was only a village. Or it might suggest that this was an outlying area near the swampy Pactolus crossing; there might still have been palaces of Hittite type elsewhere.

†L. Robert's important discussion appeared in *Nouvelles inscriptions de Sardes*, 1964, Chapter III: "Inscriptions de Synagogue."

Figure 81—Charred human bones and ashes were in this Bronze Age cremation urn at the bottom of a 35-foot pit in the Lydian Market Trench sounding, the earliest evidence of human occupation yet reached in the area of the city (1400 B.C.?). Elaine Kohler records the bones; Gus Swift, fieldbook in hand, watches workmen probe floor and earth in jar.

Figure 82—In an attempt to reach bottom in the Lydian Trench, House of Bronzes area, a deep sounding (within broken lines at right in Figure 76) was taken in terraces, each step revealing evidence of earlier occupation. In the center foreground are remains of cooking pots and hearths belonging to Late Bronze or Early Iron Age peoples perhaps ruled by legendary Herakleidai, ca. 1200 B.C.

Figure 83—Discovery of a huge Synagogue at Sardis was a high-light of the 1962 season. In the center of the picture are the platforms for North Shrine (left) and South Shrine (right). In the background part of the Forecourt colonnade is standing; the eastern end of the Main Hall is in the foreground.

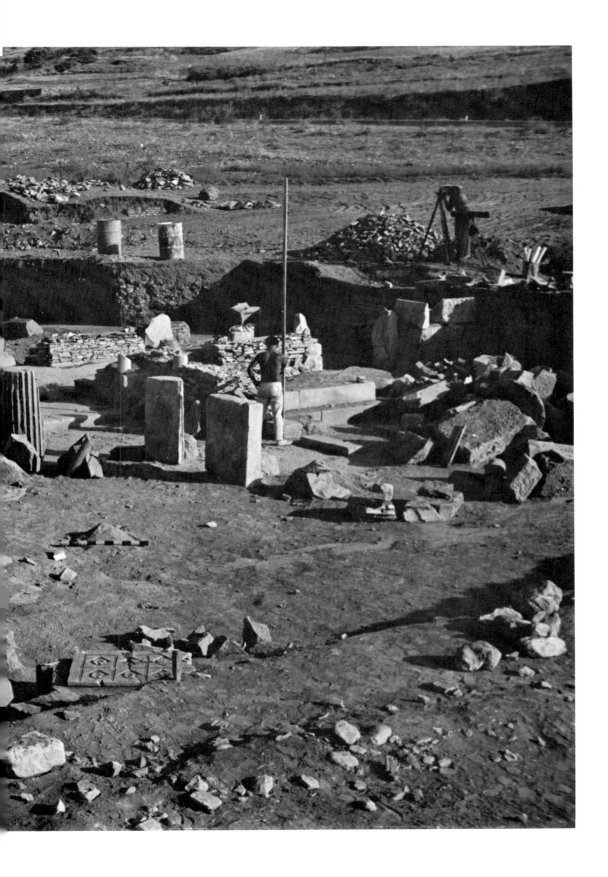

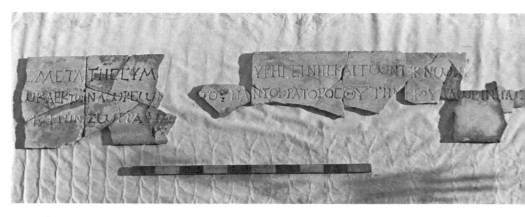

Figure 84—"I [name lost] WITH MY WIFE REGINA AND MY CHILDREN FROM THE BOUNTIES OF THE ALMIGHTY GOD GAVE THE ENTIRE MARBLE REVETMENT [of the hall] AND THE PAINTING [possibly of upper walls or ceiling]." This is the earliest (before A.D. 212) donor inscription of the Synagogue. A cast of it in presumed original position is seen in top part of restoration (Figure 182). The marble plaque was over 7 feet long, 1-1/3 feet high. Decoration of the Synagogue may have begun shortly after A.D. 166, if it was emperor Verus who on his visit to Sardis approved transfer of the hall to the Jewish community (cf. base of Verus statue, 1958, Figures 17, 18).

between A.D. 220 and 250 and rebuilt in the fourth or fifth century. Its members were highly regarded—two or three were city councillors. Its organization included Elders (*presbyteroi*) and "God-fearing Men" (*theosebeis*), and a special tribe, the Leontii. Some members of the congregation were jewelers. Not only our friend Jacob but probably also his neighbors Theoktistos and Sabbatios were Jewish merchants. Incidentally, one of their shops disclosed a huge amount of glass wares for the special benefit of Robert H. Brill of the Corning Museum, who came to study our ancient glass late in August and gave a brilliant seminar on glass chemistry.

While this was going on at Sardis, other dramatic developments ensued at the Royal Cemetery of Bin Tepe. David Greenewalt's geophysical ventures proceeded hand-in-hand with the digging of the chamber tomb of an unknown Lydian nobleman, supervised by J. G. Pedley and later by Don Hansen. Merciless heat, and mosquitoes wafted by winds from the Gygean Lake, disturbed any attempt at relaxation in the shelter and the tent we had brought out for the workmen. Still the work went on, and the tomb emerged —a beautiful, intimate two-room apartment with a corridor, built with astonishing precision *(Figure 90)*—and empty of finds, except, in the corridor, the skeleton of a small animal. Elaine Kohler thought it might be a dog, and we had trouble dissuading a Turkish journalist from reporting that we had found "the dog of Croesus." David Stieglitz did a tremendous job of architectural recording, Mike Totten photographed the tomb—and then we restored the broken ceiling, blocked the entrance, and reburied it. For the landowner warned us the peasants might carry off any available cut stones, as they have already from a number of Bin Tepe mounds.

The large sepulcher of Croesus' father Alyattes *(Figures 88, 89, Map 2)* provided the final chills and thrills of the season. We knew that in 1853 Spiegelthal had driven a tunnel into its southside, reached a system of under-

ground passages, and found an antechamber and a chamber in the southwest part of the mound. Our annual visits from 1958 to 1961 showed the tunnel entrance clogged nearly to the top. During our conferences prior to beginning the work at Bin Tepe, local landowners casually said that they had entered the tunnels. Then David Greenewalt saw four men crawl into the mound; Stuart Carter, while surveying, was startled to see another three "free lance" diggers emerge from a hole under the marker on top. Before I could make up my mind whether to risk the dangers of collapsed passages, the intrepid Vedat Kangor, tunnel crawler extraordinary, formerly in charge of our Acropolis tunnel crew, explored the entrance and reported that after a very narrow squeeze one could get into tunnels where progress might be made by alternately crouching and crawling. With Vedat I paid a visit to Alyattes the next day. Most tunnels were filled with earth leaving less than two feet of open space. Only by squeezing through a narrow opening under ceiling beams could one reach the chambers, and these ceiling beams, monsters of many tons, were all sagging—one sitting precariously on a few small stones. But everywhere were signs of recent visitations—newspapers, bottles, candles, even a doodle and date of 1962, and signs of digging in many places. A rubble collapse had buried one chamber completely and the other more than half.

Spiegelthal's publication was admirable for his time but left much unexplained. We decided to make as precise an architectural record as conditions would permit. For two days Stuart Carter, David Stieglitz, and Mehmet Ergene crawled, sweated, panted, and squeezed in the threatening underground world, hauling their instruments with them. Subsequently Mrs. Hanfmann—whose lion-like (*aslan gibi*) courage is renowned among the workmen since she made it all through the Acropolis tunnels—with John Pedley and our commissioner Kemal Bey (the narrowest passage had to be slightly widened for him) accompanied Vincent Wickwar, whose sangfroid

Figure 87—HEURON KLASAS ANAGNOTHI PHYLAXON, "Having found you have opened/having observed (guarded)—read." This admonition might be translated "Find, Open, Read, Observe" (the commandments in the Scriptures). The marble plaque was probably placed below the wooden cupboard with the sacred writings (Sefer Torah). Third or fourth century, our era. Found in 1963.

never failed, as he shot off flashbulbs and slid among rubble to take the first picture ever taken of the burial place of Lydia's mightiest king. Finally Stuart Carter and I went in for a four-and-a-half hour conference and measuring session on September 1. The same day, our workmen closed the entrance; we hope for the time being the mound may stay safe from intrusions. To excavate it would be a very difficult task; we have instead drawn a bead on the largest mound in the central part of the cemetery. There is a wonderful cold spring nearby and a work camp could be pitched there.

Cambridge   September 22, 1962

So much was written in Sardis. Now two weeks later the staff and the records are back in the United States, and we can say with profound satisfaction: "Mission accomplished."

It is time, perhaps, for a brief assessment. On June 20, 1958, we started the Sardis excavations with five staff members and fourteen workmen, our base in two rooms of the village school. Now we have just completed our fifth campaign with twenty-eight staff members, American and Turkish, and a labor force of some two hundred. We have initiated regular training of Turkish students, as well as seminar courses. We have added to our extensive camp a building for Turkish trainees. We operated with four vehicles (five, if the rented *dolmuş* to Bin Tepe is included) and, for the first time, with a Decauville railroad. We have developed specialized teams of workmen for stone work in restorations, for railroad operation, for lifting and conservation of mosaics. We have sounded or excavated at fifteen different locations in the urban area of Sardis and initiated work at the Royal Cemetery of Bin Tepe several miles away. We have made contributions to

Figure 88—Exploration of the Royal Cemetery of Bin Tepe (Figure 5) began in king Alyattes' (ruled ca. 610–560 B.C.) Mound where the masonry of the royal burial chamber reveals extraordinary workmanship of marble masonry and ceiling beams. The chamber was first entered by the German archaeologist H. Spiegelthal in 1853. The incised letters are modern, left by local villagers and other illicit visitors.

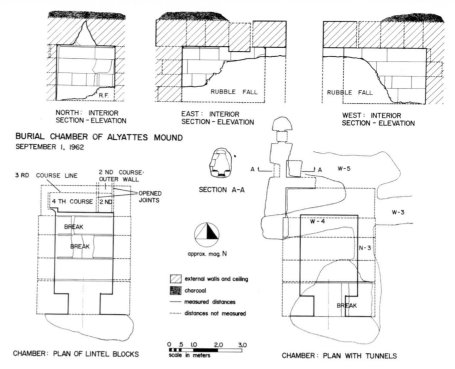

Figure 89—Architectural drawings of the marble chamber of Croesus' father. The charcoal may have come from wood used to burn funerary offerings on top of the chamber.

knowledge of this meeting place of East and West ranging from ca. 1400 B.C. to A.D. 1500. We have initiated cooperative projects in anthropology, ethnology, zoology, geophysics, geology, epigraphy, topography, and the study of glass. Written reports on last season's work by department and sector chiefs and specialists would make a 200-page book. Thirty-five plane table sheets and thirty inked drawings were prepared by our architects, several hundred drawings of objects were done, several thousand photographs taken. Four comprehensive preliminary reports, one monograph, a guide, and dozens of articles scholarly and general have appeared. In the short span of five years, the Sardis project has become a large-scale operation comparable in scope with enterprises like Ephesus and Pergamon, which have been in progress for decades.

Five years have passed since we sent out our first invitation to a number of friends to become Supporters of Sardis. At the time, one invaluable friend and benefactor had insured by his donations the existence of the Sardis excavations. For the 1962 campaign 210 contributed, and altogether over the five years 320 have helped us in our work. We think with gratitude of their faith and trust. And we recall with sorrow the passing of some of our helpers. Professor David Moore Robinson was the first to respond to our appeal. As the last surviving member of the First Sardis Expedition, we had in him a link with our predecessors of 1910–1914 whose admirable work firmly established American claim to the site. Edward L. Holsten had been known for his love for the ancient world; we rejoiced in the prospect his cooperation held when he was suddenly taken away. Katherine B. Taylor's warm interest in Sardis was an inspiration to us and to many of our friends. Like Kay Taylor, Mrs. Charles W. Phinney fought a fatal illness with unequaled courage and remained vital and cheerful to the end; we are happy that she was able to come and see Sardis, where her visit is still fondly re-

Figure 90—Southwest of Alyattes Mound is a neatly constructed tomb known locally as "the Mound Where Money Was Found" and by us as BT 62.4. Fallen on the ground in the antechamber is the stone door of the main chamber from which we are looking across to the dromos (entrance corridor). Note the beautiful joining of masonry.

membered. The passing of other friends, whose names mean much to America's cultural life, is a melancholy record: Lauriston Ward, Mrs. Clement Smith, Mrs. George Hewitt Myers, Frederick Foster, the Honorable Robert Woods Bliss. We hope that others will take their place and that in the five years to come we may rejoice in even more numerous friendships.

1963

Sardis   July 6, 1963

Kemal Bey, our commissioner, just walked in and showed me a beautiful large silver tetradrachm of Achaeus *(Figure 92)*, pretender to the Seleucid throne, who was besieged for two years on the citadel of Sardis. The coin turned up in the road that goes off from the main highway through the hollow and was used as the main east-west road in the Middle Ages. Our first gold coin of Croesus *(Figure 91)* fell into our hands from an even stranger location—a certain venerable gentleman reports finding this small but beautiful *hekte* in the public sulphur baths up on the mountain behind Sardis. Whether or not this be so, deponent sayeth not, but it is nice to know the coins exist hereabouts. To make the numismatic trinity complete, a Hapsburg gold piece was proferred to us as coming from the Royal Cemetery area of Bin Tepe *(Figure 93)*. From excavations at Sardis has come an early small Greek silver coin, with lion and incuse square, and the usual flood of bronze coins.

Were I an ancient historian, I should have started not with this last-minute news but with the omens. "During the winter before the sixth campaign, a thunderbolt from Zeus struck the capital of the column of Artemis. This was the beginning of many strange happenings"—and so it was. We found the capital of one of the two complete columns of the Temple damaged, and shall have to figure out some way of putting back the fallen parts. As to the strange happenings, the strangest was a terrific customs bill, caused by superimposed taxes and other factors. We have been fighting this battle up and down the line, with sympathetic support of various authorities and the Governor of our vilayet.

125

Figure 91—A tiny *hekte* ("sixth" of the gold unit or *stater*) with lion and bull is the only gold coin of Croesus retrieved by the Harvard-Cornell Expedition. Found by a workman in the public sulphur baths several miles away, it is only a third of an inch wide, weighs 1.85 grams.

Mrs. Hanfmann and I had flown from Istanbul to Ankara to attend to divers official business before arriving at Sardis, and to confer with the specialists of our "Fauna of Ancient Sardis" project. After two hectic days we came down to Sardis to find Gus Swift and Bill Kohler going full swing on the House of Bronzes (Lydian Trench) and Pactolus North sectors respectively. Gus has been digging since June 13, and his trench now looks awe-inspiring. Currently, the excitement centers on a well which takes off from either Hellenistic or Persian levels and keeps on going—so far twelve feet—chock full of pottery and other interesting things. Bill has been clearing another large area of Pactolus North.

Dave Mitten and Vince Wickwar arrived practically on our heels battered but unbowed after a seventeen-hour bus ride from Konya. Dave has tackled with gusto the Synagogue area—from two ends (see plan, *Figure 96*). Railroad, trucks *(Figure 94)*, and quite a gang of workmen have been rapidly bringing to light a large apse. As of today we know it has a mosaic *(Figure 95)* and a bench outside, and soon we should know whether this does or does not form an imposing conclusion for the western end of the Synagogue.

With the arrival of Noel Robertson and John Pedley, we launched the Bin Tepe project. This turned out to be an enterprise of some difficulty since the road we used to take has been battered out of recognition and viability, and the weathergod elected to turn on the heat the day we went out to build a large shelter for the workmen and a small one for the staff. Chief sufferers were Charles Waters and his USIS film crew, who rushed (jolted) out without food or water. Fortunately, we had some water left— and there is an excellent spring nearby. We discovered a better road out to the site, and the labor force will be building up now. At present John Pedley, who will take turns with Noel Robertson, is making a trench in the south side of the huge mound in the center of the Royal Cemetery *(Figure 106)*, which may be that of the founder of the great Lydian dynasty of Mermnadae, Gyges.

Figure 92 (left)—Silver tetradrachm of Achaeus who rebelled against his nephew Antiochus III and was besieged on the Acropolis, 215–213 B.C.

Figure 93 (right)—A gold ducat of the Hapsburgs minted in Holland in A.D. 1580 was perhaps lost by a sixteenth-century traveler crossing the Royal Cemetery of Bin Tepe.

The time between June 20 and July 1 was one flurry of arrivals. The Papesches made it after a trip by car through Europe; Noel Robertson had to walk up from the highway, because his telegram, naturally, followed him by a day. Ralph Iler turned up prudently on a train which was being met, which brought also a volunteer, Ayberk Araz, daughter of the governor of Manisa. The two new Turkish trainees, Arda Düzgüneş and Fikret Yeğül, architects from the Middle East Technical University at Ankara, speak excellent English; they will act as translator and draftsman respectively. With the arrival of Burriss Young, the laboratory opened its gates with an air of calm efficiency.

For three weeks now, the mosaic workshop has been alive to the sound of picks; Reha Arican, the Turkish specialist from the Istanbul Museum, is getting in shape last year's beautiful mosaics from Pactolus North (*Figures 66, 73, 74*). Mrs. Hanfmann and Barbara Papesch had quite a struggle to get the 1961 finds out in order to make room for the new season, but the recording department is now operating at full capacity. Gus Swift has set up an office to administer financial and other affairs. Ibrahim Seren, his young Turkish assistant from the Commercial College in Izmir, is also acting as postmaster.

The staff is the largest ever, and looking down the dinner table is like looking into one of those pictures by Tintoretto with an endless diagonal.

Interruption! Dave Mitten has just sent word that he has found an important inscription and Mike is needed to photograph it. The inscription is important right enough—ten lines of fine Hellenistic writing that seem to mention Zeuxis, satrap of Lydia under Antiochus III (third century B.C.).

With the season, and the finds, gaining momentum, the usual breakdowns of equipment inevitably gain momentum too. The two passenger vehicles (Landrover 1956, Jeep 1958) have just about had it; and the Citroën broke its left axle. Today seems to be the turn of the water installation. But we manage. The 1963 campaign is off to a good start.

Sardis   August 6, 1963

Henry Detweiler has just arrived and immediately infected all and sundry with his ever youthful enthusiasm. There is, to be sure, much to be enthusiastic about. We all knew that last year's discovery of the Synagogue was an event of importance but none of us had quite expected the spectacular size of the structure and the splendor of its furnishings or the surprising finds that have been pouring from this building.

Using railroad, trucks, and his sixty "troops" like a seasoned field general, Dave Mitten proceeded to clear the western end of the area. Here we had excavated a hemicycle with niches which we tentatively identified as a fountain *(Figure 96)*. To our surprise the hemicycle developed into an imposing apse with three rising benches, a spectacular mosaic *(Figure 95)* showing the tree of life growing out of a vase, and a multicolored mosaic wreath with the name of the dedicants *Flavioi, Stratoneikianos kai Synphoros*. Nor was this all. Fallen across the open end of the apse was a cascade of marble blocks, perhaps from a screening element with piers. Four of the blocks carried long Hellenistic inscriptions, two of them apparently royal communications. Under this fall there came to light a mighty marble table (four feet high, four feet wide, eight feet long), each of its massive supports decorated by a majestic eagle clutching a thunderbolt *(Figure 97)*.

Pieces of sculpture, including a battered copy of a fine female head with a crown, of Argive type of the fifth century B.C., and a capital with four little children (promptly nicknamed "Mitten's babies"), add to the excitement and puzzlement. There is a group of addorsed lions *(Figure 98)*, a relief of Artemis, and one of a speaking or praying figure of the fourth or fifth century, our era. One might doubt that the apse belonged to the Synagogue were it not for the dedicatory inscriptions, which continue to display the same formulas. Two small reliefs of menorahs have been found—and right in the apse an inscription recording the dedication of a menorah.

The table with eagles and the lions seems to belong to the actual furnishings of the Synagogue. An explanation for the other sculptural pieces was suggested by our finest sculptural find. Still cemented to a piece of the fallen north wall of the Synagogue was the lower part of a very early—and to me very beautiful—archaic *kore (Figure 101)*. I was there when the workmen found it and could not believe my eyes. But we had found previously in the Synagogue pieces of archaic Ionic capitals and profiles. Apparently (perhaps after the devastating earthquake of A.D. 17) marble parts had been salvaged from early structures and these were re-used in the Synagogue.

The overall dimensions of the Synagogue are imposing—length 270 feet, width 60 feet; the wall of the apse is preserved up to a height of 15 feet *(Figure 94)*.

I cannot begin to enumerate the diversified finds with which fortune has been favoring Dr. Mitten—"cut-out" marble inlays, bronze candlesticks, glass fused by conflagration, and two fine bronze lion heads *(Figure 103)*— not to mention hundreds of coins from the adjacent Byzantine Shops.

Along the Pactolus, William Kohler has opened a large area, and excavated with meticulous precision the Islamic levels. The first spectacular find came with the descent into the Early Byzantine–Late Roman level: a gold solidus of Justin I (A.D. 518–527) found right within a wall. Since then John Pedley and Noel Robertson have freed an additional area including a most complicated corner where a cemented structure with an arch was grafted upon what looks like an Early Roman or Hellenistic marble monument. This in turn was boxed in by Roman graves of the second or third century. The "grand layout" of ca. A.D. 400 along the strictly oriented "Street of the Waterpipes" is now seen to extend to east and west (see plan, *Figure*

Figure 94 (left)—The Synagogue being cleared with the help of Citoën in 1963. Looking west toward the Apse from the Forecourt. Length, 300 feet; width, 60 feet.

Figure 95 (right)—According to its inscription, this fourth-century mosaic decorating the Synagogue Apse was a gift of two brothers, Synphoros and Stratoneikianos Flavioi, who took the family name of emperor Constantine. Blue and red vine grows from a golden vase with blue Water of Life. Only bits of comb, tail, and feet remain of two flanking peacocks. The framing band is one rare example of crosses in non-Christian context.

75). During the last few days evidence is emerging that this layout was anticipated in Early Roman times. Tentatively, one might suggest that the area was planned after the disastrous earthquake of A.D. 17, then briefly abandoned, then replanned around 400.

From the Roman graves have come some remarkable glass vases and terracottas, including a charming figurine of a camel rider. This brings to mind the report on 5384 animal bones just received from our scientific collaborators at the University of Ankara; camel bones hold if not a spectacular yet a steady place in their frequency chart. The report, including our finds from 1958 to 1962, will serve as the basis for a publication on the "Fauna of Ancient Sardis."

The grand layout of A.D. 400 included the spectacular mosaics of a three-room suite along the street (*Figures 73–75*). Reha Arican, the expert conservator of the Istanbul Museum, has worked steadily for two and a half months to clean, back, and repair some eighty square meters of mosaics. Their display along the wall of the compound would do honor to any museum. Reha Bey has just left but will be back to lift and conserve the mosaics from the apse of the Synagogue.

Henry Detweiler has resumed study of the fascinating little Church E which was excavated to a large part last year (*Figure 75*). This is a problem not only in architectural statics but also in logistics, for the domes have to be extracted from the diverse locations where they were thrown—perhaps by earthquake. He has already developed some very interesting theories about structural peculiarities observable in the construction.

Finally, at the edge of this Pactolus North sector, we are reaching the Persian level of the fifth and fourth century B.C.

It is the Persians who account also for the most extraordinary feature disclosed by this year's greatly expanded effort in the House of Bronzes sector. Gus Swift had descended in a terraced sequence (*Figure 82*) past the

130

Hellenistic fill when a carefully built well appeared. For two weeks morning after morning, we shouted down to the "well-digger"—his voice floating up like Joseph's from the depth. The well went to 62½ feet. Then we hit water which since has been rising and was at one point successfully used to wash the sherds coming out by tons from this productive excavation. At the moment the Lydian level is being freed. There are fascinating bits of Eastern Greek, Corinthian, and Attic pottery, and the mysterious "pot hoards" (*Figure 78*). But the palm for artistic achievement goes to a Lydian head of wild expressiveness which served as the spout of a very peculiar jug.

A Lydian graffito has appeared and was duly communicated to Roberto Gusmani in whose *Wörterbuch der lydischen Sprache* it will appear as Number 62. It threatens to introduce a new letter in the Lydian alphabet.

The "Battle of Bin Tepe" has been joined but it would be premature to say that "the enemy," namely the mounds, are ours. We started on the second largest, the central mound of the five-mile-long cemetery (*Figures 5, 106*). A camp has been pitched, but everything must be trucked over some fifteen miles. The sun beats down mercilessly with no shade in sight. Shelters for staff and workmen had to be constructed right at the mound. Noel Robertson and John Pedley as archaeologists, David Greenewalt as geophysicist, and the architectural team of D. Stieglitz, R. Iler, P. P. Papesch, and M. Ergene have taken part in the gruelling ordeal.

The first plan was to locate the dromos of the big mound, but it has remained hidden. We then tried to ascertain the base of the mound which seems to be indicated by a roughly cut drop in the limestone on the north side. Following a generous offer of the Gordion expedition we sent Mehmet Ergene and a truck up to Gordion to borrow the drill that had been successfully used to determine the position of the chamber in the great mound at Gordion. We also borrowed as instructor the Gordion operator, a most engaging lanky man with a crinkly smile, Abdullah Köşe. Water turned out to

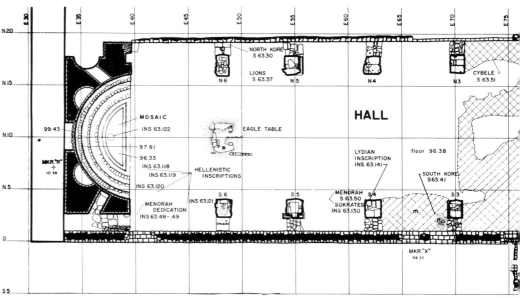

Figure 96—Results of 1963 excavations in the Synagogue are drawn in this field plan indicating Apse with niches and benches, piers, broken mosaic floor, and findspots of exciting sculptural pieces, including two seven-armed menorahs. Along the south wall is the row of Byzantine Shops.

be a major problem. A donkey train is now going back and forth from the spring one kilometer away to bring the water needed for operation of the drill, and our little house pump is somewhat inadequately performing pumping service. The worst obstacle had been put there by the Lydians themselves. The ancient Phrygians considerately built their mound of earth only; ours has scattered limestone. The drill is intended to locate stones underground, but it is as often as not stopped by these casual obstacles.

We intend to continue the experiment on the chance of locating a stone chamber by drilling, but hopes for success do not seem bright. As it would take some time to secure the materials, particularly timber, needed for shoring (timber is a government monopoly) and experienced miners needed to dig a tunnel, we have decided to postpone the major assault on the big mound until next season. We may, however, explore one of the smaller mounds which David Greenewalt had tested with electrical resistivity equipment.

As a kind of consolation prize, we have found the first considerable deposit of pottery known in the Royal Cemetery. David Greenewalt noticed that large pieces of pots were visible in a cut made by a bulldozer—the bulldozer having set out to make a piece of highway eventually planned to go across the Bin Tepe area. Under the terms of our permit we could not excavate, since we are to do one thing at a time, but we could and did collect all the pottery, which includes lydions of a type known to have been found in the chamber of Croesus' father Alyattes.

Meantime, many other activities have been carried on at the camp. The pace of finds now keeps recorders Ilse Hanfmann and Barbara Papesch working at great speed. Volunteer Ayberk Araz has been helping there and in the never ending task of sorting some twenty boxes a day at the House of Bronzes. Photographers M. W. Totten and V. Wickwar have their hands full with graves, levels, and objects as do the draftsmen, Charlotte Greenewalt and Fikret Yeğül.

132

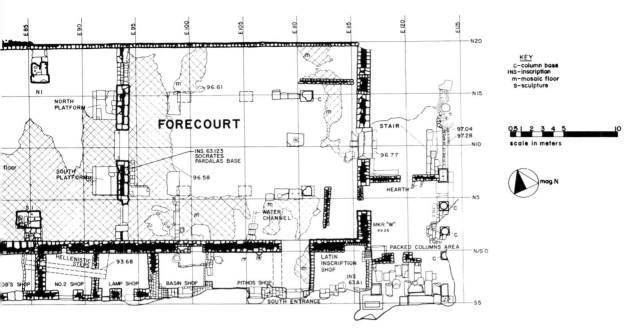

Among the many visitors to our excavation were His Excellency Nyazi Araz, Governor of the vilayet of Manisa; John T. Forbes, chief of Turkish, Greek, Iranian, and Cyprus programs for the Bureau of Educational and Cultural Affairs, United States Department of State; Edward Keller, American Consul in Izmir; Muhtar Enata, cultural affairs aide, USIS in Ankara; and many scholarly colleagues. To one of them, Homer A. Thompson, director of the Athenian Agora excavations, I owe my concluding phrase: "Sardis has the air of greatness about it."

Sardis   August 9, 1963

A unique monument of archaic art celebrating the great goddess of Lydia, Cybele, has just been discovered (*Figure 99*). To the surprise of the excavators this jewel of archaic sculpture was found among the ruins of the Synagogue of Sardis.

The marble monument, originally about four feet high, shows the great goddess Cybele in the dainty attire of an archaic Greek maiden. She stands in her shrine holding a little lion (much effaced) before her breasts (*Figure 100*). Two mighty snakes rise full height on both sides. The style of the frontal figure is that of the finest marble sculptors of Ionia. Ionic columns rise along the sides and at the back showing that the building is a shrine. Three zones of panels depict, in finely incised, light reliefs, worshiping maidens marching toward the front. Below them, on one side, are two addorsed lions sejant; on the other, two gaily dancing sileni, and below them dancing maidens with upraised arms. The reliefs continue on the back with two lions at top and two enigmatic scenes. Two eagles attack animals climbing a tree; a boar (he was said to have killed Attis, beloved by Cybele) and a lion, constant attribute of Cybele, flank another tree. Heracles wrestles

133

with the lion of Nemea, while in the next panel a bearded, crowned king drives a chariot. In the lowest panels, there is a horseman on the left and a spearman attacking a seated figure—probably Neoptolemus, son of Achilles, slaying king Priam of Troy.

The monument belongs unquestionably to the time of Croesus (561–547 B.C.) and rivals the finest Greek sculptures of the period. It was discovered by David Mitten. On the same day Gus Swift discovered in his excavation of the Lydian market area the first fragments of a Lydian archaic terracotta sculpture from a statue about two feet high—a bearded head with astonished black eyes and a leg in a red shoe, again from the time of Croesus (*Figures 104, 105*).

The Synagogue of Sardis is proving a veritable mine of archaic sculpture and architecture. We have found the lower part of a statue of a maiden (*Figure 101*), a group of two addorsed lions (*Figure 98*), sacred to Cybele, and fragments of archaic architecture, all built into the north wall of the Synagogue, which dates some eight hundred years later than these pieces, ca. A.D. 230.

Appearance of monuments sacred to the great mountain goddess Cybele recall reports by Herodotus that the Temple of Cybele was the most important sanctuary of Sardis. Its burning by Greek invaders in 499 B.C. caused the war between Persia and Greece. We surmise that remains of the archaic sanctuary must have been "stockpiled," perhaps after the disastrous earthquake of A.D. 17; the sanctuary must have been somewhere near the site of the Synagogue.

Istanbul   October 1, 1963

"There is a tide in the affairs of men" and excavations. Rising slowly like a groundswell, the wave of discoveries broke over us in August, then ebbed

Figure 98—Fragments of two pairs of Lydian addorsed lions (sixth–fifth century B.C.) were found scattered in the Main Hall of the Synagogue. This pair was found near the marble table which they guarded. Reused by Jewish community, the lions were perhaps considered symbols of the Lion of Judah. Total length 0.95 m., total height 0.63 m. Manisa Museum.

away during the last weeks of digging in September. This was meant to be a big season—the longest we ever had—and it turned out to be the biggest in results, not only in ways planned but, as is characteristic for Sardis, in ways we could hardly have anticipated.

The clearance of the Synagogue was our prime objective, for here we could safely count on achieving results of highest interest for history, religion, and the history of architecture. In the last weeks this excavation became an epic battle against time, as Dave Mitten strove in the face of a heat wave to clear the mountains of stones and labored long hours to keep up with the myriad finds. By the time Dave left, the major job was done. Our Turkish trainees, Fikret Yeğül and Mehmet Ergene, carried on, and on September 20 I saw the last major area cleared when the marble table, lying in a collapse at the Synagogue's central point, was dug out and its supports, decorated with Roman eagles (*Figure 97*), lifted by the Citroën and brought to the safety of our camp.

Free of all debris, the Synagogue looks incredibly large and light. It is large—over three hundred feet long, sixty feet across. We can now discern all major units of the plan (*Figure 96*). On the east rose a towering portico with granite columns set on tall pedestals. Passing through the portico with mosaic floors, the visitor reached a triple gate leading into the colonnaded Forecourt. The Ionic order of the massive columns was, by Henry Detweiler's calculations, relatively low, somewhat over twelve feet.

The Main Hall, reached through a second set of three gates, was lavishly decorated with mosaics, marble revetments, and (probably on the ceiling) paintings, now lost. Between the gates, within the hall, two marble platforms surmounted by railings and small temple-like structures (*Figure 83;* cf. *Figure 217*) harbored the Torah (Book of the Law) and the menorah (seven-branched lamp holder). The Main Hall featured two sets of massive piers, six along the north, six along the south side. In the focal point of this

135

Figure 99—D. G. Mitten brushing his spectacular find among the Synagogue ruins: an archaic monument to the Lydian goddess Cybele in the shape of a miniature temple decorated with reliefs. Preserved height 0.62 m. Manisa Museum.

Figure 100—Front of the Cybele monument, from the time of Croesus (565–547 B.C.), depicts the goddess standing between two snakes. The left side has registers of dancers and sileni coming to worship; on the right side (Figure 99) priestesses approach Cybele; below them are two lions, companions of the mountain goddess.

space, between the last two piers to the west, stood the huge marble table, some eight feet long, four feet wide, and four feet high. A marble pavement indicates that the reader approached the table from the west, facing the congregation. Dave Mitten conjectures that an extraordinary open-work menorah of marble, signed by one Sokrates as donor and maker (?), may have stood on the table. Adjoining the Main Hall to the west, an apse of brick still rises to a height of 15 feet. It was originally revetted with marble, was paved with a mosaic showing the tree of life, and enclosed benches rising in three tiers.

The resemblance of the plan to the plans of Early Christian basilicas is striking. Our discoveries will undoubtedly reopen the entire question of the origin of Early Christian church plans. Crucial in this context is the question whether the plan we have just described was in existence in the early form of the Synagogue. Some facts are beginning to emerge. Our epigraphist, Louis Robert, suggests that the earliest inscriptions of donors, which were placed on marble plaques in the Main Hall, belong to the late second century, our era. This might make the Sardis Synagogue the earliest synagogue preserved, Doura in Mesopotamia and the as-yet-unpublished lower synagogue of Ostia being other contenders for the "earliest" title. Donors' inscriptions in the mosaics of the vestibule make it certain that these mosaics were installed shortly after A.D. 212. Thus the Main Hall and the vestibule may be safely considered part of the original plan. The spectacular apse may have originally belonged to a different, earlier Roman building; nevertheless, at the moment we believe that the apse, too, belongs to the original plan.*

On the other hand, restoration and redecoration of the Synagogue are recorded in inscriptions. The date of this *ananeosis* (renewal) is narrowed down by the discoveries of the 1963 season. The beautiful mosaic with the tree of life was placed in the apse by two donors whose names are recorded

*For later views see *Figure 201*.

Figure 101—Lower part of a small archaic statue of a goddess or priestess (c. 580 B.C.) was built into the north wall of the Synagogue some 700 years after she had been sculpted. The two broad ribbons belong to native Anatolian dress. Height 0.4 m.

in a colorful wreath *(Figure 95)*; they took as family name the name of the House of Constantine (Flavioi). Hence the mosaic must belong to the fourth century. Then again, spectacular spoils from Sardis' most hallowed pagan shrines are built into the piers of the Main Hall. As Professor Robert points out this could occur at one time in history only: after the destruction of pagan shrines and before the decrees against building of synagogues passed by Byzantine emperors early in the fifth century. The series of piers, then, which make the Synagogue a basilica may belong to the restoration of the fourth century; but we do not as yet know whether they were preceded by an earlier series of supports.

With its gorgeous mosaics, its shining marble revetments, its high lectern flanked by statues of archaic lions of Cybele now reincarnated as symbols of the Lion of Judah *(Figure 98)*, this vast basilica could hold a community of many hundreds.

The final chapter in the history of the Synagogue was not a happy one. Sometime during the sixth century, the large entrance facade was taken down and used to make a bastion-like wall at the southeast corner. The street level outside rose, and the floor of the Synagogue came to lie three feet underground. Shops and dwellings invaded not only the outside east portico but even the Forecourt. The Main Hall, however, continued to function as a Synagogue until the entire city quarter was destroyed by the Persian invaders under Chosroes II (A.D. 616).

There is yet much to be done. The exact setting of the building to the south, north, east, and west remains to be determined by excavation. Innumerable marble fragments must be thoroughly examined to determine their position in the decoration of the Synagogue and to learn what light they may shed on earlier structures from which they were taken. A series of relieving arches in the south wall now springing from floor level pose the tantalizing possibility that an even earlier, smaller, synagogue might be

Figure 102—Native inscription of 13 lines in an unknown language resembling Lydian fell from Synagogue pier (S4 in plan, Figure 96), in which it was reused. Height: 0.86 m. It came from a large monument of sixth–fourth century B.C. The language can be read but not understood.

hiding underneath. Finally, the extent of the possibilities of restoration will require close study. For the time being, even the emergency "winterizing" is a vast undertaking; walls have to be cemented, all mosaic areas covered, and thousands of marble fragments collected and protected. A large diversionary channel had also to be dug to safeguard the Synagogue from the raging winter floods.

The finds made in the collapsed debris of the piers of the Synagogue were a bonanza beyond our wildest dreams. From late July to September 9 one fragment after another appeared, to give back to the world the archaic school of sculpture and architecture which flourished at the court of Croesus and his father Alyattes (ca. 600–550 B.C.). On September 3, I flew to Paris and was able to show our discoveries to the International Congress of Classical Archaeology,* thanks to the devoted labors of our photographers, Mike Totten and Vincent Wickwar, and to the fantastic efficiency of our associate director, Henry Detweiler, who, leaving Turkey on August 25, managed to get processed color slides back to Paris by September 5!

Eminent colleagues at Paris were delighted with these new treasures, and some (J. M. Cook, D. Levi, E. Langlotz) made the pilgrimage to Sardis to see them. Our cultural attaché, Walter M. Bastian, Jr., came just in time to witness the "unveiling" of a monumental inscription in near-Lydian writing (*Figure 102*) which stood on an archaic "Lydian" stone couch—both forming part of a pier in the Synagogue. Equally sensational, in a different way, was the discovery made by Louis and Jeanne Robert on their visit to study our epigraphic finds, in collaboration with John G. Pedley: a number of blocks with important Hellenistic inscriptions come from the front piers (*antae*) of the Hellenistic Temple of Cybele (Metroon). The inscriptions themselves reveal a chapter in the history of Sardis previously little known: after the siege by Antiochus III the city was to a large part destroyed and

*"Greece and Lydia: The Impact of Hellenic Culture," *Le Rayonnement des Civilisations grecque et romaine sur les cultures peripheriques*, 1965, plates 123–125.

punished. Then the king relented and permitted rebuilding of the city and began to give back such privileges as the use of the gymnasium (213 B.C.).

Norbert Schimmel, chairman of the Subcommittee on Sardis, Visiting Committee of the Fogg Museum, discovered, during his trip to Bin Tepe and subsequent ascent and study of the Acropolis, new technical arguments to clinch our reappraisal of the great bastion discovered in 1960—it is Lydian, not Hellenistic as we had thought (*Figure 47*).

During the month of August decisive advances were made toward completion of two important projects. At the end of four seasons' work, Steve Jacobs saw the last of the monumental architectural elements of the great Severan Marble Court "railroaded" to their appointed stations in the field outside. Steve has marked and studied some 1100 architectural pieces; their evacuation permitted him to study the basic structure and David Stieglitz to draw up the elevations. Reinforcing his arguments with knowledge gained on a visit to Baalbek, Steve first gave a masterly seminar, then submitted a report which embodies both his tentative conclusions concerning a design for restoration and his recommendations for a thorough engineering study of problems involved in the actual reconstruction of this grandiose example of Eastern Roman Baroque. Accordingly, Henry Detweiler and I have submitted to the Bollingen Foundation a proposal for the study to be undertaken by an engineering expert in 1964.

In the sector Pactolus North, Henry Detweiler led a team of architects, notably Ralph Iler and Mehmet Ergene, in the excavation and architectural recording of the fascinating Byzantine Church E. One surprise was the appearance of a rectangular space with steps and geometric wall paintings below the floor of the church; tentatively, it is interpreted as a baptistry. Henry has discovered another matter of import for the history of structural engineering: a curious grid of wooden beams under the church floor which apparently was intended as an anti-earthquake device. The liveliest seminar

140

Figure 103—Late Roman bronze lion heads (ca. 1 inch high), perhaps from a piece of furniture, were found near the Synagogue porch.

on record took place at the church as all our architects chimed in from tops of walls and domes to debate with Henry how the central brick dome of the church managed to reverse itself in midair while falling. More light on these and other aspects of the church will be forthcoming in Henry's impending Oberlin lectures on Early Christian architecture.

In addition to their normal "routine," the architects (D. Stieglitz, P. P. Papesch, R. Iler, M. Ergene) completed an essential and complicated task in tying in our various grids and triangulation systems with the survey of the Sardis area made by Turkish surveyors. Their activities on Bin Tepe, notably the survey of the big central mound involving constant clambering up and down with equipment was an ordeal in the merciless sun, but this gay and athletic group managed to survive.

Alighting at Sardis at 1:30 A.M. on August 16 after a record-speed departure from Harvard, Melvin Neville, anthropologist from Peabody Museum, went to work on our human skeletons. He was joined on September 1 by Dr. T. Çalişlar, Faculty of Veterinarian Medicine, University of Ankara, who studied the animal bones. The "bone shop" set up in the storage shed soon resounded with discussions of blood groups and various anatomical matters. Efficient, cooperative, and likable, the "zoological wing" contributed greatly to the animation of the expedition. Their mission accomplished, the experts departed leaving a legacy of boxes to be shipped for further study at Ankara, and a complete skeleton of a goat, in partial fulfillment of Mel's scientific urge for complete specimens of domestic species. Standing on the terrace to dry, the goat skeleton startled humans but not animals. Sneaking up at dawn, the Swifts' dog "Tamam" chewed off the head. The skeleton was saved by Greenie and installed in the room previously inhabited by Mel.

The final report from the Turkish geologist, Mustafa Saydamer, sets a wider framework for the question of Lydian resources in gold. Between the towns of Turgutlu and Allahiye gold is found in the alluvium of several torrents which flow into the Hermus river from the south (Map 2). "There is a close relation between the abundance of quartz formation and the gold content" of the alluvial deposits. The Sart Çay (our Pactolus) and the Tabak Çay (which flows east of the citadel) have both large amounts of the quartz pebbles. In the torrent beds descending from the Necropolis to the Pactolus "a few particles of gold have been found weighing 10 and 15 milligrams." Mr. Saydamer was conducting a general survey of the mineralization of alluvial deposits for the Institute of Mineral Resources and this task is finished. He suggests that more precise data on the gold content of the alluvial deposits of the Pactolus may be obtained by deep pits and borings in the river bed. He has, in any case, proved that there is still gold in the Pactolus.

The "Battle of Bin Tepe" was raging concurrently with the "Battle of the Synagogue" but with a vastly more complex problem in logistics. The digging was almost fifteen miles away from our camp, over poor roads. During most of the season our supply truck had to pass through an irrigation ditch filled with water. Our impermanent camp proved to be no attraction to workmen, most of whom preferred to commute by truck. Work on the shadeless mounds was exhausting and the chore of pecking away at the huge central mound disheartening. Noel Robertson's and John Pedley's operations had not revealed the hoped-for entrance or corridor on the south. The drill, generously lent us by the Gordion expedition, produced a spectacular picture of donkeys moving water up to the summit of the 200 foot high mound and a spectacular noise of two motors roaring away in the regal solitude. But the Lydians foiled us by scattering stones through the mound—stones that stopped the drill at depths where there was no chance of locating a chamber. A tunnel straight to center of the big mound will have to be the solution, which we hope to attempt next season.

Excavation of the small mound (BT 63.2) did not lack in drama. Time was running out and since a trench had produced no results at 5–10 feet, Noel Robertson started a deep pit on center. Taking over, John Pedley reported that his workmen had hit upon the edge of the ceiling of the stone chamber but a mass of rubble and earth 15 feet high still covered the rest of the grave and more rubble hung over the trench on the south. As we cautiously sought to widen the pit, a hollow revealed itself in the rubble over the grave. Our commissioner, Kemal Bey, crept in and in theatrical whispers heard all over Bin Tepe revealed to me (and all other bystanders) that he could peer into the grave through a hole in its ceiling. Great was the excitement and two State Police troopers were summoned to guard the dig day and night. Soon enough of the ceiling was excavated to wedge apart two of the hefty stone beams. As we squeezed through the ceiling we found a small chamber (9½ feet long, 4½ feet wide, 4½ feet high) built most neatly of limestone masonry with beautiful drafted edges. Parts of a wooden couch and some pottery fragments were lying about—but no treasures. In ancient times, graverobbers had tunneled daringly through the loose rubble, cut a small hole in the ceiling, and lowered a Lydian Oliver Twist who emptied the sepulcher (two of our more agile members repeated his feat in squeezing through the hole). Architecturally the monument was so interesting that we decided to clear the roof to its full length. Here we came near disaster. Overhanging rubble catapulted into the trench and only by great good fortune was nobody hurt. The architectural recording was completed and then earth brought down upon the chamber in the hope that it may escape the ever alert attention of unauthorized local diggers. The chamber has given us a novel type of Lydian sepulcher, orientated east-west rather than north-south and, as far as we can judge, without any corridor or access.

Meantime digging advanced to its appointed conclusion at Pactolus North. Supervised in turn by Bill Kohler, Noel Robertson, John Pedley, and myself, the greatly expanded excavation has thrown much light on the development

Figure 104—Bearded head and foot of a painted terracotta man of the time of Croesus emerged from a refuse pile in the Lydian Market area (Figure 76). Almost forty fragments of this terracotta were retrieved; recomposition was carried out in the camp laboratory by Mustafa Eriş (Figure 188).

of the Roman bath and on the "grand layout," the replanning of the area around A.D. 400. A new mystery popped up in the form of a marble monument with steps over which was built a chamber tomb of Late Hellenistic type. Oddly diverging in its orientation from earlier and later alignments, the monument seems to have been piously preserved by later builders. During the last days of digging, some walls and good floors of the Persian era (fifth to fourth century B.C.) appeared. There are signs that a sizable area unencumbered by later constructions is at hand. To link it with the Persian and Lydian structures known to exist a little distance to the north will be a rewarding task for 1964.

Something has been said in earlier letters of Gus Swift's mighty effort in the Lydian Trench *(Figure 76)*. The terracotta statue of a Lydian is certainly the most singular find of the season *(Figures 104, 105)*. The upper part only survives, in many fragments. As a rather short leg was found nearby, the betting is for a horseman. Equally spectacular in its own way is a large basin or bowl *(deinos)* decorated with somewhat naive but extremely colorful deer and lions (Plate III), proof that painting as well as sculpture and architecture flourished at the court of the Lydian kings. With the help of the Turkish riverine geologist Cengiz Saran (who came to advise us on well-digging) Gus has also determined that before the seventh century this area was frequently a subsidiary arm or mouth of the Pactolus, the water spilling over from the main bed and running northeast toward the Hermus.

Upon my return from Paris on September 12, I carried out the last enterprise of the season: to uncover the steps found deep below the Byzantine Shops last year *(Figure 96;* steps at E90). By this time, reserves had swung into action, some of them as short-time volunteers: Ken Frazer and Julian Whittlesey as architects, the latter fresh from underseas architecture at Bodrum; C. H. Greenewalt, Jr., as photographer; Güven Bakir as draftsman; and Mrs. Eunice Whittlesey and Miss Rosemary Lonergan as assistant re-

corders. The great majority of the workmen had left to work for King Cotton. The steps turned out to belong to a structure which disappears under the Synagogue. Their technique is superlative: each block is set on pre-incised setting lines and joined with split-hair precision. But the big protective bosses and unfinished blocks show that the building was never finished. By the finds it must be Hellenistic. Apparently the catastrophic earthquake of A.D. 17 hit the building before it was completed. In rebuilding the area, Roman architects sank incredibly deep foundation walls—at fifteen feet below floor we have not reached their bottom—and incorporated the stepped structure as footing. We have nothing to identify the structure. Only an excavation under the Synagogue might disclose whether this was a temple, an altar, a treasury, or some other kind of public building.

As white clouds lay over the Tmolus and mountain breezes swept fresh and bracing air into Sardis, the season drew to its close. Mrs. Hanfmann and her assistants caught up with the last of the nearly one thousand cataloged and three thousand "numbered" objects. The mosaic crew mounted the last of the Synagogue apse mosaics. The newly built storage shed got its doors and windows. The well with concrete caissons which we had started sinking into the Pactolus bed hit a water-bearing vein. Objects trooped into storage, trucks and Decauville lorries trooped into the courtyard. When we left Sardis on September 28 Ken Frazer was laboring in the basement over the last architectural drawings and Kemal Bey was conducting the last winterizing operations—a task which grows from year to year in proportion to the areas excavated.

1964

Sardis   July 6, 1964

On a clear day, the eye sweeps an amphitheater of mountains rising to the double-horned peaks of the Tmolus above the red cliffs of the Sardis Acropolis and Necropolis which like two sentinels stand guard over the Pactolus gap. Around the highest mound of the Royal Cemetery of Bin Tepe *(Figure 5)*, the graying yellow of cut wheatfields spreads before us punctuated sharply by the tortoise-shaped mounds. As the sun sinks, the mounds get darker and darker and little lights twinkle far away in the plain. If we turn around, another half circle of mountains comes into view with the still waters of the Gygean Lake and the last glow of sunset over the distant hills.

This is the view from the huge mound which we are attacking (Map 2, *Figures 106, 108*). We are driving a tunnel into the mound. Sounds simple but there is a world of flutter and hectic activity behind these words. Take it how you will, to dig at Bin Tepe is first of all a problem in logistics. Last year we lost much time driving workmen back and forth, fifteen miles or so, partly over poor roads. The tunnel work is set up as a three-shift job, twenty-four hours around the clock, six days a week. After our arrival at Sardis (June 11), a *portatif* was ordered; this is an approximation of a prefab but it is made with wooden boards and has a gravel floor. A house for workmen was made of reed-frame units. And a tent for the three professional miners who lead the three shifts was set up. Railway, generator, and transformer for lighting the tunnel, digging equipment, and all sorts of household things had to be supplied to maintain some twenty people out in the grand but hot solitude, far from any settlement. On June 14, Hilmi

Figure 106—King Gyges' Mound at Bin Tepe, called in Turkish Karniyarik Tepe ("Split Belly Mound" from gashes made by Roman diggers), with cut wheatfield in foreground. Harvard-Cornell expedition entered the mound from the south then joined the ancient cut (L in Figure 109) of the Roman tunnelers. The tent for the miners was later replaced by a permanent guards' house; on far right, the *portatif* house nicknamed "Bin Tepe Hilton."

Dokuzoğlu, chief engineer from the Soma Lignite Mines, and Haydar Gezik, mining engineer, came out to discuss the location, size, lighting, and shoring of the tunnel. Shoring was the stickler. Timber is a government monopoly and we owe it to the energetic efforts of our commissioner that it took only five days to get enough of it to start that task. Meantime a generator was purchased, and on June 29, about a week behind our ideal schedule, the Bin Tepe work began.

The first two days we dug in the open but on July 1 the real tunneling began. We are fortunate in having secured Haydar Bey as consulting engineer; he is going to spend each weekend at Sardis and Bin Tepe. On his first visit, July 4–5, he had a few things to correct. Our architects, Ralph Iler and Mehmet Ergene, also had something to correct—the tunnel had veered somewhat off course (*Figure 109*, lower part). We are aiming for center and have gone sixteen meters in so far, with about fifty-six to go.

I am putting Bin Tepe first; it will have absolute priority in our plans. The few of our friends and Supporters who have seen it know the irresistible fascination of the stillness and grandeur of this huge monument to the Lydian kingdom.

To come back to the beginning of the season, Jack Kroll, who dug in the Gymnasium, was rewarded by finding a painted inscription, which may prove of great interest for the units adjoining the Synagogue: it seems to say something like "Praise the Lord" (actually: "Blessed Be the People"). He is currently harvesting inscriptions, statue fragments, and glass vessels from a trench designed to clear the outside of the main gate of the Marble Court. This enterprise is in the service of Jim Yarnell, who has come out as structural expert to study the possibilities and needs for a restoration of this magnificent complex. We are beginning to hunt for heavy lifting machinery, concrete mixers, and other relevant items.

Jon Friedlaender, taken on as anthropologist, had to leave his bones and

Figure 107—GUGU monograms (ten found in 1964, twelve in 1965) read ΓΥΓΥ: gamma, upsilon repeated, left to right. These and a sixth-century B.C. poem helped to identify the central of the three huge Bin Tepe mounds as that of Gyges, Lydian king of Sardis, 680–645 B.C. (see Figures 5 and 106).

pinchhit at Pactolus North. His reward was a fine Hellenistic coin dating a curious level of broken tiles and stones. Gus Swift had encountered the same phenomenon before in the House of Bronzes area. We wonder whether this may not be the result of the destruction of Sardis by Antiochus III in 215–213 B.C., about which we learned last year through inscriptions found in the Synagogue.

Greenie (Crawford H. Greenewalt, Jr.) has resumed his slightly hair-raising excavation of the tunnels in the northern bastion of the Acropolis. For once he has real lighting, provided by our old faithful, the Onan generator of 1959, which is sitting in a niche on a cliff. At last report the tunnel, now 120 meters long, was still spiraling down.

Under Larry Majewski and Dick Stone the laboratory has been going like a house afire. They have assembled the archaic lions *(Figure 98)**, put together a panel of possibly Hellenistic painting, removed the new painted inscription from the wall, and mended Lydian terracotta sarcophagi.

The architects have an even more migratory life than usual, spending a good deal of it underground—in Bin Tepe *(Figure 110)* and in Greenie's tunnels. Andy Seager has now joined the team; Ken Frazer, whenever he has time between his duties as administrative assistant, makes archaeologists happy by shooting levels for them.

Nancy Hirschland has turned out to be a good draftsman and shows much initiative in organizing expeditions and excursions for new staff members. Our veteran draftsman and second-year trainee, Fikret Yeğül, has come from the triumph of his graduation (silver medal as best student in architecture at Middle East Technical University) and has already exerted his triple-threat talents as draftsman, architect, and archaeologist. The two new trainees, Recep Meriç (archaeologist-conservator, University of Ankara) and Metin Kunt (archaeological translator, Robert College), seem good choices.

*The lions went on being assembled (and disassembled) until 1969 as new fragments were found.

148

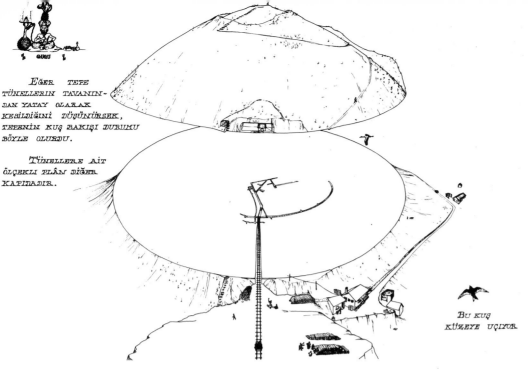

EĞER TEPE
TÜNELLERIN TAVANIN-
DAN YATAY OLARAK
KESILDIĞINI DÜŞÜNÜRSEK,
TEPENIN KUŞ BAKIŞI DURUMU
BÖYLE OLURDU.

TÜNELLERE AIT
ÖLÇEKLI PLÂN DIĞER
KAPIDADIR.

BU KUŞ
KÜZEYE UÇIYOR

Figure 108—Turkish legend in upper left corner of C. H. Greenewalt's 1966 drawing of Gyges Mound reads: "If we could suppose that the mound is sliced horizontally at the level of the tunnel ceiling, the bird's eye view of it would appear in this way. Scaled plan above the tunnels is on the other door." In the lower right: "This bird flies north." The picture shows (near center) tunnels and the "crepis," the curving Lydian wall surrounding the smaller, earlier tumulus, as well as the extent of the enlargement of the mound. Outside, near the permanent guards' house built in 1964, miners cut wood for tunnel frames.

Recep has been eagerly absorbing conservation knowledge and getting his days in the field under Gus Swift. Metin has been helpful in recording, and has put in a night shift at Bin Tepe, where we have to keep going part of the "free day."

The seminar course started off with a guidance in the topography of Sardis, on which occasion a pilgrimage was made to the much depleted site of the mausoleum of Claudia Antonia Sabina, *femina consularis*.* The tribute was however as much for the noble Roman lady as for her namesake Claudia Antonia Sabina Mitten, born to our Assistant Director and Rose Marie Mitten on June 8. Faithful to his word, Dave Mitten arrived here after a straight 21-hour flight and taxi from Boston on July 6, to plaudits of staff and local populace.

Sardis   July 30, 1964

I shall start with Jim Yarnell and the Marble Court. For six seasons we had labored to excavate this grandiose complex. Steve Jacobs had worked valiantly at the task of evacuating and recording the sea of marbles. This year about 1100 stones were staring us in the face from the field and the slopes east of the Gymnasium area, as a result of his effort. Jim arrived on July 1 and quickly got his bearings; now a majestic scaffolding is rising some forty feet in the air (*Figure 116*).

The scaffolding is to serve the restoration of the most striking feature of the entire Marble Court complex—the monumental gate at the back of the court with its four spiraling columns. But what effort and expense it takes to accomplish such a task! Take, for instance, just the question of replacing one of the monumental bases which is missing. We were jubilant when we

---

*The lower walls of this important mausoleum were preserved in 1914; its site was still visible in 1958, but it has now disappeared. See C. R. Morey, *Sardis V, Part 1: The Sarcophagus of Claudia Antonia Sabina* (1924).

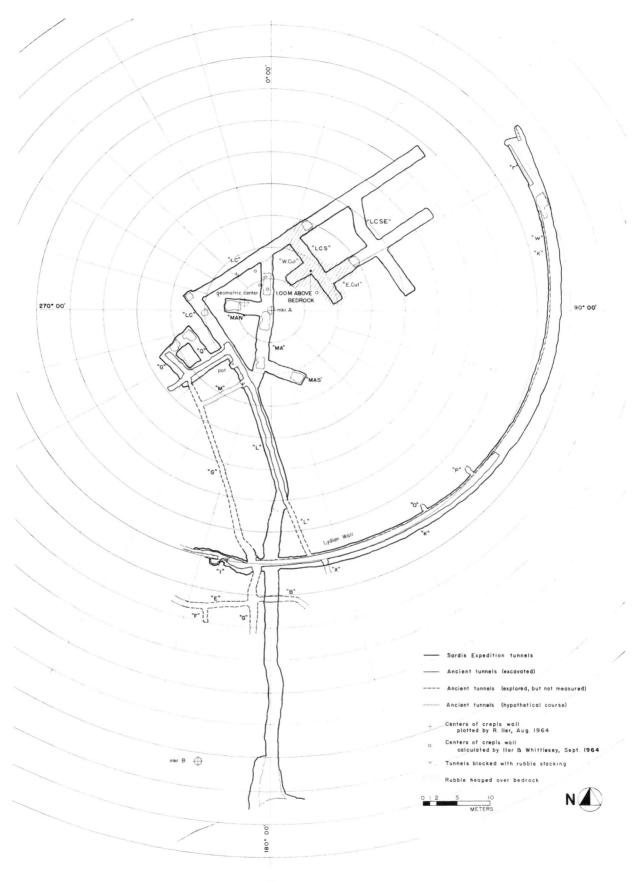

0° 00'

"r"

"w"

"K"

"LCSE"

"LCS"

"LC"

"W.Cut"

"E.Cut"

geometric center

1.00 M ABOVE
BEDROCK

270° 00'

90° 00'

"LC"

mkr. A

"MAN"

"Q"

"MA"

"G"

pot

"MAS'

"M"

"P"

"L"

"G"

"O"

"L"

"k"

Lydian Wall

"I"

"X"

"B"

"E"

"F"

"G"

mkr B

Sardis Expedition tunnels

Ancient tunnels (excavated)

Ancient tunnels (explored, but not measured)

Ancient tunnels (hypothetical course)

Centers of crepis wall
plotted by R. Iler, Aug. 1964

Centers of crepis wall
calculated by Iler & Whittlesey, Sept. 1964

Tunnels blocked with rubble stacking

Rubble heaped over bedrock

0 1 2   5   10
            METERS

N

180° 00'

mkr G

Figure 109 (left)—Plan of Gyges Mound with results of excavations through 1966. Expedition's tunnels follow or crisscross ancient robbers' tunnels (I, K, Q, G, O, P, E, B, X, M) in an attempt to locate entrance to Gyges' burial chamber. Lydian wall, now called "crepis wall" (Figure 112) enclosed a tumulus 90 meters in diameter; diameter of the mound was later increased to over 200 meters.

Figure 110 (right)—G. M. A. Hanfmann and John Sloan entering Gyges' Mound along railway track of the main tunnel behind a lorry. Hose for vital air supply at top left.

discovered that the ancient marble quarry of Sardis used for the building of the Temple of Artemis was being reopened. A long uphill walk to this romantic gorge where a crew is working elicited the information that neither the transportation from quarry to us nor the quality of marble should be counted on. Our foreman Hasan Koremaz went off to Izmir to look at some marble blocks Jim had seen there—and they turned out to be too small, not by much but by enough, and no larger ones were promised under a month.

The "hardware" for the scaffolding necessitated similar adventures. To assure delivery on time our men virtually stood guard over the machine shop at Salihli where the bolts were threaded and metal plaques drilled. Kemal Bey, our commissioner, made five trips to secure the wood needed; the longest pieces had to come from quite far away. In spite of such obstacles, Jim has gone ahead and proposed a construction schedule for August which we all hope he will be able to fulfill.

Jim is assisted by our trainee Fikret Yeğül, an excellent draftsman, who is doing the drawing and measuring. He has just been joined by our young Turkish architect, Mehmet Ergene. Steve Lattimore, in addition to archaeological supervision, has started on the restoration of the great Imperial dedicatory inscription which went around the Marble Court (*Figure 117*). Its last big piece has been unearthed just now.

At the other end of the Gymnasium area, Daoud Bey, alias David Gordon Mitten, has started work on the east end of the Synagogue and the adjacent street, amidst jubilation of his faithful workmen. Right off the bat, he had the pleasurable experience of finding the upper part of a statue of Dionysus of which he had found the lower part just before he left last summer. The fit is perfect (*Figure 115*); standing as a greeter in front of the recording shed, the boy is a fine addition to our sculpture garden.

The powers that guide the fortunes of excavators were equally favorable when David promised that he would find some glass for Paul Perrot, Di-

Figure 111—A narrow ancient (Roman) robber's tunnel made for one digger and now half filled with earth contrasts with expedition's timber supported tunnels (Figure 110), seven feet wide. The mound was composed of layers of hard red clay and softer greenish clay with chunks and chips of limestone interspersed. (Looking southeast along the Lydian crepis wall, which supported the base of the mound.)

rector of the Corning Museum of Glass, who worked with us for several days. A Byzantine shop was dug, and out came not just the usual fragments of broken glass but an entire hoard with a piece nearly intact—the Byzantine shopkeeper had considerately hidden the glass in a jar for Paul to find.

In the area above the House of Bronzes, Gus Swift has been running mighty trenches downhill (*Figure 121*) and making a section through the Lydian bazaar area (Lydian Trench). The trenches have yielded an important contribution to the urban history of Sardis. A second colonnaded street has been discovered, some twenty feet wide. This "G. F. Swift, Jr., Avenue" seems to be a diagonal artery running from the Pactolus Valley to intersect the main ("Marble") avenue (*Figure 153*). As a bonus Gus got a fine marble herm of a boy, probably Hellenistic, some small sculptures, and an immense amount of Roman pottery. But his most intriguing find came from the Lydian Trench. On the shoulder of a jug in black on red was our first painted Lydian inscription (*Figure 113*). R. Gusmani, author of "A Dictionary of Lydian," suggests that one of the four words preserved is the Lydian name of Zeus.

In the precipices of the North slope of the Acropolis, Greenie's tunnel had gone a total of 144 meters when we stopped (*Figure 70*). Greenie had discovered a subsidiary entrance and this solved, for some time, the problems of air supply and earth removal. Air could come in and earth could be thrown out. Greenie had just discovered a large "chamber" and was planning to break through its ceiling—thus assuring sufficient air for another stretch of tunnel digging—when he was called to Bin Tepe. With generators and all the other equipment required, we just could not afford two tunnel projects in inaccessible places at once. Also, there is only one Greenie. So we still have to get to the bottom of the Acropolis tunnels mystery.

The tunnels and our tunnel at Bin Tepe gave plenty of workout to our enterprising young photographers, Polly Bart and Peter Machinist. With a

152

Figure 112—Lydian or crepis wall, as seen looking west toward intersection with the main north-south tunnel. The wall was built in three courses, the lower two of rectangular ashlar masonry up to seven feet long, surmounted by an almost round "bolster" course. Note the smoothly cut slanting edge of the round piece. Use of such mighty masonry in mid-seventh-century Lydia came as a surprise.

red background cloth tied around her head, Polly is visible for miles. She and Peter struggle with sculptures weighing half a ton or so, failing generators, dragging camera transports, and other problems of field photographers.

I have been reticent about Bin Tepe—on purpose, because I had hoped we might have some news about the discovery of the tomb chamber. However, our present unusual findings are likely to reach the world via the London *Times*, whose distinguished archaeological correspondent, Mrs. Jacquetta Priestley, came to Turkey with the express purpose of reporting on Sardis. So I might as well bring you up to date, as I sit here at the so-called "Bin Tepe Hilton," in the midst of the aggregate of shelters and shacks that looks almost like a small village.

During the night of July 15, when Steve and Sherry Lattimore were out at Bin Tepe with our second commissioner, Muharrem Tağtekin, they sent word that a set of robbers' tunnels had been crossed by our tunnel and that bits of stone masonry were peering out of the wall of the robbers' tunnel to the east. Kemal Bey whispered the message through my window after midnight, and we both dashed out and stood guard through the night. The excitement ran high. As rubble was hanging overhead, it was several days before the masonry could be cleared. It turned out to be not the wall of a grave chamber, nor the corridor of a grave chamber, but a beautifully worked retaining wall, two courses high, crowned by a third course in the form of a big rounded molding *(Figure 112)*. It stands six and a half feet high, and now that we have driven a lower side tunnel along the wall, we know that the wall forms part of a circle. This is 100 feet into the big mound and we are at this point 90 feet below the surface *(Figure 109)*. On the face of the wall there is repeated five times a monumental sign, about seven inches high—but it is none of the known Lydian letters.

We think we know the solution to this mystery. Either before the famous episode when he was forced by his queen to kill his predecessor or during

153

the earlier years of his kingship, the founder of the Lydian dynasty of the Mermnadae, king Gyges (ca. 680 B.C.) apparently began to build a burial mound for himself, some 250 feet in diameter and encircled at the base by the wall we found. Either later in life, when he became powerful and famous for his gold, or else, perhaps more likely, after he fell in battle against the Cimmerians in the Sardian plain, his memorial was greatly enlarged to the present mound, which is some 700 feet in diameter (*Figures 108, 109*).

This has all sorts of sensational implications—for example, that the Lydians knew how to build monumental walls with drafted edge masonry as early as the seventh century B.C.

That the mound we are excavating is that of king Gyges appears from a fragment of the Greek poet Hipponax, whose lifespan overlapped that of king Croesus and who knew Lydia well. I have found a way of reading the sign (*Figure 107*) which appears on the wall as a monogram of GY-GY, Gugu, the name of Gyges in Assyrian annals; but there are other ways of reading the sign, and I am waiting for the experts to pronounce. We shall continue to refer to it for the moment as "Karniyarik Tepe" or "BT 63.1," because we do not wish to have clouds of witnesses around the place. As a matter of fact, the air in the tunnels is one of our problems; and the hard limestone cropping up between us and the center (with 106 feet to go, 120 passed) is another.

I am pleased about one thing. With David Greenewalt's advice on the position of the limestone and my guess as to where the base of the mound was located we drove the tunnel at a level which hit smack into the wall—wall top at sea level 188.70, bottom of our tunnel at sea level 188.25. If you remember that we had some 50 feet or more of altitude to guess at, you will see why I was having sleepless nights before.

Finding the chamber, however, is something else again. It may be off center, it may be higher or lower than our level, it may have no corridor, or it may be collapsed. We know by now that an amazing effort was made, probably in antiquity, to crisscross the entire mound with tunnels. They are filled nearly to the top with collapsed earth (*Figure 111*) and our consultant mining engineer has ruled out any systematic exploration as too dangerous. We know that two of these north-south tunnels passed near center (G and L in *Figure 109*) and that they, too, went along the wall we have found (in east-west direction). If our workmen are right, the "robbers" came in from north to south, the reverse of ours, a procedure difficult to explain if they had already found a chamber near center (unless they were looking for another).

Since July 16, the work has been conducted largely by Greenie; Dave Mitten and I take occasional stretches. We lost some time doing the side tunnel and exploring the wall for some 50 feet. We are back to three shifts, but the going is rough because of many stones and native limestone underneath. Time is the problem; keep your fingers crossed.

The two big projects—Marble Court and Bin Tepe—are costly. It is therefore with particular regret that we learned of the decision of the Trustees of the Bollingen Foundation to discontinue the support of archaeological, art, and other research programs not within the framework of the Bollingen Publication Series. Coming on the heels of the decision by the Department of State not to continue their support of archaeological projects, this leaves our enterprise, the largest in Turkey, dangling in the air.

Cambridge   September 25, 1964

In the battle of Man against Mound, the Mound won. When the last pits were dug in our tunnels on September 4, we had not found the grave cham-

ber of king Gyges. Yet we have learned much about the mound, and our unique consolation prize—the monumental wall of the earlier "mound within the mound"—has been giving us both excitement and some leads for next year.

I had left the story late in July, when, having discovered the "Lydian wall," we decided to cross it and to continue toward center. Three crews were to work around the clock in this main tunnel (*Figure 109*). An additional crew was to keep going in a crosswise tunnel toward the east. Later we stepped this up to two shifts, and their work was made easier by an ancient "robbers' tunnel" which faithfully accompanied the wall. By August 31 we had followed the wall for 180 feet. At this point the ancient tunnel alongside the wall stopped. Obviously our earlier colleagues had given up.

It is difficult to describe the uncanny and weird effect of this gigantic wall curving away in the dimly lit underground tunnel (*Figures 111, 112*). It has produced so far ten graven signs we consider tentatively to be royal monograms of king Gyges; two pairs of small, neatly incised swasticas, an A upside down, as well as a Lydian "s," all valuable evidence that Lydians knew how to write as early as the mid-seventh century B.C. As yet we have gone less than a quarter of the way around the base of the inner mound—it may form a circle of about 210 meters. We intend to continue the underground exploration of this unique wall next season.

Things were not so simple in the main tunnel. Right after crossing the wall, we found that one long robbers' tunnel toward the center of the mound was on our right, another on our left (O and L on plan, *Figure 109*). Upon advice of our mining engineer, we tried to steer a middle course between the two. Here we ran into hard native limestone and progress slowed down discouragingly as we tried to hack our way through it. Suddenly the earth collapsed on the right side at the head of our tunnel. It was the robbers' tunnel (L) higher up on our right that had veered into us. This time the

Figure 115—Roman *trapezophoros*, or table support, with ivy-wreathed Dionysus, found in "Latin Inscription Shop," Synagogue (E19; see plan, Figure 96). Height 1.04 m. Second century.

engineer advised, "If you cannot lick them, join them"; we had to step up on our tunnel floor five feet and abandon our railroad, which we had carried some 130 feet into the mound. (For those who, like myself, have not done any tunneling before, I should explain that there is always at the head of the tunnel a stretch unsupported by shoring. This is driven in three to four feet, then a timber frame is set up and linked by lengthwise beams to preceding frames. The space above and along the sides is filled with wooden boards to prevent the earth from moving. It was at the unsupported head that the earth slid down.)

What followed was like a round-the-end run; slicing along the pre-dug robbers' tunnel we made seventeen meters in a week. Portentous signs appeared in the earth filling the robbers' tunnel to its top: bits of Lydian pottery, bits of bronze, bits of charcoal. We would have bet even money that this tunnel had reached the grave chamber. Nevertheless, we decided to leave this ancient tunnel, because it was carrying us off course past the center of the mound. We struck out on our own toward center, everybody working at high speed *(Figure 109,* MA). By August 16 we had reached center under the highest point of the present mound, some 70 meters inside—nothing but the usual clay bands stared us in the face. We dug within the tunnel down to solid limestone, to make sure we had not gone over a grave chamber—to no avail.

There was time for a second guess. Back we went to the place where we had diverged from the robbers' tunnel system. Then our one and only safe evidence for the date of these extraordinary ancient tunnels appeared—a pot, broken but completely restorable, was found sitting on the floor of the ancient tunnel *(Figure 109,* pot). As near as we can determine, it is Roman.

Startling and abruptly, the robbers' tunnel L made a right turn to west, joined another long tunnel (G) which the Romans had driven toward center —and both tunnels stopped. In other words, the entire widely ramified sys-

tem of robbers' tunnels, which must have been dug over several months from the south side of the mound, stopped everywhere without reaching its goal. Why? Did they give up, or did they stop because another tunnel system driven in from the north had reached the chamber? We do not know, but a deep hollow on the northeast side of the mound (*Figure 106*, right) suggests that a second tunnel system may exist.

On our third guess, I shall on purpose be slightly imprecise. After the Lydian wall was discovered to be roughly circular, it occurred to us that the center of the earlier mound need not have been the same as the highest point of the present mound. Julian Whittlesey, Ralph Iler, and Andy Seager calculated the possible center, or rather group of centers—since the wall is not perfectly circular, measurements and calculations yield more than one. The centers of the inner mound do indeed diverge from the center of the later mound (*Figure 109*, + and o signs). Time ran out before we could test this hypothesis; to do so will be our first step in 1965.

In the meantime, steps had to be taken to secure our tunnels from the unwelcome attention of illicit diggers during the winter, whose visits are only too possible in this isolated location. A large stone portal and a big steel gate have been installed. A guard house is being built practically in front of the tunnel. Two guards will be there. Lest the timber frames rot by wetness, the tunnels will have to be opened once a week and our ventilator run to air them.

Light and air are the two great problems of tunnel digging. Toward the end, the generator kept breaking down; the more serious repairs meant long trips to Izmir. For several days the workmen struggled in near darkness with the help of flashlights and relays of automobile batteries. For several weeks in the beginning, air supply was a problem. A man working in a tunnel needs four cubic meters of air per minute, and we had ten people going in the two major tunnels. Nothing could be found on the market. Finally our chief driver-mechanic had a ventilator built in Salihli, and hitched it on to a pump motor. None of us ever calculated its exact output, but it

Figure 116 (left)—First scaffolding for restoration of the monumental entrance to the Marble Court, part of Building B, rises over the western unit of the gymnasium complex. A rotary for trucks goes around it.

Figure 117 (right)—Recomposing the great Roman imperial dedicatory inscription of A.D. 211 carved along the architrave blocks, which had been broken and scattered (Figure 53). Length of the inscription blocks was the key to ascertain the overall design of the Marble Court. From left to right: Steve Lattimore, John Pedley, G. M. A. Hanfmann (cap), Jeanne Robert, Louis Robert. For final result see Figure 207.

proved adequate to supply air through plastic tubing to both tunnels *(Figure 110)*. It is clear, however, that next year we shall need both a more powerful and a continuous source of light (probably a Diesel generator of ca. 7.5 hp—the gasoline generator had to be stopped periodically to cool off) and a stepped-up air supply.

Why not search for the chamber by digging in the open? Tentative calculations show that 50,000 to 60,000 tons of earth overlie the inner mound with the Lydian wall. Actually, about half as much again would have to be moved, were one thinking of digging away the center of the mound. We shall have to continue tunneling; and it is a consolation that at least other important items for this enterprise—the "portatif" headquarters, the shelters, and most of the equipment—are ready and will enable us to get going more quickly next year.

I make it sound as if Bin Tepe were the center of our activities. Actually this outlying territory ruled over most competently by Greenie and our second commissioner Muharrem Bey was a sort of island outpost—and our supply trucks paid dearly for traversing the rough terrain each day.

An exciting finish was put on by Noel Robertson on the Pactolus. Here under great flood deposits there emerged Lydian houses better preserved than anything we have seen so far. The area seems to have been densely inhabited, and perhaps not built over. We may be approaching there the agora of the Lydian and Persian city. This may well be the most promising sector in the immediate future. A strange monumental complex with curving walls seems to be the work of the Persians. In addition to fine Attic black-figure sherds, a charming tiny lion in rock-crystal *(Figure 114)* and lumps of rock-crystal hint at activity of skilled artisans nearby. A fierce burning seems to have terminated the earlier Lydian habitations; one is tempted again to ask whether this is evidence for Cyrus' assault on Croesus in 547 B.C. (cf. p. 231 and *Figures 176, 179* for the true explanation).

Another great destruction has been documented in the big Lydian House

Figure 118 (left)—Casting a column base at West Gate of the Marble Court.

Figure 119 (middle)—Placing part of a mended column shaft in the Marble Court with the help of a tripod. Weight of the piece is three tons.

Figure 120 (right)—Mehmet Ergene, construction engineer (right), and Hasan Koramaz, chief foreman (left), setting spiral column on base in Marble Court. Projecting modern steel bars to hold the shaft in place are being inserted into corresponding holes in column base.

of Bronzes excavation. Here a trench planned and started by Gus Swift was taken down by Steve Lattimore to the destruction of Sardis by the Cimmerians (670–650 B.C.), and on down to levels which seem to belong to the ninth or tenth century B.C., with new and colorful kinds of Lydian Geometric pottery.

Across the road, Dave Mitten ran into a very complicated situation at the east end of the Synagogue. He was able to ascertain the plan of the imposing colonnaded eastern facade and also to prove that in the present form it must belong to the fourth century rebuilding. Quite unexpectedly it appeared that the Byzantines had fortified the eastern end of the Synagogue with a tower of huge spoils and something like an outwork. Perhaps it was the assault of the Persians on this fortress in about A.D. 616 that caused that part to be burned so severely. Dave also discovered a marble-paved piazza at the southeast corner of the Synagogue. It is carefully paved, but disrupts the original northern colonnade of the "Marble Avenue." These mysteries will need to be clarified next year. A fine bronze bull's head and the lower part of a fine marble statue were among the prizes found.

To the end, the Marble Court remained a beehive of activity as Jim Yarnell and, after his departure, Mehmet Ergene strove to train the newly formed crews in the arts of building column bases of cement (*Figure 118*) and recomposing the fragments of the gorgeous spiraling columns of the monumental western gate (*Figures 119, 120*). At the same time, great strides were made in improving the designs for the prospective restoration of the court. Here a crucial job was accomplished by Steve Lattimore, who for the first time drew to scale and restored the correct sequence of the great dedicatory inscription which ran around three sides of the structure. Lively discussions of architects Yarnell, Yeğül, and Ergene and archaeologists Lattimore and Pedley (also qua epigraphists), rapid-fire correspondence by mail and telegram, and finally personal consultation with our illustrious epigraphist-en-chef Louis Robert produced a solution which greatly re-

duces the number of uncertainties in our proposed restoration *(Figure 117)*. The immediate result of these researches was to establish sizes and positions of the entablature blocks which in turn determine other important features.

On a flying visit to Ankara (total lapsed time 53 hours), I had the privilege of discussing the work of the Sardis program with United States Ambassador Raymond A. Hare, and showing him our drawings of the proposed reconstruction of the Marble Court. The new Director General of Antiquities, Ministry of National Education, Bay Mehmet Önder, expressed great interest on the part of his department in achieving this restoration. His letter of September 15 promises substantial participation by the department—about one fourth of the funds required for the restoration we plan to accomplish in the seasons 1965–1968. This will mean a genuinely collaborative enterprise, for the project will at the same time be part of the department's restoration program.

We have left the scaffold to stand over the winter in the hope of starting lifting operations early next season. Our forecast shows additional outlays for skilled personnel, special materials, and machinery.

The last week, the Sardis landscape was enlivened by a beautiful silvery giant triangle rising over various sectors. This was the novel asset to stereophotography, the "bipod" designed by Julian Whittlesey, which yielded most interesting results in photography of smaller archaeological areas presenting special problems of precise recording.

Our work on Byzantine coins was greatly stimulated this season by the welcome visit of Professor and Mrs. George E. Bates, who held enthusiastic sessions with our numismatist Jack Kroll.

John Pedley was less harassed by a flood of inscriptions this year than last, but a beautifully preserved dedication to the Emperor Caracalla, found in the hall behind the Marble Court, an inscription about mysteries of Apollo, and evidence for an important sanctuary of "The Great Mother of Gods of (all) Lydia," found at the Gygean Lake behind Bin Tepe, gave him a nice workout.

Figure 121—Middle Terrace East, House of Bronzes area, with southern colonnnade of a Roman–Early Byzantine street, now known as the HoB Colonnaded Street. Upper part of trench went through a huge dump of pottery and bones. For plan see Figure 153.

Plate III Lydian *deinos* (bowl) colorfully decorated with deer and lions attests to Lydian vase painting skill during period of the Mermnad kings. Found in the Lydian Market, House of Bronzes area.

1965

Sardis   July 10, 1965

They were drilling and drilling, doweling, watching the marble cleave and splinter, putting in reinforcing rods, building up slowly, bit by bit, the mighty shattered columns that originally bore the pediment of the gate into the Marble Court. This went on all of last season and the first weeks of this *(Figures 119, 120)*. A three-ton fragment hangs suspended from the beam of the scaffold—and still a crucial part is missing. And then, yesterday, three huge shafts of these gorgeously textured columns appeared in the excavation which Jack Kroll and Andrew Ramage are conducting behind the Marble Court upon Jim Yarnell's request. There is tension and bustle about construction, as sidewalk superintendents well know; but even greater tension about reconstruction, where so many things are unknown. Yesterday's find was the great moment of triumph of this campaign so far.

Jim Yarnell had flown in punctually from Jordan on June 18 and was joined immediately by his assistants Mehmet Ergene and Fikret Yeğül, former trainees and now staff members, coming from Harvard and Yale respectively; and by the newly appointed trainee, Tankut Akalin from Robert College, essentially "engineer in charge of procurement" for the Marble Court. Tankut raced in from Istanbul on his motorcycle, after one major spill. They all swung into action right away, and now there are not only columns on the ground but crews of masons taking down and consolidating walls, stone crews setting up on the ground pieces of the huge ornate pediment *(Figure 125)*, and master marble workers engaged in finding and fitting the fragments.

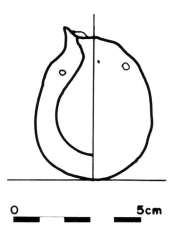

Figure 122—Drawing of an Early Byzantine pilgrim flask found in the House of Bronzes. Relief on the left shows St. Luke, seated on a high-backed chair, writing in a book; opposite him is a spiral-fluted column with volute capital. Figure on the right is St. John. Sketch shows profile and the suspension holes.

0   5cm

As usual, plans for meeting arrivals miscarried. Heavily laden with film gear, Charlie Lyman evaded a special embassy sent to the airport—two days early; but Mehmet Ergene's father proved helpful in springing Charlie from his three-hour confinement in the customs office: thus the project to make a color film was saved. A sadder delay was Ken Frazer's tangle with automobile-status questions, which delayed him almost two weeks. But arrive they did, and on June 21, Gus Swift launched his House of Bronzes dig, followed by Robert and Marcia Ascher at Pactolus North, and Andy Ramage in the imposing South Hall of the Gymnasium. The Ascher methods, developed in American archaeology, are most instructive to us and show beautiful control. With occasional assistance in linguistic matters from Metin Kunt, our archaeologist-translator, the Aschers are progressing toward the Persian and Lydian levels.

I suppose most of our friends keep their fingers crossed about Bin Tepe. The guard house constructed over the winter at the tunnel has now been taken over by Greenie and the second commissioner, Muharrem Tağtekin; its porch commands a beautiful view of the Hermus Valley and the Tmolus chain. Two miners and twelve workmen sleep in last year's *portatif*. Two cooks and two guards minister to sustenance and security. The new Landrover, generously donated by a Supporter last year, stands by, day and night, in case of emergency. But the show remains a complicated one to supply. We have not enough timber for shoring; the ventilator has already broken down once; and the consultant engineer, without whom we did not want to move in crucial matters, did not appear until July 4. We should, of course, be grateful that the tunnels and all of last year's shoring survived the series of earthquakes that shook the Salihli area in February and March.

We have solved one important problem. Last year we ran into a blockage just west of our main tunnel, where the now famous wall with "Gugu" signs runs east. Greenie has determined that the "Lydian Wall," the re-

Figure 123—Pilgrim flask detailed in Figure 122. Decorated in low relief, badly worn. Pilgrim flasks were for oil or holy water. The Sardian flasks show a variety of subjects. See Figure 185.

taining wall of the inner mound, picks up again westward. Unfortunately, the ancient "robbers" elected to tunnel to the inside of the wall, thus creating a complicated and possibly dangerous situation (*Figure 109*, at I), should we want to tunnel outside. Working with two shifts, Greenie has also driven eastward along the wall, and here signs and portents have appeared in the shape of (a) tiny jumping frogs, and (b), more importantly, a number of vase fragments. We have not, however, as yet crossed the east axis where, just conceivably, an entrance might have been located.

The "buck to center" went several meters past one group of calculated possible centers of the inner mound (*Figure 109*, +, o symbols); we are planning on several more "passes" within the central area of the mound, now that we have had the engineer's advice as to what can and what cannot be done. This is where breakdown of ventilation and shortage of timber interferes.

The floodlights flown in from Boston were tested on Monday, July 5. They had cost $25.95. Charges for airfreight, insurance, duty on both article and freight, broker, agent, transport here: almost $220. This is why we cannot airfreight material to Turkey. Anyway, Charlie Lyman, Jon Boorstin, and John Sloan, all keenly interested in film-making, have had various meetings and disputations and are now beginning the "takes."

As the study of big buildings progresses, Sardis is getting ever more architectural. It was a great comfort to have Andy Seager arrive punctually. Andy has agreed to undertake the preliminary study of the Synagogue. As we know only too well now, this means rolling, turning, pushing, and measuring stone after stone after stone.

Dave Mitten, assistant director, arrived on July 1. He is making a pit in search of an earlier synagogue and starting to free the colonnade outside the north wall. Dick Stone, our conservator, has agreed to take a hand and erect his own "office" in the Synagogue to sort the extremely rich but also

165

extremely complicated marble revetments. Incidentally, our "offices" of posts and matting were much admired by our German colleagues from Pergamon, whose delegation paid us a visit on June 23.

While we are on relations with other foreign missions: another great addition to the Sardian landscape is the fourteen-meter-high tripod most generously lent to us by the Austrian Ephesus Excavations *(Figure 149)*. There is a melancholy contrast between this kind of collaboration by an expedition which is state-sponsored, and the treatment we receive from our own authorities in matters like use of American excess property stored nearby, not used, badly needed, yet completely unavailable to us.

The most interesting finds so far come from Gus Swift's House of Bronzes: a colorful Lydian *deinos* fragment with sphinxes, birds, ibex; and for iconographic interest, a pilgrim flask with what must be one of the earliest representations of St. Luke writing the gospel *(Figures 122, 123)*.

Team work has been developing in a very gratifying manner. Thus we have now in addition to the seminars Monday night meetings on the Marble Court. A major contribution was made by Jack Kroll, whom I had asked to study the Byzantine poems and inscription (visible in *Figure 166*) which deals with reconstruction of the Marble Court. In so doing, he succeeded where archaeological and architectural investigations had failed: he discovered the exact placing of the columns which stood all around the court in pavilion-like formation. (The meeting took place despite "Crisis No. 245," the breakdown of our house generator, which has now been taken for repair to Izmir.)

Recently I woke up to sweet chirping of birds and thought how nice it was that our trees have grown enough to attract birds. Actually the birds are in a blue cage hanging in a tree; the Turks insist they are *bülbüls* (but not real nightingales). Our chief mechanic had sneaked in this melodious addition to Sardis sounds around 4 A.M. that morning.

Sardis   August 10, 1965

"George, there is a lion down here!" Undeterred by Dave Mitten's unconventional salutation I descended into the pit Dave is digging in the southeast corner of the Main Hall of the Synagogue. Immured in the cement and rubble of a foundation were a marble lion's paw and chest. The piece looks archaic *(Figure 127)*; as you may recall, precious masterpieces from the time of Croesus were found in the Synagogue in 1963, reused as building materials.

The Synagogue has been the center of many and varied activities. This season we are handicapped by insufficient means. Therefore the emphasis is exploratory, and we are laying the groundwork for a program of excavation, research, and restoration which we hope to realize during the next three years with the help of an interdenominational "Committee to Preserve the Ancient Synagogue of Sardis."

Dave has directed his small force to the exploration of areas crucial for the comprehension of the building. An important part of the colonnaded eastern facade of the Synagogue is being opened. Unfortunately, a corner of the building lies under a vineyard we do not own.

A fascinating chapter in the history of the complex is unfolding in the colonnade which ran alongside the northern wall of the Synagogue—and served at the same time as the southern colonnade of the athletic grounds (palaestra) of the Roman Gymnasium. Here Dave found a large stretch of the wall of the Synagogue lying as it had toppled to the ground *(Figure 128)*. The height of this colonnade is an important element in solving the problem of the height and roofing of the Synagogue. Some bonuses came from this excavation: an impressive Corinthian capital decorated with a

Figure 124—Scythian (?) bone plaque with twisted griffin motif from the House of Bronzes area may be associated with the seventh-century B.C. Cimmerian invasion of Sardis.

female head and two portrait heads, one Julio-Claudian, the other late antique, unfortunately much damaged.

With the arrival of Henry Detweiler, our associate director, and of Alan Shapiro, architectural consultant, of the architectural firm of Graves and Shapiro, New York, research and planning have entered an intensive phase. Daily meetings are being held at the sun-baked site and in the architectural office of the camp; already Henry's and Al's keen observations and suggestions are bearing fruit.

Andy Seager has produced two beautifully drawn tentative reconstructions, one of the two temple-like shrines (probably for the Ark of the Law and for the Menorah) at the eastern entrance into the Main Hall, which I believe to represent the original arrangement, and another of the entire 300-foot-long Synagogue structure. These drawings were made into slides and shown by me to the Fourth World Congress of Jewish Studies in Jerusalem. I was in Israel on July 28 and 29, just for twenty hours—long enough to admire the new university and the Israel Museum and to benefit from the enthusiasm and interest of archaeological colleagues in a lively discussion after my paper on "The Ancient Synagogue of Sardis."*

The problems of this impressive building are challenging. We do not yet safely know whether the earliest structure, clearly an integral part of the Roman master plan for urban renewal of Sardis after the horrible earthquake of A.D. 17, was a synagogue. We are encountering very complicated arrangements for foundations and have yet to determine whether they were built for one or two buildings. We do know from inscriptions that the Synagogue was built between A.D. 175 and 200 and rebuilt between 350 and 400. We are now seeking to determine what has survived from the original plan and construction. To give one example: the imposing apse of the

*"The Ancient Synagogue of Sardis," Fourth World Congress of Jewish Studies, *Papers*, vol. I (Jerusalem, 1967), pp. 37–42.

Synagogue is built into a Roman nymphaeum (perhaps "The Fountain of the Synagogue" known from an inscription) which in turn is built against a main wall of the Roman Gymnasium.

We are sorting out information concerning structural safety and structural measures needed for partial restoration. In noon and night discussions we are exploring various possibilities of design for the women's galleries, staircases, second story, and roofing of the Synagogue.

Herculean work lies ahead on the thousands of fragments of interior decoration. Dick Stone, our conservator has succeeded in recomposing one major element: a marble frieze some twenty feet long which features craters and peacocks in the spandrels of a series of ornate arches (seen in *Figure 212*). At present we have two men washing and joining the marbles but the great piles of this material will have to be gone over again and again before we can reconstitute the scheme of the marble-revetted interior. An expressive camel head and a dog(?) head of yellow marble (*Figure 130*) recently appeared, as well as birds and fishes or dolphins.

The perambulatory "Synagogue Study Group" has also included Jim Yarnell, whose great competence in structural engineering is of vital help, and Rick Hamann, who has been doing some of the indispensable drawing and measuring of columns and other architectural elements. Such close cooperation of architects, engineers, conservation experts, and archaeologists is not often met; we hope to carry it to ever greater effectiveness. Our major problem will be to translate the results attained into practical reality in an agrarian area where supplies of technological materials are short and the training of specialized skilled workmen takes time and effort.

August 1 was a day of triumph for the Marble Court team. Three times did the eight-ton column shaft rise into the air, as the Austrian giant tripod (*Figure 149*) and our small winch were used to maneuver the piece horizontally and vertically. Each time there was still some fault in the setting.

Figure 126—Eastern Greek potsherd with geometric "seascape," ca. 650–625 B.C., from the Lydian residential area of Pactolus North. A helmeted warrior sits in the ship; dolphins swim in the sea alongside.

Finally Mehmet Ergene, who directed the operation, set the thirteen-footer down on its base, perfectly plumb and level. He had to lift it again in the afternoon to "grout" the surfaces and make final adjustments—and nearly lost his hands and possibly worse when the column came down seconds after he had inserted a leveling piece of lead *(Figures 119, 120)*. Although the column part set is less than half of the total height, already this majestic spiraling giant evokes the vision of the splendid, monumental gate.

The four columns of the gate have become real personalities to Jim Yarnell, Mehmet, Fikret Yeğül, and Tankut Akalin—the badly shattered "No. 4" of which the lowest part just went into place, the "No. 1" still lying prostrate and being put together with much drilling and cementing (for a later portrait of No. 1 see *Figure 163*).

The top part of the gate, a heavy and ornate pediment, arch, and vault is eventually to rest on the back wall *(Figure 125)*. Examination showed that much of the wall and its piers have to be rebuilt to a height of over thirty feet. We propose to use for the purchase of the materials the allocation of TL 25,000 made by the Turkish Ministry of National Education for this restoration project within the framework (and procedures) of their own restoration program. To make the calculation drawings and the estimates was another rush job. This was accomplished before I went to Ankara for final presentation of project and estimates. A local Turkish committee is being convened and work will continue after we leave with a technical architect from Manisa and our commissioner as immediate supervisors. The Ministry of National Education has assigned as consulting supervisor Cevat Sezer, technical architect attached presently to the Bodrum Museum. His recent work has included the raising of columns of the Athena Temple at Priene and the restoration of the Genoese Castle at Ceşme. We were very happy that our hope to have Cevat Bey associated with our enterprise was realized, and even happier when he suddenly appeared at the site and imme-

Figure 127—Archaic lion of yellowish-white marble was found immured in the foundation of southeast pier in the Synagogue Main Hall (Figure 96). Length 0.57 m., width 0.19 m., height 0.37 m.

diately launched into a detailed conference with Jim Yarnell and our other Marble Court experts. As Jim has to leave August 15, it is fortunate that we are able to insure continuity with the work to be carried on by our Turkish colleagues until possibly early November.

The Marble Court is impressive with its bustling activity. "On travaille ici dans une manière digne de l'Amérique," observed a French architect who visited us.

In the Royal Cemetery of Bin Tepe the "Battle of the Mound" is in its last round. We were going to stop work at the mound of king Gyges (ca. 680–645 B.C.) on August 7 but Greenie asked for a few more days to investigate a suspicious accumulation of stones in the center of the mound. Last year's great discovery, the monumental crepis wall of an earlier inner mound, discovered 100 feet into the mound, has now run out, after we had followed it for nearly 250 feet. At the end a stretch of natural rock has been carved to simulate masonry—then the rock, too, breaks off. The different stages of carving look incredibly fresh, as if the masons had just laid down their tools.

But in the crucial central area we have put through several tunnels and covered all theoretical centers without finding the chamber (see plan, *Figure 109*).

That nomadic Cimmerian invaders from the Crimea had captured Sardis at least twice (ca. 660 and 645 B.C.) is recorded by ancient historians. We have tentatively equated a great burning, best traceable in our House of Bronzes sector, with one of these invasions. Now Gus Swift has found in a seventh century level a bone plaque showing a griffin twisted around in the unmistakable Scythian animal style *(Figure 124)*—a find as important for the dating of the origins of Scythian art as for the confirmation of the presence of the Cimmerians at Sardis. Assisted by Andy Ramage, Gus is freeing the seventh century level on a broad front—with great numbers of interesting Greek imports from Corinth, Rhodes, Ephesus, showing up.

Figure 128—Synagogue north wall fallen into the southern colonnade of the palaestra in a stereoscopic view taken with the Whittlesey bipod camera.

Figure 129—Bipod camera in operation in the Synagogue. Foreground, Eagle Table fragments; center, bipod with camera suspended from top; truck ramp going across Synagogue; J. Whittlesey guying down the bipod. Looking east.

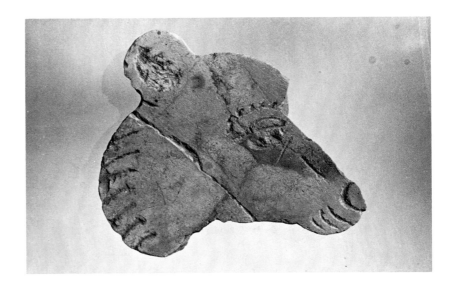

Figure 130—Dog or sheep head and a camel head from *skoutlosis*, marble revetment or paneling, third to fourth century, our era. Examples of figurative marble decoration of the Synagogue interior. No other parts of these figures have been identified. *Skoutlosis* is a late Greek term derived from Latin *scutula*, "little shield." Originally it meant the laying of shield-like marbles in patterns, came then to mean marble revetment in general.

For a while it looked as if we had guessed wrong, as if the Persian and Lydian houses which had so promisingly appeared last year on the east bank of the Pactolus torrent ("Pactolus North") might not continue—and then under Bob and Marcia Ascher's expert hands walls began to sprout everywhere. This was, indeed, a densely populated area of the Lydian capital, and the Aschers are contributing valuable observations (including such items as the offprint of an animal skin on a potsherd) toward a reconstruction of life in Lydian Sardis. Other highlights among their finds are a Lydian graffito inscription, possibly again a dedication, and a charmingly painted fragment of an early cup brought all the way from Sparta.

The hard-working Whittlesey team (Julian and Eunice) has been bringing in wonderfully precise photogrammetic and "realistic" coverage of areas being excavated—sometimes at the price of getting up at 4 A.M. to get the right light. Thus the great hall with collapsed vaulting behind the Marble Court and the foundations within the Synagogue are being recorded (*Figures 128, 129*). The thin, towering Whittlesey bipod looks like something out of a "moonshot" movie and adds a touch of the world of the future to the Sardian landscape.

Our project to make a color movie is being carried on almost single-handedly by Charlie Lyman. His activities have included such diversified pursuits as riding in a lorry in the Bin Tepe tunnels, climbing rocky pinnacles to get shots of life in the camp, and immortalizing the erection of columns in the Marble Court. A sample film roll, three minutes of glorious color, was shown to a recent staff gathering.

The picture would be incomplete if I forgot the volleyball purchased by Charlie. Every day after 5 P.M. we are sure to see a vigorous game in progress. We, the elderly statesmen, can only marvel at the energy of the young folks after eight working hours in the gruelling sun.

Sardis   September 9, 1965

The whirring of a tired generator accompanied by six clicking type-writers is the musical theme at the end of the Sardis season. One after another the members handed in their final reports and departed in a state of semi-exhaustion. David Mitten was banging away at his Synagogue report until the taxi arrived; but he had not reckoned on Charlie Lyman, who was going to go with him. Charlie had in the meantime departed to film the final act of the Marble Court drama—how Mehmet Ergene lifted in place the capital which now crowns re-erected column No. 4.

Yesterday, in the midst of it all, the new District Commissioner arrived on an official visit. This gave me an opportunity to visit our sectors. They are being winterized, walls capped with cement, column fragments and mo-saics buried again under earth. In the last rays of the evening sun the two Marble Court columns rose skyward bathed in pink light (see *Figure 163*). Somehow the capital made them appear splendid and complete, and the Commissioner remarked that this work will be an eternal monument to us.

It is well to have such encouragement, for the realities behind the work are such as to try men's hearts: the stone that first cannot be found and when found costs a fortune to transport; the cement which suddenly is unavail-able for a couple of weeks; the tangle of official regulations in which we are now involved about the Turkish government grant. But when it gets done it is going to be a monumental and beautiful thing, this Marble Court.

Toward the end, our House of Bronzes forged in the lead: the largest architectural feature yet found in that area suddenly appeared. It is a wall which apparently enclosed the entire bazaar area *(Figure 131)*. Large rooms back the wall, and all this is of venerable antiquity, dating back to mid-

Figure 131—An ambitious building program at the Lydian Market area followed upon the Cimmerian destruction by fire. A precinct wall up to six feet high and a series of large rooms may attest a forerunner of walled Oriental bazaars around 650 B.C. (The situation shown was reached in 1968.)

seventh century B.C. Gus Swift, in his excellent report, tells the story. First the wild Cimmerians from Crimea destroy and burn the area. Then all of it is covered with clay and some enigmatic industrial installations take over. The newly found wall is witness of real urban planning and in conjunction with the many fascinating finds (including a seal with what looks like writing) will give students of Mediterranean history much to chew on.

How the Lydians lived and how they planned their houses is becoming apparent at the Pactolus. Metin Kunt did fine work excavating a sizable area after the Aschers' departure. Bob and Marcia had done a most craftsmanlike job getting everything shipshape in their part before they left on August 17. Metin has linked their trench with our 1964 excavations. With the keen and observant architects Rick Hammann and Andy Seager we have begun to work out the layout of several houses. As Andy has observed, these are continuous, quite sophisticated, pretty complex houses; and though materials and building practice are in many ways the same as in the modern village around the dig, the basic planning is on a very different level. While the nicest thing found at Pactolus North remains the "Geometric seascape" showing part of a man of war going through a sea full of dolphins, of ca. 650 B.C. *(Figure 126)*, a great contribution to history comes from the fact that now we have found houses which were left as destroyed by king Antiochus III in the great siege of 213 B.C. For the first time we are getting an exact idea of how Sardians lived during the crucial transition from their traditional Lydian to the new Greek-Hellenistic culture. And our numismatist Jack Kroll was very pleased: the wholesale destruction and leveling which Antiochus inflicted on the Sardians for helping his opponent often makes it possible to give more exact dates to coins which could hitherto only be pegged down by guesswork.

In the final "beauty contest" of the season, first and second prizes were won by Dave Mitten, the first for the archaic lion *(Figure 127)*, which had

Figure 132—Early Byzantine Ionic corner capital of finest quality found split and lying upside down in the southeastern corner of the palaestra colonnade just outside the Synagogue. Replacing Roman capitals was part of the Byzantine remodeling program in the Gymnasium.

to be chiseled out of the cement of the Synagogue pier. It is small (about two feet in length) but gratifyingly complete, of cheerful disposition and, as archaic marble structures go, quite early, about 600 B.C. A German television crew who visited immediately fastened upon it but I thought we had better reserve this item. We did let them take pictures of our Cybele monument *(Figures 99, 100)* and our famous terracotta relief of a Lydian of the time of Croesus (Plate II).

Second prize went to the dramatic, chiaroscuro patterned Early Byzantine capitals from the colonnade which adjoined the north wall of the Synagogue *(Figure 132)*. Here Dave had also found a Roman capital with what must have been a very delicate female head, unfortunately much worn. But to come back to the Byzantine capitals, when our colleague Hans Buchwald of the Harvard School of Design was here he waxed eloquent about their beauty and possible Constantinopolitan origin. All three of them and the above mentioned Roman capital have been now installed in the camp.

The visit of Hans Buchwald and Clive Foss, both Byzantinists, was great fun. We were made to realize that our Byzantine monuments are something worthy of attention and even admiration. And Buchwald made a number of valuable observations on our Church E as well as on the large, unexcavated Church D. Clive Foss on his part compiled a very valuable report on our early Byzantine coins from which we were able for the first time to deduce the time at which the main avenue was renewed by the Byzantines (around the middle of the seventh century).

The departing American Ambassador, now Assistant Secretary of State for Near Eastern and South Asian Affairs, Raymond Hare, also paid us a visit, together with our Consul General at Izmir, G. Lewis Schmidt, and Mr. Kahn of the American embassy.

Upon Greenie's urging we had postponed the closing of Bin Tepe from August 7 to August 14 to August 23. We did not find the chamber but the

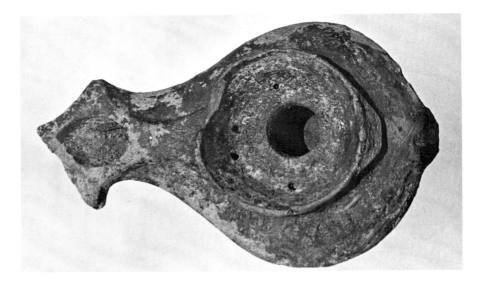

Figure 133—Roman gray-ware lamp of the first century B.C. with molded inscription (lower rim) PHOS AGATHON, "Good Light." Found in a pit dug in the Main Hall of the Synagogue. It was probably used in a building destroyed by earthquake in A.D. 17.

battle is not over yet. Everyone who enters the labyrinth of tunnels or wanders along this incredible concealed Lydian wall falls under the spell. Julian Whittlesey has already proposed the radical idea of digging away the inner mound and putting it back again—and being accustomed to large urban plans, even tried to figure out how it might be done. This will be the subject of much hard thinking over the winter. We have, in any case, to investigate and describe the cemetery as a whole, combining this, we hope, with a survey of possible Prehistoric settlements.

Only those of our Supporters who have been out to Sardis quite realize the magnitude and scope of our work. We hope more might come and more might join the ranks to help us meet what has become essentially a national obligation and a leading intercultural program.

I should like to think that our work at Sardis may be worthy to be described in the words of a find made by Dave Mitten, a lamp *(Figure 133)* on which there is written: PHOS AGATHON—"The Good Light."

1966

Sardis   July 10, 1966

The Ninth Symphony of Sardis began with an almost humdrum state-ment punctuated by slight dissonances, broke into a dramatic roll of drums, and finally unfolded its major themes.

We had met Ken Frazer and Kemal Bey in Izmir and made an unspec-tacular entry into the camp. The discordant tones were provided by the news that our consumable supplies would under a new procedure not be released for some time—they are, in fact, after a month still in customs.

The drama was provided by the change of the commissioner. On June 20, the day we started to dig, a sturdy youngish man walked in on us as we were at dinner. With his unfailing sense of drama, Kemal Bey, who had been our commissioner since 1958, arose and proclaimed: "Ladies and gentlemen, your new commissioner!" And so he was—Musa Baran (seen in *Figure 166*), formerly director of the Ephesus Museum and now assistant director of the Izmir Museum, a good friend since 1953.

To those who have been to Sardis, Kemal Bey has become a very definite image. He has worked with enormous energy and ambition to make the Sardis expedition the biggest and the best. Indeed, if he had not assumed the duties of commissioner for the period before June 20, we should never have been able to start on time this year. Our ties remain close. Kemal Bey has retained his room and is paying us frequent visits.

Our new commissioner is an archaeologist of considerable experience and has guided for several years the restoration of St. John's Basilica in Ephesus. He writes poetry and loves nature. He even moved his bed under

179

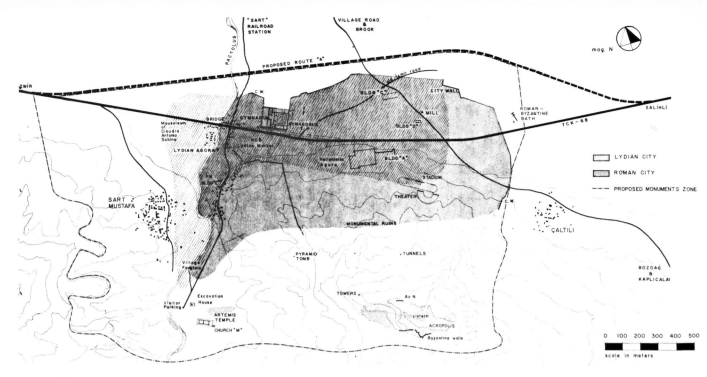

a fig tree to enjoy the outdoors at night. Whether because of increase in our wisdom or from other causes a little owl—the same as on Athenian coins—has been haunting our precincts. That night we heard it hooting vigorously. "I bet he is sitting on the fig tree over Musa," said I to Mrs. Hanfmann. I was wrong: he had sat down on Musa's knee. Our commissioner awoke to find two unblinking eyes staring at him.

As to the two major themes, the devotion of old faithfuls and new—Gus Swift, Tom Kraabel, Andy Ramage, and Larry Majewski—enabled us to start as scheduled on the digs and the work at the Synagogue; and Mehmet Ergene was at hand for the start of the Marble Court restoration.

The early laurels went to Larry Majewski whose dispatch and efficiency in cleaning and plotting the huge and much disrupted mosaic floor of the Main Hall of the Synagogue paid immediate dividends: two new inscriptions appeared on the main axis, both in key positions, one in front of the marble table before the apse, the other where we thought we had found evidence for a temporary "baldacchino" or tabernacle structure. The first is much damaged. The second is of great interest, for the donor is described as "priest and teacher of wisdom" (hiereus kai sophodidaskalos)—the latter may be a translation of "rabbi."

Tom Kraabel, R. E. Pfeiffer Fellow of the Harvard Divinity School, has shown immediate aptitude for methods and procedures of archaeology. He and a crew of some thirty men are freeing those enigmatic and tantalizing rooms which are located between the apse of the Synagogue and the main building of the Gymnasium (A, B, C in plan, *Figure 223*). A painted inscription discovered in 1964 had made it certain that they—or at least the room nearest the Gymnasium—did belong to the Synagogue. After the arduous task of earth and rubble removal, Tom has been hitting paydirt on the mosaic floors, but I shall reserve that complicated story to the next installment.

The "North Hall," a flanking unit of the Marble Court, is also down to

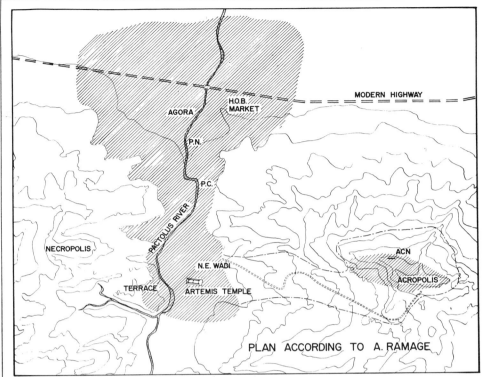

PLAN ACCORDING TO A. RAMAGE

Figure 134—A: Hypothetical plan of the ancient city. Conjectural extent of Lydian and Roman Sardis by M. T. Ergene in consultation with G. M. A. Hanfmann, R. Hammann, and A. Hyatt. Prepared with speed in support of a petition to divert the expanded highway, the tentative plan of the ancient city shows the proposed Route "A" which would by-pass the ruins area. B: There is still disagreement about the plan of the Lydian city, as is seen in the two alternative hypotheses.

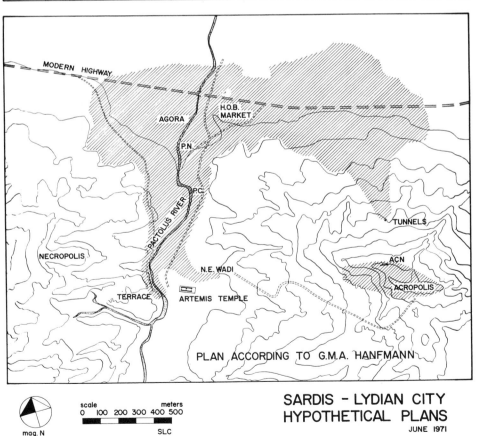

PLAN ACCORDING TO G.M.A. HANFMANN

SARDIS - LYDIAN CITY
HYPOTHETICAL PLANS
JUNE 1971

scale
0   100 200 300 400 500
meters
mag. N   SLC

floor level. We had to excavate it to permit the restoration of the Marble Court to proceed; its southern wall is also the northern wall of the Marble Court and must be investigated for structural safety prior to restoration. A melancholy tale unfolds here, for it was a major lime burning area, full of thousands of fragments of broken marbles. Four fragmentary pieces of sculpture are our consolation prizes: among them a delicate torso of a satyr and a late antique Imperial portrait. Parts of the intricate pattern of the marble floor also survive.

The Marble Court itself looks impressive with its back wall agreeably colorful: white stone jambs, red arches, gray stone wall. It was built up from September to late December by the Turkish Building Commission appointed to administer the Turkish government grant to the project and is being raised even higher at present. The third column of the monumental gate is going up. Meantime Fikret Yeğül has begun to wrestle with various problems of the design; and an important task is being performed by Nancy Hirschland, who is measuring and drawing the head capitals which we believe went on the "screen colonnade" at the eastern side of the court. Marble chips fly as master carvers execute a substitute capital, while masons have begun to put together smaller columns which went into the pavilions around the court.

Meantime Julian Whittlesey's "instrument which walks like a man" lends its silvery elegance to the busy scene, as fallen vaults and other remarkable parts of architectural and archaeological scenes are being recorded (*Figure 129*).

Rick Hammann and Alf Hyatt have launched with vigor one of our most important projects, an attempt to bring together what evidence we have dug up or observed for the urban plan of Sardis. The matter brooks no delay, for a great cloud has risen on our horizon. The new superhighway from Izmir to Ankara, known as "NATO Road," was supposed to swing around us; but upon arrival we learned that it is now to go right through the site,

Figure 135 (left)—One of the six mounds illicitly opened in spring 1966 at Duman Tepe, "Foggy Ridge," a limestone ridge about three quarters of a mile northeast of Alyattes Mound in the Bin Tepe Cemetery. The tumulus (BT 66.1) was of Lydian construction with a long entrance corridor and two chambers. (Poles of our shelter are thin trees, not antennae.)

Figure 136 (right)—Skeletal remains of 150 persons of Early Byzantine times were found buried in the chambers and corridor (shown here) of BT 66.1. Stacked in layers, they were disturbed by illicit diggers. Causes of their deaths and their burial in a Lydian chamber tomb are mysteries yet to be completely solved.

very possibly swallowing considerable parts of areas dug along the ancient main avenue. It is also absolutely certain that land prices will skyrocket making any expansion of excavations impossible not only for us but for future expeditions. Both the Turkish educational authorities and we have started writing petitions. The road is to open on August 19, but this particular stretch uses so far the present Salihli highway, not as yet widened. It may yet be possible to revert to the former plan (see *Figure 134A*).

In the Lydian House of Bronzes area, Gus Swift's great objective this year is to obtain the largest possible exposure of the earliest levels. A machine designed for this purpose is at present going through the usual birth pangs but in the meantime the place continues to furnish wonderful examples of Greek and Lydian pottery.

The vast mound of Gyges has become once again a scene of humming activity. The first visit with our mining consultant on June 19 was somewhat disheartening. The ventilator motor could not deliver enough air into the tunnels. The exceptionally wet winter had rotted much of the shoring. And there were some wrinkles about getting the miners to lead the work. All this has been fixed up, and Greenie is burrowing in the northeast central section (LCSE on plan, *Figure 109*).

Our first visit to Bin Tepe also started a new venture. One of our land-owning friends appeared out of nowhere in his green jeep and told us that several graves had been opened in the eastern area of the cemetery, near the Alyattes mound. He and other informants told of people appearing during the worst rainy season, in jeep and on foot, and digging at night. It is said that one of the graves yielded two golden earrings, four white stone alabastra, and a bronze vessel which were subsequently sold to an Izmir antiquities dealer whom many consider the guiding spirit in the enormous outburst of illicit digging in western Turkey.

We immediately appealed to the local District Commissioner (*kaymakam*) and late next afternoon the gendarmerie made a spectacular entry into our

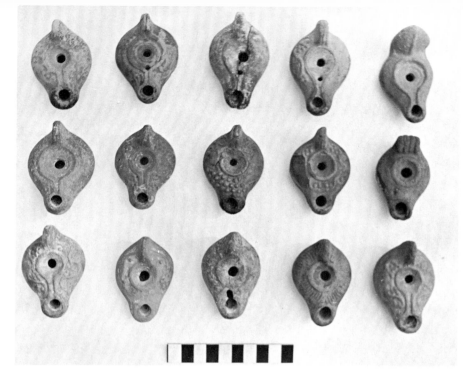

Figure 137—These lamps, found with the skeletons in BT 66.1, date the burials from Late Roman to Early Byzantine times. The newness of the lamps suggest they were lighted only during the burial rites and then placed near the bodies.

Bin Tepe camp, guns at ready—riding a tractor. The tractor was borrowed; our local law enforcement group is normally not motorized. We found the opened graves (Map 2, *Figure 135*) right enough, at least seven. This is a unique chance to study a portion of the cemetery as a unit. For several days a small detachment of workmen supervised alternately by Metin Kunt and myself have been at work starting to clear an imposing grave complex some fifty feet long. It is a beautifully built unit with a long entrance corridor *(Figure 136)*, a long chamber, and a square chamber at the end. All were left in considerable chaos by our illicit brethren.

This is perhaps as good a time as any to describe the situation, which is, indeed, hard to understand. Briefly, being outside the law, and inside the right—the wet—season, the illicit diggers hold all the trump cards. They go around with long heavy irons which pierce the ground and test for either hollows or big hefty stones. Their record at Duman Tepe—the ridge and twin mounds they tackled in February and March—was remarkable: six hits and two errors. The romantic and sinister image of invaders from nowhere digging in the dark of the night was discredited by the amount of work done, the apparent knowledge of local conditions, and the statement of one of the landowners that seventy or eighty people were working at one time.

The law requires report of any antiquities found within a week, but unless a person is caught while digging, nothing happens. And nobody feels like interfering. The landowners merely shrug their shoulders and say, "Why should I want a hole in my head?" The gendarmerie says they would never get there in time on foot over a distance of fifteen miles through the mud. It is obvious that local people must be involved. However, when asked they always speak of a mysterious shepherd, who had appeared, dug, and disappeared.

It is different when it comes to legal digging. We must go to officials, get official messages to village mayors and guards, and promise to indemnify

Figure 138—Early Byzantine bronze finger ring with representation of angel and cross supports the dating of the BT 66.1 burials at sixth to seventh century and indicates that the dead were Christians.

the owners should their crops suffer any damage. There is one cold comfort in all this. Every known investigation since 1850 has indicated that all Bin Tepe tombs have been opened, entered, and reentered time and again, from possibly as early as Hellenistic through quite modern times. The find mentioned above is what ancient and medieval graverobbers left or overlooked. On the other hand, our purpose is to secure knowledge about this unique and grandiose cemetery as a whole, about its development, about the religious and social aspects involved; and even this evidence is being destroyed both by illicit digging and agricultural activities.

Sardis   July 30, 1966

Fate has waited for Joel Savishinsky of Cornell to arrive at Sardis. She then unleashed a Dance of Death, the likes of which no previous physical anthropologist had encountered. It started slowly, with a solitary murderee; then the skeletons gathered around as at least ten individuals were found buried in a little stone enclosure, swept together in common burial in the wake of the dreadful Cimmerian destruction of the seventh century B.C. An eloquent postcript was the skeleton of a child buried under collapsing ruins and burned; the floor around was still strewn with charred wooden rafters and burned thatch from the room (*Figure 139*).

But the real shocker came with the discovery of a "charnel house" at Bin Tepe. In the Lydian chamber tomb of "Foggy Ridge" (Duman Tepe), now prosaically known as BT 66.1 (*Figure 135*), the entrance corridor, a long chamber, and apparently also a second square chamber, had been filled with layer upon layer of buried people. So far over sixty boxes of skeletal material have been dug up. Joel estimates that so far sixty to seventy individuals may be represented.

Figure 139 (left)—Examination of the burned clay floors in the Lydian Market, House of Bronzes area turned up in a seventh century B.C. stratum the partially burned skeleton of a little girl, probably a victim of the Cimmerian raid on Sardis. Ashes are from burned thatch roof.

Figure 140 (middle)—A primitive seal with goat incised in linear style on a green schist pebble was found in a twelfth to eleventh century B.C. context in the Lydian Market, House of Bronzes area. A rare example of animal figure style from the "Dark Ages" after the fall of Troy.

Figure 141 (right)—Early strata in the Lydian Market contained both imported and local imitations of Late Mycenaean (Late Bronze Age) and Protogeometric (Early Iron Age) pottery of Greece, such as the cup shown. The finds point to an early beginning of Greek influence on Lydian cultural traditions of the Iron Age.

Unfortunately for anthropologists and skeletons, but perhaps fortunately for our schedule, the recent (February 1966) graverobbers dug with vigor through all of these burials, mixing up the skeletons. Joel has spent several days underground excavating; by luck, a couple of skulls had escaped being smashed completely (*Figure 136*), and enough was left of vertebrae and long bones in some instances to show that the burials had originally been made head east, feet west. Burning lamps had been set around the dead, apparently at each burial. The illicit grave diggers supposedly found 300; our follow-up yielded about 30, some still in position (*Figure 137*).

Mystery envelops this gruesome accumulation. At first I had thought of die-hard pagans of late antiquity, secretly burying their dead in an out of the way cemetery of their remote Lydian ancestors, but a bronze ring revealed, upon cleaning, an early Byzantine representation of an angel carrying a cross (*Figure 138*). So there were Christians among the buried people. The lamps would permit a range from the third to the sixth century, our era. Eventually a close analysis of the lamps and skeletons may decide among the various possibilities: Mass burial after a plague? A family mausoleum used for several generations because of a real or fancied claim to descent from the Lydians, who had originally built the grave in the sixth or fifth century B.C.? One recalls, too, the existence of charnel houses in monasteries of Italy and Austria. So far Joel has found no clear traces of violent death, so the people do not seem to have been victims of a massacre.

The digging of this underground apartment, done chiefly by Metin Kunt, has to proceed slowly. We are now through the ten meters, seven of them roofed, of the underground corridor, and through the first, six-meter-long chamber. Still to come is the freeing of the second chamber, a picture of dire havoc, filled with stones from broken couches and floor which the recent graverobbers have piled up.

Progress has been faster on two beautifully constructed Lydian chamber

tombs on the same ridge. We are after the general plan and architecture of the cemetery, but even to plot and survey the locations of the graves is a hot and weary task. Rick Hammann, Alf Hyatt, and Necati Güler had to trudge miles to reerect the survey marker on the huge mound of Alyattes. It was uprooted and destroyed by local treasure hunters undoubtedly on the theory that an American marker must indicate if not the treasure itself, then at least some sort of hint of how to find a treasure. The distances are fantastic. Our supply truck has to make a circuit of forty miles each day, with stops at the Gyges mound tunneling show and dig at Duman Tepe.

It has been a great walking season for Rick and Alf. Fulfilling a long-cherished objective of the expedition program, they are making great strides in their attempt to record and analyze all buildings and traces of buildings which might be combined to yield an intelligible interpretation of the development of the city plan of Sardis. Already fascinating possibilities have begun to emerge: the irregular plan of Lydian-Persian Sardis, and the existence of not one but possibly as many as three regularized city plans for the Hellenistic, Roman, and Early Byzantine eras. A vast part of the groundwork of precise surveying and calculation remains to be done, not to mention the supplementary trenching and sounding needed for clarification of vital points. But it was well that Rick and Alf got off to a quick start, for suddenly their work received a very immediate practical application. I mentioned in my last letter the fight to remove the superhighway from Sardis. The Ministry of Tourism sent a request to deliver posthaste not only a plan of excavations, but a plan of all of ancient Sardis. With wonderful dispatch Alf and Rick whipped up a synthesis which is based on the best possible guesses *(Figure 134A)*. Along with some dramatic photographs by Charlie Lyman showing buses bouncing on the highway right above the ancient main avenue, this plan must by now be favorite reading in several ministerial bureaus.

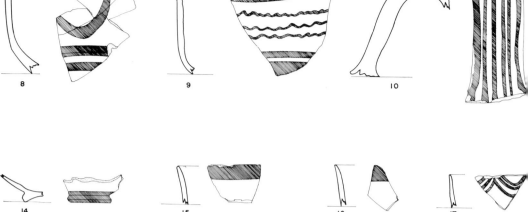

Figure 142—Profiles of mixing bowls and cups range from the thirteenth (number 8) to the ninth century B.C. (numbers 12, 19). Modeled on pottery of Bronze Age Greece, these fragments confirm the tradition that Sardis was conquered by a Greek dynasty in 1185 B.C.

This last-ditch stand is being made in the face of the announced official opening of the highway (not yet completely expanded) on August 19. In the meantime, vehicular traffic has sprung up everywhere, and the land speculation on "superhighway" prices is becoming a threat. This is a critical matter for the Synagogue, for we absolutely must secure land over its northeast corner and immediately adjacent to it.

The progress of excavation and study in and around the Synagogue has been gratifying. I promised in the last letter to tell something of the extremely important area between the western apse of the Synagogue and the great central building of the Gymnasium. Three large rooms are involved (A, B, C on plan, *Figure 223*). The one that produced the painted inscription "Blessed Be the People" in 1964 has now been completely excavated by Tom Kraabel. It appears that it was originally used by the Romans for a different purpose. A Roman silver ring with an eagle found in a second room enhances the suggestion that in the second and third century this area was an appendage of the Gymnasium. It was apparently at the height of their prosperity that the Jewish community obtained the use of this area, thus producing the most extraordinary example of penetration of a Roman Gymnasium by a Synagogue.

In Room A a beautiful mosaic was laid, and the walls painted; the inscription "Blessed Be the People" was part of this painted decoration. Later on, perhaps still in the fifth century, the room was taken away from the Synagogue and came upon evil days. A few skimpy brick walls built over the mosaic and an anvil suggest that it served as a blacksmith's shop. A crude pit in the corner was full of charcoal and animal bones, including those of pigs—evidently the blacksmith's kitchen corner.

Tom carried on other investigations and some of them paid off—in cash. A hoard of Byzantine coins was found when the entrance porch of the Synagogue was cleaned; and a gold coin of Justin II (A.D. 565–578) bright-

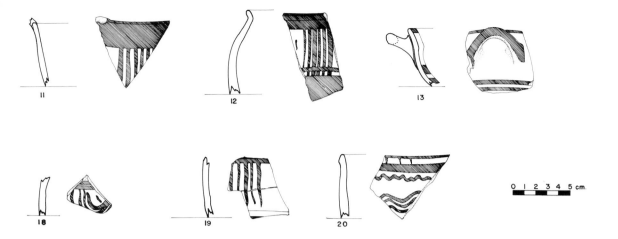

ened the day for the visit of John Coolidge, Director of the Fogg Museum.

Digging has gone on around the Marble Court to solve various architectural problems. The best sculptural find of the season was a spectacular by-product—a column capital fragment with a powerful head of Dionysus (*Figure 148*); the massive profile evokes both the portraits of Alexander the Great and those of Caracalla. It may have been intended as a mythological portrait.

Individual problems of construction and design of the great Marble Court restoration project continue to be hammered out at evening conferences and afternoon seminars. It was a great pleasure to have as "visiting critic" John Coolidge, who immediately made stimulating and provocative suggestions.

Mehmet Önder, former Director General of Antiquities and now Assistant Secretary for Fine Arts, Monuments, and Libraries, paid us a surprise visit just as a seminar on the Byzantine Church E was in progress. Mubin Beken, Director of the Research Section, Ministry of Tourism, came to look at our restoration work with R. Mensioli of the Istituto di Ristauro, Florence. They were at work on a report for UNESCO; a program directed by Piero Sampaolesi of Florence is to begin a program of restoration of several important monuments in Turkey. Carl Nylander of Upsala, fresh from his studies of masonry in Iran, delighted us by stating that the masonry of the so-called Pyramid Tomb at Sardis (*Figures 192, 193*) and of some Bin Tepe graves does have close parallels in king Cyrus' famous structures at Pasargadae.

Sardis   September 1966

Suddenly a red patch spread against the fresh green of the distant trees as the Turkish flag went up. "They are coming!" Like a rubber ball Kemal Bey,

Figure 143—Larger than life-size, this portrait head, perhaps of an emperor of the sixth century, our era, escaped the lime-burning operation set up in Room C behind the Synagogue (Figure 223). His pouting expression won him the nickname "Sourpuss."

our former commissioner, bounced in huge jumps down the dusty road from the excavations to the highway. Two black limousines slid to a stop just past the road; the third turned in. A man in a grey suit climbed out. The President of the Republic of Turkey had arrived at Sardis.

We had had short warning. Two days before an oral message had come from the governor's office in Manisa, but details did not become clear until that very morning. President Cevdet Sunay would proceed from Izmir to Ankara. He had expressed the wish to see the excavations and restoration work at Sardis. The "whistle-stop" would be short, five to ten minutes.

Our hope was to get the President right into the center of things, in front of the Marble Court, but he made for a chair in the shade of a little shelter where the stone mason cuts our stones, at the edge of the Synagogue. I shot my ammunition: a folder with photographs of the 1966 campaign, prepared but an hour before by Charlie Lyman, and two great maps of the site, one showing the alternate course for the highway desired by us *(Figure 134A)*. While Kemal Bey, present as ranking representative of the Department of Antiquities, launched into an eloquent tirade on the subject, I was frantically signaling the Marble Court crew. Finally Fikret Yeğül managed to push his way through the crowd which had formed around us with the drawings of the restoration *(Figure 150)*. Meanwhile, Charlie, who was caught way off base, having stationed himself on the wall of the Marble Court, joined the inner circle and was grinding away happily with his camera at five paces. Metin Kunt, archaeologist and personnel manager, Mehmet Bolgil, Harvard-trained architect and a Sardis "graduate" of 1960, our present commissioner Musa Bey, and the handsome English-speaking Governor of Manisa were, by virtue of being near the scene, the only people who became active participants in the audience. Our plans for welcome speeches and ceremonial introductions had miscarried, but we did fit our cherished subjects into the conversation. The President asked questions about the Marble Court, the

190

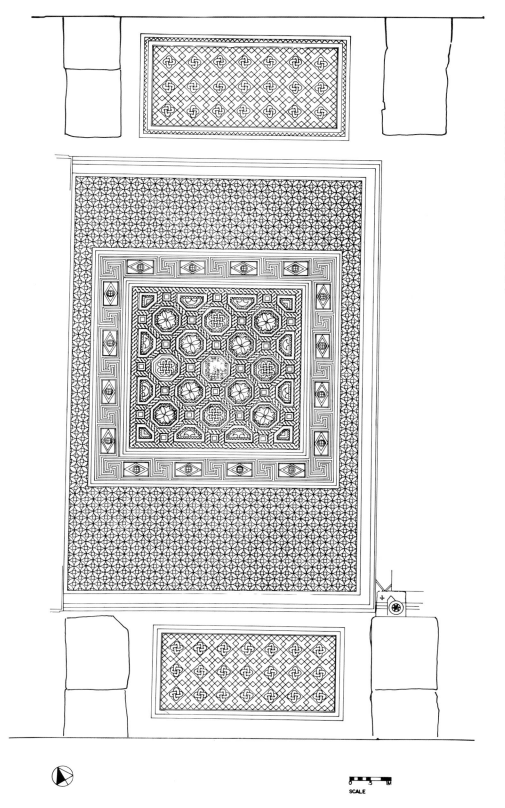

Figure 144—L. J. Majewski's drawing, based on fragments carefully preserved, reveals the magnificence and intricacy of design of the Synagogue mosaic "carpeting." The inscription, reconstructed and translated by Louis Robert, says that "Aurelios Alexandros, also called Anatolios, citizen of Sardis, Councillor, mosaicked the third bay." Synagogue decoration was pledged by donors, whose dedications preserve their names and professions and instruct us in the ancient architectural vocabulary. "Bays" were counted from west to east.

SCALE

Figure 145—L. J. Majewski, chief conservator at Sardis, works inside a *çardak* (shelter) sorting capitals from the Synagogue. Capitals and bases for seventy pilasters were recovered; eight were restored along the walls.

Synagogue, and the finds, and said he would look into the matter of the highway. In parting he wrote in our guest book: "I appreciate what you are doing for this good cause."

This was August 23. I had started this letter on August 12, the day when the House of Bronzes deep pit (down to thirty-six feet) had produced what for many archaeologists and historians will be the most exciting find of the season. For years scholars have looked for a place in western Anatolia where the transition from Bronze to Iron Age might be clearly seen, and where evidence might relate this change to the great upheaval in Greece which brought with it the downfall of the Mycenaean kingdoms. Fighting a stout battle against time and breakdowns of the earth-lifting machine, Gus Swift and Andy Ramage came upon stone walls, storage jars, and the like; but with them, broken but reasonably complete, was a very early Protogeometric Greek painted vase *(Figure 141)*. The next deeper level came up with fragments of a crater, so-called Sub-Mycenaean, or very late Mycenaean, again imported from Greece *(Figure 142)*. The skeleton of a donkey lay next to them.

To translate archaeological lingo into history: just after the time of the Trojan war, when Mycenae and the other great feudal strongholds of Bronze Age Greece were going up in flames, the Greeks were in close contact with Sardis. Greek legends reflect the restless period of migrations and wanderings, and Herodotus says that a dynasty of the "Sons of Herakles" ruled in Sardis for twenty-two generations, or 505 years (before king Gyges, ca. 680–645 B.C.), hence from the twelfth century on. There are few periods of history darker or more beset with riddles than the "Dark Ages" between the Bronze and the Iron Age in the Eastern Mediterranean *(Figure 140)*. The picture of a capital of an inland country where Greeks may have seized the rule during that period is an exciting discovery.

We had a premonition of such things from a deep sounding in 1960, but

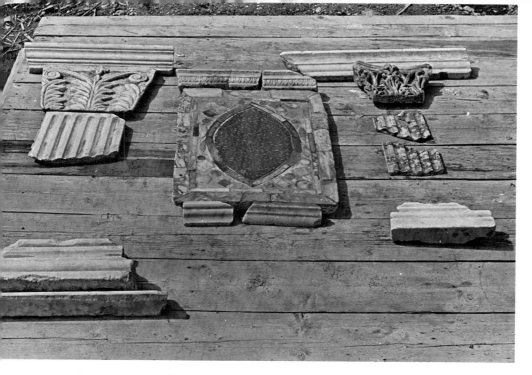

the area exposed was very small, and the handful of sherds conclusive only to those who had faith. This time there is a quantity of Sub-Mycenaean, and especially Protogeometric sherds; and the area and the division into an earlier and a later level are clear.

Three years of tunneling in the mound of Karniyarik Tepe ended on August 9, with the mound of king Gyges still defiant and its secret unresolved. After a conference with the consultant mining engineer, the inner tunnels we had dug in the central area were blocked up; but that amazing base wall of a mound hidden within the giant outer mound remains accessible (*Figures 111, 112*). (Don't rush out to Bin Tepe by yourself. First of all, you will get lost; second, Kemal Bey has the key to the tunnel door.) A late flare-up lit Greenie's last lunge. In 1965 he had tunneled along the crepis wall to a point where it seemed to break off for good in what appeared to be a natural gulch. Crossing it in a complicated tunneling feat, Greenie discovered a roughly hewn rock face going uphill—then, on the last day of this season, the monumental wall reappeared in full splendor (*Figure 109* at r). It thus continues northward. We have tunneled along some 330 feet of this base wall. As usual, the latest stop looks the most promising—could not the rock-filled crevice behind the wall be a device to hide an entrance to the chamber?

We have learned, to our sorrow, that you can miss by inches and never know it when tunneling. Greenie's heroic stand of three seasons of dangerous underground work deserved better luck. " 'Twas a good fight." The choice now is to concede defeat, install permanent tunneling (iron and cement) for the ingress tunnel and the tunnel along the wall (the present wooden shoring is rotting away), and let king Gugu sleep; or dig the mound from above, find all chambers, and put the mound back again.

Everybody says "do it by machine." On a recent trip to Ankara I asked, and the Tumpane Company kindly agreed to make a very tentative estimate.

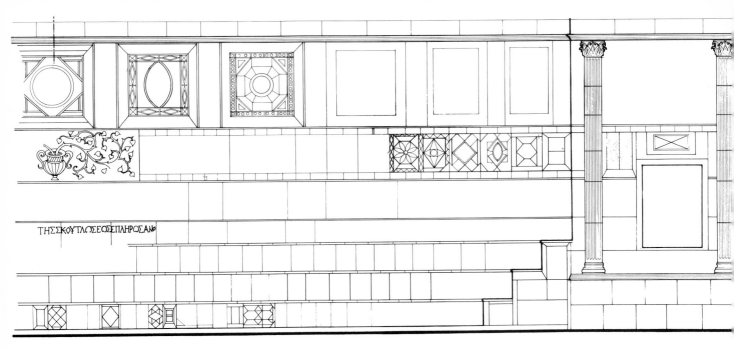

ΤΗΣΣΚΟΥΤΛΩΣΕΩΣΣΕΠΛΗΡΩΣΑΝ

It runs to $1164 per day for the machines and the men to operate and service them.

Our gentle commissioner at Bin Tepe, Muharrem Tağtekin, has built up quite a following among local folk; thus it was that a farmer brought him a pot found in his (Mustafa Seze's) field. It is the first Prehistoric pot known to us from the region of the Gygean Lake, the lake which provides the wonderful background for the cemetery of Bin Tepe.

Pursuing this lead, Muharrem Bey and Recep Meriç, assistant conservator and archaeologist, ambled along the lake shore west of the hamlet of Teke-liköy, and came back with exciting tales of sherds collected and stones observed. On August 18 Muharrem Bey excavated for just one day on a small sandy beach south of the great Western Royal Mound (we are not sure to whom it belongs). He found walls of two Lydian houses and more pottery than was found in the previous four seasons on Bin Tepe, as well as one of those fine white stone alabastra which, more than a century ago, Spiegelthal extracted from the mound of Alyattes. Here, perhaps, was the station where goods and materials were landed for the great royal and aristocratic burials. It was lucky for us that much water was taken out of the lake this summer, for the locals say that the beach is usually under water.

Although some Prehistoric sherds were found around the Lydian houses, the location of the Prehistoric settlement remained in doubt. It took a half hour to find it when I went out with Muharrem Bey on August 19. A low, water-gnawed limestone ridge, but a stone's throw from the Lydian houses, yielded so many Prehistoric sherds from an earthcut in its weathered lake front that the issue seemed settled then and there (Map 2). Two wild pear trees stand on this low (about ten feet high) hillock; as the place has no local name, Muharrem Bey promptly named it Ahlatli Tepecik, "the little hillock with the wild pear tree." It is an ideal location for a prehistoric settlement: ample fishing and fowling, enough earth on sloping fields above for

Figure 147 (left)—Tentative restoration of the Synagogue Apse wall decorations. Proper replacement of revetments was determined by impressions left in the plaster where panels had fallen off, revetment fragments found in situ, and by donors' inscriptions. The one shown states that a man and his son gave the *skoutlosis* decoration.

Figure 148 (right)—One of the capitals of the Marble Court entrance ("screen") colonnade (Figure 210), was adorned with this impressive head of Bacchus. His forerunner, the Lydian wine god Baki was born at Sardis. About A.D. 210.

primitive agriculture, and a brook nearby. The prehistory of Lydia is as yet very imperfectly known, so I should venture no more than to guess that the settlement existed in the time between 2500 and 1500 B.C.

Triumphant over this success, we returned to camp to learn that Tom Kraabel had just found in Room C behind the Synagogue apse an overlife-size late antique portrait head, obviously originally inserted into a statue *(Figure 143)*. The piece is "really wild," as our younger contemporaries would say. Rude but powerful, with that staring glance which we know from contemporary portraits from Ephesus and Aphrodisias, it may be one of the latest great marble portraits known, perhaps as late as the time of Justinian. It had been in or near a fire, and the marble had begun to decompose. Thus photographs cannot at present do it justice, but we hope to find a treatment which will permit further cleaning.

Throughout the season Andy Seager and his assistant Necati Güler patiently laid the groundwork on which future research on the Sardis Synagogue will be based—their re-survey of the building, their plans and elevations, and the catalog of all important architectural parts are fundamental contributions. With the arrival of Al Shapiro, architectural consultant, and Henry Detweiler, associate director, the Synagogue project began to shoot off fireworks. During a memorable two-day symposium Tom Kraabel gave an admirably clear and informed account of the synagogues of Asia Minor. Larry Majewski presented the results of his researches on the mosaic of the Main Hall, and suggested that the various parts of the mosaic may span quite a long period of time. He showed the magnificent drawings which he and his indefatigable schoolteacher-draftsman Hüseyin Özlü had prepared *(Figure 144)*. Larry's other great contribution, the reconstruction of the height and general character of the apse decoration, had found immediate application in the drawings of the interior presented by Andy Seager and Al Shapiro. And Larry, in turn, was able to include in his imposing

Figure 149 (left)—With the aid of a 40 foot tripod, an Ionic capital is reset on a 30 foot column of the West Gate of the Marble Court. The missing parts in concrete were later covered with tinted cement.

Figure 150 (right)—In 1966, architect F. Yeğül drew this tentative reconstruction of the west facade of the Marble Court (compare Figures 164, 165) with the West Gate only one story high.

reconstruction of the apse decoration the inscriptions restored by Jack Kroll, which apparently ran right above the three benches for the Elders (*Figures 145–147*).

The first bombshell was thrown by Jack Kroll. In a remarkably swift and penetrating study he proved that the marble plaques with the inscriptions of donors (who gave the rest of the marble revetments) belong to the third century; as they were found practically all around the hall, it follows that this huge space was built at that time.

Those who read our letters with care may have noticed I said as late as July 30 that the huge hall and the apse were built in the *fourth* century. There is more at stake than chronological quibbling. Last season we believed that this majestic and unusual composition was in some sense a reflection of the earliest Christian basilicas; but if it was built between 200 and 300, then the basilican hall of the Synagogue of Sardis becomes their forerunner, and the prime example of a Jewish basilica.

There is conflicting evidence, for some of the mosaics are shown by coins found underneath to have been laid in the fourth century. But Larry has also discovered the curious fact that the earliest mosaic donor's inscription —they were all in central panels of the seven bays into which the mosaic was divided—the newly discovered one of "Aurelius Alexandros also called Anatolios" (*Figure 144*), has to be read facing east, while most of the others were read facing west. This bears on a second important problem: was there one phase of the Synagogue when people faced east, and another when they faced west?

At the last spirited session of the Synagogue seminar, just prior to Al Shapiro's departure, Henry Detweiler threw his bombshell. Tom Kraabel's digging had revealed that two passages, later blocked up, led originally into the apse of the Main Hall. Henry pointed out that they emerged at a level which presupposed a platform, where there are now the benches for the

196

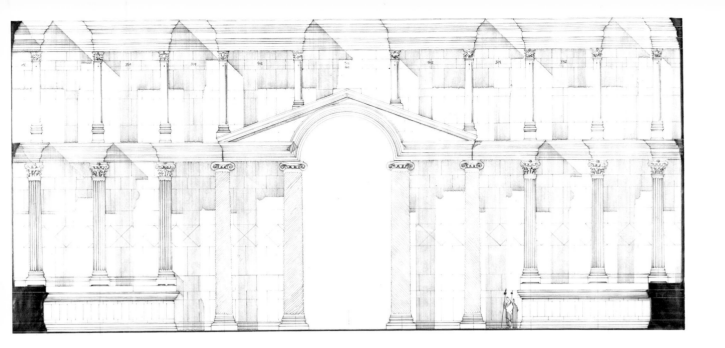

Elders *(Figure 216)*. He proposed that the apse originally contained a Roman tribunal, that the entire building was originally built by the Romans as a basilica for dispensing justice, and was then turned over to the Jewish community, which converted it into a Synagogue. This hypothesis meets many of the requirements of the evidence accumulated in 1966, but it is too early to hold any hypothesis as proved (see *Figure 201* for later theories).

Our first modest and tentative steps in restoration of the Synagogue are underway. It was finally decided to build up part of the northern wall of the Forecourt, to restore the platform of the southern of the two little shrines at the east end of the Main Hall, and to build up the wall behind it to about ten feet. All of these are preliminary steps to what was originally planned —the reerection of the eastern wall of the Main Hall with the two little shrines, a problem on which Andy Seager has done much study (see drawings, *Figure 168*). It is perhaps just as well that we have not yet been able to execute this plan, for it has become very obvious that we need a "resident" Turkish construction architect at the site, who would also do the purchasing of supplies, an immensely time-consuming matter hereabout. This position has been held by Tankut Akalin in the Marble Court Project, and his efficient work and journeyings in quest of materials have made a lot of difference.

Cars now stop, and people get out to look at the four columns of the Marble Court raising their spiraling shapes and delicately twined capitals against the towering grey-red wall *(Figures 149, 163)*. The centering for the big arch has gone up, the arch which formed the midpoint of the gorgeous pediment. We keep our fingers crossed that Tankut Akalin, who is staying until October 12, may be able to complete it. Then Kemal Bey and Ismail Kuralay, architect of the Manisa Department of Education, are taking over to carry on with the northern back wall of the court.

It looks big, acts big, and is big—in terms of men, materials, and effort

Figure 151—During road widening operations at a torrent-made gorge about 300 yards from the expedition camp, this fragment of a beautiful marble stele of the sixth or fifth century B.C. was found. It prompted a search for a Lydian cemetery. Similar stele from satrapal seat at Daskylion had reliefs with figures below the palmette lotus crown. Height 0.41 m.

—the Marble Court restoration (*Figure 149–150*). With Jim Yarnell's arrival on August 1 everything swung into high gear, and in addition to the regular splendid team of Mehmet Ergene (construction), Fikret Yeğül (design), and Tankut Akalin (construction and purchasing), we had the benefit of the energetic and enthusiastic help of Mehmet Bolgil, who came for two weeks to help—and also to help us find replacements, for next year we cannot count on the great quartet which has been carrying the show from 1964 until now. It is becoming only too clear what an intricate and unusual job this is, and how difficult it is to find people with the right qualifications and interest, and the needed time. It is perhaps the largest undertaking of this sort north of Baalbek, and will be a splendid memorial to our efforts when it gets done—but it will take some doing.

"Devil's Gorge," Şaitan Dere—that is what the villagers call a steep-walled creek which crosses the road 300 meters north of our camp (Map 2). And as the devil would have it, a bulldozer decided to go and push the earth around there. The reasoning behind this has never become clear to me, since the hillock is some twenty feet or more above the road which the bulldozer was preparing for *asfalto*, concrete surfacing. But the results were only too clear: we found two Lydian phallic markers, a beautiful finial of a Lydian stele (*Figure 151*)—not in place, but below the road where the bulldozer had pushed them—and some Roman objects.

The matter is of topographical significance, and as Rick Hammann and Alfred Hyatt have already started our long-cherished project of a reliable record of urban development of Sardis, I asked Alf to go out with Necati Güler and fix the position of the Şaitan Dere cemetery. This was quite the right scholarly procedure; but as the devil would want it, our reliable and stolid guard Ali Riza was along. He supposedly had observed the bulldozer operation, and insisted on showing us some limestone bits sticking out of the ground. With emphasis rare in him, he insisted that they were important.

Figure 152—The search at Şaitan Dere, "Devil's Gorge," revealed bathtub-shaped sarcophagus and lid, both of limestone. Skull fragments and intact Lydian vases were found inside. In background, expedition camp, and Tmolus Mountain.

Yesterday, archaeologist Meriç, shovelman Hyatt, and pickman Kunt (all staff members) discovered that it is a large Lydian sarcophagus. There was no choice. If we wanted to anticipate the local amateurs the thing had to be dug out (*Figure 152*). As I am typing, Meriç, our doorman, and Ali Riza are digging. Ten minutes ago they found a very fine Lydian lekythos in the sarcophagus. I finally fled, for there are papers to write and luggage to pack. But Sardis is certainly an unpredictable site.

This has been a great season, with thirty-five staff members and major projects in the Marble Court, the Synagogue, the House of Bronzes, Bin Tepe (actually two there, at the Big Mound and at Duman Tepe), and the urban plan program (which had the unusual distinction of being carried out in a taxi—it belongs to our chief mechanic, and thus serves at nominal rate). It has been a season in which, among the rare and wonderful sights, a grey balloon hovered over the digs for several days, another of Julian Whittlesey's irrepressible schemes to test photogrammetry. A helicopter was promised, but failed to materialize. Looking back to our arrival in June, I can hardly believe so much could have happened in so short a time.

Figure 153—Plan of Gymnasium and House of Bronzes area. Dotted lines through the Middle Terraces mark the colonnaded street found by G. F. Swift in 1964. (This road may have made a sharper turn toward the Southwest Gate.)

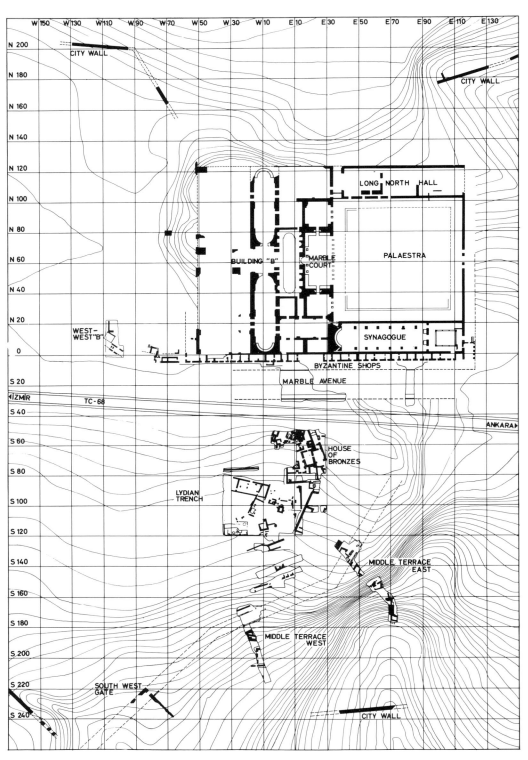

1967

Sardis   July 5, 1967

"They are finding the most beautiful little lion of bronze." The voice came whispering into my ear before I was aware of the speaker. Steve Crawford had sneaked his six-foot frame noiselessly up behind me as I was explaining the buzzing activities of the Marble Court to our most recent arrivals and colleagues, anthropologist Enver Bostanci and his assistant Fahrettin Savci, from the University of Ankara.

Steve had reason to jump up and down. The lion is a beautiful beast, about five inches long, mighty of mane, striding along with muscles playing— certainly the finest post-archaic bronze we have yet found *(Figure 154)*. And he had the good judgment to put in an appearance on Steve's birthday—a nicer present could not have happened to a nicer guy. (He got a birthday cake, too—I mean Steve.)

The lion was not the only present from the bounteous Byzantine Shops which Steve is digging *(Figure 155)*; bronze vessels and scales make pleasing adjuncts to the major aim: excavating all the shops lying along the southern wall of the Synagogue. You will recall that some of them belonged to Jewish owners such as Jacob, Presbyter of the Synagogue *(Figure 68)*, but a number of shops are still unexcavated and their ownership unknown (see *Figure 96*; *Figure 153* shows condition as of 1968).

To free the exterior of the Synagogue a second prong of excavation is advancing on the north wall. Here the wall of the Synagogue, overthrown by earthquake, was traced to as much as forty feet. Andy Seager is reconstructing its original shape from the new data, and working on the design of the doors to the Main Hall of the temple. (Compare *Figure 30*).

Figure 154—This expressive lion with a cockle shell in his mouth was a lamp of brassy bronze. Behind his neck is a hinged lid with a suspension ring. He was found in one of the Byzantine Shops. This elaborate piece may evidence a proficient local Byzantine metal industry in the fifth to sixth centuries.

A major effort of precise digging and cleaning is being devoted to the colonnaded Forecourt. Small pickmen under Recep Meriç have been uncovering two major phases in the history of this entrance area, and have just begun to reveal complex waterworks for a central fountain. Reused face downward in the marble pavement was a dedication, probably to the native Mood God (Mên Axioteinos).

Meanwhile the conservatorial wing of the Synagogue team, Dick Stone and Jim Greaves, have thrown themselves into the intricate jigsaw puzzle task of getting together the thousands of marble revetments, first into intelligible patterns, then into plausible overall designs for that once so glorious, gigantic interior. They have made remarkable strides. Their youthful assistants are assembling some very attractive decorative motifs. Slowly the building up of a specialized marble-workers' studio is getting under way.

The architectural battalion of the Synagogue is led by consultant Al Shapiro. With irrepressible good humor Al has been fighting the battle to organize a site office and supply storage, break stone masons of various undesirable habits, find the right foreman, and start the actual restoration work. At the moment he is proceeding with building the eastern (entrance) wall in the Main Hall of the Synagogue.

Equally vital was the battle of the vineyard—our neighbor's vineyard, that is. A government expropriation commission had ruled that a strip of the vineyard had been purchased by us on the government's behalf, but one of the three owners filed objection to the price. Meanwhile we needed it the worst way to make a road through the vineyard as access to the Synagogue working area. The neighbor stood (literally) his ground, and so fearful was his oratory that our head foreman and workmen were afraid of trespassing in any way. The situation resolved itself typically. We started digging along the boundary; the neighbor got tired of standing in the dust. Meantime, legal advice was secured. It turned out that the objection was not an injunction, but it was suggested that we damage as few vines as possible until the

Figure 155—Byzantine Shops, looking west along south wall of the Synagogue. These shops were excavated in 1967. Prior to numbering many were given descriptive names according to their contents, for example, the Shop of the Lion where bronze lion lamp in Figure 154 was found; others are Shop of the Brazier, of Finial, of the Frescoes, and of the Locks. Architect B. Percival is recording.

price was settled. Mehmet Ergene has laid out a short, rather elegantly S-curved road, and this is what we are using, while minding our vines and olive trees (the latter are being moved at our expense).

On his visit, the United States Consul General asked whether the Marble Court is the largest restoration project now going on in Turkey. It may well be. So great is its scope that I want to write sufficiently to explain the task, the progress, and the problems in the next newsletter. Two important linguistic finds came out of this restoration, owing to the ancient Sardians' incurable habit of reusing work of their predecessors. On May 12 Mehmet Bolgil, resident architect of the Marble Court, found built into the north wall the top of a Lydian grave stele with an inscription read for us by R. Gusmani: "This is the stele and inscription [of so and so—name lost]. Whoever [damages] this inscription to Artemis [shall pay a fine]," or words to that effect. On June 30 Mehmet Ergene appeared with a marble fragment, a new fragment from our most sensational find of 1963—the inscription in an unknown language which has become known to the linguistic world as the "Sardis Synagogue Inscription." The piece had been hiding in a heap of architectural marble fragments since 1964. It was apparently split off in antiquity, and its five letters in two lines say: *fed/et* (or *eş*). It does not seem to fit onto any line of the strange monument discovered built into a Synagogue pier in 1963 *(Figure 102)*, but it is unquestionably the same writing and the same unknown tongue, related to Lydian but not Lydian.

Guy Metraux has sailed into clearing areas in the northwest corner of the Gymnasium-Marble Court complex; this is of great importance for our knowledge of the complete plan of the complex; the counterpart of the Synagogue should lie here, and Al Shapiro and others want to know what *that* building may have been *(Figure 153)*. The architectural parts, too—columns, piers, capitals—are well preserved, and may help with the Marble Court reconstruction next door. Guy is also an asset in matters linguistic—

204

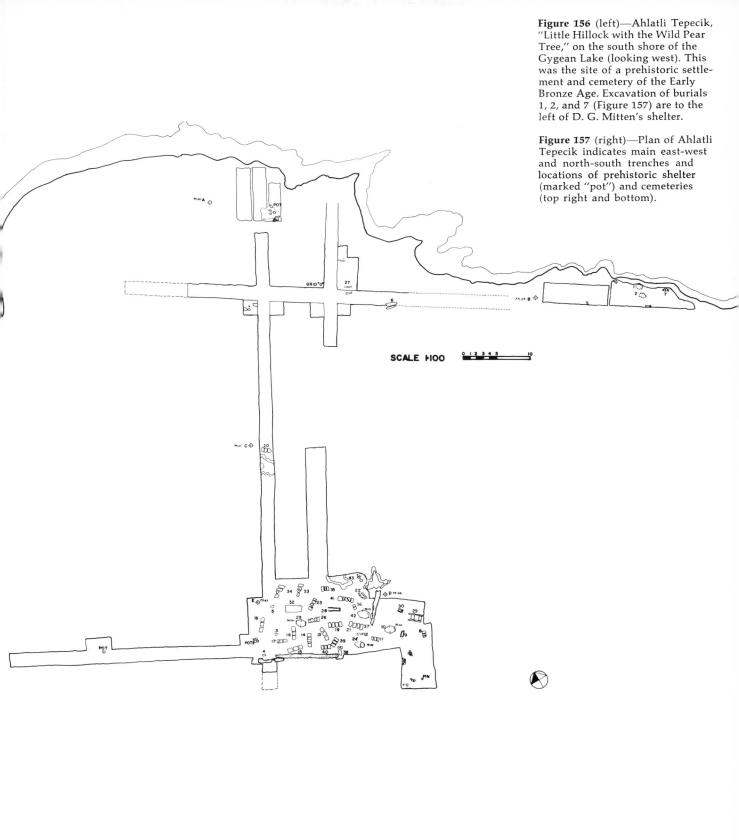

SCALE 1:100

Figure 156 (left)—Ahlatli Tepecik, "Little Hillock with the Wild Pear Tree," on the south shore of the Gygean Lake (looking west). This was the site of a prehistoric settlement and cemetery of the Early Bronze Age. Excavation of burials 1, 2, and 7 (Figure 157) are to the left of D. G. Mitten's shelter.

Figure 157 (right)—Plan of Ahlatli Tepecik indicates main east-west and north-south trenches and locations of prehistoric shelter (marked "pot") and cemeteries (top right and bottom).

Figure 158—Example of a cist grave, an Early Bronze Age inhumation (Ahlatli Tepecik 67.29; see plan, Figure 157) related to Mediterranean Cycladic culture. Here schist slabs enclose a space about two by three feet. The grave contained pottery and bones of an adult; it was roofed with slabs. Mid-third millennium.

guiding large French-speaking parties such as have recently appeared at our gates—and he is a musical addition to a staff already well endowed with voices. Our photographers, Royce Hoyle and Richard Petkun, the musical Cornellians Alf Hyatt and Brian Percival, and New York University's Dick Stone have all been raising voices in sweet harmony—especially on our Fourth of July celebration, which took place on July 3, since Tuesday is when people want to leave for their "free day" on Wednesday.

Andy Ramage has been happily deploying his labor forces on Pactolus North, moving toward his objective of clearing a city block of Lydian residential buildings in the central area of Sardis. He has been temporarily tripped by the appearance of unscheduled Roman mausolea. These redeemed themselves, however; they provided one skull and several skeletons just in time for Cornell's John Henderson to begin his career as physical anthropologist, and to benefit by the company of two physical anthropologists from Ankara. Professor Bostanci has been doing research on the ancient populations of Sardis since 1963, and has just published another report in the Turk Tarih Kurumu *Belleten*.* He and his assistant face the task of researching the material from the mass burial of 150 individuals found in the Duman Tepe-Bin Tepe charnel house last year.

Shortly after David Mitten arrived, we went on a rib-breaking jaunt (the road is washed out) to look for that promising Prehistoric site on the Gygean Lake which David is to tackle *(Figures 156, 157)*. Our first Commissioner Musa Baran gave an eloquent speech to the inhabitants of the hamlet of Tekelioğluköyü assembled in the social center, the coffee shack, and secured their good will. A venerable man in striped pajamas and skull cap, his high social status indicated by this attire and by the number of his silver teeth, is the owner of the ground and last year found there a Prehistoric pot.

*Morphological and Biometrical Examination of Some Skulls from the Sardis Expedition," *Belleten*, 31.121 (1967): 1–48.

Figure 159—Red ware jug, ca. 2500 B.C., decorated with three bosses was found intact in Ahlatli Tepecik grave 67.27. Such wares were handmade by many Early Bronze Age agriculturalists of Southwest Anatolia.

This was still June. The air was fresh. And to our great surprise, the Gygean Lake looked like the ocean, white caps whipping across and waves breaking on the limestone bluffs of Ahlatli Tepecik. The beach, where last summer we found the Lydian houses, had completely disappeared under water! We are still awaiting the second commissioner, who will come from Çanakkale; the local schoolteacher has been deputized to represent the Ministry of Education, and David was able to get going on July 1 as scheduled.

Supplying an operation twenty kilometers away takes careful timing and organization. Once food arrived hours late; another time a rain and hail storm mired the *dolmuş* currently rented for the operation. Workmen and David are staying at the camp near the big Gyges mound; the digging is about three miles away. So far no architectural remains have appeared, but numerous individual finds have, among them an unmistakable "Yortan Culture" (third millennium) spindle whorl, which gave David his greatest thrill.

We have had several visitors from Near Eastern archaeological enterprises disrupted by recent political and military events;* but I hasten to assure all parents, relatives, and friends that no untoward happening has marred our progress. The first wave of Sardian scholars, students, and scientists arrived as scheduled. New are the Synagogue's engineer and construction assistant Tolon Teker of Robert College and draftsman Hamdi Özkahraman from the Salihli school system. With the second commissioner, Dundar Tokgöz, and the architectural assistant for the Synagogue, Necati Güler of Middle East Technical University, we shall number thirty-two.

It was sitting in the bright light of the electric desk lamp. It was reading the xerox of a telegram from George E. Mylonas which Jane Scott had sent to me from the Fogg Museum. "It" was a big red scorpion. As Ilse shouted, "There is a scorpion on your desk," I smashed my desert boot into it—and

*The Six Days' War between Israel and neighboring Arab states, June 1967.

Figure 160—Several third millennium burials at Ahlatli Tepecik were made in gigantic jars (*pithoi*), three to five feet high, with vertical handles and lugs. The workmen painstakingly chip away accumulated earth to recover the contents without harm.

the lights went out (generator ran out of gas at this moment). Summer had come to Sardis.

Sardis   August 7, 1967

A Massey-Ferguson tractor, a battered truck, a Volkswagen, twenty excited dogs (one of them jumping up and down in the truck), the beating of Turkish drums and gunshot volleys into the air; all of this burst upon our sight and hearing in the bright freshness of a Sunday morning at 6:45. The people who belonged with this extraordinary display were "The Hunters' Union of Salihli." They had decided to celebrate the opening of the hunting season with a little ceremony at our public parking space. There was a brief, eloquent Moslem prayer; but they had picked a place within plain view of the temple of the hunting goddess Artemis, thus reviving a tradition three thousand years old.

A golden lamb or The Golden Calf? This thing is tiny but exquisite and to Andrew Ramage and his keen-sighted (and honest) shovel man goes the honor of finding "Lydian gold" for the first time since 1961, and of a kind we have not had before, an earring made of gold wire with this enchanting animal of thin gold sheet as an endpiece (Plate IV). Andrew has very justly written on the tag: "Catalogue, photograph, and shout!" Yesterday was a day for exquisite miniatures. In the Gymnasium colonnade next to the Synagogue, Steve Crawford found a lovely glass medallion or disk with a menorah.

The tiny and the huge. I cannot help reflecting on all the things archaeology takes in. Last summer it was decided that for restoration work we had to add to our lifting capacity. A machine was to be designed by Jim Yarnell and Mehmet Ergene. The design was sent to our engineer for the Marble

Figure 161—This burial jar (*pithos* A.T. 68.8) contained jugs for food and drink, a copper pin, and a stone pendant. Skeleton lay with head toward mouth of jar.

Court, Tankut Akalin, who came up with a counter proposal. After hectic telegram exchanges, Tankut was given the go-ahead to build the machine in Istanbul. It was supposed to be ready June 17, but as such things go, it was not. Then it had to be tensioned. Tankut went off to Istanbul and we heard nothing from him. We thought he was lost, but it turned out the machine was too big for the taste of Turkish highway inspectors and he was trying to get the proper permits to move it. Eventually it arrived—after having been fined as it went along. At the same time as the tiny earring and glass medallion were being found in the earth of our trenches, two fifty foot steel towers were being pulled upright. "Perils of Pauline" were nothing to the chills as Tankut and Mehmet Bolgil, architect of the Marble Court, wrestled with Archimedes' famous problem: to get enough power to raise two conjoined compression and tension steel towers into near vertical position. Finally it was "Citroën to the Rescue." That fabulous Citroën-Bennes Marel dumper-crane combination managed to pull the things up into the right position.

The Marble Court restoration towers, very literally, over the landscape (*Figure 165*). At present twenty-foot columns of the decorative pavilions are being lifted onto the benches. David DeLong had done a fine detailed study of the inscribed architrave parts that are to go on these column (*Figures 163–165*). Owing to the early start (Mehmet Bolgil began restoration late in April), the Turkish government grant will, for once, become available before we leave. Resident architect Mehmet Bolgil, Mehmet Ergene, Tankut Akalin, and their by now highly trained workmen strain all their efforts, but this is a big enterprise. Gluing, mending, truing, plumbing, and setting columns is hard enough. We have yet to tackle in earnest the mending, placing, and lifting of the large heavy architrave pieces which weigh up to three tons and have to go thirty to forty feet up in the air. Things get even harder when the lift is to fifty or sixty feet. We have design problems with

Figure 162 (left)—Gold, silver, and copper may have been worked at Sardis around 2500 B.C. Jar burial (EB 69.3) at Old Fishery site (see Map 2) contained golden "ear studs," silver ram as pendant, and a copper dagger, as well as pots. The dead man, perhaps a chieftain, was about 35 years old. Excavated in 1969.

Figure 163 (right)—The Marble Court 1967: At the West Gate spiraling columns and delicately carved entablature in rich Severan Baroque (ca. A.D. 200) style rise into the sky.

the second story of the gate (see *Figures 150, 164*) and the so-called screen colonnade which ran across the eastern side of the Marble Court. It will have to be built last but its dimensions have a vital relationship with dimensions of other parts of the Marble Court and so to some extent determine them.

There is now a marble saw and a marble grinder under a little shed next door to the "Shapiro Palas" (that, I learn from Jim Greaves, is now the official name of the construction office shed brought into being by Al Shapiro). To the credit of Richard Stone, our conservator who had to return to New York August 2, and Jim Greaves, his successor, the intricate parts of the gorgeous marble revetments of the Synagogue known as *skoutlosis* are being reproduced in modern marble. Dick's breakthrough was the discovery that the same pattern had been used in the hundreds of marble pieces from the revetments as in the floor mosaics. The hunt for colored marble, the training of apprentices, the quest for an experienced marble revetment worker—all entail prodigious exertions. Reconstruction of this *deluxe* feature, if only in sample panels, will challenge the generosity of benefactors of the Synagogue. Ten square feet of simple revetment paneling may range from $12 to $25; these are most beautiful, colorful patterns, each piece cut by hand.

August brought a procession of luminaries of Anatolian archaeology, among them Machteld J. Mellink of Bryn Mawr and the Karataş Expedition, friend and colleague since Tarsus, 1947. Machteld brought joy to the heart of David Mitten and John Henderson by enthusiastically endorsing as Early Bronze the great array of Prehistoric *pithoi* and other objects from the faraway lakefront enterprise at Bin Tepe (*Figures 156–162*). Despite initial disappointment, when trenches on the little hillock of Ahlatli Tepecik itself proved nearly barren, David, John, and the third (shaven) member of the Three Musketeers (David has a fine, black moustache and John a radiant,

210

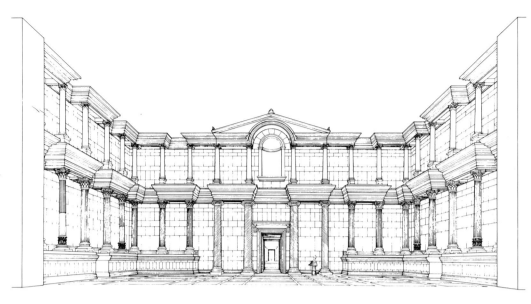

Figure 164 (left)—In the final design by D. DeLong for restoration of the Marble Court some architectural problems were solved by exchanging upper and lower entablatures and placing the arcuated pediment in the second story. For early design see Figure 150.

Figure 165 (right)—West Gate and wall and northwest corner of the Marble Court as restored in 1970. The acanthus base of first-story column on the right has been shifted compared with design in Figure 164 because parallels to this arrangement occur in other Roman buildings.

silky, red beard), Dundar Tokgöz, Bin Tepe commissioner from the Çanakkale Museum, have battled through to tremendous success. The first Prehistoric burials appeared at the edge of the lake (1, 2, and 7 on plan, *Figure 157*), but it was John's big trench uphill (at bottom of plan) toward the country road which came upon an "Ali-Baba" five-foot jar burial *(Figures 160, 161)*, followed by more jar burials and Prehistoric "cist graves" *(Figure 158)* made like a box of stone slabs. They recall graves of the southwest coast of Asia Minor, and those farther afield on Cycladic Isles of Greece. Among the goodies retrieved from this third millennium Lydian Prehistoric culture is a fine bronze dagger and all sorts of fancy pottery *(Figures 159, 162)*, stone tools and spindle whorls.

Machteld's second contribution to Sardis mysteries concerns Andy Ramage's "tower" in Pactolus North. Andy and I were puzzling: "Why is there burned mud-brick within the tower?" Machteld came up with the brilliant idea that this might be a fire altar *(Figure 169)*. Then as we looked around at the peculiar arrangements of the area around the tower, they began to take on more and more the lineaments of a sacred precinct. You will hear more of this "blow by blow" as Andy digs it up.

Alf Hyatt has just come in to report that Nuri's second taxi broke down while transporting him and Brian. Nuri's first taxi had overturned with Kemal Bey (or vice-versa) and, after sitting like an anti-accident scarecrow all bashed up in front of our camp, it was finally cannibalized and carried away. I hope this fate will not befall its twin. Brian and Alf have a grinding job to complete in the baking heat: the survey for our urban plan. This is the most important single undertaking at the present stage of our work. It brings home how much we do *not* know. They estimate that we have excavated a bit over 1 percent of the city area. By itself this is not too bad; what is vexing is that as yet we have had no chance to get digging data on the central and eastern parts of the city area. On the western bank of the Pac-

Figure 166—Payday at the Marble Court is conducted by general manager Ken Frazer (center), chief restoration architect Mehmet C. Bolgil (white cap), government commissioner Musa Baran (counting money), and chief foreman Hasan Koramaz (back to spectator). Labor force was over 200 in 1967. Inscribed on marble blocks above is an Early Byzantine poem celebrating a restoration of the Marble Court around A.D. 400.

tolus, too, coffeehouses and shops are rapidly covering the area presumably containing the Lydian agora. We might be able to make a stab or two at these problems next season.

We have been cleaning walls exposed in the high eastern bank of the Pactolus and have discovered an industrial quarter (Map 3, no. 7). Whatever was produced there required very high heat. In one place we picked up lots of "rejects"—lamps with production faults. Now two lonely workmen have the assignment of clearing the terrific vegetation from the old bridge across the Pactolus. It is pleasant work nevertheless; everything is in the shade, water channels murmur and cool the air. The bridge itself is crucial for our understanding of the course of the main avenue of the Roman and Byzantine Sardis.

Sardis   September 7, 1967

Caught in the whirlwind of departures, I kept postponing the writing of this letter. Now only the two Mehmets are left, and Ken Frazer, Ilse, Recep Meriç, and Musa Bey. A jar as tall as a man, one of David Mitten's trophies from the Early Bronze cemetery at Ahlatli Tepecik *(Figures 160, 161)*, stands forlornly in front of the showers, where I had posed it for its picture. A radiant rainbow spans the cloudy sky which breaks out in fantastic Venetian displays of dark violet and soft gold over the gashed precipices of Cemetery Hill—a mood quite unlike the hard, dry, Lydian summer heat we lived with during the campaign.

The Staff departed like an ebbing wave: today, ten people in two taxis, George and Louise Bates with Guy Metraux and David DeLong in the lead car. George had figured his time closely—the last six Byzantine coins were cataloged between 2:00 and 3:30; P.M., the taxi came at 4:00. David had worked on his beautiful drawings for Marble Court restoration deep into the preceding night *(Figure 164)*. As for Guy, he must be "beloved of Zeus," for Zeus put in an appearance twice this summer for his sake.

First Guy found the capital with an intent, grizzly head of a savage Anatolian Zeus *(Figure 208)*; then, on August 18, there appeared a reflection of that most famous original, the Zeus of Phidias. The overlifesize head is of the so-called Boston-Mylasa type, a late Classical, dramatizing revision of Phidian grandeur. The new find lends color to the thought that the Anatolian sculptor Bryaxis was the creator of this variant; there is much in common here with the style of the sculptures of the Mausoleum of Halicarnassus, where Bryaxis worked.

The second taxi was waiting for Richard Petkun. Steve Crawford and the house guards were playing volleyball on one side of the house, while on the other I was conducting the ambassador from the Netherlands, his wife and daughter, and a British student. A religious couple in quest of the Seven Churches in Asia was penetrating the center of the compound. Eventually the situation resolved itself, as everybody departed. Going with Royce and Richard were Steve Crawford, digger extraordinary in the Synagogue; Jim Greaves, conservator and chief of *skoutlosis* production; and Andy Seager, the Synagogue's resident architect.

The Synagogue team had its triumph. There had been obstacles. Fund collection lagged behind the goal; the season's objectives and labor force had to be cut back around August 15. It proved hard to find some materials, harder to find enough suitably skilled workmen; we had to quit mosaic-lifting while pushing the marble cutting. But on September 5 something new and beautiful was seen: rising in delicate, elegant completeness against the towering backdrop of the Acropolis was the small shrine on the entrance wall of the Main Hall of the Synagogue. It was probably the shrine that originally housed the Sefer Torah *(Figure 167)*.

Figure 167—A major accomplishment in 1967 was the reconstruction of the Synagogue South Shrine on a platform abutting inside east wall of the Main Hall. Bases and capitals were carved from marble after ancient fragments and column sections and the entire Doric entablature were cast in cement to bear the original pediment (shield roughened for painting).

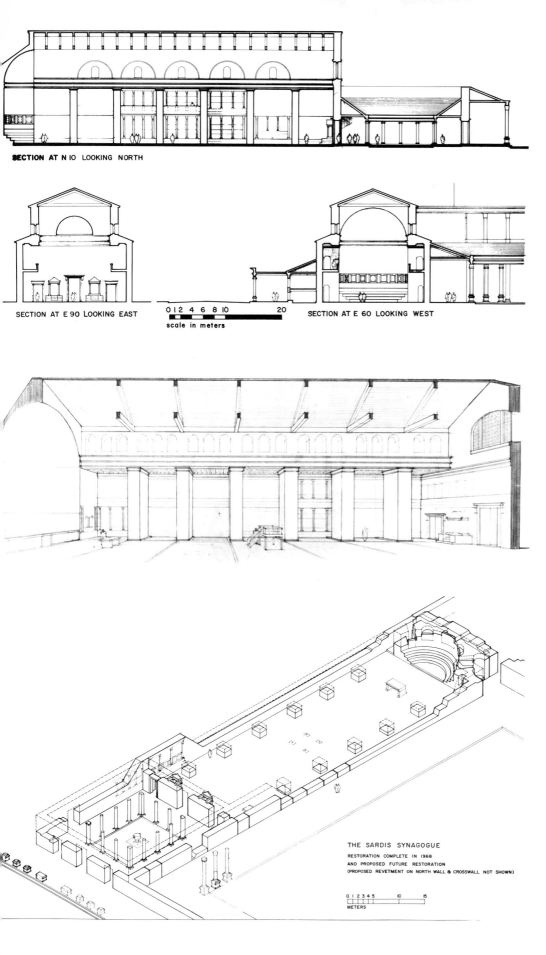

SECTION AT N 10 LOOKING NORTH

SECTION AT E 90 LOOKING EAST

0 1 2 4 6 8 10   20
scale in meters

SECTION AT E 60 LOOKING WEST

THE SARDIS SYNAGOGUE

RESTORATION COMPLETE IN 1968
AND PROPOSED FUTURE RESTORATION
(PROPOSED REVETMENT ON NORTH WALL & CROSSWALL NOT SHOWN)

0 1 2 3 4 5   10   15
METERS

Figure 168—Working out conservation and restoration of Synagogue. (A) Restoration drawings by A. R. Seager, 1966, assume galleries over the aisles, one-story colonnade in Forecourt, large and small pilasters in interior decoration, flat roof over shops toward Main Avenue. (B) Perspective of Interior of Main Hall by A. M. Shapiro, 1967. This reconstruction has no galleries, more windows. It shows the Eagle Table in front of the Apse, *bimah* (lectern) in the center, North Shrine between entrance doors. Looking north. Perspective suggests the vast spatial effect of this hall which rose to over 70 feet. (C) The program adopted for conservation of the Synagogue; A. M. Shapiro, 1966, revised by A. R. Seager. It called for clearing and restoring columns of porch and Forecourt, building up east wall between Forecourt and Main Hall, reerecting two shrines, placing samples of interior decorations on south and north walls next to entrance wall into Main Hall, building south and north wall to about 10 feet, consolidating the walls of the Apse at even height. (Deviations from the 1966 proposal adopted in actual restoration: north wall was built to only 4 feet; piers of the Hall were left at varying heights.)

For two summers Andy Seager had worked to find the fragments and to design the most plausible solution. The mending of the two porphyry-like columns, the carving of the small bases and capitals, the casting of the dainty Doric entablature, and the lifting of the ancient, nearly complete pediment were supervised by Mehmet Ergene, using all the skill he had developed during his four seasons as constructor-restorer-conservator of the Marble Court. Andy and Mehmet were assisted by Tolon Teker and Recep Meriç, assistants for construction and conservation respectively.

Working overtime, Jim Greaves and his two marble pattern cutters produced all seven marble pattern panels for the decoration of one bay of the Main Hall (in place in *Figure 182*), though we could, for lack of time, do no more than display them on a hastily devised easel-like support; and Recep cast the first shaft for the pilasters of the interior, of which we have so many bases and capitals.

The workmen cheered when this display went on for photography, two days before the end of the Synagogue season. In principle, we have developed the technical capabilities for the proposed partial reconstitution of the wonderful interior decoration; but we need sufficient means to realize even the modest goal of restoring two bays of this fifteen-foot-high marble-decorated wall.

Their dig at Ahlatli Tepecik *(Figures 156–161)* had stopped on August 15, but David Mitten, John Henderson, and Dundar Tokgöz kept going to Bin Tepe. Coming back sunburned each evening, they hauled in a cloud of witnesses for Prehistoric life on the Gygean Lake: mighty *pithoi,* spindle whorls, and tools. Fostering of cordial relations with local inhabitants, a forte of David's, paid off great dividends to scholarship. At least three Prehistoric cemeteries and a major settlement were pointed out by local well-wishers. Owing to Dundar Bey's interest and foreman Emin Cavuş' skill beyond the usual surface picking, they were able to excavate sample burials.

The finds open exciting vistas of trade and commerce northward to the Troad, eastward to Hittite lands, and southward to wild Lycia.

In Homer, one hero appears and has his *aristeia*, where he shines in deeds of valor; and then another is given pride of place. The next *aristeia* is that of Steve Crawford. By pits made in the second half of the season he has proved that the building which became the Synagogue was designed from the beginning with an apse, and that all its major walls go deep enough for us to give up. The deepest pit Steve dug up was well over twenty feet and the north wall of the Synagogue kept going down; it was even more surprising to see the same thing happen when we cut through the three benches in the apse and went down, down, down. There never was another building on this site. This hall was planned and the immensely deep terracing built by Roman engineers for fear of earthquakes, after the great earthquake of A.D. 17. (For later views see pp. 243, 247, and *Figure 201*.)

We cannot yet be dogmatic about the exact time of the construction of the apsidal hall which became the Synagogue—anywhere from A.D. 20 to 200. Henry Detweiler did, however, during his stay, point out several cogent parallels for diagonal passages into the apse among Roman civil basilicas: the best conjecture is still that the hall was built as a Roman basilica and then turned over to the Jewish congregation, possibly during the visit of the emperor Lucius Verus in A.D. 166. I. Rabinowitz of Cornell thinks that one of the few Hebrew inscriptions may bear the name of the emperor—honored perhaps for giving his permission to turn over this huge basilica to the Jewish community.

Looking most mysterious, a large vaulted passage runs clear across the entire width of the Synagogue, under the floor. "There is nothing like a drain"; for this is what the huge passage is—taking water off the main avenue, off the Byzantine Shops, and running on, perhaps for over 400 feet across the entire Gymnasium.

Figure 169—First Lydian sacral precinct found at Sardis in Pactolus North is dominated by altar 11 feet long dating from the time of Croesus, 561–547 B.C., and later enlarged after damage by flood. Burnt matter from sacrifices was found inside; a half lion sat on far right corner.

Figure 170—When the Pactolus North altar was rebuilt during the Persian occupation at Sardis, two and one half archaic lions were immured at its corners, carefully packed with schist and limestone chips. Apparently four lions had originally adorned the top of the altar. This lion's flank was blackened by flames during sacrificial rites in honor of Cybele, tamer of lions. A Lydian inscription to *Kuvava* (Cybele) was found nearby.

"Keep walking" was the slogan of Brian Percival and Alf Hyatt as they trudged up hill and down dale to put Sardis ruins on the urban plan, much to the detriment of Alf's feet. This down-to-earth mode of travel brought discovery—almost 400 feet of the ancient city wall fronting on the Pactolus (Map 3, nos. 6, 9, 7). It was Alf who casually queried: "Is not this the city wall before it turns up to the Acropolis?" (In fairness I must add that H. C. Butler's admirable surveyor, Lloyd B. Emory, showed something of a wall in his map of Sardis in 1913, but surprisingly very much less than that has become visible now.) At the same time, workmen who were clearing the remains of the ancient bridge produced evidence from ancient coins that the bridge and adjacent city wall were built in one swoop around A.D. 400. This transformation of Sardis into a fortress was a masterpiece of Late Roman defensive military design. We are just beginning to get an inkling of the changes in the city pattern which such a transformation may have entailed.

"Don't you think it is about time that we disembowel the tower?" Andy Ramage was putting the question, and his next "anatomical operation" would have deserved that "blow by blow" account which I rashly promised in the last letter. Suffice to state: August 25, Andy discovers nearly complete lioness in the southeast corner of the "tower-altar"; August 26, Andy discovers nearly complete lion in the southwest corner; August 28, Andy puts back the masonry removed to extract the lions; dig ends (*Figures 169, 170*).

An extraordinary picture has emerged. Once upon a time, in the days of king Croesus, there was an archaic altar with four lions, one at each corner, or maybe two pairs, lion and lioness, all lions roaring eastward. As fire sacrifices went up in the center of the altar, the flanks of the lions turned toward the fire were blackened. Then the altar was damaged, perhaps by enemy action, quite certainly by flood. When it was repaired, the new,

221

larger altar rested in part on two feet of gravel deposited by the flood. During this repair the two and one-half lions surviving were carefully immured near their original positions but became quite invisible. Who was the original owner of the altar? The Goddess with Lions par excellence is Cybele or Kubaba, the greatest goddess of Sardis; representations of a sphinx-taming goddess and of lions have been found in Pactolus North. But Artemis, honored by the huge temple upstream, also tames lions.

Andrew has been able to outline an entire sacral precinct, however despoiled. In the emptiness of noon, these reddened clay floors and altar walls are strangely eloquent. Did the Persians after their conquest of Sardis (547 B.C.) convert the altar from worship of a native goddess to the more abstract cult of fire? Competition of various religious traditions at the cosmopolitian city of Sardis is a story yet to be told.

A tantalizing glimpse of these complexities flashed up during the last days of the excavation. Lying symmetrically to the Synagogue—which occupies the south side of the Gymnasium—is the Long North Hall (see plan, *Figure 223*). Guy Metraux had been able to prove that unlike the Synagogue, the North Hall had no apse at its western end; he was just beginning to unravel the plan of the hall when time ran out. At the eastern end, he had found the corner of a colonnaded entrance court, an atrium. On the entrance step, crudely graven, was a cross with long, archangel-like wings; a lion jumps toward the cross from the left; from the right, a human figure with extended hand touches the wing of the cross. Might not the Long North Hall have been converted into a church? Synagogue and church would then have flanked the entrance to the formerly pagan Gymnasium in perfect and symbolic symmetry. We have to excavate the Long North Hall completely before we can know.

"The sheep did not bother me any," remarked Brian Percival judiciously to David Mitten at breakfast. "It was when I heard you at 3 A.M. hollering in the bushes 'Push him the other way' that I really woke up." The "him" was a ram. It seems that for two nights running, shepherdless sheep had invaded the porch of the Swift House. Their milling and bleating brought David and Andy Ramage out of bed; after a spirited battle in the dawn's early light, the two Ajaxes routed the invaders.

Nobody will deny that the Temple Party in the Tenth Year was the most talented of all temple parties. Torches and flashlights were footlights as in a complete surprise there sounded from the threshold of the temple the familiar strains of South Pacific to words familiar to none. "The South Pactolus or Sardian Pacific" (conductor Brian Percival and the seven stars could not agree which title was right) was a smash hit.

David Delong, G. Metraux (billed as Mary Metraux), Bonnie Henderson (who emerged as "The Dame"), Jim Greaves (the original instigator), Mehmet Ergene, John Henderson (who scored a triumph in his brief appearance as Bloody Mary), Alf Hyatt, and music director Brian Percival sang harmoniously and danced vigorously, but it was the hilarious verbal adaptation to the local scene which had the audience in stitches.

The Great Review was followed by a Turkish comedian, who also serves as the truck driver for the Prehistoric Bin Tepe project. The "International Festival" ended with Turkish dances.

Under Croesus and under the great satraps Oroitas and Tissaphernes, the ancient Royal Road brought everyone to Sardis. Now the Izmir-Ankara highway brings a procession of archaeological potentates, the directors of the Iasos, Aphrodisias, Pergamon, and Hierapolis excavations and our Turkish colleagues from the Old Smyrna dig, all stopping by at Sardis going west; a Belgian mission to Apamea in Syria was headed east. We appreciated the stimulating research possibilities outlined for us by Clarence Wendel, minerals attaché of our embassy in Ankara, who went to look for possibilities of Lydian mines around Sardis. Professor Verzone of the Italian

Figure 171—Most of the staff photographed in camp during celebration of the tenth anniversary of Sardis campaigns. Lower row, from left, G. E. Bates (kneeling), K. Z. Polatkan, A. H. Detweiler, G. M. A. Hanfmann (clasping hands), R. Meriç, Ilse Hanfmann, A. Ramage (kneeling). Middle, left of column, Louise M. Bates; between column capitals, A. R. Seager; standing on the right, J. S. Crawford, D. DeLong, B. Percival. Upper row, seated on column, F. K. Yeğül; half-head behind him, A. Hyatt; G. P. R. Metraux, T. Akalin (standing). Two overlapping heads on left of tree: M. C. Bolgil (front), C. H. Greenewalt, Jr. Seated on right, K. J. Frazer (cap), J. L. Greaves.

Hierapolis mission kindly gave of his time to serve as a critic in a lively session on our Marble Court restoration project.

The sessions in our seminar on conservation and restoration were both top-flight and up-to-date. We heard Ken Frazer (with first-hand pictures) on the restoration of Abu Simbel, Henry Detweiler on international legislation relating to monuments and his experiences as adviser on architectural preservation, and Larry Majewski (again with pictures) on "Flood Damage and Emergency Restoration at Florence." Brian Percival's observations on architecture and archaeology in Malaya, based on his Peace Corps experience, tied right in with this theme.

The Tenth Campaign at Sardis has fled with astonishing rapidity *(Figure 171)*. We have had first-rate results in digging and preservation; it also had a new component—intensive work toward final publication. Enver Bostanci, George and Louise Bates, Fikret Yeğül, and C. H. Greenewalt, Jr., showed the pattern of visiting experts who will engage in this task. In record time, Enver Bey cataloged more than 150 skeletons, George and Louise cataloged 1070 Byzantine coins, Fikret advanced remarkably in the colossal task of the final publication of the Marble Court and its environment, Greenie composed a draft for a publication of Eastern Greek pottery found at Sardis. To make permanent and known to all what we have discovered is publication: the quintessence of all our work and effort. This activity will greatly increase after 1968 and is likely to continue through the second decade of the archaeological exploration of Sardis.

The Tenth Campaign has clarified several matters.

1) *Large-scale digging* may well stop after 1968. This always will be an arbitrary decision, and some small-scale digging will be indispensable for 1969, possibly 1970. We hope to excavate all necessary things in and around the Synagogue and to clarify the North Hall enigma in 1968.

2) *Small-scale digging* and cleaning for final publication and completion of the urban plan will continue in 1969–70, possibly 1971.

3) Unresolved is the situation at the *mound of Gyges* tunneled in 1964–66. The Department of Antiquities urges continuation until the chamber is found. For the moment we are doing nothing to preserve the tunnel which goes around the 100-meter Lydian wall, one of the world's most fantastic sights.

4) The *Synagogue* requires one more season of digging (1968), two of study (1968–1969), three of conservation (1969–1971?).

5) *Marble Court.* M. C. Bolgil has made most valiant efforts to speed up the job; upon my request, he has prepared time and cost estimates for several phases or options. Even the minimal emergency option with only the first story restored will, on realistic schedule, carry over into 1969. We favor an intermediate solution which would include restoration of the impressive pediment in the second story.

6) *Preparatory work for final publication.* This summer revealed the need for yet another project: study of the Sardis city wall as an example of Late Roman military architecture. After observing experts at work, considering that boxed and packed up materials have to be made available both at the Sardis camp and at the Manisa Museum, and noting what is involved in research and production of illustrations, I feel that the camp at Sardis may well have to stay open during the coming decade. We will plan on continuing research (and possibly training activities) at least until 1976.

1968

Sardis   June 30, 1968

"You cannot step twice into the same waters." One leaves Sardis with its people and activities suspended in one's mind, like a silent movie that stops, showing a man with his leg in the air. Somehow, one expects that everybody will be where you left him, waiting for you to come. Meantime, the film of life has run on, and these people have been moving on their own paths, following their own plans and their own aspirations.

We were happy to see Ken Frazer's familiar form, a merry twinkle in his eye, as we alighted at sundown into the empty vastness of Çigli Airport at Izmir; but at Sardis some of the key population had changed. Our camp superintendent is no longer the liquid-eyed Halil Ibrahim; he has become an official with the government Cotton Office. The new majordomo, Cengiz Ersöz, has a crew cut and a stern look, and has been a radar operator in the airforce. He used to be our gatekeeper and a bit of a wild boy, but after army service he developed into a first-rate administrator. Last year's lab assistant, Erol Yurdakoş, shifted from teaching school to attending police school in Izmir. One of the two boys who were patiently taught to cut marble patterns has gone to a school in Istanbul. We shuffle around, find replacements, and eventually get things on an even keel. In a way, the upward movement in life of our Turkish assistants is a compliment to things they have learned at Sardis.

Mrs. Hanfmann, Ken, and I came to Sardis on June 13, a strange, hazy, sticky day. Eliminating the fearsome serpentines at ancient Nymphaion, the new road shoots straight as an arrow to Turgutlu—almost an American highway. Far off at the edge of the plain are the five picturesque towns and

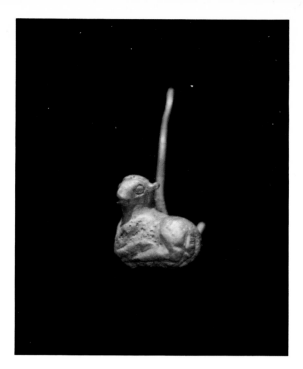

Plate IV A tiny (0.01 m. long) couchant golden ram or lamb with gold wire, perhaps part of an earring, found at Pactolus North. During the Mermnad Kingdom goldsmiths and jewelers may have worked here, near the Lydian gold refinery.

villages which cut themselves into memories of all trips from 1957 on: Kemal Paşa, named after a victory of 1922; Armutlu, "Pear Village"; Ören, with its park full of camels when the villagers brought grapes down in August; Yiğitler, "Heroes," charming with its bubbling brook and fresh green, and its scary bridge consisting of two beams with nothing in between; Parsa, whose pavement was all early medieval cobblestones with sharp tips pointed upward—nothing faster than first gear would get you across. Their names were an evocation; but driving through them was abomination.

Entrenched at Sardis we found a little "family" who had started restoration work on the Marble Court early in May: supervising architect Mehmet Bolgil, M.A. of Harvard School of Design, he of swaying gait, driving energy, and irrepressible laughter; Ken Frazer, our general manager and genial spirit of the camp; Kemal Ziya Polatkan, now associated with us as chairman of the Turkish Commission for the Marble Court Restoration, whose ebullient temper and manifold deeds since he became our first commissioner have made him a legend; and one of our photographers, Elizabeth Gombosi, newly arrived on the Turkish ferry boat *Truva* ("Troy"). Elaborate plans had been made to meet Elizabeth in Izmir, but she zoomed all the way to the coffeehouse at Sart before Ken caught up with her.

The little group mushroomed as Gus Swift (our senior archaeologist), Brian Percival (architect from Cornell), Andy Ramage, Elaine Gazda, and Steve Crawford (archaeological Harvardians) all poured in on one afternoon. The population explosion has been continuing ever since, leading up to the ultimate thirty-eight or forty members. Naturally, people had their adventures: Gus's bags went to Hongkong and Andy left his passport in the Istanbul Exchange Office. Still, even the notebook on conservation which Sid Goldstein left in a taxi turned up, having been forwarded through a chain of various hands to the excavation house.

As usual, during the first two weeks everybody scurried around getting

Figure 172—Lydian gold refinery discovered: conservator R.E. Stone and archaeologist A. Ramage detect a tiny bit of gold (at end of workman's trowel), found within strange greenish concentric rings of earth ash and fired clay, just south of the lion altar (Figures 169, 170) at Pactolus North. Driblets and bits of gold foil proved that metal purified in the refinery was gold.

organized—locating last year's materials and gear, such as the tent invented for the photographers by our amazingly explicit deaf-and-dumb carpenter; discovering that there are no more little white bags for bones, and that Mrs. Hanfmann has to cut 200 of them from a new bale of cotton; filling up the medical kits for each of the new sectors. In the midst of this activity, formally ushering in a new Sardis season, the generator broke down when overloaded by a would-be English-speaking electrician.

It is almost unbelievable how much Mehmet Bolgil has managed at the Marble Court in six weeks: column after column and pavilion after pavilion are growing upward in this, the most monumental of all restorations going on in Turkey. We had a seminar there yesterday, a very successful one, and the rosy evening light on the golden marble was sheer poetry.

The digging was launched on June 20. There had been doubt whether many workmen would work for the wages paid last year. Enough showed up, however, and they stayed after the rates were announced.

Our four experienced excavators have been making good headway. In the fascinating sacral area of the Lydians on the Pactolus, Andy Ramage has found a step on the west side of the altar he freed last year, modernistic little terracotta heads, a room full of pottery, and a powerfully stylized bronze head of an eagle, archaic, small, and filled with lead.

Gus Swift's main purpose is to secure more data on the plan and precinct wall of the seventh century B.C. Lydian bazaar (*Figure 131*), very important for the history of urbanism. A strange and macabre discovery has added unexpected information. Gus was looking at the deep pit he dug in 1966 when like Hamlet he found a skull at his feet. More bones were sticking out of the gravel in the side of the trench laid bare by cascading winter torrents. Careful digging and brushing have revealed several individuals, victims, we believe, of that terrible onslaught and fire when the city was stormed by Cimmerian nomads in the seventh century B.C. Two are complete; of other

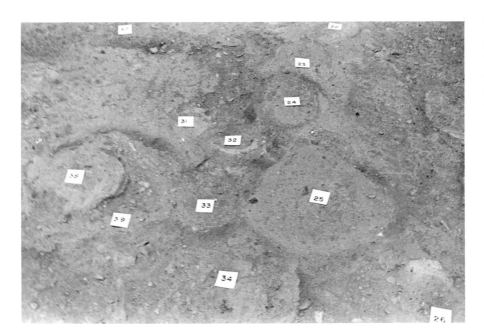

Figure 173 —Depressions (here still filled with earth) were identified as cupels—fire-resistant crucibles for the purification of gold and silver from base metals. Nearly three hundred were found, measuring 6–8 inches in diameter and 3–4 inches deep.

individuals there are only parts. One man was lying face down, the others in strange twisted positions. Were they innocent bystanders, or were the well-preserved skeletons those of Lydian warriors, or even of the enemy killed in or after the battle? Ray Liddell and Elizabeth Gombosi have been covering the gruesome scene in photography and Elaine Gazda has made a careful drawing. David Finkel, anthropologist from Cornell, arrived just in time to start his researches with this sensation.

One strange contribution came in the hands of a young boy. His skin was a clear, light brown with red on his cheeks, his eyes were large and beaming, and his smile full of charm. He was a very clean-looking little boy. He had come dashing down the slope where his father was winnowing. In his hand he clutched the terracotta figurine of a little boy. He gave it to me. I said that his father should come to the camp house to get paid in presence of the Turkish commissioner. For we only purchase things for the Manisa Museum and strictly according to the commissioner's advice. Three minutes later he was back, gasping, tears in his voice: "Abe ("Older Brother") give it back or give me the money." I gave back the figurine but later asked the commissioner to talk to the father. We bought it on behalf of the Museum, but the commissioner says it is a forgery made partly from ancient molds by an enterprising school teacher in Turgutlu some twenty-five miles away. I fear the commissioner is right. But we must know about the local forgeries too.

Note to tourists: A United States Embassy circular for Americans sums up the legal position toward the disastrous antiquities trade: "You cannot take it with you." It is illegal to take any antiquities out of the country.

At this point we should introduce this year's representatives of the Turkish government. Blond, blue-eyed, hollow-cheeked, the senior commissioner Osman Aksoy comes from the Ankara Museum, and is a veteran of many archaeological expeditions. He has already done a lot of running

Figure 174 —The cupellation process: gold was probably collected from the ore by placing the crushed ore over the surface of a partly oxidized bath of premelted lead. The slag and earthy impurities were then skimmed off the gold-bearing lead; and the metal, kept at a temperature near the melting point of gold, was further oxidized by exposure to air. The molten lead oxide dissolved the oxides of all the other metallic impurities as they were formed, and was either drained off or was absorbed in the porous bone ash lining of the cupelling hearth. The unoxidizable gold or silver remained behind in the form of a cake or globule of high purity. (Drawing by F. K. Yeğül from a sketch by R. E. Stone with additional suggestions from Professor Cyril S. Smith, Massachusetts Institute of Technology.)

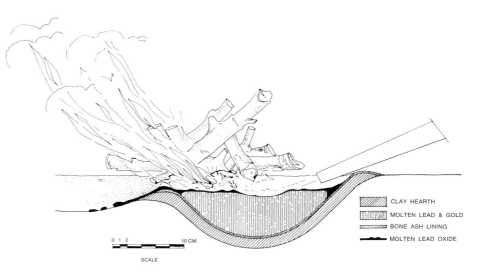

CLAY HEARTH
MOLTEN LEAD & GOLD
BONE ASH LINING
MOLTEN LEAD OXIDE

SCALE

around with me to the various government offices in Izmir and Salihli, culminating in a visit to the new Governor of Manisa. The second commissioner is a young archaeologist from the Istanbul Museum, Miss Güldem Yüğrüm. Three American-trained architects and three students from the Middle East Technical University and Robert College serving as engineering and architectural assistants complete our Turkish roster.

Dick Stone arrived from southern Turkey, where he was conserving mosaics; Andy Seager arrived from Iowa, where he had been teaching. As conservator and architect for the Synagogue project respectively, they have been wrestling with the conservation of the building and recomposition of samples of its gorgeous interior decoration. As always, we are working against time, and this year also against lack of funds. A lot of intensive study and drawing is going on. Masons have started raising higher the wall for the sample bay of marble revetments *(Figure 182,* center). A suitable white revetment marble has been located and partly bought, but it is amazing how much trouble it can be to find the right kind of black and colored marbles. Our boys are acquiring considerable respect for the ancient marble cutters —especially when a modern marble establishment refuses to try their diamond saw on some of the ancient materials.

Sardis   August 6, 1968

To stand where the wealth of Croesus was made; to watch his craftsmen squat at little fires, pumping at the bellows, purifying the gold in cupels, pouring it out of crucibles—this could happen only in a dream. Yet this is the scene we have discovered and can prove by tiny but telling clues.

It all began on July 6, when archaeological detective Ramage, tenderly brushing a clay floor, perceived the outlines of little greenish rings *(Figure*

230

Figure 175—Proof of effective technology for treating metals are fragments of a clay bellows-nozzle for collecting a large volume of air and iron blow-pipe for concentrating heat on a small area.

173). They proved to be depressions lined with clay and ashes. Some heavy, grey matter adhered to the inside of one of them. Ramage's hunch that the little hollows had something to do with metalmaking set off the hunt. The Importance of Having the Right People at the Right Place in the Right Time was gloriously upheld, as scientific detective Dick Stone developed the technical interpretation of clues and detective Sid Goldstein ran the tests to prove them.

The grey matter proved to be lead slag with traces of silver. The depressions, Dick felt sure, were cupels, fire-resistant containers for purification of gold or silver. Cupellation involves extracting impurities out of silver or gold by heating them with lead *(Figure 174).*

For a week or so, we had the theory, the cupels, the lead, and the traces of silver, but no gold. Then keen-eyed assistant Halis Aydintaşbaş spotted a tiny speck of gold. As the technique of sifting and searching the clay floors and industrial refuse became more proficient, more and bigger specks of gold appeared *(Figure 172).*

One of the thrills came just as Consul General and Mrs. Guy A. Lee and Vice Consul and Mrs. Charles J. Pitman visited Pactolus North, the area we have dug since 1960 on the east bank of the Pactolus whose gold-bearing sands were so famous in antiquity. They were leaving when Sid Goldstein suddenly jumped and waved wildly. For a horrible moment I thought he had been bitten by a scorpion. Actually, he had the largest piece of gold foil yet found, roughly triangular, almost an inch long.

More important than these scattered gold bits are the traces of gold left in cracks of crucibles (clay vessels). They prove beyond doubt that gold was being treated and melted here. By the number of cupels—now over 300 —Dick surmises that the amount of gold handled was substantial. He thinks we may have in the thin gold foil *(Figure 178)* indirect evidence for cementation, a process for separating gold and silver. And king Croesus is known to

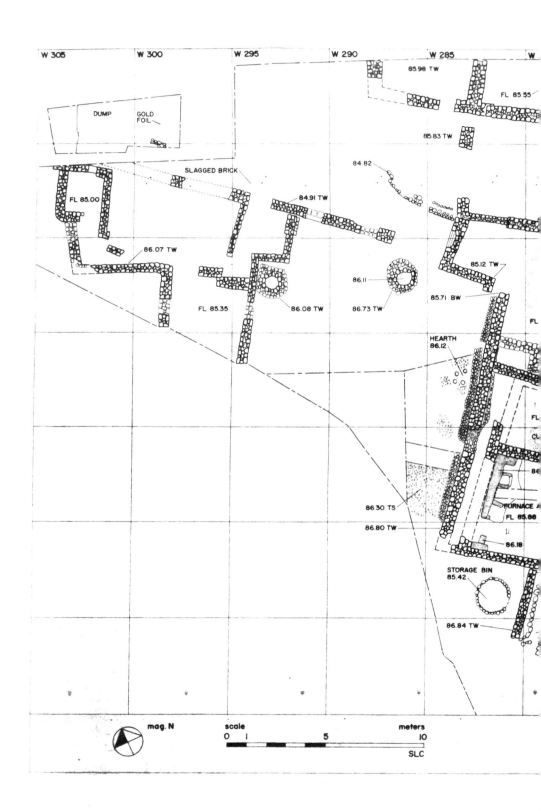

W 305   W 300   W 295   W 290   W 285   W

85.98 TW

FL 85.55

DUMP   GOLD
FOIL

85.83 TW

84.82

SLAGGED BRICK

FL 85.00   84.91 TW

86.07 TW

85.12 TW

86.11

85.71 BW

86.08 TW   86.73 TW

FL 85.35

HEARTH
86.12

FL

CL

86

86.30 TS

FURNACE
FL 85.88

86.80 TW

86.18

STORAGE BIN
85.42

86.84 TW

mag. N

scale
0   1   5   meters
                              10

SLC

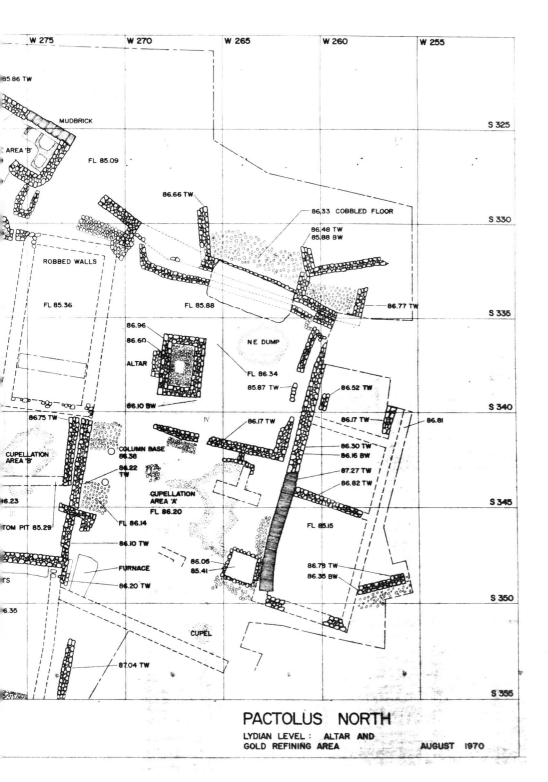

Figure 176—Plan of the gold refinery of the time of Croesus with Lion Altar (W 270, S 340), Pactolus North. The refinery was enclosed by walls forming a quadrangle (W 260–283, S 330–347). Dotted areas contained cupels for removal of base metals. Parting of silver from gold (cementation) was probably carried on with aid of small furnaces (Furnace Area A, W 280, S 345; Area B, W 275, S 325). The oblong structures flanking altar may be priests' dwellings (built after refinery was abandoned). Dump of metallurgical debris in upper left corner suggested another refinery was nearby.

have been the first to mint gold and silver separately. His predecessors who invented coinage had to strike an alloy of gold and silver, since they were unable to separate the two.

This gold refinery of king Croesus was protected by Cybele, the great goddess of the mountains who guards the ores and metals (*Figures 176, 177*). The most striking feature of this installation is her altar which towers amidst the "cupellation floors," the same altar which so surprised us by yielding the immured lions of Cybele in 1967 (*Figures 169, 170*).

The substance of the great discovery is clear. To work it out will take time. We are not equipped for microscopic photography, yet this is what is needed to illustrate gold dendrites and other remarkable phenomena which will tell how Croesus' gold was extracted, purified, and worked. Only the simplest tests can be done here at Sardis; yet modern metallurgy has an enormous range of investigative techniques—in the advanced scientific laboratories.

The second thrill of the season: On July 16 Mehmet Ergene was testing the foundation and the stylobate in the colonnade of the Synagogue Forecourt. He turned over one of the marble steps—and found himself face to face with two majestic goddesses, Artemis and Cybele (*Figures 180, 181*). A relief, three feet high and two feet wide, had been used as a building stone, lying face down. Both goddesses are frontal, archaic statues, crowned and veiled. Artemis, the taller sister, holds a hind in her crooked right arm; Cybele, echoing the gesture, holds a recumbent lion. On the right two smaller profile figures, a man and a woman, raise their arms in adoration. There was great excitement as Elizabeth Gombosi rushed to immortalize the scene, looking herself like a young Artemis as she was shooting away with her camera. The relief is heavily sintered and is now soaking in a big wooden tub. It will go down in history as an extraordinary document of Lydian art and religion.

234

Figure 177—Pactolus North: an overall view of the Lydian sacral area with gold refinery and the altar to Cybele (center). Probably a number of such small refining units lined the east bank of the Pactolus. Just right of altar, a system of channels for water supply. Foreground and left: Byzantine Church E and Roman bath.

We were lucky with goddesses this season, Another one, with veil, is holding a snake in her hand. She appeared on a small pilaster capital of marble which we got from a peasant who found the piece. The Lydian pantheon is getting more diversified by the hour.

Scientific deduction from minute clues celebrated another triumph when David Mitten and Güldem Yüğrüm, discovered proof that by 6000 B.C. hunting and fishing folk were prowling on the shores of the Gygean Lake (*Figure 156*) behind the Royal Cemetery. The oldest man-made object yet found in the Sardis region is a tiny carnelian Mesolithic lunar tool; it took experienced Prehistorians to recognize it.

"Davoud Bey," alias David Mitten, David Finkel, and Güldem hanım* are commuting to the lake site of Ahlatli Tepecik in a blue microbus. Prehistoric burials and much other Prehistoric material continues to be found; and splendid imported objects (a perfume flask with dancers imported from Corinth) show the place was subsequently an important Lydian settlement. David Mitten is toying with the idea that this might have been king Gyges' hunting and fishing lodge from which he could watch his huge mound being built.

The mound (*Figure 106*) is less than a mile from the lake shore at Ahlatli Tepecik. We went there with the party of the American Consul and found that the tunnels we had dug and shored up in 1964–1966 (*Figures 109, 111*) are deteriorating. The tunnel curving around alongside the great wall of the inner mound buried some 100 feet deep is a most uncanny sight; how to preserve it is one of the hard nuts we have yet to crack.

Preservation work in the Synagogue has given us a great display of varied activities. As I was passing through the building yesterday, the door frame for the ten-foot southern door into the Main Hall was going up. Pilasters were being fitted on to a resplendent dado of marble revetments on the

*hanım, "Lady," "Miss," "Mrs.," is put in Turkish after the first name.

235

Figure 178 (left)—The gold of Croesus. The Pactolus North refinery area produced gold lumps, globules, dribbles, and foil—shown here—whose presence in conjunction with furnaces and pitted foil suggests that during Croesus' reign the Lydians developed the so-called cementation method for separating gold and silver. This piece weighs only 30 milligrams.

Figure 179 (right)—Mudbrick furnaces kept temperature at 700° C during cementation, a process for separating gold from silver. Gold was hammered into thin foil-like sheets, stacked in vessels with a salt or alum solution, and heated for a long time. Eventually, the silver combined with the chloride or sulfate and pure gold was the residue. Croesus was the first in history to strike separate coins of silver and of gold.

adjacent wall (*Figure 182*). A team of mosaic workmen was cleaning a mosaic in the Forecourt. Behind them, the "stone crew" was pulling part of a column into place. These combined operations are being directed by Dick Stone for interior decoration, and for construction by Mehmet Ergene, whose great qualities as trainer of skilled workmen and construction architect have previously served the Marble Court restoration. But lack of means for the Synagogue project has meant fewer workmen, thus slowing down the pace. (We had hoped for $40,000, but obtained only $11,000 in 1967–68.) In general, all prices and wages have been rising in Turkey. After careful comparisons and discussion with government and other advisers we granted a general increase on August 1, to a somewhat reduced labor force. In terms of current wages the increase was thoroughly justified, but it does add a substantial percentage to the field expenses.

Dick Stone designed, after existing ancient pieces, a marble panel with green and red marbles. To find the green and red marbles, our newly appointed, energetic engineering assistant, Emin Balay, traveled several hundred miles north to Gemlik, south to Mylasa, and finally east all the way to Ankara. By a stroke of great good fortune he had the advice of Turkey's leading specialist on marbles, Arhan Tekvar, who providentially turned up here because he is working in the vicinity and because he is a friend of our Marble Court architect M. C. Bolgil. (Arhan Bey's splendid "Inventory of the Marbles of Turkey" with color plates is strongly recommended to all interested in marbles.*)

Emin Bey's great moment of triumph came one evening when a splendid array of gleaming, regal porphyry-colored slabs leaning against the wall of the camp house greeted the astonished Sardis staff as they returned from work. Emin and Arhan Bey got the last available block in Ankara, and

*Arhan Tekvar, *Türkiye Mermer Envanteri, Maden Tetkik ve Arama Enstitüsü Yayinlarindan.* (Publications of the Minerals Research Institute no. 134; Ankara, 1966.) Preface by S. Alpan. Survey of marble deposits, with map, and color plates.

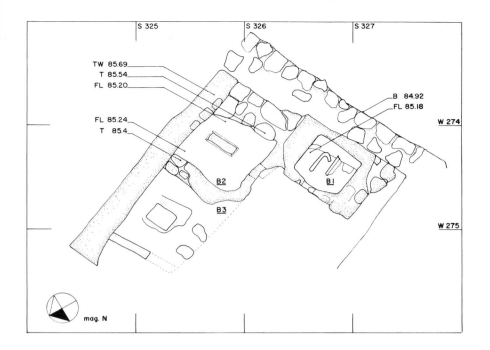

ISOMETRIC   FURNACE B1

PACTOLUS NORTH

FURNACE AREA B   AUGUST 1969

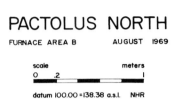

datum 100.00 = 138.38 a.s.l.   NHR

carted a half-dozen big marble slabs to Sardis—on a public bus, having persuaded the bus company that this was a legitimate equivalent of personal luggage.

Meantime, a quantity of white marble had arrived for the three-foot dado of the wall. "But who will detail this marble revetment?" mused Dick. "I have done this kind of work," volunteered Halis Aydıntaşbaş from Middle East Technical Institute, Ankara, whom we had engaged as architectural draftsman for the Synagogue. Here was a lucky break. Deliberate, persuasive, and determined, sporting a remarkable blue velvet sports cap, Halis Bey has been standing guard over the craftsmen who are putting up the backing and pinning the marble plates to the wall—and lending a hand himself.

Dick Stone has just departed, leaving a scattering of brilliant inspirations for a variety of our projects. Larry Majewski, director of New York University's Conservation Center, arrived punctually on July 28 to take over the conservation guidance. He has already spotted one potential sensation—there may have been figurative mosaics in Guy Metraux's enigmatic Long North Hall, that tantalizing counterpart to the Synagogue (Figure 153). Was it once a church with images of saints?

Another of our old pros, Axel von Saldern, came, researched, and completed with awesome efficiency by August 5 his prepublication field work on the glass accumulated by our excavations. In a brief, lucid, and cogent seminar presentation, Axel revealed that well over 3000 objects are represented by the glass fragments, from one or even two local factories of the Early Byzantine period.

Axel got great support from the cast of "depo dwellers," who live in our recording shed: Elaine Gazda, who drew some two hundred glass objects; our photographers, Elizabeth Gombosi and Ray Liddell, who coped with a big rush assignment; and Mrs. Hanfmann and her assistant, Chip

Figure 180—Turning over a block from the stylobate (at right) of the Forecourt colonnade, the Synagogue crew discover a relief of Artemis and Cybele. Engineer Ergene, conservator Stone and assistant director Mitten are amazed.

Figure 181—The two great goddesses of Sardis. Dating to the first half of the fourth century B.C. this votive relief from the Synagogue Forecourt (Figure 180) depicts on the left Artemis, taller, cradling a deer in her arms, and on the right Cybele holding a lion. Two worshipers approach the goddesses from the right; a tympanum hangs in the upper right corner. The column on the left, forming part of the framework, and the platform on which the figures stand may indicate a temple front. Hitherto some scholars thought Artemis and Cybele were one and the same goddess at Sardis. Height 0.99 m.

Goldstein, who produced both the stores of glass and the information about them.

You cannot bite the hand that feeds you. Thus when our cook Rüştü, who feeds more than thirty staff members and fifteen house personnel five meals a day (tea at 10 and 5 included), asked our architects Mehmet Bolgil and Mehmet Ergene and assistant Emin Balay to join him in an embassy, they could hardly refuse. Together with the middle-aged cook, these gentlemen (none of whom is married) were to sue for the hand of a village beauty on behalf of the cook's assistant. Two visits, each lasting from 9 P.M. until midnight, covered a variety of agricultural subjects in conversation. But in the end, this example of the village ritual ended in a failure—the father would not consent.

Gus Swift's Lydian Trench begins to look like part of a real Lydian town; Mehmet Bolgil's Marble Court is about to set the speed record for erection of one of the decorated pavilions; and Dave Mitten had brought a beautifully worked archaic limestone tripod from the Royal Cemetery—but I must leave these and a multitude of other matters for the final letter. Tonight, the three days' break we grant our staff for travels has ended. Larry Majewski, Fikret Yeğül, and Andy Ramage have just staggered in after an adventurous journey to our colleagues at Cnidus. Tomorrow, everybody will be off on the final spurt of this great campaign.

News from home indicates that ticket sales for the Sardis benefit exhibition, "Gods and Heroes: Baroque Images of Antiquity," are progressing well. You may recall that this exhibition will be at the Wildenstein Gallery in New York, from October 30 through January 4. As the proceeds go to support the culmination of the Sardis excavations, we hope that friends and Supporters of Sardis will be sure to come, and that they will stimulate the widest possible attendance among their friends. A gala preview the evening of October 29 is being organized by a nationwide benefit committee, under the leadership of Mrs. Edward M. M. Warburg and Mrs. Arthur A. Houghton, Jr. The exhibition will examine the diverse ways in which artists of the Baroque period re-interpreted classical antiquity. Two years of careful planning by John Coolidge, former director of the Fogg, Agnes Mongan, acting director and curator of drawings, and Baroque specialist Eunice Williams have resulted in our assembling a spectacular array of paintings, sculptures, and drawings by masters of the period, including Rembrandt, Poussin, Claude, and Caravaggio. A handsomely illustrated, informative catalog by Eunice Williams will be available at the gallery. And there will be a display of photographs and color slides of Sardis arranged by Jane Scott.

Sardis   August 1968

With thirty-seven staff members and assistants, a labor force over two hundred, and a great variety of projects, "Sardis 1968" is probably the most comprehensive among the numerous foreign archaeological projects in Turkey. The material being worked on spans several thousand years: David Mitten is finding pottery equivalents of Troy I (ca. 3000 B.C.) in his test excavation of Ahlatli Tepecik on the shores of the Gygean Lake, while C. H. Greenewalt, Jr., is working with Late Byzantine and Islamic remains as he investigates the citadel of Sardis for final publication. Between these two ends of the spectrum lies the most important epoch of Sardis, that of the Lydian Kingdom, to the knowledge of which the 1968 campaign has brought major contributions: at the Lydian Bazaar Gus Swift is revealing a highly unorthodox and striking pattern of architectural planning in Sardis of the seventh century B.C.; while on the Pactolus, the joint efforts of archaeologist Andrew Ramage and conservators Dick Stone and Sidney Goldstein have resulted in the detection of an area which may be an industrial establishment having to do with treatment of gold.

The 1968 effort was intended as the culmination of a decade of large-

scale digging. It also marked the beginning of a terminal phase of the two restoration projects: the grandiose example of a monumental Roman exterior in the Severan Marble Court of 211–212 in the Gymnasium, and the challenging attempt to recompose at least a sample of the resplendent interior of the gigantic Synagogue of Sardis (A.D. 166? to 250 for its earliest phase). Both will continue in 1969. Work on key points in the urban plan of Sardis was carried on by Brian Percival and Richard Penner. Several probes to locate the diagonal street which joined the main east-west avenue near the Synagogue were undertaken by M. T. Ergene.

Supplementing the topographical and architectural work, research on various groups of finds is gaining momentum. Professor and Mrs. George E. Bates will come soon to finish their study of Byzantine coins. The most heartening symbol of our progress toward publication was the printed sample page of George's catalog, sent here recently by Harvard University Press.

The publication of "Paintings and Mosaics of Sardis" will have some fascinating material. Larry Majewski has just drawn the paneled wall painting of the Romano-Byzantine bath "CG," and has started work on the paintings of the Early Christian Peacock Tomb (discovered in 1961, *Figure 61*).

The attempt to reconstruct the marble revetments in one bay of the south wall of the Synagogue, adjacent to the cross wall between the Main Hall and the Forecourt, was preceded by considerable research. Since 1966, Larry Majewski, Dick Stone, J. L. Greaves, and now Halis Aydıntaşbaş have tackled the much neglected subject of design and techniques of Roman marble paneling. It is fortunate that Halis had experience in modern use of marble revetments. He and Dick Stone designed the technique used by us to combine modern conservation standards with craft practices known in Turkey now. When the study of marble revetments appears, it will be based on practical experience.

242

Figure 182—Sample of interior decoration being restored in the Synagogue Main Hall. Marble panels on the South Wall include one bearing the dedicatory inscription of Regina and her husband who donated all the marble revetment and painting of the ceiling (Figure 84), above the four pilasters and colored panels over a dado of white marble slabs (Figure 146). On the left are the restored South Shrine with Doric columns and the partially reconstructed North Shrine, its Corinthian columns already in place.

The Synagogue rather than the regular excavation sectors has produced inscriptions and marble sculpture. Two Hellenistic inscribed sepulchral stelae were found built into the south wall of the Synagogue. According to Louis Robert they are from the third century B.C., one of an Arcadian, the other of a Samian. The Arcadian stele retains traces of red painted background. Used face down as a block of the stylobate in the Forecourt was the sculptural find of the season: the relief showing the great goddesses Artemis and Cybele, one holding a hind, the other a lion. The faces of the goddesses were intentionally damaged. I have the feeling that the Jewish builders used the piece with some feeling of triumph when they put it in as a building stone during the renovation of the Synagogue around A.D. 400 (Figures 180, 181).

Andrew Seager has come up with important new observations resulting from his detailed study and recording of the structure. The chief item of contention is the evidence that prior to serving as a Synagogue the hall may have opened in several gates or arcades into the southern colonnade and court (palaestra) of the Gymnasium. Another important, still controversial point is the exact sequence of events in the construction of the apse, which is such a striking feature in the plan of Sardis Synagogue. Last year we found that an apse had been foreseen in the foundations, possibly executed in the second century, our era; yet there are strong reasons to think that the apse was not really part of the original Gymnasium plan, and clear evidence that the apse superstructure was built after the long walls of the Synagogue Main Hall. (For latest solution, see Figure 201.)

Corresponding to the Synagogue on the south side is the Long North Hall on the northern side of the Gymnasium palaestra (Figures 222, 223). Here Guy Metraux has already shown that there was no apse. A division into several large bays is emerging which may correspond to the scheme suggested for the "pre-Synagogue" by Seager. Decorated with mosaics on walls and ceiling, the Long North Hall may have been an apodyterion, a dressing

243

room, according to Metraux's tentative interpretation.

Excavation of the walls of the Synagogue is almost complete with Steve Crawford's clearance of the eastern entrance porch and the remaining Byzantine shops along the south side (see plans, *Figures 153, 222, 223*). The entrance porch is still encumbered with secondary walls and with architectural pieces, piled up as the Byzantine soldiers left them during their final defense of the building against the Persian onslaught in A.D. 616.

Visitor after visitor comments on the large scale and diversity of the Marble Court restoration activities, as our homemade crane lifts tons of marble and some fifty workmen are seen dispersed at heights varying from ground level to fifty feet up in the air. Mehmet Bolgil drives ahead with great speed. One of the great pavilions (or aediculae), the best preserved one, was just re-erected in only five days—preceded, of course, by weeks of assembling and mending work on the ground.

Soon we shall have a design committee session on the one great problem remaining: the colonnade which screened the entrance side of the court (*Figures 210, 211*). David DeLong, who taught during the past year at the Middle East Technical University, Ankara, is this season's design architect for the Marble Court, but the matter also ties in research undertaken by Yeğül, Metraux, and Bolgil.

In the lively discussions of matters architectural and archaeological, one authoritative voice was much missed this summer at Sardis. Henry Detweiler, our associate director and former president and now life trustee of the American Schools of Oriental Research fell ill in May. His illness cast a shadow over our departure and we were much relieved when news came that he was recovering, news confirmed by a call from the indomitable Henry, who had a telephone installed at his sick bed as soon as the doctors would let him. We shall be looking forward to seeing Henry here again next year.

After writing these lines I reflected that the major finds of the season apparently had come to an end. Then Steve Crawford came walking down the corridor. "Open your hand," said he, and dropped into it a gorgeous earring, gold with green and red stones, and tiny pearls. He added: "It is the best the Izmir Five-and-Ten can offer." For a dreadful moment, I half swallowed Steve's kidding. Actually, he had found the earring in a probe two meters below the floor of the Synagogue near the apse in Early Roman fill. Not to be outdone, Guy Metraux came up with a charming bronze dog from his Long North Hall. At tea Andy Ramage and Sid Goldstein brought another crucible fragment, with traces of fire and bits of gold inside, the most cogent proof of gold working. And just after tea the Landrover came puffing up the terraces of the camp with an Ionic capital which Greenie had sent down from the Acropolis.

Sardis   September 7, 1968

Everybody at the luncheon table got up and applauded. For David De Long had pinned to our "blackboard" his perspective drawing of the Marble Court, just off the drawing board. The accolade was well earned: this is a beautiful drawing which shows the court as it is being restored and was very complicated to make. But a standing ovation should also be given Mehmet Bolgil, restoration architect, who is drawing close to the optimum objective of the season: all eight pavilions and four half-pavilions of the first story to be completed by October 1. When you come from the east on the highway you see from afar that a Roman building stands there; "we did not realize it was so big," is the visitors' typical comment when they enter the gymnasium area and are engulfed by the hustle and bustle of vehicles, wires, electric drills, and lifting gear. We are now determined to see the thing through its most challenging step: to put into position in 1969 the beautiful pediment over the second story of the monumental gate at the

Figure 183—Carpet rollers of the Synagogue. Using a new, speedier technique, mosaics are lifted for cleaning and repair. They will be backed by concrete and reset on cement bedding (Figure 200).

back of the court. This will get the building through what we consider restoration Stage II. It will then be one of the great sights of Roman architecture anywhere (see *Figures 164, 211*).

"You have now trained at Sart a whole school of restoration specialists," remarked Professor Ziegenhaus, architect of the Pergamon Expedition, on his recent visit, and this is true enough. This flowering of marble menders, stone movers, mosaic restorers, and so forth who were trained in the Marble Court restoration is now a great asset to the work at the gigantic Synagogue, as became quickly evident after Mehmet Ergene took over the construction side of the Synagogue project. He has been training these village workmen since 1964, and under his guidance restoration of the Forecourt jumped forward with impressive results. Nevertheless, Mehmet in his report rightly observes that his progress was handicapped by lack of labor. The truth is that we had raised less than a third of the funds needed for the 1968 work in the Synagogue. So something had to give. We were fortunate to have engaged our specialized staff, and thus most of the objectives are being reached, in particular erection of the four heart-shaped corner columns in the Forecourt. Now Emin Balay has taken over the construction, since Mehmet returned to Cambridge. Emin is an engineering student from Robert College, and has already restored two of the intermediate columns. We hope that next year the Forecourt can be completely "reconditioned" after we lift all mosaics and then put in the central fountain with marble paving around it. It will be the most complete room of the Synagogue.

To lift the mosaics, Larry Majewski is using a new technique in which the mosaic is rolled off like a carpet (*Figure 183*). It could be put back the same way, except that we keep "looking under the rug" and finding things. For Andy Seager has been waging a battle to unravel the "prehistory" of the building—the story of the structure before it became a synagogue (*Figure 201*). Andy, Dick Stone, Steve Crawford and Guy Metraux have been

Figure 184—R. Meric, Larry Majewski, and Mustafa Eris, take measurements for casting a new base for the marble fountain crater which will grace the Forecourt of the Synagogue. This is the original from which a cast was made.

"pitting" under the floors. They and Mehmet Ergene have turned up indications that a different arrangement of piers had been envisaged on the north side of the Main Hall; and that the earlier building has the east wall of its Main Hall several feet to the east of that of the Synagogue. The critical question is whether the earlier building was really a civil Roman basilica which was turned over to the Jewish congregation in A.D. 166 under the emperor Lucius Verus, or whether there was an earlier synagogue somewhere after all, or whether this was originally meant to be a dressing room for the Gymnasium—which is what its counterpart, the Long North Hall, seems to have been.

I have told something of the adventures involved in getting the marbles for the one bay of interior decoration which we are at present attempting. Halis Aydintaşbaş has been driving on, and will go about ten days overtime. The effect will be most striking. The panel with those hard-to-get green and dark red marbles turned out gloriously. We have now established the sources of supply and developed the rather intricate technique. For 1969 we are considering one more bay and just possibly the apse.

The completion of the North Shrine, that remarkable little aedicula set against the east wall of the Main Hall, was for a long time delayed by a column. It was to be turned by August 7 in a marble shop in Izmir. Not since Job had a man been hit by a series of misfortunes to rival the owner of that shop. His workmen got sick or ran away; his lathe refused to work; he himself got a heart attack. And he also wanted 100 TL more than we had originally agreed upon. So the column did not get done until late August (it is visible in place in *Figure 217*, left of main door).

Under Larry Majewski's expert direction the furnishings of the Synagogue have made much progress. The huge fountain crater has acquired a foot (*Figure 184*). The two pairs of lions, which flanked the great marble table, have been disassembled—because more pieces were found—and reassembled

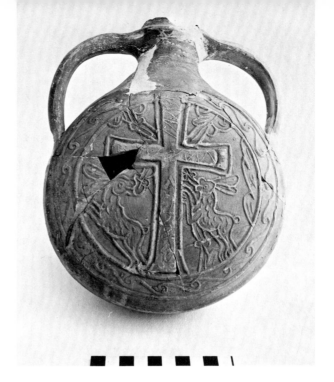

Figure 185—Large pilgrim flask of the fifth or sixth century with cross and hares nibbling flowers was found in a Byzantine Shop probably owned by a Christian.

again *(Figure 98)*; they have also been cast so that copies could be set up when the time comes. Larry is a kind of miracle man. When we got back from Izmir after our last not really free day, he unveiled before the astonished crowd beautiful wall paintings which he pulled off the walls of the Peacock Tomb *(Figure 61)*. These are most attractive pictures of peacocks, partridges, and baskets filled with roses, and more roses scattered over the white background. They had to be removed from the tomb to be saved; somebody had got into the mausoleum despite lock and key and tried to cut out the best picture of birds. Larry has already mounted these striking paintings, which are probably Early Christian, fourth or fifth century, so there will be no difficulty about displaying them in the Manisa Museum.

Another of Larry's discoveries will have to be taken up in our 1969 program. Under the highest pinnacle of the citadel there is a large vaulted room cut into the rock and filled with gravel; at the lower end is a sizable hole. We had confidently advertised this as a cistern, but Larry discovered painted wall stucco, and not one but several layers. He suggests this might be a Christian chapel. Time and labor were too short now at the end of the season but we would like to clear at least a corner to see if Larry is right.

I was writing some of this in the Kismet Hotel in Izmir when the phone rang. It was the Center for Nuclear Physics at Çekmece, Istanbul. I had been trying to contact them to see if we could arrange for neutron activation tests of some of the minute gold specimens we found. I was about to give up the struggle with overwhelming static and the chirping Turkish of the lady at the other end of the line, when the assistant director came on the phone in English. As a result we got a telegram today: "Earliest date for sample analysis November. . ." We shall, of course, accept.

Other specimens and associated materials (slag, earth from cupels) are being examined and analyzed at Ankara's modern Institute for Minerals Research. Larry Majewski, Mehmet Bolgil (who had architectural business

Figure 186—Mehmet C. Bolgil, supervising architect of Marble Court restoration, peels a latex print from the inscription (Figure 207) which recorded the dedication in A.D. 211 to (THEOI)S PATriois (Gods of our Fathers) and Most Familiar (Members) of Our House, Our Lords, the Emperors (KAI OIKEIATATON KYRION HEMON).

with the Antiquities Department), and I flew to Ankara, where in company of Clarence A. Wendel, minerals attaché, United States embassy, we called on Dr. Sadrettin Alpan, director of the institute. In a few minutes we were having an animated Turkish-English discussion with Dr. Nilüfer Baycin of the Research Laboratory and another scientist, Miss Nurgun Güngör. Having accomplished this and gone through an extensive agenda with the Department of Antiquities (permissions for gold testing, future of the Marble Court project, the fight to remove the highway TC 68 from the Sardis ruins) we returned to Sardis after a total absence of thirty-five hours and fifty minutes. Such speed was possible because of the wonderful help of Mr. Wendel, who understands our excitement over the discovery of gold-making in the time of Croesus. He even managed to fit into our tight schedule a pleasant visit at his home and a lunch in the club where we had a chance to talk with Dr. A. L. Tinnin, the cultural affairs officer.

The little gold specimens kept coming up as long as Andy Ramage continued to dig above, below, and around the cupellation floors. An important finding of his precise and delicate work: the gold refinery was active for a fairly short time—dating by pottery, about 570–550. This almost exactly coincides with Croesus' reign (561–547). But Andy had to pay a price for his good fortune. "O scorpions, O serpents"—the aria from *Idomeneo* might have been this summer's theme song. In a mean and cowardly manner a scorpion stung Andy twice when he was in bed. Greenie dashed with Andy through the night to the Salihli hospital; he survived the experience with more discomfort from injection than from the scorpion. Before that, Guy Metraux was a victim—apparently the scorpions decided that a decade of Sardis staff immunity was too much.

The season rose to a crescendo of discovery in mid-August. Just as Larry was finding his Christian chapel on the citadel, Greenie discovered evidence for glorious staircases at the Lydian wall on the Acropolis (*Figure 47*), evi-

Figure 187—View of Acropolis of Sardis from the north. The piers in the foreground are the remains of a Roman building; the wall in the background marks the location of the Roman civic center (points 30 and 24 in Map 3). The Acropolis, first fortified in the eighth century B.C., had in Lydian and Persian times a triple system of defenses admired by Alexander the Great. Soils around Sardis are now mainly for grazing of goats and sheep and for crops including cotton, eggplant, figs, grapes, melons, olives, peppers, sesame, tomatoes, and wheat.

dence which came out through his meticulous cleaning. The reexamination disclosed too that the Lydian architects used an intentional two-color scheme—green sandstone and white limestone. It is becoming ever more probable that architects and masons went from Croesus to Cyrus, from Sardis to Susa, to build the first monumental masonry palaces in Persia.

Drafted to serve as archaeologist in an attempt to detect the direction of a major street, Mehmet Ergene discovered an inscription of signal importance for the Late Roman and Byzantine city plan. Set between Christian crosses, the text seems to say that "a gate was leveled and a colonnaded street built . . . up to the Tetrapylon." A tetrapylon is a fourfold gate which traditionally occurs at the major intersection of avenues in a Graeco-Roman city. This intersection may well be by the eastern end of the Synagogue, or at the place where the inscription was found.

In the Byzantine Shops along the south wall of the Synagogue *(Figure 155)*, where the lion-shaped bronze lamp was found last year *(Figure 154)*, Steve found a majestic pilgrim flask decorated with a large cross and small crosses, and two hares eating flowers *(Figure 185)*. It seems that Jewish and Christian shops were interspersed in this shopping center. From their forays into the Prehistoric past at Ahlatli Tepecik in the Bin Tepe cemetery, Güldem Yüğrüm and David Mitten brought fascinating evidence of metallurgy of the third millennium B.C., a silver tube and a fine copper dagger, as well as masses of pottery. And in the very last days of the season, Gus Swift's Lydian Market sprouted forth with a series of large units strung along a precinct wall *(Figure 131)* at strange angles. The rooms are filled with choice Lydian and Greek pottery. Gus also found an enigmatic iron object a yard long; guesses have ranged from scepter to table leg to steelyard for weighing.

Then the whole team turned to intensive research and report writing, punctuated briefly by the temple party, a late one this year. Turkish drum

250

and *zurna* and an Eastern Anatolian dance executed under the small moon by Emin Balay, Necati Güler, Elaine Gazda, and Elizabeth Gombosi highlighted the party.

The volleyball net is down. Mattresses and blankets are being aired on the tea table. Our pine trees wave in autumn wind and petals are falling from the rose bushes around the house. The time for parting has come. It was a very good year. We had shot for a smashing campaign, setting goals good and high. Despite political perturbations, economic oscillations (remember the travel restrictions?), and the rise of prices and wages in Turkey and the United States, we achieved most of our objectives. Yet as the days ticked away in August, it became ever clearer that we shall have both unfinished business to complete and some new goals to attain in 1969.

The largest tasks were foreseen and foreseeable: the restoration of the Marble Court and conservation of the Synagogue. We shall try for Stage II on the Marble Court: putting the glorious pediment on top of the great gate. The Synagogue needs intensive combined operations; this year operations in the Synagogue like the lifting of mosaics paved the way for surprise results in research. As we prepare for publication, urgent salvage work must be done along with research on the precinct of Artemis. We hope to clean up the messy situation left by the first Sardis Expedition—pardonably —in 1914, and repair recent damage (this year stairs had fallen off the Temple during the winter). Cleaning up the Altar of Artemis should provide key knowledge for its date. We shall have more excitements as our clean-up crews (small compared to digging teams) tackle our own earlier doings. Work on the urban plan needs to be completed. Our educational program, run with much success by Gus Swift this season, has been bolstered by four traineeships granted through Cornell University by the Ford Foundation. The big expenses now are for research at home and field work here in Turkey.

1969

Sardis   July 12, 1969

A grove of fig trees, tall reeds and grasses, prickly bushes, a flowering wilderness of impenetrable green—this was the sector CG on June 22, 1969, nine years after we had stopped excavating *(Figures 39–40, 54)*. It looked as if nature had totally repossessed the ruins of the Romano-Byzantine complex which Harvardians Jane C. Waldbaum, Duane W. Roller, and I are to restudy for publication. But once the valiant foreman Mehmet Yavuz, had started to fight with fire and scythe against this overpowering jungle, the lineaments of huge masonry began to reemerge. Now Dick Penner and Peggy Darnall, architects from Cornell, are clambering about, placing grids and levels on the main structure, while thirty feet below, in a green pool, a concert is given by splendid-voiced frogs. Vaults and arches are festooned with plumb bobs carefully planted and anchored by Ken Frazer, our general manager and architect. Several small crews supervised by Duane are digging up features critical for a recheck of what was done from 1958 to 1960, and for new information.

Rustic vignettes from the season's opening: wheat stacks had invaded the area. When we approached to try to work out a compromise between agriculture and archaeology and explain what we were about, a wizened little man appeared, flayed the air with his arms in the direction of the Pactolus, and squeaked, "I know, I dug there." We had unearthed another survivor of T. L. Shear's 1922 campaign. Meanwhile, the farmer to the north of us was cutting off another area of ruins by digging a water canal. His horse-cart is moored to a wall of the ruins. His baby, parked in a cardboard box under the last extant fig tree, has visibly grown since we started digging.

What is going on at CG is fairly typical of the phase of "digging for publication." This takes up to sixty workmen, as against 150–200 during our large-scale digging campaigns. About the same number are working at the Marble Court restoration and Synagogue projects.

Financial footnote: A new minimum wage regulation, effective July 1, has raised wages all around and wiped out much of the economies from our cutback.

"We got accustomed to its face"; members no longer shriek with delight when Andy produces another tiny driblet of gold out of his pocket, but the orange clay of small furnaces for parting gold from silver (we think) and the telltale rings of cupels for removing base metals are still coming to light at Pactolus North (Figures 172–179)—along with other evidence for scientific history. Andy is to finish clearing this exciting area during this campaign. (After our reports about the gold refinery a Turkish newspaper had me cry exultantly: "After twelve years I shall find the Treasure of Croesus!" We have talked ourselves hoarse explaining that the Persians took it away long ago.)

Steve Crawford has completed his supplementary digging of the Sardis commercial center, picking up "a touch of Venus" along the way—a pretty head and a prettier midriff of marble. He had an unusual reexcavation on his hands when he began to look for the marble seats of the Byzantine latrine which adjoined the shops (Figure 45). Everybody had forgotten where they were left. Finally, the chief foreman, Hasan, remembered burying them in a little-frequented part of the Gymnasium; thus vital information on an integral part of the Sardian economic center was saved.

Shortly after we started work at Bin Tepe a day of hurricane weather was followed by wild crashes of thunder and a deluge at midnight. The roads have become murderous and our red truck had to be dragged out once by a tractor from neighboring Tekelioğluköy. Mellon patches are blocking resumption of digging at Ahlatli Tepecik. David Mitten, who is spelled by David Finkel, is testing around the Balikhane (Map 2; on the Gygean Lake) in search of a habitation site. Having passed through mixed Romans and Lydians, the two Davids have just hit the Bronze Age. Their joys of discovery (*Figure 162*) and their jolting journeys are shared by the Muharrem Tağtekin, our second commissioner, veteran of many campaigns at Bin Tepe.

The facades of the Marble Court have grown a lot since Mrs. Hanfmann and I came to Sardis early in May. We had rushed out immediately to see what damage the severe earthquake of March 28 might have done. Fortunately, the major tremors had swung north and east of Sardis and thus no great harm had ensued. To lay plans for beginning the Marble Court program on May 20, supervising architect Mehmet Cemal Bolgil had flown to Sardis straight from his honeymoon in England, where the parents of his bride then lived. Mehmet has brought his young wife to Sardis; Zerrin hanım has proved a first-rate worker and a great asset to the expedition in the administration and recording departments.

The remarkable crane constructed by our engineer, Tankut Akalin, has grown a longer arm and is capable of sixty-foot lifts. Columns of the second-story pediment are now proudly rising into the sky.

Andy Seager came from Indiana and Halis Aydintaşbaş came from Spain (he was there on a fellowship) to pick up the threads of last year's work on the Synagogue. Halis has just completed the pediments of the two little shrines in the Main Hall and is starting on the lowest course of revetments in the Main Hall. Andy has just studied reconstitution of the floor of the Forecourt, and now he is starting tests to solve some of the mysteries in the earlier history of this unique building. Meantime, Sidney Goldstein, conservator from Harvard, is laying out in the Synagogue the appealing dove-and-crater frieze which we hope to put, at least in part, on the Forecourt wall.

Figure 188—The most memorable man on the expedition staff, village potter Mustafa Eriş became a skillful conservator of antiquities. A hunchback with artistic hands who had dreams and visions, Mustafa was a mainstay of our laboratory from 1959 until his sudden death in 1969. Here he is repairing pottery.

Sidney and his wife Chip, assistant recorder, arrived on July 3. Until then, the laboratory was closed. In other years our beloved Mustafa Eriş had opened it. But Mustafa Eriş died last spring. A round head, hair standing on end, nose like a stork's beak, the luminous eyes of a child, a cavernous bass rumbling unexpectedly out of the small hunchbacked body, and the long, sensitive fingers of an artist—this was Mustafa *(Figure 188)*. He came to the laboratory in 1959, a potter by trade. Once he grasped that we preferred broken old pots to his new ones, he became a superlative craftsman-restorer. Completely dedicated to his work, he was like a beneficent gnome inhabiting the laboratory—perhaps the only place where he was truly happy.

With the kind of digging we are doing we are not supposed to find many objects, but the objects come to us. First ever popular Dave Mitten was summoned by a village friend to bring in a handsome relief stele. It shows a young man named Nympheros with athlete's gear; then no less than five inscribed Hellenistic funerary urns came streaming into David's net. He was given, too, a collection of vases, quite intact, assembled by his friends at Bin Tepe over the winter.

Dave and I were sitting in front of the Swift House when a boy ran up— the same appealing little boy who sold us a fake terracotta last year. (I have since learned that terracottas and lamps made in Turgutlu are not meant as fakes; you can buy them, with proper identification as imitations, at the official tourist pavilion in Izmir.) The boy flung two pieces at us: one an incomplete Lydian perfume jar, the other a biggish sherd on which we discerned under the mud which caked it the countenance of a painted sphinx. We knew Greenie would never forgive us if we did not secure this masterpiece of Lydian Orientalizing drawing *(Figure 190)*, and we promptly purchased the two pieces for the Manisa Museum. A couple of days later, the boy appeared with another bit of the sphinx and more Lydian pottery. Now Greenie began to urge action to locate the source of such goodies. After

some detective work on our side the boy's father led us there—at a price.

The boy had covered about fifty yards in a straight line from the spot of discovery to the spot of sale. The heap of pottery was wedged in by hard earth and stones in the side of a creek known as "Northeast Wadi" (*Figure 189*), not far from the Artemis Temple. H. C. Butler (1914) and T. L. Shear (1922) reported Lydian houses here, deeply buried. I had explored it in 1953 and marked it for action in 1958, but abandoned the plan in favor of another area. Now Greenie has started digging.

The first great find of the new Sardis excavations was the Lucius Verus inscription discovered by Tom Canfield on July 11, 1958 (*Figures 17, 18*). As the fiercest hot south wind imaginable howled through the camp, July 11, 1969, ended in a blaze of archaeological glories. Greenie's Northeast Wadi detection; David Mitten's triumphant announcement of a big Bronze Age level at Eski Balikhane in Bin Tepe (Map 2); Andy Seager's and Halis' recovery of a relief of a goddess used in the Synagogue as a wall revetment—these came one after another, unfolding a new chapter in the unpredictable saga of Sardis.

Sardis   August 11, 1969

The moon never shone more brightly over Sardis than in those momentous days of July, but the "moon fever" that had seized the United States was only a spasmodic affliction at Sardis. One reason was that the few radios at hand got more noises than news. There would be paroxysms of excitement—Larry Majewski rushing out of his room shouting, "They have landed!"—but then only a dribble of news via the radios of the Turkish personnel and workmen. Still, we toasted the astronauts in the evening of July 21, and Dr. Ali Ataseven, our expedition doctor, was so enthusiastic

Figure 189—Archaeological detection: following up the clue of pottery (Figures 190, 191), we discovered Lydian houses in a dry gulch, the "Northeast Wadi," right behind the camp. Parts of two houses are seen here running across the gulch; a circular storage bin is at upper left. Findspot of the pottery was between the two crossing walls.

about the success of the moon voyage that he sent a congratulatory telegram to our embassy.

We used to measure the passing of our season by the progress of threshing on the village threshing floors (Figure 55) between the city wall and the Pactolus North dig—but this year the high pitched monotone of the mechanical thresher was heard through the land and into the night. There was a truck standing in each field to take away the harvest. Ours may well be the last generation to see the biblical round of labors in the fields, orchards, and vineyards of Lydia—the twig-woven, basket-like cart so similar to the carts of the land and sea peoples who invaded Egypt about 1200 B.C.; or the threshing sleigh, set with "Neolithic" flint teeth. Now, heavy traffic rushes on Route TC 68 through the ruins of Sardis. (Honesty compels me to say that after the rented threshing machine left, the horse and the ox teams came out for the clean-up.)

Leopards, dolphins, hares, lions, and yellow-green birds (they are recognizable quails)—new life and color has come to our camp from the dozens of tall mosaic slabs that line the walls of the camp enclosure, the storage shed, and the terrace of the house. Larry Majewski has mobilized the crew which usually moves heavy columns at the Marble Court to extract this spectacular display from the shed where about a hundred mosaic pieces had been stacked since the time when, several seasons ago, they were lifted from the villa at Pactolus North and from the Synagogue. Larry's purpose is to study them for his publication of "Mosaics and Wall Paintings from Sardis," but he has also reminded us what a treasure house of mosaics we have amassed.

At the Synagogue, Halis Aydintaşbaş and Larry have combined forces to repair the top and cast the legs of that enigmatic object, the table with reliefs of Roman eagles adorning its legs and a beautiful egg and dart decorating its top (Figure 97). The top, seven feet long, weighs about two tons.

257

Figure 190—This ten-inch-wide sherd with snooty sphinxes brought by a village boy set off the search in the Northeast Wadi. It is a piece of a Lydian "Orientalizing" (because of Oriental monsters) jar, sixth century B.C.

Halis has made the brilliant observation that in style and size it greatly resembles the ornaments still to be seen on the great Hellenistic Temple of Artemis at Sardis. Was the temple already falling into decay (in the fourth century?) when the Jewish community secured one of the temple parts to use as a lectern (or as support for a menorah) in front of the apse of the Synagogue—precisely where the altar was located in early Christian churches? (See *Figure 216*.)

The lifting and consolidation of the mosaics in the Forecourt and Main Hall is pivotal for the research and conservation of the Synagogue; for lifted and consolidated they must be before they can go back to their places. At the same time, any probing under the floor, any quest for earlier buildings can be done only after the mosaics have been lifted. Andy Seager, architectural researcher for the Synagogue, remarked half-humorously, half-plaintively that he and Halis, archaeological investigation and concomitant restoration, are playing leap frog, jumping over each other to keep out of each other's way. Now that Larry Majewski has activated a larger mosaic crew, the roll back of mosaics is going faster *(Figure 183)*. Andy had eagerly waited for several crucial mosaics to be lifted and had then the supreme satisfaction of seeing under the floor walls and piers which he had predicted on grounds of architectural logic *(Figure 201)*. As a burning sunset gleamed through the Synagogue door, we sat in the apse and listened to Andy giving a superlative disquisition into the intricate history of this ever astonishing edifice.

"The less we dig, the more we find." For a while it looked as if every stroke of a pickax was bringing to light Lydian pottery, some of it painted in enchanting Orientalizing style—wild goats, lions, and a very small sphinx. Greenie's Northeast Wadi has revealed Lydian walls and other evidence that a big settled area of Sardis was up that creek *(Figures 189, 191)*. Meantime, Andy Ramage came forth with some choice items from his gold refinery on

258

the Pactolus—among them a most intriguing stone mold to cast jewelry. More Lydians chimed in from Bin Tepe, from Dave Mitten's dig and from two graves at the "Three Mounds" (Üçtepeler), with a great assortment of pots and a fine bronze mirror—the last lot an offering from local peasants.

Professor Roberto Gusmani from the University of Messina, world-renowned specialist and author of a dictionary of the Lydian language, sneaked into camp during pre-lunch commotion. Gusmani is blond, blue-eyed, and looks very young for one of such attainments. He has already made a number of fascinating suggestions about our Lydian inscriptions. And yesterday he wowed our crowd with a superlative talk on "How to Read and Write Lydian" (actually "Lydische Inschriften und Graffiti"), which everybody agreed was as clear a statement as anybody could make about a language that uses "enclitica piled up after the first word of a phrase."

Men are digging stepped trenches up and down the steep slope of the Pyramid Tomb (Figure 192), and a net of strings intersects and weaves above them. Sandor Kasper, a leading archaeological architect long associated with the excavations of the German Archaeological Institute in Turkey, is giving a terrific demonstration of digging and measuring techniques. He is assisted by Mrs. Kasper, a student of archaeology at Munich. Her keen eyes have already discovered an interesting sign: a second swastica on the eastern side of the steps on which the presumed pyramid stood.

We have invited Sandor Kasper to make a stone by stone survey and drawing of this monument and to investigate its surroundings because it has become the center of great interest and controversy. This strange array of steps, excavated first by Butler before 1914 and again by Greenie and Chris Reagan (1960–1961), displays amazing technical resemblances to buildings constructed by Cyrus, king of the Persians, at Pasargadae, his capital in Iran. Having visited Pasargadae late in May, I can swear that our Lydians were

active there—probably because Cyrus carried them off after he had captured Sardis in 547 B.C.

The day was gray and the Gygean Lake unquiet. The little promontory and the pebbly beach were strewn with oxygen tanks, diving gear, and all sorts of mechanical equipment. A generator rattled away and a man was talking on the radio. Fifty yards downwind, almost hidden by tall sesame stands, was one of the typical local shelters, *çardaks*, serving as D. G. Mitten's field office, with about half of the Sardis Expedition members swarming around it. By strangest coincidence two American teams had arrived on the little promontory within twenty-four hours and had settled within fifty yards of each other. David Mitten, David Finkel, and their commissioner Muharrem Bey had come to salvage from oblivion a Bronze Age village of 5000 years ago; a team of salvage experts from NATO had come to raise a plane that had fallen into the lake four weeks ago (the pilot had bailed out).

Dave Mitten made the introductions, and then asked, "Sergeant, can you tell us about your plans?" The muscular giant was laconic and to the point: "High winds have driven off one of our pontoons. As soon as we get it back, we will put pontoons under the plane, buoy her up, and tow her to the end of the lake. Then the plane will be put on a truck and towed away." (And so it happened, too.)

We went out to view Dave's Bronze Age discoveries at this place called "The Old Fishery" (Eski Balikhane). Though brief in time and limited to an open patch in the vegetation, the dig has brought forth mighty pithoi and finds the full impact of which will be considerable for our knowledge of technology and religion of the Early Bronze people of this region. The best find was the burial of a man of high status, about thirty-five years old. He lay flexed in the big jar, legs bent. At his temples were the enigmatic "ear plugs" or "studs" of gold beaten over a core of bitumen or similar material.

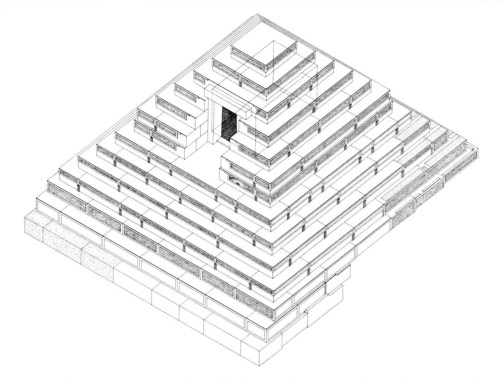

Figure 192 (left)—The Pyramid Tomb was surveyed and leveled inch by inch in 1969. This remarkable limestone masonry structure may be the funerary monument for a Persian nobleman who fell in battle for Sardis (547 B.C.). Trenches were run down the hillside and along the brook to retrieve parts fallen downhill. On top of tomb, architect S. Kasper drawing. See also Figure 62.

Figure 193 (right)—Meticulous observation of incised setting lines and wear of stones has led S. Kasper to propose a new reconstruction of the Pyramid Tomb. Entered from the north, the burial chamber was under a pyramid with seven steps.

At his mouth was a perforated silver pendant in the shape of a ram. At his hip was a copper dagger. Similar "gold studs," presumably signs of high rank, have been found in burials of "Troy II" date (2500–2200 B.C.) in southern and central Turkey. To prevent undue uproar, Güldem hanım with great presence of mind declared to the workmen that the studs might be of brass *(Figure 162)*.

July is the month when we drive hard and all our projects advanced at a hot pace. Then we took a break from July 30 to August 2. Staff members journeyed to Ankara, Gordion, Bodrum, Cnidus, Istanbul; they returned full of gratitude for the generous hospitality of other excavators. As work picks up toward the final spurt, we are having a hard look at things done and to be done. And it comes to pass that things look you in the eye and say: "You cannot finish with us this season—you need more time." Thus together with Mehmet Cemal Bolgil and Ken Frazer we are considering whether in the Marble Court restoration we can or cannot go on beyond Stage II— which is currently being implemented as the central part of the second story goes into place. "Stage III" would call for putting up the other pavilions, the wings of the second story. We have the equipment, we have the crews specialized in this complicated job for the last five years—and if we move the present equipment set-up and disband the crews, they cannot be brought again to the same level in less than five years. But there is Mehmet Bey's supervising time—he has already made considerable sacrifices by agreeing to take out five months a year from his architectural practice and has done so three times; and there are the steadily rising costs. Other matters have hitherto been left aside: repairs are needed of all the major architectural pieces not used in the reconstruction; visual links are needed to the immediately adjacent parts of the Gymnasium; the gray-red austerity of supporting walls calls for treatment (they were revetted with marble in antiquity); and then there are the ancient marble floors (at present safely buried under pro-

Figure 194 (left)—Relief, four feet wide, waterworn, found under bed of Pactolus torrent. Left half of the marble pediment of a temple-like mausoleum, made when Sardis was the western capital of the Persian Empire. The relief shows husband reclining on couch, food on the table, drinking cup in his right hand; wife at his feet; two daughters on another couch. Around 400 B.C.

Figure 195 (right)—Setting the keystone of the ornamental arch in the pediment over the West Gate of the Marble Court on August 12, 1969, six seasons after restoration began. Completing the pediment entailed a 70 foot lift.

tective earth cover)—not to mention the tricky problems of drainage. All of this adds up to 1970. At the moment, everybody is excited—after six years of work, obstacles, and frustrations, the keystone of the pedimental arch of the second story is scheduled to go into place at 4 P.M. on August 11.

The setting of the white marble decoration of the Synagogue Apse has begun—a most important step in our efforts to recreate something of the antique splendor of the interior (for its condition in 1970, see *Figure 216*).

P.S. Mehmet Bolgil has just found a little marble Muse with a lyre to provide a harmonious conclusion for the day.

Sardis   September 6, 1969

The red excavating machine had stood for some time in the village, at the corner between the coffeehouse and the fruitstand. It belongs to the railway department and it seemed stranded at this intersection where a yellow sign says: "To Sardis Ruins." Suddenly, the long-armed thing took off and emerged in the middle of the Pactolus bed, just a little below the steep bank where in 1959 and 1960 we dug Lydians, Romans, and Byzantines at Pactolus Cliff (*Figure 31*).

The machine started digging a canal some ten feet below the present bed of the Pactolus. We kept an eye on it but nothing happened until one morning Mehmet Bolgil rushed by in the beige Landrover. He had gotten word that a sculptured piece was being found. "Being found" is the right description; the piece, very oddly shaped, was sticking out only a foot or so from the bank of the freshly dug canal, and the next whack of the machine could cover it up again.

There was some diplomatic palavering and it was agreed that the villagers would go on digging their canal but would protect the piece—against a con-

sideration, to wit: a contribution to the cost of the canal (which is to bring drinking water to the lower village). Mehmet and I thought we had discerned on the visible part of the piece some kind of horsemen or horses, while Greenie and Fikret Yeğül said it was a reclining man. They were right. The relief turned out to be the left half of a small pediment, about four feet long (*Figure 194*). There is, indeed, a man reclining on a couch, looking left; three women of decreasing size are seated *en échelon* looking toward him—surely his wife and two daughters. The style of the large, soft figures is of the Persian period though largely Greek in inspiration; it is tempting to think of the man as one of Sardis' famous satraps. As the pediment came from a building only about ten feet wide, and as the "Funerary Meal" is a standard theme of sarcophagi and reliefs of that era, it may well have adorned a mausoleum. It is a unique piece for Sardis—but so eroded by water that one only divines its originality and elegance.

For a while things were popping. If we turned over a marble slab, it turned out to be a long inscription in honor of one Iulius Lepidus. If we tried to set straight a stone left stranded by Butler in 1914, it turned out to be a Hellenistic stele—with a Greek inscription. And if we just cleaned a bit of a wall, Lydian monograms and masons' marks jumped out. It was a good thing we had Gusmani at hand; he managed to make just three Lydian signs yield the reading: "he wrote to (or "for") Artemis."

I ended the last letter with the keystone of the gorgeous "Baalbek" arch almost going up to crown the second story of the Marble Court. It went up the next day, August 12 (*Figure 195*). What an occasion that was! Martha Hoppin sat on top of the southern wing of the Marble Court dangling her feet and providing official photographic coverage. High over the keystone, exhibiting complete sangfroid as he insinuated himself amidst, beside, and above the crane operators, was Paul Woolf, gray kerchief waving under his cap; he was providing superofficial coverage. Naturally, way up there was

Figure 196 (left)—On the same day that the keystone of the Marble Court arch was set (seen at top, and Figure 195), the two-ton table top was hoisted into place on the most controversial furnishing of the Synagogue, the Eagle Table. According to some it served for mystery rites involving wine, others say it was used for display of the menorah or reading of Scriptures. The top may have been taken from a pagan temple.

Figure 197 (right)—Interior of Early Christian Church M (ca. A.D. 400) looking east through window of inner apse. On the left is an unexplained niche. A marble pavement and traces of painted stucco survive. Probably a martyr's chapel, this is the earliest Christian church extant at Sardis.

Mehmet Cemal Bolgil, the man who made the Marble Court shoot up; and Hasan Koramaz, chief foreman, master mason, and a man who loves difficult stone jobs more than anything else. As I did not wish to be found wanting, the arch looked as if it had about a dozen statues on top of it. It was a proud moment as we remembered those who had done so much for the Marble Court: Henry Detweiler, who first identified the stones of this arch; Steve Jacobs, who so methodically laid the foundation for the entire restoration project; Jim Yarnell, who got the restoration show going; Mehmet Ergene, who carried it on after Jim.

The same afternoon a different but equally momentous lifting took place in the Synagogue. I wrote in my last letter about the controversial "Eagle Table"—confirmation of a mystical Judaism for the late Erwin Goodenough; for some, a lectern; a stand for a menorah for others. With a heave the stone crew lifted the two-ton table top into place. It was amazing how strong and monumental this table turned out to be, how much dignity it has added to the view of the apse and, indeed, of the Synagogue *(Figure 196)*.

The table stands on axis with the fountain. I was driving by and did a double take; then stopped and jumped out, and still could not believe my eyes. Standing in its pink-yellow, soft marble beauty in the middle of the Forecourt colonnade, its rounded contours at once counterpointing and harmonizing with the rise of the slender columns, making an emphatic accent in the long perspective toward the center of the apse, the fountain crater seemed completely and incredibly right, giving meaning and proportion to the entire Forecourt (Plate V). Yet I was looking at a marble-tinted cast made by Larry Majewski and indistinguishable from the original, which currently stands on a terrace of our camp.

There are more wonders to be seen in the Synagogue: the bird frieze with the same kind of water-of-life crater as marks the fountain; the marble benches of the Elders (they are being revetted with marble); and the new bay

of interior decoration, over which will rise the second of our donors' inscriptions, the one of Hippasios the Second, "the most monumental . . . of all the later inscriptions of the Synagogue," of which some thirteen feet are preserved. "I, Hippasios the Second, A Citizen of Sardis, with my wife . . . because of the pledge, gave the marble revetments for the ornament of the House," says the text *(Figures 199, 216)*.

Fireworks will no doubt continue as our probes into the past of the building yield all sorts of controversial material. As some 125 square meters of mosaics were being lifted under Larry's supervision, coins began to appear under the mosaics in quite considerable numbers. (We are told that to this day in some regions of Turkey some money is put under a new floor in a house.) We found a great number of coins of the fourth century under mosaics of the Forecourt previously thought to have been put down some 150 years earlier. The Battle of the Mosaics is the one thing that will make the conservation project in the Synagogue go on not only in 1970 but probably also in 1971. We now have enough experience to know that the lifting and consolidation simply cannot be hurried, especially when things keep showing up underneath. But the great coherence and the coloristic glow that the mosaic floor will add to the building are worth the time and effort.

There is a structure of red sandstone in front of the Artemis Temple which Butler called "The Lydian Building" and left in something of a small size chaos—our predecessors at Sardis did not anticipate the outbreak of World War I. (We now have a picture of Howard Crosby Butler and his crew of 1913 as a principal display in our salon by courtesy of Mrs. Seymer, daughter of William H. Buckler of Baltimore, who was Butler's inscription specialist.) We had said in our permit application that we should like to put the monument in order. Snatching a couple of workmen released from the Pyramid Tomb, Duane Roller and our stone crew went to work. It is the stepped altar of the Artemis Temple all right *(Figure 202)*; but side trenches

and the clearing of a central hole dug by Butler revealed that there is nothing underneath but our eternal enemy, riverine deposits of gravel. A bit of a lamp from the fifth or late sixth century B.C. is the only datable evidence in surprisingly barren soil. This is a fine monument, not yet properly studied; and with Ken Frazer's architectural expertise we hope to make progress on this job—which includes all sorts of tantalizing problems about the relation of the altar (fifth century B.C.?) to the Hellenistic Temple of Artemis. (Just to tease us, right under the surface of the Roman extension of the altar there appeared an exquisite bit of architectural ornament: a marble fragment with a delicate late archaic or early classical lotus and palmette.)

It is a long step from the altar of Artemis at the west side to the little Christian Church M tacked on to the southeast corner of the giant temple (*Figures 67, 197, 198;* Map 3, no. 18). Peggy Darnall and I were doing some studying of the structure for Steve Jacobs, who tried to preserve the church when he was at Sardis in 1960 and 1961, and has agreed to publish or republish it. The church, quite an early one (fifth century), is remarkable for having a second apse tacked on to the original one (*Figure 198).* Peggy mentioned that Butler's drawing (but not his summary text) showed a grave orientated north-south in this second apse, and now Steve would like to know whether there was really a grave in that place. I ordered our one and only workman to scratch around a bit; to our surprise there came out tiles and under the tiles a skeleton—but lying with head to west, toward the apse. Well, perhaps he wanted to be near the saint in the original church. But then a second skeleton showed up, in line with the first, head to west, and conforming in all details to Turkish Islamic burials. The poser is that the church was completely covered by a landslide from the ninth century until 1912 when Butler dug it out. Villagers are noncommittal, and no venerable ancient has yet come forward to identify the skeletons, but my suspicion is that they may have been buried there at some time between 1918 and

Figure 198—Church M was built when Artemis temple (column on right) was abandoned. Recent graves were found, between the damaged outer (left) and repaired inner apse. The projecting rectangle may have been a room for priests. The church was repaired and cleaned in 1961 and 1970. (A different view from south is Figure 67.)

1924. Instead of solving a mystery we have another mystery on our hands.

The one but last battalion is about to depart: the Goldstein team from lab and recording, Martha Hoppin and Elizabeth Gombosi from their hectic race around the precincts to meet all last minute photography requests, Duane Roller to his Norton Fellowship in Athens, we back home via Germany. Still carrying on will be the Kaspers, Ken Frazer, Lee Lort, the Bolgils (to complete this season's Marble Court aims), Halis Aydintaşbaş (same for the Synagogue), and this season's popular engineer and purchaser, Teoman Yalçinkaya (Robert College), who will take on the constructional supervision of both projects in 1970, with Mehmet Bolgil and Andy Seager as consultants. In 1970, too, we aim to get the Acropolis study done, deferred this year by the sudden discoveries in the Northeast Wadi; to do the prepublication work on that great economic Lydian area, the House of Bronzes or Lydian Market; and keep on going on several fronts for publication of objects.

It is already clear that this intensive stage of study and preparation constantly yields new finds and results: finds in the ground, from cleaning—like the Roman paintings in a tomb near the Artemis Temple which were undetected when Larry Majewski started his inventory of all wall paintings from Sardis, though the tomb had been known; finds above ground, from clearing, as when Peggy Darnall, Dick Penner, Martha Hoppin, and I discovered the first and only round tower in the city wall (at the cost of being prickled by thorns and thistles); finds inside, in our own boxes, as when pieces of fine pottery or sculpture found in different years come together to form a meaningful whole. The joys of discovery never cease.

1970

Sardis   July 11, 1970

For the first time in Sardian history there were fireworks on the Fourth of July. The ancient Tmolus Mountain resounded in nightly darkness to the popping of firecrackers, and madly twirling candles lit up marble fragments in our courtyard. Ken Frazer had conjured the firecracker show. Larry Majewski, after a brief rehearsal at Artemis Temple, led a medley of patriotic songs celebrating with considerable vocal emphasis Larry's native Iowa and Martha Hoppin's native Ohio. A last minute crisis—no bubbly wine for toasts—was narrowly averted by a scouring of all shops and restaurants in Salihli.

This may sound as if the Sardis campaign is off to a normal start. It is. On June 1 we did not yet know whether and when we might be able to begin; by June 22, twenty-three expedition members and the two Turkish commissioners had appeared, and digging activities started on schedule. The camp had never seemed more peaceful and idyllic, trees waving gently, birds singing. The faithful house staff headed by the remarkable Cook Rüştü (originally an electrician and plumber who fixes generators and pumps as well as menus) seemed to work with smooth efficiency. Old members slipped into the agreeable Sardis routine; new members seemed to adjust readily to the "early to bed, rise at dawn" schedule. Everybody seemed more relaxed. After the strife and tension of American college campuses, Sardis in its narrow Pactolus valley, with its green vineyards and piping shepherds, felt like a hidden vale, a place to let the world go by.

But the world does not wish to go by. The verses of Horace about black worry clinging to the rider went around in my head as we shot along the

Figure 199—Synagogue, 1970: restoration of the mosaic floor. Center ("Bay 3"), mosaics are freed from earth cover, lifted (Figure 183), and mounted on concrete blocks. Mounted mosaics stand against the wall. To the right ("Bay 2"), stone bedding and cement backing are laid. In "Bay 1," in front of marble revetted Apse, mounted mosaic parts are maneuvered back into original positions.

nearly empty highway in the leaden summer haze of the Anatolian highlands. Late in the evening an urgent summons to Ankara "to discuss an important problem" threw me into a dither. Near midnight, our favorite Salihli taxi driver, Pertev, was fished out of the local coffeehouse, and at five A.M. Gerry Olson, soils specialist from the Department of Agronomy at Cornell, and I took off. Somehow, this summons came tied to a report that peasants had complained to the Governor about Gerry's digging holes outside the excavation.

The important problem turned out to be the measures which the Turkish authorities wished to have taken internationally to suppress illicit traffic in antiquities. They left no doubt that the matter is paramount in their view of cultural relations with the United States. We took the opportunity to ask for additional legitimation of Gerry's soil-sampling activities. This was done by letter to the Governor of Manisa. Now, with determined step accompanied by two Turkish assistants, Gerry is ranging up hill and down dale sampling the soils of Sardis (Figure 219). In Ankara, he made contact with Mesut Özuygur, director of the Institute for Soils Research and an ardent alumnus of Cornell (1948), who put him in touch with the Soils Conservation Division (Topraksu) in Ankara and Manisa.

Our day in Ankara ended with a fine study in contrasts. We sipped elegant tea in Özuygur's modern apartment, one of five hundred in a pentagonal block, as red evening light poured into the light shaft. Then we elbowed our way through the heaving, clamoring mass of humanity in Ankara's new Central Garage, which is planned like New York's West Side Terminal. Seven hours later the superlatively springed, modern bus, complete with "Captain" (driver) and a hostess, put us at the village road to the Sardis camp, as sunrise broke the long dawn.

From last September to June this had not been a good year. The worst

269

Figure 200—L. J. Majewski (left) supervises positioning of Synagogue's mosaics in Bay 1. According to an inscription (Figure 144), mosaics were counted in "bays" (*diachorema*) from west to east. The Main Hall had seven bays.

blow was Henry Detweiler's death. It is hard not to think of him as present here at Sardis, where so many of his Turkish friends still ask about him—and where his and Catharine's room was across from ours.*

Months of uncertainty about the current permit policies of the Turkish Department of Antiquities made planning difficult. Yet here we are and hard at it. Restoration architects Mehmet Cemal Bolgil and Teoman Yalçinkaya were already going full tilt when we arrived. The exhilarating clangor of drills and chisels still emanates from the Marble Court of the Roman Gymnasium. The court grows in size and beauty as the second story is being finished. Its bulk lords it above the highway—a sudden vision of Roman urban magnificence rising out of Sardian vineyards (*Figure 226*).

Andy Ramage had to perform acrobatics to check the reading of the dedicatory inscription of A.D. 212 on the Marble Court's first-story aediculae (pavilions) before removal of the scaffolding (*Figure 207*).

In one corner of the Synagogue, near the apse (*Figure 216*), where the marble "usta" is finishing the revetment for the benches of the Elders, Andy Seager, architect in chief, is exercising photographers Elizabeth Gombosi and Martha Hoppin in photography of overlapping walls and periods. Lindley Vann is intently watching prize pickman Durmuş dig under a newly found marble floor—a floor earlier than the famous mosaics which decorated the

*Albert Henry Detweiler, Professor of Architecture and Associate Dean of the College of Architecture, Art, and Urban Planning, Cornell University, died of a heart ailment in New York on January 30, 1970, at the age of 63. As president of the American Schools of Oriental Research he secured in 1955 the sponsorship of the Schools for the Sardis project and subsequently induced Cornell University to join. His great experience in the field and his extraordinary administrative abilities were placed unstintingly in the service of Sardis, first (1956–58) as field adviser, then as associate director (1959–1970). He had a wonderful knack of communicating his enthusiasm for people and life to others; and many will remember the evening conversations with Henry on the excavation house terrace, where he was as willing to share his thoughts as to listen to the interests and needs of others. If you asked Henry to do a thing it was as good as done, so quick and effective was he in his actions. He was a wonderful colleague as well as a very dear friend.

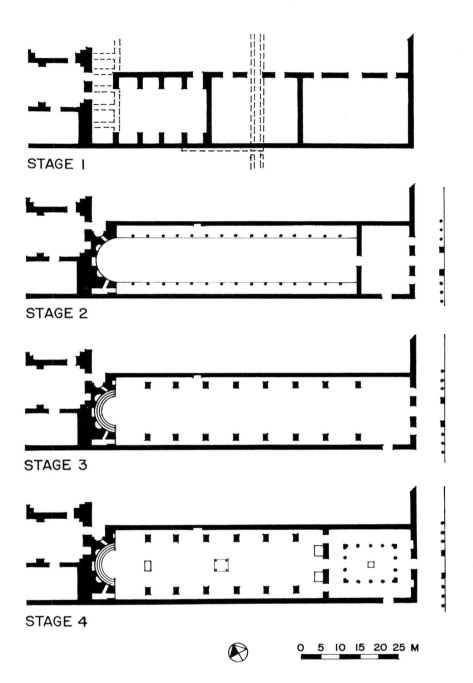

STAGE 1

STAGE 2

STAGE 3

STAGE 4

0 5 10 15 20 25 M

Figure 201—From dressing room to Synagogue? Through detective work on traces of earlier construction, A. R. Seager discovered four stages in the development of the building. Stage 1: After A.D. 17 three rooms, possibly dressing rooms or lecture halls, backed the southern colonnade of the exercise court (palaestra), part of a gymnasium perhaps never completed. Stage 2: Foundations for a hall with apsidal nave and two aisles, perhaps separated by colonnades, and a small entrance room. A. H. Detweiler suggested that in the second century a Roman civil (court) basilica was planned for this hall. Fragment of Hebrew inscription honoring emperor Verus (A.D. 166), found in 1962, might refer to a gift or sale of the hall to the Jewish community. Stage 3: First phase of the Synagogue (A.D. 170–250?). Possibly with benches for Elders; earliest marble revetments and mosaic pavement. Stage 4: Renovation (*Ananeosis*), mentioned in inscription, ca. 350–400. Colonnaded Forecourt and fountain, north and south Shrines, *bimah*, Eagle Table, and parts of interior decoration.

Figure 202—Lydian Altar of Artemis. A stepped sandstone structure, the altar already existed in 401 B.C., as the younger Cyrus and a Persian nobleman had sworn oath of friendship here earlier. The platform was enlarged to an oblong in Late Classical times.

Synagogue's Main Hall (*Figure 199*). Lindley has turned up a coin of Trajan under the floor which may have considerable bearing on the complex history of the Synagogue (*Figure 201*). The Synagogue Forecourt is getting more beautiful as Larry Majewski lays the colorful mosaics lifted and consolidated in previous years (*Figures 212, 213* and Plate V).

At the beginning of the season we had quite an argument whether to install a roof over the colonnade of the Forecourt (for restoration plan see *Figure 168*), but finally decided against it, since time would not suffice this year (and without it the columns look more striking against the blue sky).

A little digging, and a lot of architectural drawing—a lot of major prepublication recording is to be done by our nine (or ten) architects. Hidden under pointed native headgear, Gus Swift's familiar figure ranges again after a year's absence over the huge Lydian Market trench. Stuart Carter, Sardis "graduate" of 1961–62, and young giant Leon Satkowski from Cornell are Gus's architectural team preparing plans of a sequel which spans urban life at Sardis from the Bronze Age to the Early Byzantine era. Gus has come up with the best find so far: a half-life-size Hellenistic bearded marble head of delicious workmanship (*Figure 220*).

Stuart and Leon will also be servicing Pactolus North, where Andy Ramage with just three workmen has been giving a model demonstration of what prepublication digging should be. This will be our closest approach to Sardis' Lydian and Persian civic center.

Peggy Darnall and David Van Zanten are the counterpart team doing chiefly the precinct of Artemis and other assorted structures—the Southwest (Map 3, no. 8) City Gate and Church M.

Under enthusiastic guidance from Ken Frazer as architect-archaeologist and Greenie as archaeological finds expert, the tantalizing Altar of Artemis (*Figure 202*) is beginning to reveal its secrets—and put before us new ones. Ken had noticed last year that the inner altar of early masonry may have had

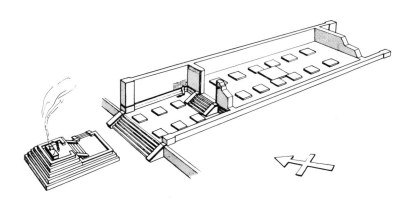

Figure 203—Reconstruction of archaic altar and hypothetical archaic temple by K. J. Frazer. The actual altar was a table on the platform; the priest prayed toward the cemetery, which according to Lydian inscriptions the goddess was to protect.

ARTEMIS TEMPLE
In its Archaic and first
Hellenistic building phases.
LA in its Archaic form.

SCALE : Perspective.
Pronaos : 17.96m (NS) x 17.65m (EW)
Cella   : 18.11m " x 38.85m "
Altar   : 7.60m   " x 14.00m " (Hypoth.)

KJ F
AT 50
Dec'r 1971

pyramidal form. It was partly to check this matter and partly to see whether the expansion of the altar into a 20 by 10 meter oblong was Lydian, Hellenistic, or Roman that the present digging got going. We are sure that we will overturn previous views of the shape and development of this, the earliest structure of the sacred Artemis precinct, before which the Younger Cyrus and Oróntas swore their fragile oaths of friendship (407–401 B.C.) and which Xenophon and his Ten Thousand must have seen.

The last of our architects, Fikret Yeğül, just arrived after what he termed a "Kafkaesque experience": he was measuring the waterflow of a well for the Turkish airforce when the pump broke down, postponing his furlough by several days. He is now pushing ahead on his publication work on the entire Gymnasium which he is co-authoring with Steve Jacobs, our associate director.

Laboring in the camp laboratory and shuttling to Manisa for objects are Sid and Chip Goldstein. Mrs. Hanfmann, under a *çardak*, is nearly engulfed by a flood of Hellenistic pottery fragments. Jane Scott from the Fogg Museum has set up a lamp shop in the Küçük Depo ("small storage"). She also has a stamp shop, open after dinner in the "big salon"—Jane has been elected postmistress of the Sardis camp. Jane, who with precision arrived exactly on time, has proceeded with equal competence with her research on lamps. Nancy Ramage had a wonderful time supervising the first phase of the Artemis Altar excavation. She has now shifted to drawing the many accumulated objects.

Thus the campaign is advancing on its multiple fronts—though the feeling of urgency is slightly wilting in the constant heat.

Accompanied by the District Commissioner and legislature member for Salihli, the genial Governor of Manisa arrived for dinner at 5 P.M. He promptly raced off to Bin Tepe with our friend Kemal Bey, director of Manisa Museum, our two commissioners, Güldem hanım (Istanbul Mu-

seum) and Erol Bey (Izmir Museum), the *kaymakam* (District Commissioner), and myself in attendance. He enjoyed the chills and thrills of the Gyges Mound tunnels *(Figures 109–112)*. The record crowd at the lively dinner included Lee Lort from the Fogg and a charming couple from the textile factory in Salihli. Everybody was in a cordial mood, and his Excellency gave a delightful little speech. He missed our presence on earlier visits, he said, and hence had dispensed misinformation about Sardis calling the Roman Gymnasium a Lydian building. The conversation veered toward the mixture of Turks and Americans at our table: "Now, here is a typical Turkish girl," said the Governor pointing an unerring finger at olive-tanned Seattle-born Elizabeth Gombosi, our photographer.

"My dear Mr. Commissioner, please settle this matter by noon." It was the Vali speaking again, but this time from his office and over the phone. The matter at stake was electricity for the Marble Court electrical tools. On June 15, just as we were driving out for our first dinner at dusk, little twinkling lights suddenly came on by the threshing floors at the ancient city wall. That very day, electricity had come to Sardis. Yesterday, July 10, the village mayor (muhtar) in pink-orange shirt and billowing black mustache handed us a red and silver card—and we became Subscribers No. 47 to the Electrification of the Village of Sart Mustafa. (Electric wire posts can be discerned in *Figure 216*.)

But in between, not all was sweetness and light. Last Sunday, Teoman came driving up to the Artemis Temple, and by the way he "reined in" the beige Landrover like a galloping messenger bringing his horse to a sudden stop, I could tell something dramatic and traumatic was afoot. "The muhtar says he is going to stop the electricians and overturn our electric poles. Shall I speak to him harshly or softly?" I asked Teoman and Güldem hanım to do the parlaying. We petitioned the village for admission. The muhtar countered with the demand that we cover the entire amount the village still

owed the government on the electrification scheme (the villagers pay one third of cost). Eventually, our subscription was settled at one fourth of the initial demand. It took the joint efforts of Governor, District Commissioner, and state electrical engineer as well as hectic rides to Manisa and Salihli, but the matter was arranged between 7:45 A.M. and 1:45 P.M. (The outcome was entirely according to all rules, regulations, and reasonable estimates of other subscriptions—but I did push for proper settlement because I do not believe in the theory that Americans should always pay more.)

Sardis   August 5, 1970

"He needs a lot of coin envelopes"; the remark floated to me in the pre-luncheon milling about. I pricked up my ears. Lindley Vann had just moved from the interior of the Synagogue to its southeast corner. "Yes, I had about ninety this morning," confirmed Lindley. In five days he and Andy Ramage, who was spelling Lindley, had collected some 420 very small bronze coins. There were imprints of a "strong box" of bronze, and of a lead container (for silver and gold?), and the coins were scattered in a few square feet in the so-called "Packed Columns Area" (*Figure 96*, lowest right). This corner of the colonnade had been made into a small narrow room—we used to think by Byzantine soldiery—parts of fallen columns packed tightly side by side were put down as a floor and flimsy brick walls built. Andy has a theory that a thief broke the strong box and finding nothing but pennies dumped them in disgust. Was this the treasury and poor box of the Synagogue? Or the army paymaster's small change?

In any case, for numismatists it is a hoard. Seven years ago the first part of it, some 150 coins, had been found—but we were unable to dig and lift the packed columns. Since then George Bates and Clive Foss had both

Figure 206—Two horned, bearded snakes flanking a sacrificial bowl. This relief, found just across the Pactolus from the expedition camp, attests worship of ancestral heroes envisaged as snakes. It is perhaps of the Hellenistic or Early Roman Period.

studied the 1963 find; it was thought that the latest coin was of A.D. 602. The very great majority from the present run is from the late fourth century, but Andy Ramage is not through studying the entire hoard yet.

Under Andy Seager's and Lindley's guidance, a fearsome pile-up of architectural parts has been cleared, and there is now a beautiful open space and marble pavings and platform at the southeast corner of the Synagogue.

Somehow, the expanse of a city street paved with magnificent marble blocks brings back the sense of city life as buildings alone cannot. Here the Main Avenue of Sardis advanced toward a triple arch, or perhaps even a Tetrapylon, a quadruple gate, at the major intersection with the so-called East Road *(Figure 222* shows one possible reconstruction) which ran past the facade of the Synagogue. This was the most important intersection of the city. From the facade of the Synagogue a marble paved platform, perhaps for public ceremonies, was pushed out some fifteen feet into the East Road. We have just restored and preserved two parts of this extraordinary feature by building brick supports for the earth on which the platform rested.

The Avenue rewarded Andy Seager and Lindley for getting it free. Written in a wreath on a mighty marble pillar was the acclamation AUXEI H TYKHE SARDEON, "Long Live the Fortune of Sardis." It was deciphered by joint efforts of the two Andys (Seager and Ramage), Larry Majewski, and our incomparable epigraphist *in absentia* Louis Robert—via a letter from Paris. The inscription was brought in triumph to the compound as a good omen.

Reused as a paving block was another inscription mentioning HADRIANOS OLYMPIOS ANTONINOS—presumably the Roman Emperor Antoninus Pius. Another paving stone yielded three ponderous Early Byzantine verses about somebody who built a foundation (it is not clear of what); a lion head and other sculpture fragments followed.

In his incessant struggle to learn every fact about the Synagogue, Andy

Figure 207—A. Ramage traces in red the carved inscription on the entablature of the Marble Court. It commemorates the dedication by the METROPOLIS TES (Asia's), the city of Sardis, in the upper band and a benefactress ANTONIA (Sabeina) in the lower. The dedication ceremony was in A.D. 211.

Seager has been going through the great accumulation of architectural fragments and stone furnishings housed in the Synagogue shed. He is recomposing many fine pieces. The most exciting find is the upper parts of the model of a building over twenty inches high—a shrine or arch with four piers surmounted by a domed baldachino with a pyramidal roof. There were metal adornments attached to its four elaborate pediments. Such was the shrine of the Famous Tyche (Fortune) of Antioch, perhaps also of the Tyche of Sardis—or perhaps even the Torah shrine of the Synagogue? The famous ciborium at St. Peter's, too, was derived from this type. Or might this not be a model of the city's great tetrapylon known to us from an inscription?

The inscription was found two years ago in a place where during the past few weeks Gus Swift has deployed a small labor force. Lying across a Roman colonnaded road, overthrown by earthquake, was a mighty brick arch *(Figure 204)*; its keystone is a cross cut in white marble *(Figure 205)*. Was this the tetrapylon? Surely this arch was part of the great Byzantine rebuilding "from the street of Hypaepa to the tetrapylon" mentioned in the inscription.

The main battle which has raged, still rages, and will continue to rage in the Synagogue is the battle of mosaics. Assisted by indefatigable village school teacher Hüseyin Özlü, who is devoted to the task of drawing mosaics for Larry Majewski, Larry has brought together wonderful documentation for the Synagogue mosaics. At the same time, he has pushed ahead with his specialized mosaic crew on the lifting *(Figure 183)* and with the equally specialized stone lifting crew on the setting of the mosaics *(Figure 200)*. Most of the Forecourt mosaics have now been set. For sizable missing areas Larry outlines the major panel units in black and then fills the areas with a mixture of white cement, river sand, and marble chips; this results in a scatter mosaic effect compatible with the original mosaics *(Figures 212, 213)*.

Small losses in the mosaics are repaired with old mosaic cubes; the boys who are doing this are getting to be quite expert. The preparation, which involves laying stones, gravel, and cement bedding for proper drainage and foundation before the actual setting of the heavy concrete-backed mosaic slabs, is quite a time consuming undertaking.

We hope to get all of the Forecourt and three bays of the Main Hall done; there will remain to be done four bays of the Main Hall and the entrance porch of the Synagogue—"to be done" means to be cleaned, rolled up, backed, cured; and then set as described above. Totaling over 600 square meters, this floor is a mighty task for 1971.

Structural work on the Synagogue, on the other hand, is nearing its end; the walls of the apse are being now evened out, and the six pairs of piers brought into varying stages of repair (*Figures 216, 217, 223*).

Every visitor to our camp will remember the cheerful marble faun (*Figure 44*) grinning at him from the upper terrace in front of the lab; and Supporters who have not met him in the flesh (or stone) have met him on our invitations to the Wildenstein Benefit in 1968 (a beautiful shot taken by our late friend Dr. Edward Graeffe). I caught my breath—here was our marble faun suspended from a chain, grinning at me in the morning sun, some thirty feet in the air (*Figure 210*). The scene was the Marble Court where the last major structural feature, the one-row screen colonnade, is now receiving its chief adornment—Corinthian capitals decorated with heads of divinities (*Figures 208, 209*). We are using some of the original capitals but not the most precious ones; it was a cast that had risen so triumphantly over the scene.

Future visitors to our camp will not find our genial faun at home. After presiding over our teas and other activities for twelve years he has left this morning for the Manisa Museum whither our masterpieces will increasingly migrate.

278

Figure 208—Larry Majewski completing the capital with Zeus head from the North Room of the Gymnasium. A cast was taken and installed on a pier of the room.

"I suppose," said an Austrian professor of architecture, on his way back from Aphrodisias, "your Marble Court is really the biggest restoration of this kind, next to the Italian reconstruction of the theater in Sabratha (North Africa)." Now when it is getting finished in its major lineaments, the restored Marble Court seems a miracle *(Figures 211, 226)*. One remembers five disheartening seasons (1959–1963) when the wild helter-skelter of fallen architecture was being evacuated, never endingly, with railway and Citroën *(Figures 53, 116)*; the even wilder seasons when everybody was running for supplies and materials; the heart-searching sessions to gain the major *points d'appui* for design *(Figures 150, 164)*; the bafflement over means to lift the heavy loads to forty-, then sixty-foot heights *(Figure 195)*; the even greater bafflement in trying to find an architect who could be at the site longer than two months. Slowly, through wonderful enthusiasm of many men, these tangles were being unwound, all obstacles cleared. There is a long phalanx of friends to be remembered, from the first excavators, Henry Detweiler, Dave Mitten, Tom Canfield, and Tony Casendino, through Steve Jacobs' great effort at systematic research and his report which laid the foundation for restoration; then the restoration phase sparked and organized by Jim Yarnell, with Mehmet Ergene as his faithful lieutenant in construction, Fikret Yeğül in design, and epigraphists Steve Lattimore and Jack Kroll, who settled some of the basics of the entire building by correlating the architecture and the dedicatory inscription *(Figures 117, 186, 207)*; and the never failing Ken Frazer involved in both architecture and supplies. The new era that is now carrying the project to its goal started in 1967 when Mehmet Cemal Bolgil took over for five-month stretches with Fikret Yeğül and David DeLong doing important design work, and engineer Tankut Akalin and now Teoman Yalçinkaya surmounting technical difficulties. (Yet to this day each bag of cement, each brick has to be carried to the top of the building by hand.)

Figure 211—Panorama of the Marble Court at the end of October 1970. Scaffolding is down except at the screen colonnade and north and south rooms. On far left, Synagogue with Apse.

The upper parts are at present hollow and one can run through uncanny corridors and admire the skill of masons who are putting up the last part of the structure.

Nancy Ramage has been a one-woman team for study and restoration of capitals. Since she has published the definitive article on the subject, she was rushed to the Marble Court to see that the right capitals got the right faces—namely the gods that were represented on them. She has also drawn that famous capital of the Artemis Temple which was brought down by lightning in 1963. Sallie Carlisle has been getting her teeth into the drawings of pottery. Although her southern accent remains unaffected, her Turkish is increasing, and every morning she dispatches the Turkish errand messenger in fine style for shopping in Salihli. It was Sallie's luck to find the final solution to a baffling crime: a dead mouse in the bottom drawer of the office file. It was apparently slain by the weight of red tape.

We have had excellent seminars. One of the most unusual was that of Jane Scott—four ancient lamps burned briskly on the table. Jane, Larry, and Gus had experimented and discovered that olive oil just oozes out of the lamps, that putting water under oil does not quite do the trick either, and they concluded that castor oil is the most satisfactory fuel.

Yesterday, Greenie and Güldem hanım galloped out to Bin Tepe to rescue remains of an Early Bronze Age burial and bring in two fine archaic vases, one a Greek alabastron from Corinth. Meantime the middle part of a Venus came in from an area above the theater.

Lindley Vann and a couple of workmen are launched on a tough project known as "Unexcavated Buildings" (Map 3, nos. 23, 24, 25, 26, 27, 29, 30). Under an onslaught of vineyards and construction, these buildings are vanishing fast. Our intention is to rescue what information we may. The tough part is that there is a lot of walking uphill to be done. Lindley started with the so-called Odeion (Music Hall) and promptly discovered two subterranean chambers. (*Figure 187* shows unexcavated Basilica C, no. 30 on Map 3).

Sardis   September 7, 1970

Suddenly the lights were on and the generator was throbbing. The night was dark, and it seemed as if we had gone to bed only minutes ago. It was, in fact, 4:30 A.M., and time for Lindley and David to depart to catch the earliest plane. It dawned by the time we poured out to say good-bye. "Two more leaves have fallen," Kemal Bey never fails to observe. We are now down to a little company of eleven to close the show. Golden sunshine fills the Pactolus Valley, raisins are drying on the roof of the village house by the road, and with cooler breezes there is an etched clarity in the views of the Tmolus Mountain and the sweep of the royal mounds of Bin tepe. (At this point came the call of the Muezzin, with four loudspeakers pointing to the four winds from each minaret; we heard every call, especially the one at 4 A.M.)

There was an upsurge in temperature and in work all through August, as one staff member after another wound up his work and departed. Larry Majewski went laden with mosaic drawings. Jane Scott left a wonderful collection of lamps, which have now been shipped to Manisa by Kemal Bey who is most eager to have the world's largest number of lamps on view in the Manisa Museum.

Gerry Olson departed somewhat apprehensively for Ankara in our green Landrover piloted by the son of our former chief driver Mehmet Gülergül, who knows no English but knows Ankara from having done military service there as chauffeur for a general. They returned in triumph having performed all missions and delivered the soil samples to all appropriate places. Whereupon Gerry zoomed off to Rome and the United States. We are all looking forward to his study of over one hundred samples of Sardis soils and their bearing on the ecology of the ancient city.

Sid Goldstein conferred with Izmir geologists and scientists, cleaned up the last shelf and object in the laboratory, and even wrapped some of the outdoor sculptures in plastic sheets. To him, Chip Goldstein, and Greenie fell the task of constantly back-stopping other research by bringing most of our object material from 1958–1962 back from Manisa to Sardis for study preparatory to publication. On the other hand, we have shipped some 350 objects, including many sculptures, mosaics, wall paintings, and jewelry to the Manisa Museum. Sid did considerable work on difficult and diversified preservation of metal objects and proceeded with his own research on technological materials especially materials for gold refining. Chip, who is a speed demon on the typewriter, was also typing manuscripts for various people—a major part of our work is now the preparation of drafts for publication.

Before they left, Andy Ramage and Stuart Carter produced plans of the Gold Refinery Area and other Lydian remains at Pactolus North *(Figure 176)*. The same kind of closely coordinated research was carried on at the House of Bronzes by Gus Swift and Leon Satkowski. Gus gave an admirable seminar in which he presented the three major phases of Lydian archaic culture discernible at the Lydian Marketplace. He places them from the early seventh to the early sixth century B.C. The array of buildings and walls, including some new units and a monumental building of mud brick, was truly impressive. Together with Andy Ramage's more complicated but equally rewarding industrial and sacral installations near the Pactolus, we have gained real insight into some aspects of Sardis in the times of Lydian greatness.

The great harvest of this season are architectural drawings. Some seventy were made by Stuart Carter, Peggy Darnall, David Van Zanten, and Leon Satkowski; special sets of Synagogue drawings were done by Andrew

Figure 212 (left)—West portico of Synagogue Forecourt with (left) three gates to Main Hall. Missing squares of mosaics held inscriptions of "God-Worshiping Men" (*Theosebeis*) who gave mosaics. They will be replaced by copies. Square at bottom of the back wall was left open to show earlier wall fresco underneath the fifth century marble revetment. Part of the arcaded bird-and-vase frieze was tinted red to visualize original background effect (top of back wall).

Figure 213 (right)—Southeast corner of Synagogue Forecourt. Large missing areas of mosaic were filled with terrazzo approximating texture of mosaic. Small areas were restored with ancient mosaic cubes. The marble threshhold belongs to a wall later built over the mosaic. All Synagogue mosaics showed vegetable or geometric ornaments (no animals or humans).

Seager, and of the Marble Court by Fikret Yeğül; and a majestic unfolded perspective was made by Mehmet Cemal Bolgil—with the striking additions of this year's screen colonnade with its head capitals and the North and South Halls.

All this required a lot of measuring and surveying, a lot of cleaning, and some digging. Peggy Darnall and I reopened the Southwest Gate first dug in 1966 (Map 3, no. 8), and were rewarded not only with better understanding of the plan but also with a very pretty Early Christian pilgrim flask. (Lest the many visitors who are looking for St. John's Church of Sardis be prematurely encouraged, this object with two crosses is of the fifth or sixth century.)

We went first to the vineyard—and he was not there. We went to the mill—and he was not there either. We went to the coffeehouse—and he had just zoomed past us on a motorcycle. We were looking for Hüseyin Yağren, miller, who told Fikret Yeğül that he had dug up a marble street just like the Main Avenue which we have exposed near the Gymnasium (*Figure 64*). He had been told by the then antiquities guard to re-bury the street. It runs apparently under the water channel of the mill. As it passed at the foot of the mighty platform with Church "D," possibly the Cathedral of Sardis, the matter is of considerable urbanistic interest (Map 3, just north of 29). But there is no time left to dig.

Two bearded, horned snakes rear at the sides of a sacrificial bowl (*Figure 206*) brought in by a farmer. The relief looked at first old enough to be Lydian, though at present I should settle for Hellenistic. The farmer led us straight across the Pactolus where he had found the stone when he was building a water canal. The ancient wall he pointed out was under a mighty canopy of prickly thorns. Later Greenie got over and cleaned the place; the recognizable walls proved to be late Roman or Byzantine, though we had found plenty of Lydian sherds in the scarp. We know very little about the

Figure 214—Fragment of a marble revetment incised with two twittering birds, found in the Synagogue. Fifth century, our era.

west bank of the Pactolus but we do suspect that a Lydian road followed the torrent here as on the eastern side (Map 3, across from no. 15).

The furnace-like sirocco was blowing. We had all sorts of company, marching in queues in and out of our "small salon"—where they were being hydrated with *gazos:* Father Benedikt Schwank of Beuron Abbey with Bible-seeking ladies; three soils engineers from Manisa in quest of Gerry Olson (who had left); Gus and Eleanor Swift with their long announced guests, the Calvin Sawyers from Chicago; two professors of classics from New Jersey; Professor John G. Pedley of Michigan, who had just completed his book on Ancient Literary Sources for Sardis; a Harvard student of government; and our own Miranda Marvin of Wellesley. Our vehicles as well as Teoman and Lindley Vann were long overdue for lunch.

"They are fighting a big fire in the theater" (Map 3, no. 26). We rushed out when Lindley came in. The fire had broken out in the theater, at the edge of which farmers were harvesting, and had raced through the dry shrubs up the Acropolis. Teoman and chief foreman Hasan had rushed over a crew of our workmen. Teoman had got the forestry chief and a forester from Salihli to come. It looked like a scene out of hell—or a modern movie: figures moving through black smoke billowing high above precipices over our heads. After four hours the fire was finally stamped out. Lindley and Leon had been surveying in the "Odeion" (Map 3, no. 27) quite a bit away when the fire broke out.

Every visitor to Sardis is struck by the sight of two towers which seem to totter on the brink of a ridge against all laws of gravity (*Figure 218,* Map 3 no. 22). People free from dizziness can make it to these structures, but there was no jubilation when I announced that they must be drawn and described. Stuart and Greenie were both having the usual desperate spurts to finish drawings and reports. They had one quick look at the towers and Greenie said that they and Elizabeth Gombosi would go up bright and early

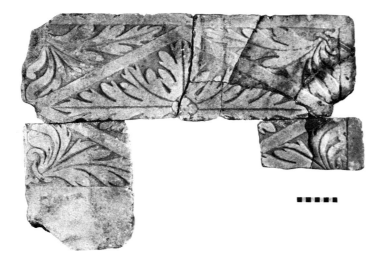

Figure 215—A great variety of marble revetments *(skoutlosis)* was used in the Synagogue. Heavily undercut acanthus plants in lozenge and in four corners stood out against tinted background. Fifth century.

but be back for the visit of Consul General and Mrs. Thomas McKiernan. Ken Frazer was guiding our very amiable guests (who had en route picked up the distinguished German septuagenarian Professor E. Langlotz) through the beautifully exposed mysteries of the Lydian Altar *(Figures 202, 203).* We were just returning for tea, and I wondered out loud whether Greenie got back. "Well, there is your answer," said Ken. I looked up and saw three tiny figures dancing on top of one of the towers. They did get back and Stuart did make a plan.

We have by now packed up and closed the books, but at this point our charming and energetic commissioner (she also tells everybody's fortunes from coffee grounds after dinner with great effect) Güldem Yüğrüm burst into the office: "They are bringing a really interesting stone." And so they did, on a gaily painted horse cart. The piece is unusual right enough—a very beautifully carved part of an inscription in Greek on one side, a reclining and parts of a standing figure on the other. The inscription looks to be of Roman Imperial age but no word is complete. It is a puzzle how this two-sided monument was used.

Discoveries kept being made at the Synagogue. Under the mosaics, coins of the third century up through the reign of Claudius Gothicus (A.D. 268–270) dated the first three bays of the mosaics of the Main Hall. And we found an inscription to "Germanicus, God" in the pavement of the "grand piazza" at the southeast corner of the Synagogue. Louis Robert elucidated this to mean the famous nephew of the emperor Tiberius, who was in command of the Eastern Provinces; he made a visit to the oracle of Claros dramatically described by Tacitus, and died suddenly in Antioch in A.D. 19.

Andy Seager has been able to show that there was a mighty arch spanning the Main Avenue from the corner of the Synagogue entrance southward. A very striking sight it is to see the vehicular part of the road rising to go through the central passage. Andy also set afoot a great project for studying

Figure 216—Apse area of Synagogue in October 1970, looking southwest. Benches for Elders and part of Apse have been revetted, the Eagle Table (lectern?) re-erected, and the south wall consolidated. Small reconstructed door led into rooms belonging to Synagogue (a ritual bath and a hostel?). Holes in mosaic floor are for drainage. Condition restored is ca. A.D. 400.

Figure 217—Main Hall of Synagogue, October 1970, looking east. In foreground, Eagle Table and three bays of reset mosaics. The north wall has been consolidated at a height of four feet, the south wall at ten feet. Samples of interior decoration in the far corners with (south) and without (north) internal paneling. Four bays of mosaics are covered with earth. Compare the restoration proposal, Figure 168.

Figure 218—Perched on eroding conglomerate, the "Flying Towers" (West Ridge) held a key position on the ascent to the citadel. This Byzantine (sixth–seventh century) fort was built partly of earlier structures. Recorded and drawn for the first time in 1970.

Figure 219—Soils research at Sardis. Exposed soils profile at edge of recent landslide scar, some 150 meters upslope from the Pyramid Tomb, on the western side of the Acropolis (Map 3, no. 14). The platy structure typical of landslide-prone soils is seen on the left (behind shovel). On the right, soil structure has been severely disrupted by recent landslide.

and repairing the Synagogue furnishings, which include at least twenty huge round marble offering trays, and all sorts of striking decorative pieces.

Just now the casting of the top slabs of the two wings of the Marble Court has been completed, and there is a great race to finish the large and beautiful entablatures over the entrances of the North and South Halls, the two units flanking the Marble Court *(Figure 211)*.

On August 25 Mehmet Bolgil and I met with the Director General of Antiquities in Ankara to present illustrated reports on the present situation of the Marble Court and Synagogue projects. We found genuine appreciation of the effort and means it had taken to bring the Marble Court project to its present state. But our desire to bring the finishing phase (revetment of bench, of the facades, and of walls; restoration of pilasters; clearing and consolidating of the marble floor; and minimum outlining and landscaping) entirely under the Department of Antiquities was met only by assurance that the present Turkish Trust Commission collaborating in the project can count on TL 60,000, twice the present grant, for next year. We also predicted that two seasons will be needed for the mosaic program and most necessary cleaning and clearing measures in the Synagogue.

This year's twenty-six members were an enterprising team. Martha Hoppin lead numerous archaeological forays on free days under the slogan "This may be my last chance to see . . ." (insert any of twenty archaeological sites). Elizabeth and Martha immortalized us in the Synagogue Forecourt and in our "sculpture-gardened" camp.

We were expecting General and Mrs. Paul Harrell, NATO commander in Izmir, when a tremendous blast of horns was heard. A big cavalcade roared into the parking lots and began to circle madly. "My, they must have brought the entire NATO!" I hardly had time to think when out jumped our old driver-mechanic Nuri, and out poured from each taxi (all six taxis of Salihli made up the cavalcade) a crowd of children, mostly little boys gaily

Figure 220—This lively head was found in a stone heap in the House of Bronzes. It is probably from a small Late Hellenistic (first century B.C.) statue of Zeus.

waving and shouting. The visit turned out to be the first part of circumcision festivities which included three little boys of our cook. They had come on inspiration to have photographs taken—gay, spirited children—Elizabeth and Martha promptly obliged. And off they went yelling and shouting with glee: "Bye, bye." About fifteen minutes later General Harrell's big black car appeared noiselessly and sedately.

Rembrandt's Nightwatch, Jan Steen's festivities, Dürer's Mother, and Homer's Palace of Odysseus—all these came to mind when sixty relatives, thirty children, twenty friends, and eleven Sardians (plus our entire house staff) met at our cook's house to celebrate the occasion that night. In the enchanting intimate couryard of Rüştü's house in Salihli tables groaned with food. And Mrs. Hanfmann lead Turkish women in Turkish dances.

We had started the season with a program of huge scope especially for architectural recording and completion of several manuscripts. This year's exceptionally harmonious team accomplished a lot, but midway through the season we had to cut back from maximum objectives.

We knew at the beginning that the Synagogue mosaics and other restoration work would take us into at least 1971; we know now it will be 1972. The goal for the Marble Court will be reached in the main. A phase of transition to Department of Antiquities–Trust Commission management is necessary. There is a lot to be done in the Gymnasium area before we can open it to the general public: small scale digging, cleaning, clearing. Greenie has put in a remarkable performance as assistant director of the 1970 season, and he did yeoman work on the Altar of Artemis and on a manuscript on the Lydian new structures. But the tying together of the work on the Acropolis must remain until next year. David Van Zanten, working closely with Ken Frazer, tackled and finished all assignments in the Artemis Temple, including the finest detailed plan ever made of any structure there, that of the archaic (LA I, 550 B.C.) and that of Late Persian or Early Hellenistic (LA II,

292

fourth century B.C.) Artemis Altars. These new datings are the result of Ken Frazer's and Greenewalt's sustained and meticulous digging and observation. Yet at the last moment it appeared that the overall plan of the Artemis Sanctuary drawn up by the First Sardis Expedition (1913) and subsequently used by us cannot be sufficiently trusted and a new survey is necessary. I did not get around to checking and completing the description of the city wall. The Roman and Byzantine phases of Pactolus North and the House of Bronzes sectors remain to be described, mapped, and pulled together in detail.

There is work to be done on the final mapping and checking phases of our Prehistoric survey and Lydian finds at Bin Tepe, checking of archaeological data on the Synagogue, and the completion of data on the urban plan and unexcavated buildings.

There is even more ahead on the study of objects for publication which can only be carried out here—about half of the sculpture, metal objects, Lydian pottery, and architectural and other terracottas are yet to be done. Still to be studied are Greek and Roman coins now assigned to Professor and Mrs. T. V. Buttrey of Michigan; several kinds of Greek pottery (esp. Corinthian), Hellenistic pottery other than relief ware, all Roman, Byzantine, and Islamic wares, and Islamic coins. When Greenie and I sat down just before his departure, we drew up a list of twenty-one staff and administrative members that will be needed for jobs to be done in 1971.

We have accumulated valuable and exciting material, riches of knowledge for many branches of scholarship. We have to do it justice. This kind of field work may be less sensational but the great and lasting benefits lie here—and in setting our excavations and restoration in such an order that when they do become generally accessible to public inspection, we can take pride in what the Sardis Expedition has done.

Figure 222—Monumental Roman urbanism at Sardis. Reconstruction of central and eastern part of the Gymnasium by A. R. Seager. The design probably goes back to a masterplan made after earthquake of A.D. 17. The Synagogue and its Forecourt stand at the intersection of Main Avenue and East Road. In the center is the palaestra (exercise court); to the west of it is the Marble Court, and a section through Aleipterion and main central building of baths. Across the palaestra from the Synagogue stands the Long North Hall. The western part of the complex was not excavated.

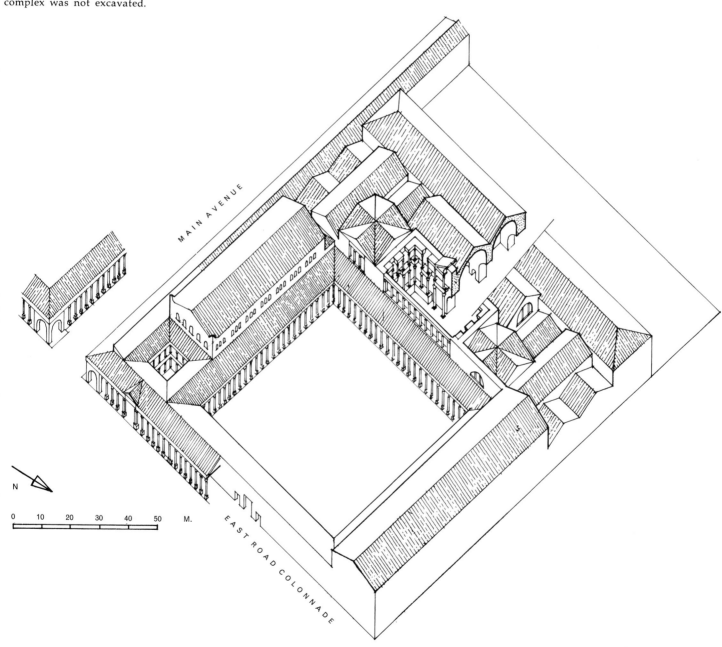

MAIN AVENUE

EAST ROAD COLONNADE

N

0   10   20   30   40   50   M.

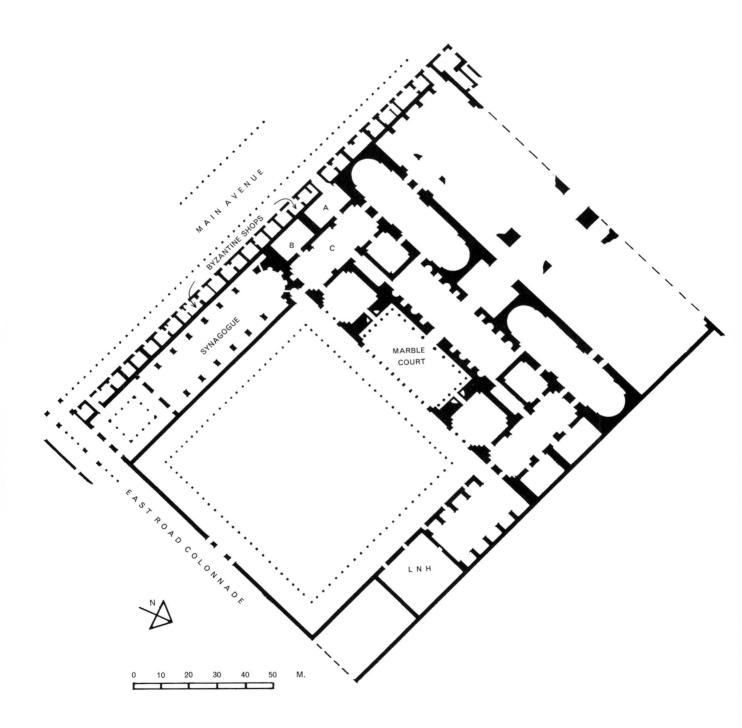

Figure 223—Plan of the Gymnasium complex.

MAIN AVENUE

BYZANTINE SHOPS

A

B

C

SYNAGOGUE

MARBLE COURT

EAST ROAD COLONNADE

L N H

N

0 10 20 30 40 50 M.

Figure 224—Structural diagram of the West Hall, behind the Marble Court, showing how the vaulting and arch system of concrete and brick distributed the weight of the massive building (walls about ten feet thick). "U" is ultimate load, "R" is weight of the vault, and "W" is the weight of the wall. Roman builders showed skillful utilization of the load-bearing capacities of different materials. (The figures at the right are levels measured from the arbitrary level of 100.)

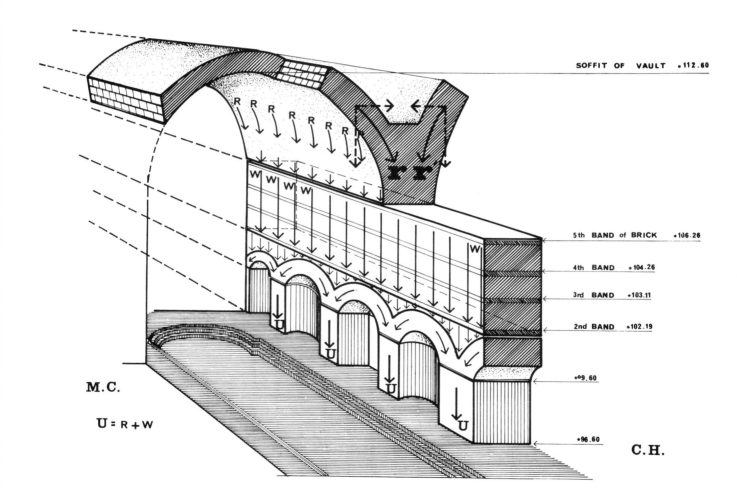

SOFFIT OF VAULT ·112.60

5th BAND of BRICK ·106.26

4th BAND ·104.26

3rd BAND ·103.11

2nd BAND ·102.19

·09.60

·96.60

M.C.

U = R + W

C.H.

Figure 225—Suggested plan and circulation pattern of the Gymnasium baths by Fikret K. Yeğül. The circulation pattern consisted of a roughly circular route from east to west—from cold to warm and hot and back again to tepid and cold. The bather proceeded from the large Palaestra on the east (1) into room 2 and on to rooms 3 which might have served as *apodyteria* (changing rooms). Passing through a long monumental hall (4), he entered a suite of heated rooms (5) which converged into a single caldarium (hot room) (6), placed on the major east-west axis of the complex. He continued into room (7) which might have been a tepidarium, through a hall (8), and completed his bathing routine in the frigidarium (9) with its huge swimming pool. The bather now had the option of returning to the dressing rooms (3) or moving out through the Marble Court (10) into the open Palaestra for outdoor exercise. The plan of the complex offered a great number of variations on this "typical" bathing procedure. The direct and repeated movement between the swimming pool and the exercise ground was facilitated by the construction of a monumental gate connecting the Marble Court to the frigidarium.

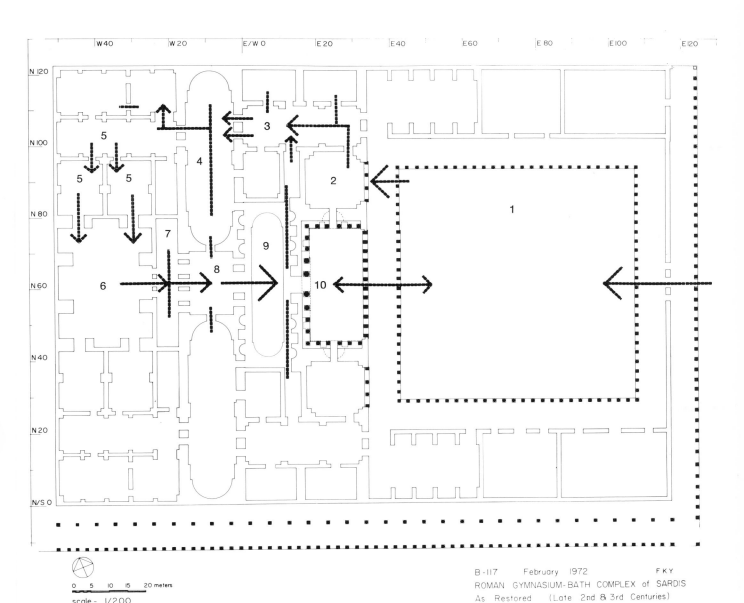

B-117   February 1972   F K Y
ROMAN GYMNASIUM-BATH COMPLEX of SARDIS
As Restored   (Late 2nd & 3rd Centuries)

scale - 1/200

0   5   10   15   20 meters

1971

Sardis   July 18, 1971

It was dusk and we had just come home from the first Acropolis ascent. Greenie went up on the spur of the moment to show his future field of operations to Ted and Anne Buttrey (numismatic experts from the University of Michigan) and quite a crowd went up with him. In the freshness of the June evening, in the glow of the flaming sunset, the old citadel of Croesus cast its spell as strongly as ever. Now we were back in the darkness of the valley.

Some stones were lying by the *depo* (storage shed). "What have they dragged in now?" I wondered to myself. Thirty seconds later I was jumping with joy. What we had not been able to find in thirteen campaigns was delivered to our doorstep: one of the longest Lydian inscriptions known, nineteen lines of it *(Figure 227)!* We encouraged with suitable reward the youthful finders who had discovered it in the spring, supposedly a couple of hundred yards upstream from us in the Pactolus bed. It may be well to explain that we pay rewards for objects found in the Sardis region which then become property of the Manisa Museum. We always ask our commissioners to conduct the negotiations and set the amounts so as to leave no doubt that this is an official transaction and made with approval of appropriate Turkish authorities.

As a result of our enthusiasm, one little painted horsecart after another drew up at the gate to deliver the winter and spring "harvest." A strange stele with a Gorgon's head and a rather attractive Hellenistic funerary relief were among the highlights. The relief showed a tall mother and smaller

Figure 227—A surprise find of 1971. The Lydian inscription, one of the longest yet to be found; half of its sixty words are hitherto unknown. According to R. Gusmani, it treats of property agreements among the members of a family.

daughter in identical "Pudicitia" postures, holding their veils with one hand, and a son in citizen's cloak and orator's posture.

But what does the Lydian stele say? We have sent photographs and a copy to the supreme authority on Lydian, Roberto Gusmani, and shall await the result with impatience.

There was another unexpected development. Just as our advance battalions were arriving at Sardis, a Lydian chamber tomb was discovered at the village of Başlioğlu Köy, a couple of miles up the Pactolus valley. Upon official request of the superintendent of the region and of our commissioners, Andy Ramage and Ken Frazer dug it, finding the first Lydian funerary couch we have ever seen in situ (*Figure 228*). It is a very pretty chamber tomb and the mound is one of at least five. The location, on the lowest slope of the Tmolus, commands a magnificent view of the Pactolus valley, of the citadel of Sardis, and of the Hermus plain beyond. This may have been a cemetery of a feudal family owning land nearby. Now it is a mountain hamlet with a few houses, presenting a fascinating mixture of mudbrick and stone, architecture of the plains and architecture of the mountain. The finds were few, the tops of two alabaster flasks, two bits of sherds, just enough to confirm a general dating to the sixth or fifth century B.C.

It was not without trepidation that Mrs. Hanfmann and I scheduled our arrival here two weeks later than usual. We need not have worried. Owing to the good services of Ken Frazer, Kemal Bey, Mehmet Cemal Bolgil, and Andrew Ramage the place was running full blast when we arrived.

Larry Majewski, his assistant Philip Lins, our former trainee and now commissioner Recep Meriç (Ephesus Museum) and Jim Wrabetz were lifting mosaics and digging up subfloors in the Synagogue. Because he has an eagle eye for such matters, Larry discovered that a piece of wall which had smashed into the mosaic floor contained about a hundred cubes of mosaic, mostly of glass. This is the first definite proof that the upper walls of the

Figure 228—Lydian furniture in stone. Leg of the couch on which the dead man was put to rest. From a sixth or fifth century B.C. chamber tomb constructed of limestone found about two miles southwest of Sardis in the foothills of the Tmolus range (Map 2).

Synagogue were decorated with magnificent mosaics, possibly with a vegetable pattern. Together with the polychrome marbles of the lower story this must have made a glorious interior.

Another objective for the season was to look for more coins in and under the mosaics of the Synagogue. Over a hundred have been found already in the entrance porch, largely late Roman small coppers.

While on the subject of the coins, the Buttreys are a very hard-working numismatic couple. They hold outdoor offices—Anne for "Greek" issues of Roman times under a çardak, Ted fighting the niagara of Roman coins at a little table in the open sun. Numismatic lore is flying back and forth: "You should see this really phony Alexander," and so forth. They have found to their and the expedition's good fortune a most adept amanuensis in Theda Vann, our recording assistant who is rapidly becoming a numismatist.

Mehmet Cemal Bolgil as supervisor-consultant had started work on both the Synagogue and the Marble Court. As you may recall, the tops of the end walls were not yet restored in the Marble Court, and we had thought of doing some of the revetments. In the meantime, the Turkish government had doubled their grant, usable this time for both labor and materials. (It was for materials only before.) We had several sessions on the season's program, the last one with Steve Jacobs, our associate director and architectural expert from Cornell. We have let go of the revetments because much more detailed study of all the fragments and the extant imprints would be required than we can now make. Instead, Mehmet Bolgil is reconstructing several of the five pilasters which correspond to the columns of the gate and of the pavilions. We have also decided to outline the athletic exercise court, the Palaestra, so that at least the overall plan would be visible to the public.

In the service of research, the freeing and recording of the beautiful and elaborate marble floors of the Marble Court was added to this program. They had never been uncovered completely, and we had piled earth over them, quite high, during restoration. To record them is the current task of Lindley Vann and Paul Zygas, architects from Cornell.

Here, too, unexpected finds popped up. The strangest were incised inscriptions right on the floor. Between a sun disk and a tree we read: "Place of the Senate" (gerousias), "of the meeting place" (symphorio), "Place of the Council" (topos boules). All sorts of problems attach to these scribblings. They are not well enough cut to represent the official reserved seats or even standing room notices. But they do suggest that the highest official bodies of the city came to attend ceremonies in the Marble Court and the adjacent "oiling hall" (aleipterion) (Figures 222, 231).

There was a nicely cut bit of a hip and belly—in marble, of course—and this led to Mrs. Hanfmann's triumph. The piece reminded her of something. Five minutes later we had a more complete (but still headless) satyr, one part found in 1965, the other in 1971.

Ruth Thomas (Research Fellow, Fogg Art Museum) has established herself in the "Skullery," where the bone man used to sit. Alternating this habitat with the terrace of the house and with excursions into the Artemis Sanctuary, she is writing our "Report I" while also getting her fill of field archaeology. Ruth has already given to our seminar an admirably lucid account of an obscure subject: the way in which the Artemis Sanctuary was buried in Late Roman times.

David Van Zanten had recruited our lab assistant, Recep Ertetik, as a rod boy and was shooting the Artemis Precinct survey anew, a most crucial task. He has now switched to a study of the city wall, a job which gives full scope to his climbing as well as his drawing powers. The study of the city wall was started in 1969. One matter left undone—"get dimensions of Sections 15–17"—sounded simple, but turned out to rival the Martyrdom of St. Sebastian. In this, the northern section, the city wall is submerged in a thicket of thorny vegetation; and when Steve Jacobs, David, and I reemerged from it, we were absolutely pickled in thorns. It will take a bushcutting team a couple of days to penetrate this jungle.

On July 11, anniversary of our first big find in 1958, NBC television crews had appeared in force at the Marble Court and Synagogue. They had come up the week before, led by Doris Ann, producer. The television program is about the Seven Churches of Asia and is to be shown in the spring. Steve Jacobs was drafted to give a statement to the television people on his own special project: the little Church M behind the huge Artemis Temple (*Figures 197–198*). (To make sure that this historic event was not lost to posterity, we had Elizabeth Gombosi take pictures of the interview.) Steve has really saved this little, very early church from ruin by his timely restoration measures in 1961, and he gave a penetrating discussion of it in our seminar yesterday. Apparently, there is a good chance that the western, original part dates from the later fourth century, which for churches is very early indeed.

Afterwards, the NBC people were doing the Roman and the Jewish background for the Church at Sardis at the Gymnasium and the Synagogue, and it was my turn to answer three well-chosen questions. With all that television gear sticking out of microbuses, and professional characters wandering all over the lot, the Marble Court looked like a set for a Cecil B. De Mille extravaganza, with the difference that the stage set was real.

Now that Greenie has gone up the Acropolis (on July 15) to start cleaning and follow-up digging on our one and only Lydian house floor there, and Andy Ramage is studying the Hellenistic and Roman periods at Pactolus North, the season's enterprises are at their peak.

There are changes in the Sardian picture. The biggest surprise was an automobile road which now runs up the left bank of the Pactolus, from the great Izmir highway into the mountains and across the Tmolus range to Ödemiş, near ancient Hypaepa (Map 2). We see the dust of the cars across the Pactolus from our camp. The road puts the Pactolus Valley as traffic artery back where it was in Lydian times. I used to boast of this as a "secluded vale" and a classic contrast to modern jet travel: "It takes fourteen hours from New York to Sardis, and fourteen hours on foot from Sardis to the springs of the Pactolus"—but that is no longer true!

Another example of change: As I was driving down to the Marble Court through the upper village of Sart Mustafa a brand new red microbus stopped in front of me. Out of a mud-brick hut came six women and girls with traditional kerchiefs and peasant dresses. They stepped from their door into the microbus and went off into the brave new world.

Postscript. Gusmani's letter about our new Lydian stele has just arrived. He says "This is a very important find not only because of the length of the text . . . About *half of the sixty words were hitherto unknown* . . . The text belongs to later Lydian cursive writing . . . *Saristroś* possibly a divine name (compared by Vetter with Zarathustra which is not particularly persuasive); *tavśēn* is always a divine epithet. The text has resemblances with the ordinances of Mitridastas from the Artemis Temple (*Lyd. Wörterbuch* Nos. 23–24) . . . Apparently property matters are involved . . . *śfēnal*, property, appropriated . . . Relatives are mentioned: *kaña*, 'woman' . . . *taada*, 'father' . . . I should emphasize the difficulty of the text . . . it has some striking departures from normal Lydian verbal forms."

Sardis   August 5, 1971

The minute Larry Majewski turned his back and went to Mount Athos, and Mrs. Hanfmann and I went on the "break" to Nicomedia (Izmit) and Nicaea (Iznik), mischief reared its head. First Elizabeth Gombosi discovered a Jewish count and then Stuart Carter discovered a Lydian palace (?) wall. Elizabeth, Stuart, Greenie, and Ken Frazer were the skeleton crew who stayed at Sardis while most of the others wandered off during the three free days we usually intercalate in the middle of the season.

Elizabeth had climbed up on a ladder to photograph one of the mosaic fragments. "Hey," said she, "is this not an inscription?" And so it was. On a fragment banged into a cocked hat by the fall of bricks when the building collapsed there was written large, "The vow of Paulos the Count" (*Euche Paulou Kometos*). It is a very pretty mosaic, the tablet with inscriptions flanked by triangles in black, red, and light blue. It lay just off the central axis of the Main Hall of the Synagogue; there may have been a counterpart inscription, but that is lost. The inscription reads toward the west, in the direction of the apse with the seats of the Elders. Hidden by fallen bricks, the mosaic escaped detection in 1963, when this part was excavated. It is an emphatic reminder of the high standing of the Jewish community of Sardis that there was a count among them.

That this inscription was found is a testimony to the care and accuracy with which Larry Majewski, Jim Wrabetz, and Larry's assistant Phil Lins have been "looking under the rugs." As you may recall, Larry lifts the mosaics first, backs them with concrete, and puts them aside; meantime archaeological workmen carefully excavate whatever appears under the mosaic floor, looking especially for coins; then the restoration crews take over, put in a new stone bedding, cover this with a cement bedding, and then maneuver the mosaics back into their old place. This complex and complicated combined operation got going under Larry, Phil, Jim, and Recep Meriç, a student trainee with us several years ago and now assistant at the Ephesus Museum.

Recep is such a keen archaeologist and conservator that our Austrian colleagues, for whom he was commissioner in the Ephesus Excavations, got him a fellowship to the University of Vienna. It turned out that prior to Vienna, he had to study German at the Goethe Institut in Blaubeuren—and

had to get there by August 2nd. Thus, suddenly, on July 29, off went Recep. Our plan was that he would stay through the season helping to supervise the mosaic work after the supreme expert, Larry Majewski, left. Things looked bleak for our Synagogue work schedule. To our great relief, Faruk Akça was available to step in. Faruk had been working in the firm of Mehmet Bolgil. He had previously studied and worked in America for several architectural firms. Faruk's idiomatic American makes the language barrier a lot smaller for Jim Wrabetz and Phil Lins, and the work is really moving. At the moment, mosaics are being set in Bay 4, beddings for mosaics are being poured in Bay 5, and the ancient underpinnings are being explored in Bay 6. Bay 7 of the Main Hall remains to be done, as well as the entrance porch to the Synagogue. It will be a tight race to get it all done by September 30. The Synagogue is such a unique building that we also want to try to learn as much as possible during this floor-lifting operation (see *Figure 217*).

In a way, Stuart Carter's Acropolis discovery came about through our associate director, Steve Jacobs. He had gone up with Stuart for a last glimpse of the citadel (Map 3, no. 20). At "Acropolis North" (Map 3, to right of no. 22) there was a white worn stone shining out from the dark top soil, only ten feet or so above the place where Don Hansen had discovered the magnificent royal palace or fortress wall of drafted masonry in 1960 (*Figure 47*). Stuart is architect for the Acropolis; together with Greenie as archaeologist it is their task to clean and record what was excavated from 1960 to 1962. In his gentle way, Stuart would not rest until Greenie set a workman to cleaning this stone. When it was cleaned, out came a stretch some thirty feet long of magnificent courses of masonry, the southeast corner of a terrace. Both ends of the masonry run back into that old enemy of ours, the native conglomerate rock of the Acropolis (*Figure 229*).

The new wall is high over the northern slope, with magnificent views of the Sardian plain (Map 3, to right of no. 22). It is clearly a higher step of the

Figure 229—Was there a Palace of Croesus on the Acropolis after all? The discovery in 1971 of a second splendid Lydian wall just above the one found in 1960 suggests that a vast terraced complex rose up the north slope of the citadel in Lydian times. Length of new wall about 30 feet. See Figure 47.

same general complex as the Lydian wall Hansen found in 1960. As one looks at these two terraces, diagonally aligned, there rises before one's mental eye a kind of Tower of Babel structure up and up the steep slopes of Sardis' citadel (Figure 230). There are letters and signs cut on the rusticated faces of the masonry blocks, similar but not the same as the royal monographs on king Gyges' wall in the great mound of the Royal Cemetery (Figure 107).

The scary thing is this. Don Hansen in 1960 dug right and left of this great wall, running into native rock everywhere. Yet just a few feet higher up a parallel wall was concealed in a pocket of earth.

The north side of the Acropolis is more gentle than the precipices on the east and west sides; its upper part is overgrown with dark shrubbery and dwarf oak. This slope is several hundred yards wide (east-west) and a couple of hundred yards long in its upper part (south-north). Then it breaks in towerlike scarps on the downward descent toward the Hermus valley. Short of burning down the whole vegetation, stripping the surface (and thus starting erosion on that whole hillside), and rooting out every possible stone or earth pocket—work for several summers—one cannot be sure that more of such walls might not be hidden under the brush. Who knows, perhaps considerable parts of the plan of the Royal palace or castle might yet be retrievable from disjected fragments such as the two we found. Or, again, one might find nothing (see Figures 3, 6, Plate I).

This Acropolis North situation is quite a contrast to the central flattish part of the citadel (Map 3, no. 20) where we had dug about half of the area uncovering Byzantine houses and graves. Greenie's careful recheck did not add any Lydian remains to the single Lydian house wall known since 1961, but brought clearer insights into the housing of the Byzantine garrison.

Greenie also cleared a corner of that vast cave within the highest peak of the Acropolis which used to be considered a cistern until Larry Majewski found superposed wall paintings in one corner. This was a domed and vaulted space cut right into the gritty rock and then presumably stuccoed. Several burials appeared under floor. Larry's conjecture that this was a chapel has gained in probability.

Lindley Vann and Paul Zygas were trying to catch up with Fikret Yeğül's (research assistant for Gymnasium publication, now at Harvard) requests about the dimensions of the central building of the Gymnasium. Fikret had sent a beautiful color plan on which just a few missing lines were to be filled in. It was discovered that some of the dimensions were missing because those parts were never excavated. Optimistically, I persuaded Mehmet Bolgil to put a couple of men on clearing some of these vital statistics, just to draw two little lines for the door into the central Gymnasium unit. A week later, two men were still laboring forlornly before the huge wall. In their eagerness, they dug away one of our most precious survey and level markers, causing me to gnash my teeth and go up in the air. More happily, their research produced a lovely piece of architectural decoration from top of a pier in the South Hall of the main Gymnasium building: an exquisite rendering of the famous Erechtheum palmette-lotus anthemion. In the end, a big spurt for a couple of days by six workmen and the Citroën resulted in the appearance of two arches. They show that the entrances to the west side were spaced differently from those of the east side.

One forgets how dreadfully massive the big Roman buildings are, how many hundreds of tons of bulky debris of stone and cement they pile up in their collapse. It is really only dozens of men and a fleet of trucks which can successfully excavate these complexes.

While the jungle fighting action at the city walls was put into operation, David Van Zanten really took over. At the well-preserved wall stretch above the House of Bronzes (Map 3, no. 9) he dug a pit to supplement our sounding of 1960 so that a complete section can now be drawn. He has

Figure 230—This view of the Acropolis north walls includes peak where Christian chapel and graves from Byzantine times were hidden.

walked and climbed the full length of the wall, has found new pieces, and has explained the general layout and construction. He has noticed, too, important comparisons in the city walls of nearby Philadelphia (Alaşehir) and Aphrodisias.

We have not quite decided whether it was the Goths in A.D. 253 or the Goths in A.D. 398 who scared the Sardians into building this three mile long, thirty foot high wall. (Map 3, no. 9, shows extant wall remains in plan.)

With quiet determination, Andrew Ramage has been doping out the secrets of the Roman-Byzantine bath at Pactolus North. Paul Zygas is putting them down in a very complicated plan. Andy, who has already done the earlier Lydian and Persian buildings of that sector, gave a fine seminar on the spot. Other educational events of this series were David Van Zanten's brilliant discussion of the city wall and, as an extracurricular event, Ken Frazer's thrilling account, with slides, of the late Brian Emery's excavation of Imhotep sanctuary at Saccara. We were all duly staggered by the prospect of discovering one million two hundred and fifty thousand mummified ibises.

The new Governor of Manisa came to visit Sardis. He brought us a welcome present, a book on the Manisa vilayet. He also very promptly made inquiries with the Highway Ministry about that hardy perennial, our fight to remove the main highway from Sardis ruins *(Figure 134A)*. It sems that the diversionary route, already staked out, may yet get going in 1972. (It had been scheduled for 1971.) The Governor was full of very lively reminiscences of his recent trip to the United States made in the company of five other governors under the auspices of the Agency for International Development (AID). He told us of a project in Manisa which will stir the hearts of Classicists: a tourist highway is being built up to the top of legendary Mount Sipylos, home of the Anatolian Mother of Gods (the mountain top is 1517 meters high, and 19 degrees centigrade cooler than Manisa—Magnesia ad Sipylum—lying at its foot).

Figure 231—The resplendent marble floor of ninety-one panels briefly revealed in the Marble Court in 1971, and preserved in a dramatic shot by Elizabeth Gombosi, Sardis photographer. It had to be covered up again pending the decision whether the laborious work of consolidation should be undertaken.

Ken Frazer brought me a nice slip, in three colors, blue on the left, green in the middle, red on the right. It says, gasoline: 110 krs (1969); 146 krs (1970); 154 krs (1971). That is how costs have gone up. There was a petition from our workmen for a wage raise. After considerable calculation, we have granted something like 15 to 20 percent for the lower grades and lesser amounts for the higher brackets, as of August 1. We all got together for the brief address on the subject delivered by Mehmet Cemal Bolgil in bright earliest morning, with the small crowd of about seventy workmen against the big walls of the Marble Court. We hope to get through the season on that arrangement (unless there is an official wage increase all around).

Sardis   September 7, 1971

There is a quiet radiance over the serene September days at Sardis which is just right. We really should have our grand opening of the Marble Court and Synagogue restorations in September. It would be a fine occasion to bring our friends here on one of those popular travel tours. Two archaeological missions have called recently, the Ephesians (Austrian) and the Milesians (German). Professor H. Vetters and his colleagues now propose to reerect at Ephesus the famous library of Celsus (c. A.D. 135). They paid us the compliment of seeking information on our restoration procedures at the Marble Court. They were followed the next day by Professor Gerhard Kleiner, director, and Miss Agatha Hommel, "Hausfrau" and conservator of the German Miletus excavations, who were eager to find out about our techniques in lifting and resetting mosaics in the Synagogue. They have to conserve mosaics of the newly found church of St. Michael and also plan to restore part of their Sacred Road and the Nymphaeum (Fountain House). We have become if not "The School of Hellas," as Thucydides said of

Athens, then the "School of Asia" for large-scale restoration.

In Turkish, the word *müfetiş* (mufettish) has a dire and foreboding sound, with overtones of "investigator" rather than "inspector." It was not without curiosity that we heard rumors about an inspector from the Department of Antiquities approaching Sardis after visiting other excavations at some length.

On the morning of August 19, a light blue Landrover pulled into the Marble Court, and out came a statuesque lady in a dark blue suit, Süheyla Keskili, former director of the Antioch Museum. For those who had expected the inspector to be heavily mustachioed and fierce, this was a bit of a comedown. Süheyla hanım went right to it and paced over the site with us. She then held conferences at the camp, first with her department's commissioner (also a lady), then with us, taking up major features of digging, restoration, storage, and security. The visit was well timed. We had made an appointment with the Director General for August 24, and the suggestions of the inspector brought into focus most of the major issues, both long and short range.

The inspector's report was on the desk of Hikmet Gürçay, Director General of Antiquities, when Mehmet Cemal Bolgil, our architect-in-chief and consultant on restoration, and I called. Hikmet Bey read it to us sentence by sentence. The report was short and constructive, and Hikmet Bey was moved to remark that Sardis had come off best of all the missions visited so far by his inspectors.

Incidentally, this was our first visit to the Department of Antiquities since it was transferred from the Ministry of National Education to the new Ministry of Culture. The move seems well justified, since the huge problems of primary, secondary, and higher education are really quite different from the equally pressing needs for promoting scientific archaeological and art historical work and waging war on illicit diggers.

Figure 232—Marble Court with
Palaestra cleared to permit delin-
eation of its originally colonnaded
area (Figures 222, 223).

Both the Director General and the inspector had emphasized the need for a clear-cut demarcation line between excavated and unexcavated areas. While we were straining all our efforts to accomplish the Marble Court restoration, much of its vicinity was a construction site piled with materials. You could not see what had and what had not been excavated before. Nobody remembered that Tom Kraabel ran out of time before completing the excavation of a major room between the Synagogue and the main Gymnasium building, or that the large hall with a long swimming pool, just behind the Marble Court, ended up looking like a bombed-out ruin. Now we have to clean up these things and make the join with the unexcavated part of this huge complex look presentable.

To create an intelligible approach to the towering structure of the restored Marble Court, something has to be done about the large athletic court, the Palaestra, which prefaced the main building of the Gymnasium (*Figures 222, 223, 232*). This season, the western colonnade PAW (Palaestra West) has been excavated and the northern (PAN) and eastern (PAE) colonnades outlined at their front edge by Mehmet's and Faruk's indefatigable men. We have promised to remove about two feet of earth to the level of the Palaestra's apparently well-preserved marble floor, but did not promise to expose it. For it would have taken several crews and many seasons to lift, consolidate, and reset such very fragile marble *opus sectile*.

Storage is becoming a serious problem. We have been getting away with one lockable storage shed with shelves for the more valuable Synagogue fragments. Now we have to do something about the incomparably larger number of the columns, friezes, and capitals from the Marble Court and the Gymnasium generally. We are extending the locked shed along the Synagogue wall and starting an open air, roofed shelter for a number of others.

We have to start worrying too about bringing in the people in orderly fashion. At the moment, the Gymnasium area is delightfully but dustily bounded by a vineyard on the east, a pretty chaotic uphill-down-dale strip of land on the south, and stubbly field where we do some dumping on the west. We can manage the vehicular entrance; for the pedestrians we plan to clean an original side gate of the main entrance to the Gymnasium from the east which was partly dug in 1966.

Two of the Synagogists have just departed—Paul the architect, Jim the archaeologist. Jim was typing until 4:20 A.M. prior to his departure. He had previously discovered sizable fragments of the face and neck of a beautiful (Constantinian?) overlifesize statue in the Main Hall, and immense amounts of small change as well as a nice draped torso of the "citizen-orator" type in the porch, the torso having been built into a late wall.

Jim and Faruk have determined that there is a well-like contraption in a room behind the Synagogue, a matter of interest because of the existence of rooms with ritual baths in other synagogues. This, too, is "to be continued" in 1972.

Sculpture is a manly art but Nancy Ramage and Elizabeth Gombosi are definitely ladies. Nancy, now in Cambridge, studied our sculptures last year, and I am continuing our joint prepublication work this summer. Both Nancy and Elizabeth pleaded for strong men as assistants and I am now seeing why. "Drop a nice torso and lose your toes"—all these poetic and aesthetic creatures weigh a ton! None are heftier, more smashed, and more smashing than the fragments of colossal heads, legs, and bodies from the Artemis Temple. There is a superb Hellenistic head of Zeus; a striking Roman head of emperor Antoninus Pius, who was either successor or co-tenant with Zeus in the temple; possible parts of an Artemis; and a less colossal but still overlifesize torso of a man in a toga. All these treasures come from the First Sardis Expedition and almost none has been studied. Our former conservator W. C. Burriss Young had collected them from the old excavation house in 1961. Among them Mrs. Hanfmann has found part of an archaic siren, and Ken Frazer discovered a little archaic Lydian lion.

Fortunately our conservator, Phil Lins, is a strong man and so did not mind washing, mending, dangling from tripods, and mounting on bases the new stone inhabitants, some of whom now stand very lifelike among the trees on the terraces of our camp.

We have finished a lot of work in the last two campaigns: all sectors outside the city walls, the city wall itself, the Artemis Precinct (but not the Temple), the Acropolis, most of the work on the Pactolus North and the House of Bronzes-Lydian Market areas. The work on the Gymnasium and the Synagogue is greatly advanced. Of the large classes of finds, the Byzantine coins have been published, the study of Greek, Roman, and Islamic coins is well launched. Glass, lamps, metal objects, and sculpture are all coming along.

I have enumerated what we have to do in 1972: finish all restoration work and research in the Gymnasium, Synagogue, and Pactolus North sectors— the last including a special study of a Byzantine church. As to objects, we have the jewelry, the terracottas, the miscellaneous, and the enormous field of pottery to do. Part of it will remain for 1973–1975; and so will the architectural research on the last Roman-Byzantine phase of the House of Bronzes, and the prepublication work on Prehistoric and Lydian settlements and cemeteries on Bin Tepe and the Gygean Lake. We are thinking of an official opening of the Marble Court and Synagogue restoration for 1973.

Epilogue

The letters end with 1971 but not the work. Still, after fourteen campaigns one may well look back and see what has been done. When we wrote our glowing forecasts in 1958, we were overoptimistic about the speed of excavating. Paper is patient; it takes ten minutes to write a paragraph promising excavation of a building; it might take ten weeks or ten months of work or even ten years and tens of thousands of dollars to do the job.

We had envisaged in our three-year Phase A a freely ranging program of soundings all over the site. We were able to do some but not nearly as many as we had planned. There were good reasons. A very important one was the present Turkish Antiquities permit regulation which stipulates that one cannot dig and then fill in excavated areas. They are to remain open. The farmers, on the other hand, are not anxious to sell land and to withdraw it from cultivation: "What will our children and grandchildren do, if we sell?" was a question we frequently heard.

Then, in some ways, Sardis turned out to be a complicated site. Earthquakes and erosion have upheaved the slopes *(Figure 219)*, and floods have deposited heavy overburden in the plain. One might almost say that what looked good turned up bad, and what looked bad turned up good. The Upper Terrace (Map 3, no. 5) was covered on the surface with Lydian sherds but turned out to be a colossal Roman dump (1959). The melon patch along the highway looked like nothing at all; yet it hid not only the rich House of Bronzes but also one of our prime objectives, the Lydian Market *(Figure 4)*. Everybody was raring to dig on the Acropolis in 1958. Three archaeologists brave and true ate their hearts out and each wrote at the end of his season

·that the Acropolis was so much damaged by nature and upended by the Byzantines that it hardly warranted continued digging. Yet in 1971, the northern slope of the citadel suddenly revealed another palatial Lydian wall (*Figure 229*). What looked like an uninteresting patch of burned Hellenistic debris at Pactolus North led Andrew Ramage to the Lydian lion altar (*Figures 169, 170*) and eventually to the gold refinery of the Lydian kings (*Figures 172–179*, Plate IV).

We had made one bad guess in this preliminary phase. I had deduced from Butler's and Shear's accounts and my own visits in 1953 and 1957, when I had picked some archaic sherds out of the bank, that the Northeast Wadi was the place to start looking for Lydian houses (Map 3, no. 16)— except for the scary prospect that they were supposed to be buried under more than twenty feet of earth and gravel. When Don Hansen got through with the Artemis trench in 1958, we considered the matter. In the glaring summer sun, the dry gulch looked most uninviting. Don and Henry Detweiler opted for flat-topped Kagirlik Tepe (Map 3, no. 19) which looked so much like a Mesopotamian tell—and yielded an unspectacular Roman cemetery. I consoled myself with the idea that toward the end, when low on funds, the gulch, so near the camp, might still be a possible small-scale dig. When we finally were compelled to look into Northeast Wadi (*Figures 189–191*), vineyards—most expensive of all cultivated land—had sprung up on either side, so we did not attempt to extend the excavation although it is certain that the archaic quarter is not too deeply buried (six to ten feet) and, given its location so close to the later Artemis sanctuary, this region might be of great importance.

We have learned much about the western part of Sardis but we never did get to excavate in the central and eastern part of the site. That brings us to the third and most important limitation. As in war so in archaeology: you have to decide where and how you are going to commit your forces. Already during our exploratory years, there developed a double-pronged attack. For the early periods, we committed ourselves to massive penetration down into the Lydian and Prehistoric strata in the House of Bronzes-"Lydian Trench" area *(Figures 81, 82)* and to extensive digging of Lydian and Persian levels in the Pactolus Cliff *(Figure 31)* and Pactolus North *(Figure 177)* sectors. In tackling the vast Gymnasium *(Figures 53 and 211)* and the big bath complex CG *(Figure 40)*, we were trying to do justice to the later cultures, to the Hellenistic, Roman, and Early Byzantine Sardis, and to the big architecture which was so representative of these phases. The simultaneous surprise discovery of the giant Synagogue *(Figures 216, 217)* and the beginning of the work at Bin Tepe *(Figures 106–112)* preempted our forces and resources. During the height of our excavations (1962–1967) no further expansion into other parts of the site was feasible.

Finally, there was something else we had not clearly foreseen in 1958. With the opportunity thrust upon us, we adopted in 1964–1965 a program of restoration for the Marble Court and (less ambitiously) for the Synagogue; with this we had really added to our plans a "Restoration Phase C," which is still continuing. Such a restoration program called for a new array of experts, of skilled labor, and of expensive machinery and materials. Running restoration activities side by side with large-scale excavation really strained staff and camp capacity.

By 1968 it was becoming clear, too, that the most vital duty of an expedition, the final scientific publication of results, could no longer be delayed. Digging is fun but an unpublished excavation is no better than an illicit graverobber's dig.

Since 1968 we have been engaged in "Publication Phase D," and it will continue for several years in the field, and probably some more years at home, until all the twenty volumes, ten monographs and ten reports, on our excavations have appeared.

What have we accomplished? There is, I think, no doubt that the discovery of the gold refinery on the Pactolus is as fundamental a contribution to economic and technological history of the Lydian kingdom, and, indeed, of the ancient world, as we had any right to expect. We are, literally, standing on the ground where Croesus' wealth was made *(Figures 172–179)*. Next in importance is something less easily defined—the gains in knowledge of Lydian architecture and urbanism, which have revealed a curious division in quality and materials, with cheap riverstone and mudbrick used for the houses of the living *(Figure 131)* and monumental stone masonry for the apartments of the dead *(Figures 90, 112)* but also for what seem to be palatial structures on the Acropolis *(Figure 229)*.

We are still arguing with each other about the exact size and shape of the City of Croesus *(Figure 134)*. Andrew Ramage thinks it did run up both banks of the Pactolus, while I believe it had a kind of cross pattern, with the Pactolus street intersecting the east-west artery. But we do know what some parts of the city were like and a book on domestic and industrial architecture of the Lydians can be, indeed, has been written.*

We have found thousands of objects the Lydians made and used in their daily lives and we can now speak with some assurance of the way they lived. We have obtained some interesting evidence for their curious rituals *(Figures 78, 169)* and gods *(Figure 181)*.

Fewer Lydian inscriptions came our way than had been found by Butler but the 1971 stele has provided one of the longest and most challenging texts known. The discovery of the "Synagogue Inscription" in an unknown tongue is a major event for the linguistic studies of ancient Asia Minor. It seems to be in a dialect related to Lydian. G. Neumann thinks the tongue might be Torrhebian,† described by Dionysius of Halicarnassus *(Antiquitates*

*Andrew Ramage, "Studies in Lydian Domestic and Commercial Architecture at Sardis" (unpublished dissertation, Harvard, 1969).
†G. Neumann, "Ein weiteres Fragment der Synagogen-Inschrift aus Sardes," *Kadmos*, 8 (1969): 95.

Romanae I.28, quoting the fifth century historian Xanthos of Lydia) as bearing the same close relation to Lydian as Doric to Ionian in Greek. Or one might think of "Maeonian." It is Maeonians not Lydians whom Homer knew on the Gygean Lake (*Iliad* XX. 389–392), and the poet Hipponax says "Hermes the Dog Throttler" (cf. p. 110, *Figure 78)* was called Candaules *Maeonisti,"* in Maeonian language."

Quite as striking was the discovery of a number of Carian inscriptions (another very poorly known language) incised on Lydian bowls found in the Lydian market. These people lived to the south of the Lydians and served as their mercenaries—Croesus' wife was a Carian princess.

Out of an unexpected treasure trove, the walls and piers of the Synagogue, has come a series of sculpture and architectural pieces from the time of Croesus and the Persian era which throws entirely new light on the mythology, history, and religion of the Lydians and on the origins of the Ionic order of Greek architecture *(Figures 99, 100, 101)*.

Going back in time, our finding of Mycenaean, Submycenaean, and Protogeometric levels disproved the ancient tradition that Sardis was founded after the Trojan wars, and confirmed the Herodotean (I.7, 13, 91) story about Heraklid invaders and that of Nicolaus of Damascus about the seer Mopsos*—presumably errant Bronze Age Greeks who were fighting natives and Hittite dependencies in the twelfth and eleventh centuries (see pp. 192–193, *Figures 140–142)*. We have shown, too, by Gus Swift's pits in the Lydian Market area, that huts and cremations of a Western Anatolian culture were built on the site of Sardis not later than the fourteenth century B.C. and possibly earlier.

We may still do some work on the Prehistoric mounds of the Gygean Lake tracked by Dave Mitten; but already his discoveries there of the huge jar burials with gold, silver, and copper objects *(Figure 162)* and cist graves on the Gygean Lake *(Figure 158)* have given the Lydians a firm place in the

*F. Jacoby, *Fragmente griechischer Historiker*, Part IIA (1926) no. 90. F. 16.

advanced Early Bronze Age cultures of the third millennium in Western Anatolia, parallel to Troy I and II—fulfilling the prophecy of Heinrich Schliemann, founding father of Aegean archaeology, when he wrote that Sardis "is bound to throw much light on the Trojan antiquities."*

In the great scheme to survey and record all of the hundred or so mounds at Bin Tepe *(Figure 5)* we have made at least partial progress and have pinpointed and excavated some representative examples of Lydian chamber tombs *(Figures 88, 90, 112)*. The big mound, to be sure, has refused to yield its chamber, but the discovery of an inner wall with its monumental masonry and monogram is revolutionary for our knowledge of early Lydian attainments in architecture.

For the Hellenistic period, we have learned that the Lydian culture continued in its material manifestations way past Alexander the Great. We have learned from inscriptions built into the Synagogue piers that it was Antiochus III who in 213 B.C. totally destroyed the western part of the city in punishment for its rebellion and then ordered his powerful viceroy Zeuxis to supervise a *synoikismos*, a new founding of Sardis, apparently farther east. We have found the debris of the destruction at the House of Bronzes and Pactolus North. The repopulating of Sardis at least in part with Jewish families from Mesopotamia is the ultimate cause for the least expected discovery of the Expedition—that of the giant Jewish synagogue of Roman times, far and away the largest known from the diaspora.

Whatever its exact date, a synagogue which is an integral part of a Roman gymnasium is an amazing find *(Figures 222, 223, 226)*. This architectural situation alone would make the find one of signal importance; but we can add furnishings of mysterious and controversial significance (the Eagle Table, the pairs of sculptured lions, the bimah in the center as with Sephar-

*From a letter dated August 22, 1879, in E. Meyer, *Heinrich Schliemann: Briefwechsel, II, 1876 bis 1890* (Berlin, 1958).

Plate V Synagogue and Marble Court (background) in 1972. Columns in the Synagogue Forecourt are partly originals, partly cast. Preserved mosaics have been mounted on concrete slabs and replaced. The fountain was cast in marble chips and tinted cements after the original.

dic communities), the mosaics and marble decorations, and above all some eighty inscriptions—three in Hebrew, the rest in Greek—disclosing much about the organization of the Synagogue and about the social status of its members. One was a count; some were high officials of Imperial administration, several were city councillors, most were citizens of the city of Sardis. There were goldsmiths among them and probably glass makers as well.*

It is this discovery, rather than the appealing but less informative finding of a possible Early Byzantine baptistry *(Figure 33)* and of two unidentified churches, which is of importance for the history of the Church of Sardis. For it is to such communities as Sardis that Paul and Barnabas traveled, and also St. John of the Revelation; and it is against such background of prosperous and powerful "Hellenized" Judaism that the development of the earliest Christian communities took place. The curious form of the Sardis Synagogue, itself perhaps a Roman basilica, is of considerable importance for the question of origins of Christian basilicas and of such features as the *synthronon* (benches for the clergy).

In the broad view, the Late Roman–Early Byzantine city was continually alive and prosperous from the great earthquake of A.D. 17 to its destruction by Sassanian Persians in A.D. 616. Masses of glass ware seem to have been used widely and continually. It is only with the reign of Heraclius (A.D. 610–641) that the Classical city came to an end. The precise dating of this event is a new discovery made possible by the coins found in the Byzantine shopping center.

*"Nothing in the remoteness of Qumran or Dura (with its otherwise important synagogue) can compare with this procession of empires and developed, rich civilizations. If the Jews are in Sardis as early as the date of Obadiah, then Anatolian Judaism is a participant in the variegated history of Persian and Hellenistic Asia Minor from the beginning," says A. T. Kraabel in his discussion of the significance of Sardis for our knowledge of Judaism in Asia Minor. ("Judaism in Western Asia Minor under the Roman Empire," unpublished dissertation, Harvard, 1968.)

There is a temptation in archaeology to neglect the impoverished periods of decline in favor of the glamorous periods of prosperity. We have tried not to succumb to it; we have thus secured evidence for a slight revival of industrial activities and for the building of a church ("E," near the Pactolus; Map 3, no. 11) in the tenth, eleventh, and twelfth centuries. There is, on the other hand, a pathetic air about the densely packed burials of the Byzantine Age we found within the citadel walls on the Acropolis—mute witnesses of times of sieges, when inhabitants fled to the shelter of great walls and steep cliffs.

Finally, for the Islamic era, we have proved by a hoard of Turkish "feudal" coins that the citadel was still being used around 1420 after the alleged destruction by Tamerlane (1402);* and we have been able to show that making of glass objects went on at the village workshops which had been installed in the little Church E until the domes of the building were overthrown by an earthquake perhaps as late as the eighteenth century.

Because the Fogg Museum of Art was one of the institutions which have pioneered the concept of scientific conservation of art, we had a particular obligation to try to set up standards of conservation of objects as high as conditions in the field might permit. We were fortunate in having a series of conservators, first from Harvard, later from the Center for Conservation at New York University, who sought to maintain this ideal. We were fortunate, too, in that our association with the College of Architecture, Art, and Planning at Cornell permitted us to offer to students, American and Turkish, training in field architecture. Without the expert knowledge of Professors Detweiler, Jacobs, and Yarnell from Cornell and L. J. Majewski from New York University, and without the dedicated work by student trainees who subsequently became staff members and even supervising

*George C. Miles, "Note on Islamic Coins," *BASOR*, 170 (April 1963): 33–35: joint issue of Ghāzi Djunaid b. Ibrāhīm (1403–1415) and Muhammad I (Ottoman sultan, 1402–1421); and Ilyas b. Muhammad, Menteşeoglu (1402–1421).

architects (M. C. Bolgil, A. M. Shapiro, M. T. Ergene, T. Akalin, A. R. Seager, F. K. Yeğül, R. H. Stone, H. Aydintaşbaş, S. M. Goldstein, T. Yalçinkaya), we could not have accomplished the restoration of the Roman Gymnasium and the preservation of the Synagogue.

The philosophy that one can dig up buildings and then leave them to the mercy of the elements and pilferers is going out. Our aim was to re-create one example of an outstanding Roman exterior (the Marble Court of A.D. 211) and an interior which would include samples of the glorious decorative system of marble revetment that had developed in Roman Imperial times; the unique historic significance of the Synagogue gave additional impetus. Together, these two structures are already becoming major attractions for the general public as well as scholars; we believe the result justifies the time, funds, and effort spent in realizing the plan.*

The full impact of our finds upon a great variety of disciplines will become evident as publication progresses; but already a dozen or so diversified publications each year attest to the interest of the Sardis finds. Architecture, archaeology, anthropology, epigraphy; geophysics, geology, and metals analysis; study of languages and religions; history of all kinds—these are but a few of the general fields involved. To bring all of these together in the final synthesis on Sardis will be a high aim to strive for.

"There have been excavations at Sardis but Sardis has not been excavated"—that is how I really should have started this book. Our guesses on

*There is no better way of learning about a building than to try to build it. After much training, the local workmen—and the migrant master masons and marble sculptors, who nowadays come from very few locations—caught on to the procedures of their Roman predecessors. A great scholar of Roman architecture, John B. Ward Perkins, confessed that as he first entered the Gymnasium area, for a moment he had the illusion of seeing the Roman builders finishing the Marble Court. Apart from the metal (instead of wooden) crane and tripod, electric tools, and quality of the cement, not very much had changed from Roman times in the equipment and processes we used.

the area we have explored have ranged from 1 to 6 percent depending on how big you assume the Roman city to have been.

How much more can or should be done? There are many prizes still hidden in the soil of Sardis but with each passing year obstacles to excavation will increase. I have pointed out that we have not excavated any sectors or buildings in the central and eastern parts of the urban area. They are known to contain the Hellenistic-Roman civic center (Map 3, nos. 24, 25, 26, 27), the theater, the stadium, and a row of major public buildings east of the Gymnasium. We have a favorite contender for the location of the Palace of Croesus in the flat-topped hill now crowned by a Byzantine fort (Map 3, no. 23). It stands over what may have been an ancient temple platform, and the tunnels of the Acropolis (*Figures 69, 70;* Map 3, no. 21) lead in this direction. There is the vast cathedral at the eastern edge of the city (Map 3, no. 29) and a Roman Basilica in the plain (Map 3, no. 30). In 1970 we were shown the location, just below the great church, where an east-west Marble Avenue was briefly seen by the landowner. Of the areas we have probed, the Northeast Wadi (*Figures 189, 191*) and the area north of the Artemis Temple seem to have much to offer for the Lydian and Persian periods. Not nearly as denuded as its central and southern parts, the northern slope of the Acropolis beckons with promises of more palatial walls (*Figure 230*).

The difficulties, however, are becoming formidable. There were hardly any buildings on the site in 1948. The new highway, constructed in 1952, has acted as an irresistible magnet attracting new construction. In 1969–1970 alone, some thirty housing units were built on the western bank of the Pactolus over the presumable location of the Lydian agora. Vineyards, most expensive of all crops, have been planted in recent years over the cathedral, the stadium, and civic center, all being farmed under old land deeds. Under a similar deed, the theater has been put under cultivation. Somehow, the ruins in these areas begin to melt and disappear. The situation is changing even more rapidly in the Royal Cemetery of Bin Tepe, where each year some more mounds are brought down, sometimes by farmers, sometimes even by state road builders. And these ravages are exacerbated by widespread illicit digging both in the mounds and on Prehistoric sites.

We have started one phase of research at Sardis and this we must finish. There is much left that a new generation of archaeologists may discover at Sardis—if the site is preserved.

Staff List

Publications on Sardis

Illustrations

Index

Staff List, 1958-1971

Titles and institutional affiliations or home towns are given as of the time of work for the Sardis expedition. ST signifies a Turkish student trainee under a P.L. 480 grant by the State Department, STF a trainee under a Ford Foundation grant. METU stands for Middle East Technical University, Ankara; MTAE for Maden Tetkik Arama Enstitüsü, Ankara (Mineral Research Institute).

Tankut Akalin	Robert College	ST, restoration engineer	1965–67
Faruk Akça	Moran and Bolgil	assistant architect for restoration	1971
Osman Aksoy	Archaeology Museum, Ankara	first commissioner for 1968 campaign	1968
Arif Akyel		lab assistant in conservation	1958–1963
Claire Albright (Mrs. Fuller)	Fogg Museum	assistant recorder	1959
Turhan Alper	University of Ankara	ST; recording	1963
Frederica Apffel	Harvard (Fogg)	assistant recorder, Cambridge	1959
Ayberk Araz	University of Ankara	assistant in archaeology	1963
Mehmet Ardos	University of Izmir	gold macrophotography	1968
Reha Arican	Archaeological Museum, Istanbul	conservator	1962–63
Marcia Ascher (Professor) (Mrs. Robert)	Ithaca College	archaeologist, assistant recorder	1965
Robert Ascher (Professor)	Cornell	senior archaeologist, anthropologist	1965
Aysu Ataseven	University of Istanbul	assistant in recording	1961
Halis Aydintaşbaş	METU	assistant in architecture	1968–69

Güven Bakir	University of Ankara	ST, draftsman, archaeologist	1958–62
Emin Balay	Robert College	assistant architect, engineer	1968
Musa Baran	Izmir Museum	first commissioner for 1966 and 1967 campaigns	1966–67
Polly Bart	Radcliffe	photographer	1964
George E. Bates (Professor)	Harvard	specialist for Byzantine coins	1963, 1967–71
Louise M. Bates (Mrs. George E.)	Boston	assistant for Byzantine coins	1967–71
Nilüfer Bayçin	MTAE	gold analyses	1968
Hugh Blackmer	Harvard	faculty aide, Cambridge	1963
Mehmet C. Bolgil	Harvard; Moran and Bolgil	ST, architect, supervisor of restoration	1960, 1967–71
Zerrin Bolgil (Mrs. M. C.)	Istanbul	assistant to field director, recorder	1969
Jonathan Boorstin	Harvard	photographer	1965
Enver Bostanci (Professor)	University of Ankara (Institute for Palaeanthropology)	specialist for project on human skeletal remains	1962–65, 1967–70
Brenda Bragdon (Mrs. Joseph H.)	Harvard (Fogg)	financial administration, private funds records, Cambridge	1970
Heinrich Bremer	University of Izmir	gold macrophotography	1969
Robert H. Brill	Corning Museum of Glass	specialist for glass	1962, 1964
Theodore R. Buttrey (Professor)	University of Michigan	specialist for Roman coins	1969–71
Anne E. M. Johnson Buttrey (Mrs. T. R.)	University of Michigan	specialist for Greek coins	1969–71

Erol Çakir	Izmir Museum	second commissioner for 1970 campaign	1970
T. Çalişlar	University of Ankara	specialist for project on fauna	1963
Thomas H. Canfield (Professor)	Cornell	architect	1958–59
Sallie Carlisle	Harvard (Fogg)	executive secretary, draftsman	1969–71
Stuart L. Carter	Cornell	architect	1961–62, 1970-71
Anthony B. Casendino	Cornell	architect	1959–60
John S. Crawford	Harvard, University of Delaware	archaeologist	1967–69
Margaretta J. Darnall	Cornell	STF, recording architect	1969–70
Mario Del Chiaro	University of California, Santa Barbara	archaeologist	1959–60, 1962
Mrs. Christina Del Chiaro	Santa Barbara	assistant recorder	1960
David DeLong	METU (Fulbright Scholar)	architect	1967–68
Mrs. A. S. Denholm	Harvard (Fogg)	work on ancient sources	1960
A. Henry Detweiler (Professor)	Cornell	field adviser and chief architect, associate director	1958–70
Mrs. Catharine Detweiler (Mrs. A. Henry)	Cornell	numismatist	1958–62
Yaman Dinçtürk	Salihli	assistant for architecture and conservation	1961–62

Sabri Doguer (Professor)	University of Ankara, Faculty of Veterinary Medicine	specialist for project on fauna	1962–65
A. Düzgüneş	METU	ST, archaeologist, translator	1963
Dennis Egnatz	Harvard	student assistant	1959
Talat Erben (Professor)	Çekmece Nuclear Research Center	gold analyses project	1968–69
Asim Erdilek	Izmir College	ST, archaeologist, translator	1962
Mehmet T. Ergene	Robert College; Harvard	ST, architect, assistant for Marble Court Restoration, construction architect	1962–68
Mustafa Eris	Sart	lab assistant in conservation	1959–68
Cengiz Ersöz	Sart	assistant in recording	1963
Recep Ertetik	Sart	lab assistant	1969–71
David J. Finkel	Cornell; University of Oregon	anthropologist	1968–69
Clive Foss	University of Massachusetts, Boston	Byzantine specialist	1969–71
Kenneth J. Frazer	British School at Athens	administrative assistant (Turkey), architect, general manager	1962–71
Jonathan Friedlaender	Harvard	anthropologist	1964
Lee Garrison	Harvard (Fogg)	administrative assistant, secretary	1968–69
Elaine Gazda	Harvard (Fogg)	archaeologist, draftsman	1968
Jean Gilmartin	Harvard (Fogg)	photographic documentation, Cambridge	1969–71
Margaret Golding	Harvard (Fogg)	collection of ancient and modern references to Sardis	1958

Clare W. Goldstein (Mrs. Sidney)	Harvard (Fogg)	assistant recorder	1968–70
Sidney M. Goldstein	Harvard	STF, archaeologist, conservator	1968–70
Elizabeth Gombosi	Harvard (Fogg)	photographer	1968–71
J. L. Greaves	New York University	conservator	1967
M. Greene	Harvard (Fogg)	recording	1963
Charlotte Greenewalt (Mrs. David)	Massachusetts Institute of Technology	draftsman	1961–63
Crawford H. Greenewalt, Jr.	University of Pennsylvania; University of California at Berkeley	archaeologist, assistant field director, 1970–71	1959–71
David Greenewalt	Massachusetts Institute of Technology	specialist in geophysics	1961–63
Necati Güler	METU	assistant in architecture and conservation	1962, 1966–68
M. Gültekin (Professor)	University of Ankara, Faculty of Veterinary Medicine	report on fauna	1963
Roberto Gusmani (Professor)	University of Messina, Italy	specialist for Lydian and epichoric inscriptions	1969–71
Frederick B. Hammann	Cornell	architect	1965–66
George M. A. Hanfmann (Professor)	Harvard	field director	1958–71
Ilse Hanfmann (Mrs. George M. A.)	Harvard (Fogg)	recorder	1958–71

Donald P. Hansen	Harvard; Oriental Institute, Chicago	archaeologist	1958–62
Bonnie L. Henderson (Mrs. John S.)	Cornell	assistant recorder	1967
John S. Henderson	Cornell	anthropologist	1967
Martha Hoppin	Harvard (Fogg)	photographer	1969–70
Richard Hoyle	Harvard	photographer	1967
A. H. Hyatt	Cornell	architect	1966–67
Ralph K. Iler	Cornell	architect	1963-64
Erol Izdar (Professor)	University of Izmir	gold macrophotography	1968
S. W. Jacobs (Professor)	Cornell	senior architect, associate director, 1970–71	1961–63 1969–71
R. Clark Johnsen	Harvard	student assistant, Cambridge	1960
Anne M. Johnson (see Buttrey)			
Jean Johnson (Mrs. Sherman E.)	Church Divinity School of the Pacific	assistant recorder	1958
Sherman E. Johnson (Professor)	Church Divinity School of the Pacific	epigrapher, archaeologist	1958
Russell Jones	Harvard (Fogg)	photographic documentation, Cambridge	1969
Elizabeth Kalinoski	Cambridge High and Latin	assistant for records, Cambridge	1969
Alexander Kasper	German Archaeological Institute	architect, archaeologist	1969–71

Bärbel Majer Kasper (Mrs. Alexander)	German Archaeological Institute	assistant archaeologist for Pyramid Tomb publication	1969–70
Orhan Kaya	University of Izmir	gold macrophotography	1969
Lenore Keene	American College for Girls	assistant recorder	1958
L. Klein	Cornell	architect, Ithaca	1962–63
William Collins Kohler	Harvard	archaeologist	1961–63
Elaine H. Kohler (Mrs. William C.)	Boston University	assistant recorder and anthropologist	1961–62
Alf Thomas Kraabel	R. E. Pfeiffer Fellow, Divinity School, Harvard	archaeologist	1966
John H. Kroll	Harvard	numismatist, archaeologist	1964–66
Metin Kunt	Robert College	ST, archaeologist, translator	1964–66
Sherry Lattimore (Mrs. Steven)	Radcliffe	assistant recorder	1964
Steven M. Lattimore	Princeton	archaeologist	1964
Harry Lau	Ohio State University	assistant in project for photogrammetry	1966
Robert P. Lewis	Harvard	architectural documentation, Cambridge	1969
R. Liddell	Harvard	photographer	1968
A. P. Lins	New York University	STF, archaeologist, conservator	1971
Sally Loomis	Harvard (Fogg)	executive secretary	1957–67, 1968–69 part-time

Emily G. Lort (see Lee Garrison)			
Charles P. Lyman	Harvard	photographer, in charge of film project	1965–66, 1968
Peter B. Machinist	Harvard	photographer	1964
Lawrence J. Majewski (Professor)	New York University	senior conservator	1964–71
Nancy Mason (Mrs. John)	Harvard (Fogg)	assistant for private funds, Cambridge	1970
Michael Mathers	Harvard	photographic documentation, Cambridge	1969-70
Robert A. Mayers	Cornell	architect	1960
Recep Meriç	University of Ankara	ST, conservation trainee, assistant commissioner 1971	1964–67, 1971
Guy P. R. Metraux	Harvard	archaeologist	1967–68
George C. Miles	American Numismatic Society	specialist for Islamic coins	1971
David Gordon Mitten (Professor)	Harvard (Fogg)	archaeologist, assistant to director, 1963, assistant director, 1964–	1959–71
Rosemarie Mitten (Mrs. David G.)	Harvard	conservator	1963
Ann D. Moffett (Mrs. Christopher)	Harvard (Fogg)	part-time assistant	1960
Charlotte B. Moore	University of Pennsylvania;	preparation of records, Cambridge	1969

338

(Mrs. Gordon T.)	Harvard (Fogg)		
S. Myers	Harvard	photographer	1966
James R. McCredie	Harvard	photographer, archaeologist	1959
Melvin Neville	Harvard	anthropologist	1963
Sevim Okar	Çekmece Nuclear Research Center	gold analyses	1968–69
Baki Öğün	Department of Antiquities, Ankara	assistant commissioner	1958
Gerald W. Olson (Professor)	Cornell	soil scientist	1970
Mrs. Brooks Otis	Fogg	Sardis Expedition Records, Cambridge	1963
Akay Özbaşi	Salihli	lab assistant in conservation	1962
G. A. Özbay	METU	assistant in engineering and procurement	1966
H. Özkahraman	Salihli school system	draftsman	1967
Sabri Özkan	Salihli	assistant in conservation and recording	1963
Hüseyin Özlü	Salihli school system	draftsman for mosaics	1966–68, 1970
Mesut Özuygur	Soils and Fertilizer Research Institute, Ankara	soils research project	1970
Barbara Papesch (Mrs. Peter)	Harvard (Fogg)	assistant recorder	1963
Peter P. Papesch	Harvard	architect	1963
John G. Pedley (Professor)	Harvard; University of Michigan	epigraphist, archaeologist	1961–64, 1969–71
Richard H. Penner	Cornell	architect	1968–70
Brian Percival	Cornell	architect	1967–68
Paul N. Perrot	Corning Museum of	specialist for ancient glass	

	Glass		1964
Richard Petkun	Harvard	photographer	1967
Aydin Polatkan		assistant in conservation and recording	1963
Kemal Ziya Polatkan	Director, Manisa Museum	first commissioner, member of Turkish government commission for Marble Court Restoration	1958–65 1966–71
Andrew Ramage	Harvard; University of Massachusetts, Boston	archaeologist	1965–71
Nancy Hirschland (Mrs. Andrew Ramage)	Radcliffe; Harvard; Boston University	draftsman, archaeologist	1963–71
Charles Reagan	Cornell	archaeologist	1961
Jeanne Robert (Mrs. Louis)	Institut Français d'Istanbul	assistant for Greek and Latin inscriptions	1958–71
Louis Robert (Professor)	Institut Français d'Istanbul; College de France, Paris	specialist for epigraphy	1958–71
Laura F. Robertson (Mrs. Noel D.)	University of Cincinnati	assistant recorder	1964
Noel D. Robertson	Cornell	archaeologist	1963–64
Charles F. Rogers, II	Cornell	architect	1960–61
Marga R. Rogers (Mrs. Charles F.)	Cornell	architect	1961
Duane W. Roller	Harvard	archaeologist	1969
Elizabeth Root	Harvard (Fogg)	faculty aide, Cambridge	1962
Marion Dean Ross (Professor)	University of Oregon	architect	1958

Cengiz Saran	Ministry of Water Works, Turkey	specialist for riverine geology and water search	1963
Leon Satkowski	Cornell	STF, architect	1970
Fahrettin Savci	University of Ankara	assistant, human skeletal remains project	1967
Joel S. Savishinsky	Cornell	anthropologist	1966
Mustafa Saydamer	MTAE	specialist for geology	1963
Holly Lee Schanz	Harvard	assistant recorder	1966
Jane Ayer Scott (Mrs. Wellington)	Harvard	specialist for lamps, research editorial assistant, acting administrator	1969–71
Andrew R. Seager	Cornell; Ball State University	architect, in charge of Synagogue design and publication	1964–71
Muzaffer Şenyürek (Professor)	University of Ankara	consultant in anthropology	1958–60
Ibrahim Seren	Izmir Commercial College	administrative assistant	1963
Alan M. Shapiro	American Schools of Oriental Research	fellow for architecture, consultant on Synagogue	1959, 1965–67
John Sloan	Cornell	architect	1965
Bonnie T. Solomon	Harvard (Fogg)	photographer	1961
Ingeborg Sonn	Harvard (Fogg)	Sardis Expedition records	1963
Arthur R. Steinberg	Harvard; University of Pennsylvania	archaeologist	1958–59
David Stieglitz	Cornell	architect	1962–63
Richard E. Stone	New York University	conservator	1964–65, 1967–68

Alice B. Swift	University of Chicago	assistant recorder	1961
Eleanor Swift	Chicago	assistant recorder	1961
Gustavus F. Swift, Jr.	Oriental Institute, Chicago; Fogg Museum	senior archaeologist and administrative officer	1960–71
Gustavus Swift, IV	Chicago	assistant in photography	1961
Muharrem Tagtekin	Manisa Museum	second commissioner for 1963–66 and 1969 campaigns	1963–66, 1969
Erol Tan	Sart	assistant in conservation, architecture, recording	1963
Charles P. Taylor	Harvard	photographic documentation, Cambridge	1969
Tolon Teker	Robert College	engineering assistant for Synagogue	1967
Ruth S. Thomas	Harvard (Fogg)	research fellow, coordinator of research material and records	1970–71
Dundar Tokgöz	Canakkale Museum	commissioner for the Prehistoric project, Bin Tepe	1967
Michael W. Totten	Williams College	photographer	1962–63
Hüseyin Turudoglu	Salihli	assistant for architecture	1961
Gülercan Ugurluer	Robert College	administrative assistant	1971
Şükran Umur (Mrs. Aydin)	Harvard (Fogg)	assistant recorder, Cambridge	1959
David Van Zanten	Harvard; McGill; University of Pennsylvania	STF, architect	1969–71

Robert L. Vann	Cornell	STF, archaeologist, architect	1970-71
Theda Vann	Ithaca	assistant for numismatics and assistant recorder	1971
Axel von Saldern	Corning Museum of Glass	specialist for study of ancient glass	1960, 1968–70
Jane C. Waldbaum	Harvard (Fogg)	editor and research fellow (Classical art and archaeology)	1968–71
John Washeba	Harvard (Fogg)	conservator	1958–59
Lucy Weaver	Harvard (Fogg)	financial administrator	1969
Robert H. Whallon, Jr.	Harvard	anthropologist, photographer	1960
Eunice Whittlesey (Mrs. Julian H.)	New York	assistant for photogrammetry	1963–67
Julian H. Whittlesey	Whittlesey and Conklin	specialist for photogrammetry	1963–67
Vincent Wickwar	Harvard	photographer and faculty aide	1961–63
Paul Woolf	New York	specialist, photographer	1969
James Wrabetz	Harvard	STF, archaeologist	1971
Teoman Yalçinkaya	Robert College	assistant for Synagogue and Marble Court restoration	1969–70
James W. Yarnell (Professor)	Cornell	specialist, supervisor for Marble Court restoration	1964–66
Fikret Yegül	METU; University of Pennsylvania	ST, architect, specialist for Marble Court design and publication	1963–71
W. C. Burriss Young	St. Paul's, Baltimore; Harvard	conservator	1960–63
Güldem Yügrüm	Archaeological Museum, Istanbul	first commissioner; Bin Tepe commissioner, 1968	1968–71
Erol Yurdakoş	Sart	assistant in conservation	1962–63, 1966
Paul K. Zygas	Cornell	architect	1971

Publications on Sardis

READING ON ASIA MINOR AND LYDIA

E. Akurgal, *Ancient Civilizations and Ruins of Turkey* (Mobiloil Turk, Istanbul, 1970).

———— *Die Kunst Anatoliens von Homer bis Alexander* (W. DeGruyter, Berlin, 1961).

G. E. Bean, *Aegean Turkey, An Archaeological Guide* (Praeger, New York, 1966).

C. H. Greenewalt, Jr., "Sardis," *Grolier Encyclopedia*, forthcoming.

R. Gusmani, *Lydisches Wörterbuch* (Carl Winter, Heidelberg, 1964).

G. M. A. Hanfmann, "Greece and Lydia: The Impact of Hellenic Culture," Huitième Congrès International d'Archéologie Classique, *Le Rayonnement des civilisations grecque et romaine sur les cultures périphériques* (E. de Boccard, Paris, 1965) pp. 491–500, figs. 1–3 (Cybele monument), pls. 123–125.

———— "Sardis," *Encyclopedia Britannica* (1966), 19:1069.

———— "Sardis," *Encyclopedia Judaica* (forthcoming).

———— and D. G. Mitten, "Sardi," *Enciclopedia dell' Arte* (1966), pp. 498–501.

———— and J. A. Scott, "Sardis," *Princeton Dictionary of Classical Archaeology, A Guide to the Sites*, ed. R. Stillwell (Princeton, Princeton University Press, forthcoming).

Herodotus, *History* I.6–94: Mermnadae from Gyges to Croesus (77–92, 152–161: Persians in Sardis; 93: gold dust from Tmolus, Alyattes' tomb; 94: coinage).

S. E. Johnson, "Christianity in Sardis," in A. Wikgren, ed, *Early Christian Origins: Studies in Honor of Harold R. Willoughby* (Quadrangle, Chicago, 1961) pp. 81–90.

A. Thomas Kraabel, *Judaism in Western Asia Minor under the Roman Empire* (Studia Post-Biblica, Leiden, ed. J. C. H. Lebram; forthcoming).

H. Metzger, *Anatolia II: First Millennium B.C. to the End of the Roman Period*, trans. J. Hogarth (Ancient Civilizations, London, 1969).

H. Muller, *The Loom of History* (Harper and Brothers, New York, 1958).

G. Neumann, "Lydia," *Der Kleine Pauly* (1967), p. 158.

J. G. Pedley, *Sardis in the Age of Croesus* (Centers of Civilization Series, University of Oklahoma Press, 1968).

Revelation 3.1–6.

"Sardis," *Turkey: Nagel's Encyclopedia Guide* (Geneva, 1968), pp. 430–432.

A. Tekvar, *Türkiye Mermer Envanteri, Maden Tetkik ve Arama Enstitüsü Yayinlarindan* (Publications of the Minerals Research Institute No. 134; Ankara, 1966). Preface by S. Alpan. Survey of marble deposits, with map, and color plates.

GENERAL PUBLICATIONS ON THE SARDIS EXCAVATIONS

G. M. A. Hanfmann, "The Ancient Synagogue of Sardis," *Papers of the Fourth World Congress of Jewish Studies*, 1 (Jerusalem, 1967): 37–42.

———— "Digs Expose Ancient Lydian Capital," *Natural History*, 72 (December 1963): 18–27.

———— "Excavations at Sardis," *Scientific American*, 204 (June 1961): 124–135.

———— "Golden Sardis," *Horizon* 5 (September 1963): 82–89, 10 figs.

———— "Lydiaca," *Harvard Studies in Classical Philology*, 63 (Cambridge, Harvard University Press, 1958), pp. 65–68.

———— "Sardis und Lydien," *Akademie der Wissenschaften und Literatur, Mainz, Abhandlungen der geistes und sozialwissenschaftlichen Klasse* 4, (1960), pp. 493–536, 24 ills.

———— and A. H. Detweiler, "Excavations at Sardis," *American Turkish Topics*, November 1958.

———— "From the Heights of Sardis," *Archaeology*, 14 (1961): 3–12, 14 ills., 1 pl.

———— "New Exploration of Sardis," *Archaeology*, 12 (1959): 53–61.

———— "Sardis through the Ages," *Archaeology*, 19 (1966): 90–97.

G. M. A. Hanfmann and J. C. Waldbaum, "Kybele and Artemis: Two Anatolian Goddesses at Sardis," *Archaeology*, 22 (1967): 264–269, 11 figs.

Illustrated London News, May 30, 1959; July 9, 1960; April 1, 1961; April 7, 1962; March 9, 1963; March 14, 1964; March 21, 1964; March 20, 1965; March 27, 1965; September 17, 1966; September 24, 1966; April 6, 1968; April 13, 1968.

D. G. Mitten, "A New Look at Ancient Sardis," *Biblical Archaeologist*, 29 (May 1966): 38–69.

SPECIALIZED PUBLICATIONS ON THE SARDIS EXCAVATIONS

Final publication of the excavations by the Harvard University Press is currently in progress. Of the series of ten monographs and ten comprehensive reports, the following have appeared:

G. E. Bates, *Byzantine Coins*, Sardis Monograph 1 (Cambridge, 1971).

J. G. Pedley, *Ancient Literary Sources on Sardis*, Sardis Monograph 2 (Cambridge, 1972).

Results of the annual campaigns have been reported by G. M. A. Hanfmann with contributions by expedition members in the *Bulletin of the American Schools of Oriental Research* (BASOR): 154 (April 1959): 5–35; 157 (February 1960): 8–43; 162 (April 1961): 8–49; 166 (April 1962): 1–57; 170 (April 1963): 1–65; 174 (April 1964): 3–58; 177 (February 1965): 2–37; 182 (April 1966): 2–54; 186 (April 1967): 17–52; 187 (October 1967): 9–62; 191 (October 1968): 2–41; 199 (October 1970): 7–58; 203 (October 1971): 5–22.

Reports of the excavations by G. M. A. Hanfmann, A. H. Detweiler, and D. G. Mitten have also appeared in the *Türk Arkeoloji Dergisi (Dergi)*: IX.1 (1959): 3–8, pls. 1–18; X.1 (1960): 3–20, pls. 1–18; XI.1 (1962): 18–22, pls. 12–24; XI.2 (1962): 40–45, pls. 29–38; XII.1 (1964): 26–33, pls. 32–43, XII.2 (1965): 8–23, 16 figs.; XIII.2 (1965): 58–63, 29 figs.; XIV.1 (1965): 151–154, 15 figs,; XV.1 (1966): 75–78, 30 figs.; XVI.2 (1967): 77–84, 92 figs.; XVIII.1 (1969): 61–64, 19 figs.

Summaries in M. J. Mellink, Annual Reports on Archaeology in Asia Minor, *American Journal of Archaeology*.

W. F. Albright, "Albert Henry Detweiler," *BASOR* 198 (April 1970): 2–4.

E. Bostanci, "An Examination of Some Human Skeletal Remains from the Sardis Excavation," *Antropoloji*, 1.1 (1963): 121–130.

_____ *Study of the Skulls from the Excavation at Sardis and the Relation with the Ancient Anatolians* (English and Turkish) Ankara Universitesi Dil ve Tarih Cografya Fakültesi 185 (Ankara, Universitesi Basimevi, 1969).

G. H. Chase, report on pottery, in H. C. Butler, "Fifth Preliminary Report on the American Excavations at Sardis in Asia Minor," *American Journal of Archaeology*, 18 (1914): 432–437.

_____ "Two Vases from Sardis," *American Journal of Archaeology*, 25 (1921): 111–117.

A Choisy, "Note sur les tombeaux lydiens de Sardes," *Revue archéologique,* 32 (1876): 73–81. Chamber tombs excavated by G. Dennis at Bin Tepe.

V. L. Collins, ed. *Howard Crosby Butler, 1872–1922* (Princeton, Princeton University Press, 1923), a memorial volume with biography by V. L. Collins; bibliography by H. S. Leach reprinted separately as *A Bibliography of Howard Crosby Butler* (1924).

A. H. Detweiler, *A Manual of Archaeological Surveying* (American Schools of Oriental Research, New Haven, 1948).

C. H. Greenewalt, Jr., "Lydian Vases from Western Asia Minor," *California Studies in Classical Antiquity,* 1 (1968): 139–154.

———— "Orientalizing Pottery from Sardis: The Wild Goat Style," *California Studies in Classical Antiquity,* 3 (1970): 55–89, 18 pls.

G. M. A. Hanfmann, "On Late Roman and Early Byzantine Portraits from Sardis," *Homages à Marcel Renard, III, Collection Latomus,* 103 (Brussels, 1969) pp. 288–295.

———— and S. W. Jacobs, "A. Henry Detweiler, 1906–1970," *Newsletter,* Society of Architectural Historians (1970).

———— and O. Masson, "Carian Inscriptions from Sardis and Stratonikeia," *Kadmos,* 6:2 (1967): 123–134, pls. 1–4.

———— and J. C. Waldbaum, "New Excavations at Sardis and Some Problems of Western Anatolian Archaeology," *Near Eastern Archaeology in the Twentieth Century: Festschrift for Nelson Glueck* (New York, Doubleday, 1970) pp. 307–326.

N. L. Hirschland, "The Head Capitals of Sardis," *Papers of the British School at Rome,* 35 (1967): 12–22.

A. Thomas Kraabel, "Hypsistos and the Synagogue at Sardis," *Greek, Roman and Byzantine Studies,* 10 (Spring 1969): 81–93.

D. G. Mitten and G. Yügrüm, "The Gygean Lake, 1969: Eski Balikhane, Preliminary Report," *Harvard Studies in Classical Philology,* 75 (Cambridge, Harvard University Press, 1971).

S. Okar and A. Aydin, "Sart Hafriyatunda Bulunan Altin Numunelerinin Notron Aktivasyon Analizi," Center for Nuclear Research, Istanbul Cekmece, May 1969, 14 maps and charts. (Neutron activation tests of gold specimens from the Pactolus refinery.)

G. W. Olson and G. M. A. Hanfmann, "Some Implications of Soils for Civilizations," *New York's Food and Life Sciences Quarterly,* 4.4 (1971): 11–14.

H. F. Osborn, "Howard Crosby Butler," *Dictionary of American Biography* 3 (1929) : 361.

L. Robert, *Nouvelles Inscriptions de Sardes*, fasc. 1 (Librairie d'Amérique et d'Orient, Paris, 1964), pp. 5–62, pls. 1–11.

A. R. Seager, "The Building History of the Sardis Synagogue," *American Journal of Archaeology* (forthcoming).

T. L. Shear, "Sixth Preliminary Report on the American Excavations at Sardis in Asia Minor," *American Journal of Archaeology*, 26 (1922): 396–400. Pot of gold.

J. F. M. Von Olfers, "Uber die Lydischen Königsgräber bei Sarden und den Grabhügel des Alyattes nach dem Bericht des Kaiserlichen Generalconsuls Spiegelthal zu Smyrna," *Abhandlungen der K. P. Akademie der Wissenschaften zu Berlin*, 1858, pp. 539–556. Summary in G. Perrot and A. Chipiez, *History of Art in Phrygia, Lydia, Caria, and Lycia* (London, 1892), pp. 258–266.

A. Von Saldern, "Glass from Sardis," *American Journal of Archaeology*, 66 (1962): 5–12.

J. H. Whittlesey, "Tethered Balloon for Archaeological Photos," *Photogrammetric Engineering*, (February 1970) p. 181.

FINAL PUBLICATIONS OF THE PRINCETON EXPEDITION

H. C. Butler, *Sardis I: The Excavations. Part I: 1910–1914* (E. J. Brill, Leiden, 1922).

H. C. Butler, *Sardis II: Architecture. Part I: The Temple of Artemis* (E. J. Brill, Leiden, 1925).

C. R. Morey, *Sardis V: Roman and Christian Sculpture. Part I: The Sarcophagus of Claudia Antonia Sabina* (Princeton, Princeton University Press, 1924).

E. Littman and W. H. Buckler, *Sardis VI: Lydian Inscriptions. Parts 1 and 2* (E. J. Brill, Leiden, 1916, 1924).

W. H. Buckler and D. M. Robinson, *Sardis VII: Greek and Latin Inscriptions. Part 1: Seasons 1910–1914* (E. J. Brill, Leiden, 1932).

T. L. Shear *Sardis X: Terra-cottas. Part I: Seasons 1910–1914.* (Cambridge, England, 1926).

H. W. Bell, *Sardis XI: Coins. Part 1. Seasons 1910–1914* (E. J. Brill, Leiden, 1916).

C. D. Curtius, *Sardis XIII: Jewelry and Gold Work. Part 1: Seasons 1910–1914* (Sindacato Italiano Arti Grafiche, Rome, 1925).

Illustrations

Note. Unless otherwise noted all photographs are by the Sardis Expedition.

Figures

351

352

Plates

Maps

Index

Butler, Howard Crosby, 6–7, 10
Byzantine fort ("Flying Towers"), 326, Fig. *218*, Map 3

Carians, 97, 321
Chase, George Henry, 8
Christians in Sardis: art, 39, 53, 55, 60, 166, 186, 250, 285, 323, Figs. *23, 33, 122–123, 138, 185*; baptistry (Byzantine Shops), 55–56, Fig. *33*; bishop's palace (?) (House of Bronzes), 39; chapel (?), 248, Fig. *230*; Church of Sardis one of Seven Churches of Asia Minor, 4, 39, 303, 323; Church D, 285; Church E, 101, 130, 140–141, 324, Figs. *75, 177*; Church M, 266–267, 303, Figs. *67, 197–198*; crosses, 55–56, 186, 250, 277, 285, Figs. *23, 33, 138, 204–205*; funerary ritual, 186, Fig. *137*
Church D, 285
Church E, 101, 130, 140–141, 324, Figs. *75, 177*
Church M, 266–267, 303, Figs. *67, 197–198*
Cimmerians, 154, 159–160, 171, 175–176, 185, 228–229, Figs. *124, 131, 139*
City Gate (CG), 30–31, 33–34, 67, 70, 319, Figs. *22, 39–40, 54*
City Wall, 66, 267, 302
Claudia Antonia Sabina, 149
Coins, 125, 275–276, 324, Figs. *21, 91–93, 179*
Conservation of art, *see* specific items
Copper: dagger, 250, 261
Croesus: city of, 320, Fig. *134B*; coinage, Fig. *179*; and Cyrus, 1, 77–78, Fig. *48*; and Cybele monument, Fig. *99*; gold refinery at Pactolus North, 230–234, 249, Figs. *172–179*; and Lydian art and architecture, 139, 321, Figs. *71, 104–105*, and palace on Acropolis, 326, Figs. *69, 229*; and sacral precinct, Pactolus

North, Fig. *169*; treasure of, 43–44
Cybele: altar of, 222, Figs. *169–170*; archaic shrine monument of, 133–134, Figs. *99–100*; and Artemis relief, 234, 243, Figs. *180–181*; Hellenistic Temple of, 139–140; lions sacred to, 134; protector of gold refinery, 234; Figs. *176–177*; Temple of in Herodotus, 134
Cycladic culture, Fig. *158*
Cyrus: conquest of Croesus and Sardis, 2, 77–78, 159, Figs. *48–49*; and Lydian masonry, 250, 259–260
Cyrus the Younger, 273

Dark Ages, 192, Fig. *140*
Dennis, George, 5–6
Detweiler, Albert Henry, 12–13, 270

Earthquakes: of A.D. *17*, 3, 130, 168, Fig. *133*; and Acropolis landslides, Figs. *67, 70*
Eski Balikhane, 260–261, Fig. *162*

First Sardis Expedition, sculptural finds of, 315–316. *See also* Butler
"Flying Towers," 326, Fig. *218*, Map 3

Germanicus, 287
Glass, Byzantine: beaker, 60, Fig. *36*; factories, 37, 237, 323
Gold: associated with Sardis in antiquity, 1; coins of Croesus, 10, 125, Fig. *91*; dust from Tmolus mentioned in Herodotus, 2; Lydian jewelry, 85, 208, Fig. *57*, Pl. IV; modern resources near Sardis, 141–142; "pot of" found by T. L. Shear, 10; prehistoric from Eski Balikhane, 260–261, Fig. *162*; refinery of Croesus, 230–234, 248–249, 320, Figs. *172–179*
Goths, 4, 309
Graffiti, 29, 99, Figs. *11, 68*